The Cambridge Companion to
Modern Latin American Culture

The term Latin America refers to the Portuguese and Spanish-speaking
states created in the early 1820s following the wars of independence,
states that differed enormously in geographical and demographic
scale, ethnic composition and economic resources, yet shared distinct
historical and cultural traits. Specially commissioned essays by leading
experts explore the unity and diversity of the region's cultural
expressions. These essays analyse history and politics from the
nineteenth century to the present day and consider the heritage of
pre-Columbian and colonial Latin America. There is a particular focus
on narrative as well as on poetry, art and architecture, music, cinema,
theatre, and broader issues of popular culture. A final chapter looks at
the strong and rapidly expanding influence of Latino/a culture in the
United States. A chronology and guides to further reading are included,
making this volume an invaluable introduction to the rich and varied
culture of modern Latin America.

Cambridge Companions to Culture

The Cambridge Companion to Modern German Culture
Edited by EVA KOLINSKY *and* WILFRIED VAN DER WILL

The Cambridge Companion to Modern Russian Culture
Edited by NICHOLAS RZHEVSKY

The Cambridge Companion to Modern Spanish Culture
Edited by DAVID T. GIES

The Cambridge Companion to Modern Italian Culture
Edited by ZYGMUNT G. BARAŃSKI *and* REBECCA J. WEST

The Cambridge Companion to Modern French Culture
Edited by NICHOLAS HEWITT

The Cambridge Companion to Modern Latin American Culture
Edited by JOHN KING

The Cambridge Companion to
Modern Latin American Culture

edited by
JOHN KING

CAMBRIDGE UNIVERSITY PRESS
Cambridge, New York, Melbourne, Madrid, Cape Town, Singapore,
São Paulo, Delhi, Dubai, Tokyo

Cambridge University Press
The Edinburgh Building, Cambridge CB2 8RU, UK

Published in the United States of America by Cambridge University Press, New York

www.cambridge.org
Information on this title: www.cambridge.org/9780521636513

First published 2004

A catalogue record for this publication is available from the British Library

Library of Congress Cataloguing in Publication data
The Cambridge companion to modern Latin American culture / edited by John King.
    p. cm – (Cambridge companions to culture)
Includes bibliographical references and index.
ISBN 0 521 63151 3 – ISBN 0 521 63651 5 (pbk.)
1. Latin American – Civilization. 2. Arts, Latin American, I. King, John, 1950– II. Series.
F1408.3.C283   2003
980.03 – dc21   2003053229

ISBN 978-0-521-63151-8 Hardback
ISBN 978-0-521-63651-3 Paperback

Transferred to digital printing 2010

Contents

Illustrations

Notes on contributors

CATHERINE BOYLE is Reader in Latin American Literary and Theatre Studies at King's College, London. She is the author of *Chilean Theatre 1973–1985: Marginality, Power and Selfhood* (1992) and has published widely on Latin American theatre. She is a co-founder and editor of the *Journal of Latin American Cultural Studies*.

CATHERINE DEN TANDT Associate Professor of Hispanic Studies in the Department of Modern Languages and Literatures at the University of Montreal. Her research focuses on contemporary Caribbean culture, especially the Hispanic Caribbean. Her current project explores how Caribbean culture and Caribbean culture critics have responded to the pressures of globalization. She has written on Puerto Rican and Québécois cultural politics, on women's writing, race and identity in Puerto Rico and on Caribbean popular music.

JAMES DUNKERLEY is Director of the Institute of Latin American Studies, and Professor of Politics, Queen Mary, University of London. Amongst his books are *Americana: The Americas in the World, around 1850* (2000), and (edited with Victor Bulmer-Thomas) *The United States and Latin America: The New Agenda* (2000). He is currently preparing a study of the Bolivian Revoluton.

VALERIE FRASER teaches at the University of Essex and is co-director of the University of Essex collection of Latin American Art. Publications include *Drawing the Line: Art and Cultural Identity in Contemporary Latin America* (with Oriana Baddeley, 1989), *The Architecture of Conquest: Building in the Viceroyalty of Peru 1535–1635* (1990) and *Building the New World: Studies in the Modern Architecture of Latin America 1930–1960* (2000).

RANDAL JOHNSON is Professor of Brazilian Literature and Culture at the University of California, Los Angeles. He is the author of *Literatura e Cinema: Macunaima do Modernismo da Literatura ao Cinema Novo* (1982), *Cinema Novo x5: Masters of Contemporary Brazilian Film* (1984), *The Film*

Industry in Brazil: Culture and the State (1987), and *Antonio das Mortes* (1998) and is editor, or co-editor of *Brazilian Cinema* (1982; expanded edn, 1995), Pierre Bourdieu's *The Field of Cultural Production* (1993) and *Black Brazil: Culture, Identity and Social Mobilization* (1999).

JOHN KING is Professor of Latin American Cultural History at the University of Warwick. He has authored and edited some ten books on Latin American cinema, literature and cultural history. His most recent publications include *Magical Reels: A History of Cinema in Latin America* (expanded edition, 2000) and, co-edited with Sheila Whitaker and Rosa Bosch, *An Argentine Passion: The Life and Work of María Luisa Bemberg* (2000).

GWEN KIRKPATRICK is Professor of Latin American Literature in the Department of Spanish and Portuguese at the University of California, Berkeley. She has published on Spanish American *modernismo*, primarily on Leopoldo Lugones, Julio Herrera y Reissig and Delmira Agustini; modern poetry (Neruda, Storni, Cabral de Melo Neto, Vallejo, etc.); and other topics in literature and gender studies. Her most recent writings have focused on contemporary Chilean literature.

GERALD MARTIN is Andrew Mellon Professor of Modern Languages at the University of Pittsburgh and president of the International Institute of Ibero-American Literature. Publications include *Journeys Through the Labyrinth* (1989), critical editions of Miguel Angel Asturias's *Hombres de maíz* (1992) and *El Señor Presidente* (2000), as well as several major contributions to the *Cambridge History of Latin America*. He is currently completing a biography of Gabriel García Márquez.

ANTHONY MCFARLANE is Professor of Latin American History at the University of Warwick. Publications include *Colombia Before Independence: Economy, Society and Politics Under Bourbon Rule* (1993) and *The British in the Americas, 1480–1815* (1994). He is completing a study of the Wars of Independence in Spanish America.

WILLIAM ROWE has taught at the universities of San Marcos (Lima), Liverpool, King's College London, Universidad Iberoamericana (Mexico) and is currently Anniversary Professor of Poetics at Birkbeck College, University of London. At King's College he was Professor of Latin American Cultural Studies and founder of the Centre for Latin American Cultural Studies and the *Journal of Latin American Cultural Studies*. The author of many books on Latin American literature and culture, his most recent work is *Poets of Contemporary Latin America: History and the Inner Life* (2002).

VIVIAN SCHELLING is Senior Lecturer in the Department of Cultural Studies at the University of East London. She is the co-author, with

William Rowe, of *Memory and Modernity: Popular Culture in Latin America* (1991). She has recently edited *Through the Kaleidoscope: The Experience of Modernity in Latin America* (2000).

ILAN STAVANS is Lewis-Sebring Professor of Latin American and Latino Cultures at Amherst College. His books include *The Hispanic Condition* (1995, expanded edition 2001), *The Oxford Book of Latin American Essays* (1997), *The Riddle of Cantinflas* (1998), *Mutual Impressions* (1999), *On Borrowed Words: A Memoir of Language* (2001), and *Spanglish: The Making of a New American Language* (2003). In 2000 Routledge published *The Essential Ilan Stavans*.

JASON WILSON is Professor of Latin American Literature at University College, London. He has published extensively on Latin American poetry, surrealism, travel writing and literary translation. His most recent publication is an edition and translation of Bernardin de Saint Pierre's *Journey to Mauritius* (2001).

RICHARD YOUNG teaches courses in literature, film and popular music in the Spanish and Latin American Studies programme at the University of Alberta. He is author of several books including *Octaedro en 4 tiempos* (1993). He has edited *Latin American Postmodernisms* (1997) and *Music, Popular Culture, Identities* (2002) and has been editor of the *Revista Canadiense de Estudios Hispánicos* since 1996.

'internalizing aspects of European modern movements such as Fauvism and cubism, but transforming them into paintings that are Brazilian in form, colour, content and intention' (p. 214).

In this brief snapshot – to use Cendrar's image – of Brazil in the 1920s, we can see some of the many and varied cultural practices that this book seeks to introduce and develop, from samba to high modernist poetry, from self-conscious naive art to polemical essay, from the earliest rudimentary moving images to contemporary cinema, from the *favelas* in Rio to the literary salons of Paris, where many Latin Americans travelled, in actuality or in imagination, through reading. How to map this field, without falling into taxonomy or arbitrary selection? The Argentine writer Jorge Luis Borges wrote a very short story about a group of cartographers who were charged to produce a map of the empire. They achieved this task, but only by producing a map the size of an empire.[2] Overwhelmed by the 'uselessness' of such exacting precision, subsequent generations allowed the map to disintegrate. Fragments of the map soon blew across the kingdom and became a shelter for animals and beggars, their meaning eluding interpretation. The editor's task must be to find reference points between the two extremes imagined by Borges: of total coverage, or of fragments that become meaningless without adequate contextualization.

The format chosen is a series of discrete but overlapping chapters on history and culture that, read together, offer different pathways into a rich and complex area of study. This introduction has chosen to concentrate on one 'story', that of 1920s Brazilian modernism, but many others can be found by making links across the chapters. The analysis of Latin American narrative is here given somewhat more space than other areas. This reflects the nature of the current academic field, where courses on Latin America are almost invariably based on Latin American novels or short stories, texts that are used as stepping-stones to the appreciation of broader cultural concerns. The same is true of the wider interested public: the first exposure to Latin America is still likely to be a novel by Gabriel García Márquez or Isabel Allende, although salsa classes and the football skills of a Maradona might justifiably lay claim to question the pre-eminence of the written word. Such an emphasis does not imply, however, any hierarchical relationship in the analysis of different artistic practices and movements.

It is necessary from the outset to clarify the title 'modern Latin American culture'. Following orthodox historiography, this book takes the creation of independent Latin American states in the 1820s as the starting point of the 'modern' period, although neat 'beginnings' must, of necessity, look to continuities and breaks with the past. For this reason the book includes a framing chapter on pre-Columbian and colonial Latin America for, as its author Anthony McFarlane notes, these newly independent states, 'took political control of societies which, during three hundred years of Spanish and Portuguese rule, had been formed by interaction between peoples descended from the Amerindians, who were the original peoples of the Americas, the Europeans who came to settle and the Africans who were forcibly carried across the Atlantic into slavery' (p. 9). No appreciation of the 'modern' can ignore this legacy, the most obvious examples of which are the dominant languages of Spanish and Portuguese. Different chapters explore the continuing presence of the colonial past, in particular those dedicated to popular culture, to art and architecture and to music.

As several contributors point out, the term 'Latin America' is a European invention of the middle of the nineteenth century, initially employed as a way of differentiating Spanish- and Portuguese-speaking societies from the Anglo-American world, in particular from the growing power of the United States. Yet, as James Dunkerley argues in chapter two, these Latin American states varied widely in terms of geography, demography, ethnic composition and economic development: 'Populations and economies . . . remain very varied in size and any idea of a Latin American communality should always be qualified with respect for the region's diversity' (p. 29). Indeed, as all the chapters reveal, any search for a communal 'Latin American' culture has remained an elusive, somewhat quixotic ideal. Gwen Kirkpatrick notes that in the nineteenth century, 'independence leaders like Francisco de Miranda and Simón Bolívar envisioned a unified Spanish America joined together by a common linguistic and occidental cultural heritage. Some of the most notable writers of the century were passionately committed to a cultural unity that surpassed national borders, but invented and real national differences have inevitably marked our readings over a century later' (pp. 60–61). Just before his death, Bolívar would wearily remark that such an impulse to unity was like ploughing the sea. Indeed, the widespread survival of indigenous languages, from Mayan languages in the south of Mexico and Guatemala, to Quechua and Aymara in Peru and Bolivia, to Guaraní in Paraguay, contested the 'Latin' domination in the region and questioned any easy invention of even a 'national' cultural unity. Cultures in the plural would always be the defining characteristics of the region, cultures marked by their heterogeneity, to use the term of the critic Antonio Cornejo Polar. In the same way, the 'non-Latin' strains of African culture continued to define many cultural practices, especially in Brazil and in the Spanish Caribbean.

With all these provisos, many of the artists and writers analysed in this volume embrace the term Latin American and seek to define its distinguishing features, as being inside and outside the Western tradition. To take one example: in an essay discussing the work of the Colombian painter and sculptor Fernando Botero, the Peruvian writer Mario Vargas Llosa argues that,

> culturally Latin America is and is not Europe . . . it cannot be anything other than hermaphrodite . . . The radical denial of European influences has always produced in Latin America shoddy pieces of work, with no creative spark; at the same time, servile imitation has led to affected works with no life of their own . . . By contrast, everything of lasting value that Latin America has produced in the artistic sphere stands in a curious relationship of both attraction and rejection with respect to Europe: such works make use of the European tradition for other ends or else introduce into that system certain forms, motifs or ideas that question or interrogate it without actually denying it.[3]

Botero's work is seen by Vargas Llosa as exemplary in this respect: reinvented memories and images of Botero's Colombian childhood, meld with his fascination with Italian Quattrocento art to produce a unique, hedonistic and optimistic vision of the world that radiates from his benign, inflated figures.

What of the term 'culture'? In one of the finest novels of modern Brazil, Clarice Lispector's *A hora da estrela* (1977; *The Hour of the Star*), two relatively mute and 'uneducated' characters are struggling with the meaning of words. The female protagonist, Macabéa, is always inquisitive, her boyfriend, Olímpico, by contrast, is aggressively dense and defensive. Like many poor immigrants to the big cities, their access to entertainment and to knowledge is through the culture industry: television and, in Macabéa's case, her radio, which acts as a comforter and a talisman:

> – On the radio (says Macabéa) they discuss 'culture' and use difficult words. For instance, what does 'electronic' mean?
> – Silence.

- I know what it means, but I'm not telling you.
- ... Radio Clock says that it broadcasts the correct time, culture and commercials. What does culture mean?
- Culture is culture he replied grudgingly. Why don't you get off my back?[4]

Macabéa's question is a good one and however much an editor, faced with the complexity of the term, might feel tempted to reply like Olímpico, some clarification is in order. The main emphasis of this volume concentrates on what Raymond Williams calls, 'the more specialised if also the more common sense of culture as "artistic and intellectual activities"', concentrating on the literary, visual and performing arts, while not excluding the broader sociological and anthropological definition of culture as a 'whole way of life' of a distinct people or other social group.[5] Vivian Schelling's chapter on popular culture in particular offers this wider perspective. In her definition, popular culture refers to 'a very broad and diverse array of forms and practices such as salsa, samba, religious ritual and magic, carnivals, *telenovelas* (television soaps), masks, pottery, weaving, alternative theatre, radio, video and oral narrative, as well as the "whole way of life", the language, dress and political culture of subordinate classes and ethnic groups' (p. 171). She also explores the main ways in which theorists of popular culture analyse the field, as 'folk culture', 'mass culture' and 'culture and power'. The other chapters in the book also remain porous to the mixing of cultural forms and practices. There is no better way of understanding the effects of the 'culture industry' on local communities than by reading the novels of the Argentine Manuel Puig. In the same way, the Paraguayan writer Augusto Roa Bastos has written a monumental novel, *Yo el Supremo* (1974; *I The Supreme*), seemingly the high point of literary modernism. Yet the work is suffused by the tension between writing and orality, the written and the spoken word, the dominant oral language of Guaraní and the literary, official language of Spanish. Artificial barriers between high and low, elite and popular, break down as soon as they are erected. It is the case, however, that in this companionable-sized volume, many examples of material culture such as food and drink, sport, fashion or other rituals of daily life are simply not covered. Those interested in such areas should refer to the recent, very comprehensive *Encyclopedia of Contemporary Latin American and Caribbean Cultures*, edited by Daniel Balderston, Mike Gonzalez and Ana M. López (London, 2000).

The last chapter in the book analyses Latino/a culture in the United States. Ilan Stavans's account is both a personal odyssey and an academic mapping of the fields of literature, popular music and language, showing the ways in which the cultures of Latin America are transformed in a new environment. As Stavans remarks: 'Latino literature offers different challenges to its Latin American counterpart: Latinos are at once an extremity of Hispanic civilization in the United States and also an ethnic minority – north and south in one' (p. 320). To be a Mexican or a Cuban in America is very different to being a Mexican-American or a Cuban-American. What is life like 'on-the-hyphen', to borrow the book title of Gustavo Pérez Firmat's exploration of the 'Cuban-American way'? Are these cultures on a collision or a collusion course?[6] The arguments for a consideration of Latino/a culture in this *Companion* are overwhelming, for, as James Dunkerley points out

> [a]ccording to the US Bureau of Census, what it calls the 'Latino' population of the country is growing at such a rate that by 2050 it will be half that of the 'white' citizenry and double the number of African-Americans. At the turn of the century Los Angeles is amongst the most important of the cities of Latin America, and Miami is best understood not just as a major conurbation of Florida (bought from Spain in 1819) nor even as a Caribbean entrepot but as a continental metropolis. (p. 29)

This concluding chapter, therefore, analyses one of the most important cultural issues of the new century, between North and Latin America and within the United States itself.

The final word of introduction should be given to Jorge Luis Borges, who, in a slightly more cerebral version of the cannibal image that opened this discussion, sought to define modern Latin American culture in terms of creative irreverence, turning the periphery into the centre, or, rather, arguing that there are no centres, for the centres can be located everywhere:

> I believe that our tradition is the whole of Western culture and I also believe that we have a right to this tradition, a right greater than that which the inhabitants of one Western nation or another may have . . . I believe that Argentines and South Americans in general . . . can take on all the European subjects, take them on without superstition and with an irreverence that can have, and already has had, fortunate consequences.[7]

The 'fortunate consequences' of these artistic practices are the subject of the following pages.

Notes

1. Nicolau Sevcenko, 'From Canudos to Brasília', in V. Schelling (ed.), *Through the Kaleidoscope: The Experience of Modernity in Latin America* (London and New York, 2000), p. 95.
2. Jorge Luis Borges, 'On Exactitude in Science', in his *Collected Fictions* (London and New York, 1998), p. 325.
3. Mario Vargas Llosa, 'A Sumptuous Abundance', in D. Elliott (ed.), *Fernando Botero* (Stockholm, 2002), p. 24.
4. Clarice Lispector, *The Hour of the Star* (Manchester, 1986), pp. 49–50.
5. Raymond Williams, *Culture* (Glasgow, 1981), pp. 11–13.
6. Gustavo Pérez Firmat, *Life-On-the Hyphen: The Cuban-American Way* (Austin, TX, 1994), p. 6.
7. Jorge Luis Borges, 'The Argentine Writer and Tradition', in *The Total Library: Non-Fiction, 1922–1986* (London, 2000), p. 426.

1

Pre-Columbian and colonial Latin America

The concept of 'Latin America' is a mid-nineteenth-century European invention, conjured up as a convenient means of distinguishing the Spanish- and Portuguese-speaking countries from the Anglo-American world which, after the American Revolution, found its most powerful expression in the United States. However, if 'Latin America' was a novel term in the nineteenth-century political lexicon, the societies to which it referred were far from new. The independent Latin American states created in the early 1820s took political control of societies which, during three hundred years of Spanish and Portuguese rule, had been formed by interaction between peoples descended from the Amerindians who were the original peoples of the Americas, the Europeans who came to settle and the Africans who were forcibly carried across the Atlantic into slavery. None of these states was the same: they differed in geographical and demographic scale, ethnic composition and economic resources and potential. But they shared one fundamental feature: their societies, economies and cultures had all been profoundly marked by relations with the Iberian colonial powers in the centuries before independence. Indeed, the Latin America that came into being in the early nineteenth century was, in key respects, still redolent of an older world, with roots that went back to the European discoveries of the late fifteenth and early sixteenth centuries, and beyond, into the past of the Amerindian societies which had developed over thousands of years before Columbus. Any appreciation of modern Latin American culture must take account of that historical experience.

The crucible within which Latin America took shape was created by the Iberian colonial powers following Columbus's discovery of America in 1492. When, in the wake of his voyages, the monarchies of Spain and

Portugal claimed sovereignty over territories in the 'New World', they set out the broad boundaries within which Latin America was to develop its fundamental linguistic and cultural characteristics. Henceforth, Spain and Portugal were to be the sources of the dominant languages and cultures, displacing – though not eliminating – the tongues of the native Americans whom the intrusive Iberians now claimed the right to rule.

At its broadest level, the new linguistic and cultural geography stemmed from the territorial division etched on to the world map in the late fifteenth century when Spain and Portugal agreed to divide the world into two spheres of influence. In 1494, at the Treaty of Tordesillas, Spain and Portugal accepted an imaginary line of demarcation that divided the Atlantic Ocean from north to south: Ferdinand and Isabella, the Catholic Monarchs of Aragon and Castile, claimed rights to sovereignty over all lands that lay west of the line, leaving Portugal to develop its exploration, trade and settlement to the east of the line. This imaginary boundary, drawn up before Europeans were fully aware of the extent or significance of the lands which Columbus had found, was to divide the Americas into territorial spaces which, in time, became the two great zones of European influence in Latin America. One was Portuguese-speaking and foreshadowed the modern state of Brazil; the other was Spanish-speaking and spawned all the other Latin American republics. In this sense, modern Latin America is the unforeseen consequence of diplomacy between two medieval European monarchies which could not imagine the historical outcomes of their agreement.

In the early decades of European colonization in the Americas, Spain took the lead and the lion's share of territory. Spaniards were quickly captivated by the opportunities for individual and imperial aggrandizement in this supposedly 'New World', and took their language, customs and religion wherever they wandered. As their explorations, conquests and settlements soon spanned much of the Western hemisphere, the reach of their culture was correspondingly great. Within a half-century of Columbus's landing in America, settlers, merchants, missionaries and crown functionaries had moved beyond Spain's first bases in the Caribbean, fanning out over the continental mainlands in pursuit of lands to settle, precious metals to plunder, subjects to rule and souls to convert. Incoming Spaniards left a trail of destruction in their wake and, amidst the ruins of Amerindian societies, implanted their language and culture. Indian languages and cultures survived, sometimes on an impressive scale, but now had to face strong, sometimes overwhelming, competition from the

European newcomers, and the Spanish language eventually spread over vast areas of South America, Central America and Mexico, becoming the mother tongue of most Latin American nations.

Portugal developed its American colony more slowly and on a smaller scale, though it too was eventually to grow into a great adjunct of the Iberian Atlantic world. At Tordesillas, Portugal's aim was simply to push Spanish exploration as far into the western Atlantic as possible, in order to ensure Spaniards did not interfere with their activities in Africa and Asia; however, in so doing, its negotiators unwittingly carved out a space for Portuguese colonization in America. For, when Pedro Alvares Cabral, bound from Lisbon for India in 1500, swung out westwards into the Atlantic and touched a hitherto unknown land that lay east of the Tordesillas line, he promptly claimed it for Portugal. At that moment, Portuguese America was born at an isolated point on the north-east coast of Brazil, which Cabral took to be an island comparable to those found by Columbus in the Caribbean. In the short term, this affirmation of Portuguese sovereignty meant little. Decades passed before Portugal showed much interest in its American territory; its merchants preferred to concentrate on developing the rich Asian trades opened by Vasco de Gama's voyage to India in 1498. In the long term, however, Cabral's landfall had momentous consequences, for it provided the base from which was later to emerge the rich society of Brazil, formed from a distinctive blend of Portuguese, Indian and African peoples. From the late sixteenth century, this society became the world's first great producer of sugar for export to Europe, cultivated in plantations owned by whites and worked by black slaves; to this society on the coasts another was added during the late seventeenth and early eighteenth centuries, when gold attracted settlement into the interior and added a new dimension to Brazil's wealth.

Spanish and Portuguese colonization did not merely transfer the languages of the Iberian peninsula to the Americas; it also engendered social structures and implanted cultural values which were to become deeply entrenched in the territories ruled by Spain and Portugal. The societies which emerged under the aegis of the Iberian monarchies were built, first and foremost, on the exploitation of subject peoples. Societies in which Europeans lorded it over native communities – coercing their labour, appropriating their resources and disparaging their cultures – were pioneered by the Spanish, starting in the Caribbean islands. The colonization of Hispaniola and Cuba which followed from Columbus's initial encounters with these lands and their peoples set a pattern which was followed, to a greater or lesser extent, wherever substantial numbers of Europeans settled in the American continents. Despite being lauded by Columbus for their innocence and hospitality, the Arawak peoples of the islands were reduced to virtual slavery by settlers eager to enrich themselves by exploiting local gold deposits. Within a couple of generations of Columbus's arrival, native communities had all but disappeared in the islands colonized by Spaniards, succumbing to the irreparable damage inflicted by Old World diseases against which they had no immunity, and unremitting exploitation against which they had no protection.

The larger indigenous societies of the American mainlands, though stronger numerically, were also highly vulnerable. At first, they seemed capable of resisting the incursions of Spaniards. Indian communities on the fringes of the Caribbean – on the coasts of modern Colombia, Panama and Venezuela – withstood the first exploratory probes made by small groups of Spaniards and impeded exploration and settlement in the South American interior for several decades. However, even the most powerful indigenous states were unable permanently to resist the advance of Spanish explorers and conquistadors. The first great Indian state to fall was in Mexico. Between 1519 and 1521, Cortés and his expeditionaries penetrated the Aztec realm and, allied to Indian auxiliaries, devastated the Aztec kingdom by taking its capital, Tenochtitlán, and overthrowing its empire. After destroying the Aztecs' military might in battle, Cortés then appropriated their symbolic power by building a new Spanish capital on the ruins of Tenochtitlan, thereby putting down the foundations for the Viceroyalty of New Spain that was established in 1535. Little more than a decade after Cortés's conquest, Francisco Pizarro and his cohort of conquistadors had an equally dazzling success in overcoming Amerindian power, when they entered the heart of the Andes and seized control of the Inca state in 1532–5, creating the base upon which the Viceroyalty of Peru was founded in 1543. From these vantage points, at the core of the greatest Amerindian kingdoms in Mexico and Peru, Spaniards fanned out over Mesoamerica and Central America, and spread throughout the South American continent.

The range of Spanish exploration was remarkable. Starting with an array of islands and coasts, the sixteenth-century Spaniards soon converted these peripheral settlements into a transcontinental empire. They quickly advanced from the Caribbean and circum-Caribbean shorelines and drove deep inland, lured by the promise of gold (the legend of El Dorado continued to be a sharp spur to exploration in South America until well into the sixteenth century) and the discovery of large, well-ordered native communities and rich resources in the continental interiors. In little more than half a century, Spaniards had ranged over the vast and enormously varied lands that lay between Mexico in the north and Chile in the south, and had also traversed the continents from east to west. Crossing mountains, deserts and forests, Spanish explorers not only reconnoitred huge stretches of the American continents, but they also opened frontiers for settlement across a wide compass of distinctive physical and climatic environments. The Portuguese, by contrast, were slower to explore the resources of their American territory and initially reluctant to move far from the coasts. Their settlements in Brazil were small and scattered, looked to the sea rather than the continental hinterland and drew their manpower from imported African slaves rather than from the Indian populations, who, resisting enslavement, retreated inland. Thus, while Spanish America became a constellation of extensive territories, each of which bore the marks of the Indian societies on which it was built, Portuguese America turned its back on the seemingly inpenetrable fastnesses that lay inland and, until the bandeirantes searching for Indian slaves and gold opened the interior in the late seventeenth and early eighteenth centuries, Brazil remained no more than a strip of widely separated coastal towns that fused European and African, rather than European and Indian, cultures.

The heartlands of colonial Latin America were, then, formed primarily by Spanish settlement, most of which was in place by the second half of the sixteenth century. Exploration and conquest opened the continents to fresh streams of Spanish immigrants who spread over America in a sprawling archipelago of towns and cities, replicas of the urban centres of the Mediterranean world from which most of the new immigrants came. Some of these – Mexico, Bogotá, Caracas, Lima, Santiago, Buenos Aires – were to become major cities during the colonial period, and the platforms for the great capitals of modern Latin America. But they were exceptional. The great majority of the population lived in small provincial towns, villages and hamlets that were usually isolated from the exterior and often had little contact with each other. Indeed, one of the enduring effects of the spread of Spanish settlement as it spread deep into mountainous interiors, following the contours of the social geography laid down in pre-Columbian times, was to create a fragmented world of inward-looking regions. Difficulties of transport and communication across harsh terrain, particularly in the Andean regions, meant that many people lived isolated lives in communities whose identities were closely bound to their immediate environments and whose small economies had scant possibilities for growth.

Towns and cities were, nonetheless, the cutting edge of social and cultural transformation in the Americas. In Brazil, the cities of the coast – at Pernambuco, Salvador (Bahia) and Rio de Janeiro – became focal points for an entirely new form of economy and society: an economy geared to the export of a single agricultural commodity – sugar – and a society built on the slavery of Africans. In Spanish America, the major urban centres were less directly dependent on overseas commerce and had an important political role as centres of colonial administration. However, unlike the pre-Columbian American cities from which native kings had once extended their authority, such as Cuzco or Tenochtitlan, Spanish cities were more than simply strongholds from which to demand tribute and hold political sway. With them came entirely new ways of thinking and behaving which, combined with the Spaniards' confident sense of European cultural superiority, required the utter transformation of pre-Columbian America.

The impact of life ways translated from Spain to the Americas was felt in all major areas of social life. In pre-Columbian America, economic life had been geared primarily to subsistence production by peasant communities, whose agricultural surpluses supported relatively small groups of artisans, traders and leaders. With conquest and colonization came new concepts of property and exchange that revolutionized economic and social life in the Americas. Spaniards set up individual landholdings in the form of farms and estates; they introduced the cultivation of new crops brought from Europe, such as wheat and sugar, and brought cattle, sheep and horses which transformed both the use of land and the means of transport and communication; they geared their production, in part at least, to selling in urban markets or, where they could, in overseas markets; and, to lubricate their economic activities, they introduced metal currencies which provided a new medium for storing value and conducting commerce. These innovations were, moreover, accompanied by the development of a new industry, that of mining. Once the Spaniards discovered hitherto unexploited deposits of precious metals, these became the base of mining enterprises which fuelled an unimagined and unparalleled boom in gold and silver production. From the middle of the sixteenth century, gold and silver became Spanish America's principal commercial products. The gold mines of Colombia, and the silver mines of northern Mexico and the Peruvian mountain sites, especially at Potosí, entered into a century-long opening cycle of growth that, in the world's first great episode of economic 'globalization', bound the Americas and Europe into an Atlantic economy. Thus the occupation of American lands and the subordination of their peoples was consummated by the creation of great mining enterprises which, by financing trade with Europe, stimulated the growth of American towns, agriculture and commerce; moreover, by providing the Spanish crown with rich revenues from taxation, mining also paid for the construction of a complex structure of royal governance.

Economic boom and political innovation reshaped the world of native Americans, but brought them few benefits. For, with the rising tides of Spanish settlement, focused on cities and organized around patriarchal family units, came a rapid diminution of Indian populations, involving the extinction of some communities and the permanent mutilation of many others. Such destruction was partly the direct result of Spanish economic exploitation of native societies: Indian communities were deeply, sometimes fatally, disrupted by Spanish appropriation of their land and coercion of their labour. But the greatest dissolvent of Indian society and culture came from Old World diseases disseminated by Europeans wherever they went.

Over the course of the sixteenth century, epidemics caused demographic damage on a scale without historical precedent. In some regions, particularly those on the coasts fringing the Caribbean and the Pacific or in areas, such as Western Colombia, where Spanish gold mining imposed special burdens on native peoples, whole societies were wiped out in the passage of a few generations. In other regions, such as the highland regions of central Mexico and the Andean regions of southern Peru and Bolivia, native communities proved better able to withstand the onslaught of disease, but were still scoured by extraordinarily high rates of morbidity and mortality. Repeated attacks by epidemics of smallpox, influenza, measles, typhus and other imported diseases not only had horrifying short-term effects – a Spanish cleric reported from Mexico that the Indians 'died in heaps like bed bugs' – but they also inflicted lasting long-term damage by undermining the social integrity, economic productivity and reproductive capacity of the communities exposed to their impact. The catastrophic impact of disease is difficult to measure adequately; however, reasonable estimates suggest that the native population of central Mexico fell from around 25 million in 1519 to fewer than a million in 1630, while the population of Peru probably fell from 10 to 12 million to little more than a million over a comparable period. Not all communities were equally badly hit; nonetheless, contact with Europeans carried a phenomenal human cost everywhere in the Americas, and native peoples never fully recovered from the immense losses inflicted by the waves of deadly illnesses that swept through their societies in the century after the Europeans' arrival.

The impact of European settlement on indigenous societies was not confined to demographic devastation. Physically enfeebled native societies were also prey to far-reaching cultural changes. During the early years of discovery, the Catholic monarchy sought moral justification for its claims to sovereignty over the New World by promising to convert its pagan peoples to Christianity, and under Charles V and Philip II this evangelizing endeavour unfolded with great fervour, as missionary orders sought to convert entire Indian societies to Christianity. In this task, the missionaries were, superficially at least, enormously successful. At a time when the Protestant Reformation began to transform the religious landscape of Europe, the Catholic Church not only retained its power in the Iberian world but installed itself as the sole legitimate source of spiritual authority throughout the Americas, imposing a rigid orthodoxy supported by a militant clergy. While the Spanish settlers and their descendants exploited the bodies of the Indians, the clergy sought to take hold of their minds, promising eternal salvation in return for acceptance of Catholic doctrine and recognition of the Spanish crown as God's servant on earth. Thus, while Spanish towns, mines and estates were the vital building blocks of hispanicization in material life, the churches installed in native communities were the vanguard of an equally important hispanicization in the cultural sphere. Willingly or not, native communities were assimilated into a monotheistic Christian world which demanded that they abandon beliefs and practices which, however central to their cultures, were not consonant with Catholic doctrine.

This intolerant 'spiritual conquest' transformed the cultural landscape throughout those regions where the Church was able to muster significant clusters of missionary priests. Native temples and objects of worship were destroyed with unblinking zeal, to be replaced by Christian churches and images; native priests were persecuted and native elites subjected to heavy pressures to convert, in the belief that commoners would follow where their leaders went; whole native communities were resettled in *congregaciones* or *reducciones* as a means of breaking down barriers against acculturation to Europeanized, christianized ways. But the missionaries did not entirely dismantle Indian cultures and identities. For, in their quest to subvert pagan beliefs and practices, missionaries were willing to learn and preserve Indian languages and customs, and, by seeking to protect their neophytes from the corrupting influences of Hispanic society, they helped to preserve the social cohesion of Indian communities even as they sought to transform their mental worlds.

While helping to conserve elements of pre-Columbian America – albeit within the shell of Christianity – the clergy also set out a defence of the Indians which came to occupy a significant place in Latin American intellectual and political life. In the disputes over the nature of the Indians which took place in the middle of the sixteenth century – most famously when the Dominican Bartolomé de las Casas defended the Indians' right to be regarded as fully rational beings against imperialist thinkers who cast them as 'natural slaves' incapable of equality with Europeans – we may detect the first signs of a concern with the question of Indian rights that persistently resurfaced in Latin American states after independence. Much of the debate which took place in the nineteenth and early twentieth centuries was to be conducted on terms analogous to those set down in the early colonial period. Conservatives clung to attitudes shaped by Spanish imperialism, regarding the Indians as irredeemably ignorant, backward and incapable of fully contributing to, or participating in social progress; liberals took a stance akin to that of Christian humanists, recognizing the Indians' rights to equality before the law and to full participation in society, but only on the terms set down by the dominant society; finally, thinkers influenced by socialist ideas adopted a perspective which, by focusing on the poverty of the Indians while attributing special qualities to them (notably their communitarianism and isolation from the corruptions of capitalism), sounded distant echoes of those missionary efforts, especially strong among the Franciscans in Mexico and the Jesuits in Brazil, to defend the Indians against exploitation while insisting on their unique virtues of innocence, piety and closeness to nature.

The missionaries who lived and worked among the Indians (and among black slaves) were only one wing of a Church which grew increasingly wealthy and powerful under Iberian colonial hegemony. Unlike the Anglo-American colonies in North America, which became a haven for religious dissidents and where the established Anglican Church competed with many other Protestant churches, the Iberian colonies were dominated by a single, established Catholic Church which tolerated no deviation from its doctrines or practices. In return for its privileged position the Church underwrote the legitimacy of Iberian governments in America, and its clergy provided the religious framework for instilling obedience to the Spanish and Portuguese monarchs. While missionaries attended to the Indians, the secular clergy under its bishops provided for the spiritual, educational and some of the material needs of the rest of society. The Church was physically present throughout society, visible in a multitude of churches, convents and monasteries, and contributed to the structure of social life through its many religious and social activities. The crowded calendar of religious observance was not only a source of spiritual guidance; it also structured community life and, through processions and other religious celebrations, offered important occasions for public spectacle and public solidarity. And the Church was, of course, the leading agency for attending to the poor and providing education. The clergy sustained schools and universities for the elites, though its lack of concern with the education of the vast majority ensured that colonial Latin American societies had very low rates of literacy.

Although Catholicism proclaimed the fundamental equality of humankind in the eyes of God, the Church's emphasis on the divide between Christians and non-Christians interacted with civil society's ideas of social hierarchy in ways that emphasized ethnic difference and inequality. The preoccupation with ordering ethnic difference into a hierarchy was influenced by the Spaniards' special concern with *pureza de sangre* (purity of blood) in their own society, where, in the later fifteenth century, the crown and nobility sought unity behind one monarchy and one religion by focusing animosity on Jews and Muslims who were persecuted for refusal to convert to Christianity. In America, such intolerance of other beliefs and customs tended to translate into attitudes of ethnic superiority. The desire among Iberian elites to avoid the taint of non-Christian blood surfaced among the creoles of Latin America in another form: avoidance of marriage with non-whites. Indeed, despite the struggle of members of the missionary clergy to defend the Indians against imputations of inherent inferiority, both the Spaniards and the Portuguese brought a strong strain of ethnic intolerance to the Americas, where it was strengthened by the imperatives and habits of colonial domination. Neither the Spanish nor the Portuguese were racists in the modern sense: they did not regard Indians or Africans as biological inferiors whose birth condemned them to a permanently subordinate role in social life, as 'scientific' racists were later to insist in the nineteenth century. Nonetheless, the Spanish American and Brazilian white elites regarded Indians and blacks as cultural inferiors and converted their prejudice into incontestable norms; thus Hispanic and Luso-Brazilian cultures contained the germs of racist attitudes which carried into post-colonial Latin American cultures and have, to this day, proved difficult to eradicate.

Nonetheless, despite the Iberian disparagement of Indians and blacks, one of the most remarkable features of colonial Latin America was the extraordinary extent of ethnic mixing that followed the arrival of Europeans. From the later sixteenth century onwards, the advance of Hispanic and Luso-Brazilian cultures was buoyed up by the growing numbers of people of mixed ethnic origins who identified with Iberian rather than native ways. Mestizos born of European and Indian descent and mulattos of white and African descent occupied an ambiguous and uncomfortable position in the social order. They suffered discrimination, being blocked from educational opportunity and all but the most lowly political and ecclesiastical office, but had greater potential for social mobility than Indian peasants and black slaves. For, although mestizos and mulattos were accorded a social status lower than that of whites, they were regarded as superior to the mass of the Indian peasants and black slaves whose inferior legal standing relegated them to the lowest rungs of the social scale; furthermore, as free persons, they tended to take to creole ways of thinking and behaving. This did not mean that they completely shunned contact with Indians and blacks. In urban environments, free people of colour lived side by side with Indians and blacks and formed plebeian groupings which shared antagonisms towards the white elites and even on occasion joined in rebellion against them. Indeed, in the urban uprisings of Mexico City (1624 and 1692) and in the great eighteenth-century rebellions in South America, popular political action crossed the lines of caste and class and created alliances that posed serious threats to colonial government. Such alliances were short-lived, however, and the ethnic divisions propagated by Iberian colonial rule remained a formidable obstacle to constructing shared social identities and common political goals.

While ethnic mixture created substantial social layers that stood between the European, the Indian and the African, it did not submerge the cultures of the indigenous and the enslaved. Although Indians were forced to accept government by whites, they were not simply passive victims of colonialism. In some regions, such as the frontier zones of northern and southern Mexico, northern Colombia, southern Chile and the plains of Argentina, Indians continued to resist white incursions at the end of the colonial period, so that strong enclaves of independent Indian culture still existed when the first Latin American states were formed in the early nineteenth century. Equally if not more important was the persistence of Indian cultures within Hispanic societies. Unlike the English colonies in North America or the Portuguese settlements in Brazil, where surviving Indian communities retreated in the face of attrition, the Spanish colonies included native peoples who, as their populations recovered during the seventeenth and eighteenth centuries, became a substantial part of larger colonial societies without being fully integrated into them. Spanish legislation allowed Indians to retain independent corporate landholdings and, though imposing tribute and labour levies, left Indian communities with a degree of autonomy under their own leaders. Such communities did not entirely reject European ways: they incorporated European crops and livestock into their economies, often actively participated in the market economy and adopted forms of community solidarity – notably the *cofradía*, or religious confraternity – introduced from the Iberian Peninsula. However, where Indians sustained cohesion as communities, they preserved important elements of their past, whether in material forms such as housing, diet and dress, or in the cultural spheres of language, custom and belief. Indeed, the 'anti-idolatry' campaigns conducted in the seventeenth century and Mexican and Andean Indian rebellions during the eighteenth century revealed the presence of heterodox beliefs and practices which show that Indians had succeeded in shielding elements of pre-Columbian belief, usually by blending them with Christian teachings.

Another important contribution to the formation of Latin American society was made by Africans and their descendants. More than 7 million Africans were carried across the Atlantic into American slavery from the sixteenth to the end of the eighteenth century, and were distributed throughout the continents for employment as agricultural workers, miners, artisans and domestic servants. By far the largest numbers went to Brazil, to work in the sugar plantations which, from the middle of the sixteenth century, became the mainstay of Brazil's economy; later, they were also employed in cultivating the coffee that became Brazil's principal agricultural export after independence. Europe's insatiable demand for sugar spread slavery into the Caribbean during the seventeenth century, and in the eighteenth century, the Spanish island of Cuba followed where the English and French West Indian planters had led. But, if Cuba was a relatively late developer of slave-based plantations, slavery lasted longer there than elsewhere in the Caribbean. The conversion of Cuba into a slave society inhibited Cubans from joining the movements towards independence in Spanish America in 1810, and Cuba retained both colonial rule and slavery until both were overthrown at the close of the nineteenth century. Smaller but substantial numbers of slaves were also found in other areas of colonial Spanish America: in Venezuela, slaves were employed on cacao and coffee plantations; in Colombia, they were used in gold mining and tropical agriculture; and in Peru, where slaves were utilized on the haciendas of the Lima hinterland and other areas on the Pacific coast.

Although enslaved, Africans and their descendants were, like native American peoples, a vigorous presence in Iberian colonial societies. Not surprisingly, their influence was greatest where slave numbers were highest, but their impact was felt wherever slaves were employed as servants, artisans and field hands. This was largely contained within a world dominated by slaveowners or, in urban settings, by societies in which blacks were a minority. Torn from many different African cultures and thrust together in an alien environment, slaves – who were mainly young males – could not reproduce their own societies in American settings. Some slaves sought to escape from slavery by joining together in runaway communities (known as *palenques* in Spanish America and *quilombos* in Brazil) which did have some of the characteristics of African social life; however, the majority lived in societies dominated by the language and culture of their Iberian masters. This environment was of course far from friendly to the slave, but the system of slavery in Latin America was arguably less hostile to slaves than its British and French equivalents. Iberian societies were already familiar with the institution of slavery long before the African slave trade and plantation agriculture turned slavery into a major institution in the Western hemisphere, and had developed customs and laws that allowed the slave a moral and legal personality, and even encouraged slaves to seek manumission and their owners to grant it. This did not eliminate violence and cruelty towards slaves, but it at least enabled slaves to assert some minimal rights while allowing some to become free persons. And, over time, sexual relations between blacks and whites, though often forced on slave women by their white masters, added another stratum to colonial society, that of the mulattos. The emergence of this mixed-race group did not signal the absence of prejudice and discrimination: on the contrary, free blacks and coloureds were barred from many of the privileges which whites took for granted. It did, however, forestall the erection of formal barriers of racial segregation of the kind that were later constructed in the United States, and ensured that interaction between whites and blacks was more frequent and open in Latin America.

Clearly, then, Indian and African influences made an important contribution to shaping the cultural character of Latin America. At the end of the colonial period, Latin America was still far from being wholly 'Latin'. In Peru and Bolivia, large numbers of people continued to speak Quechua and Aymara; in southern Mexico, Mayan languages were widely spoken; in Paraguay, most of the population spoke Guaraní; and, throughout Latin America, including Brazil, a host of other languages survived, albeit sometimes among small groups living on distant frontiers. Moreover, strains of African culture continued to flourish long after the end of colonial rule, especially in Brazil and the Spanish Caribbean. Brazil was by far the largest importer of slaves in Latin America in the colonial period – close to two and a half million between 1500 and 1810, compared to about one million for the whole of Spanish America – and, like Cuba, sustained the institution of slavery until the closing decades of the nineteenth century. In such societies, African cultural practices continued to be transmitted from generation to generation, and were kept alive not only in the communities of slave runaways which existed on the margins of colonial society, but also at its core, in the African-influenced dialects, work practices, religious beliefs, music and dance which were present wherever substantial numbers of slaves and free blacks were concentrated.

The simplicity of the divisions that separated Indians, Africans and Europeans in the early years of Iberian colonization thus gradually gave way to complex colonial societies with structures and cultures that distinguished them sharply from their metropoles. And, within their increasingly diverse societies, the creole elites of Spanish and Portuguese America became more aware and assertive of their own identities. This was partly a consequence of a decline in the ability of the metropolitan powers to impose economic dependence and political control; both Spanish and Portuguese power waned during the later seventeenth century while the colonies enjoyed growing diversity and relative prosperity. The picture was not everywhere the same, but in Brazil and in the most prosperous colonies of Spanish America – the silver-mining economies of Mexico and Peru – creoles took a growing share of wealth and power in their own societies. In Brazil, where the crown had always allowed colonials a wider margin of self-government than in Spanish America, creoles used their wealth to buy their way into important administrative positions and by the end of the seventeenth century had acquired influence at the highest levels of colonial government. In Spanish America, too, creoles penetrated into the upper ranks of the royal bureaucracy, taking advantage of Spain's financial weakness to purchase positions in the audiencias (colonial high courts) and the royal treasury, from which they could exercise political influence commensurate with their economic and social standing.

Matching this political advance was a growing cultural self-confidence. This was particularly conspicuous in Mexico. There, a few leading writers sought to articulate a distinctive creole identity by constructing a version of Mexican history which, by exalting the ancient Indian world and giving Mexico a special religious significance, sought to assert Mexico's cultural equality with Spain. The readiness to identify an American culture as a blend of the Spanish and Indian pasts did not, however, have any immediate political implications. Admiring Indians in the past did not mean accepting Indians as coevals in the present, and creoles did not yet imagine that they might join with other ethnic groups in a common future as one 'nation' under independent government. In Spanish America and Portuguese America, creoles wanted recognition of their equality with metropolitan whites and acknowledgement of their fitness to take a leading role in governing their own societies. In short, they wanted recognition of their status as a ruling class within the colonial system, not an autonomous political life outside it.

The barriers to building a sense of unity in societies with disparate ethnic identities were strengthened by the political systems of empire. Neither Spain nor Portugal allowed any form of representative government in their dominions; local participation in government was formally confined to small municipal corporations which, over time, usually became self-regarding and self-perpetuating oligarchies, dominated by the same creole families from generation to generation. Latin America's colonial societies thus lacked political institutions which might have nurtured supra-local, proto-national solidarities in the way that the provincial assemblies did in British North America, and political perspectives and aspirations tended to express the views and interests of creole families and peer networks rather than the larger societies of which they formed part.

This is not say that Latin America was politically dormant throughout the colonial period, or transfixed in a prolonged 'colonial siesta'. At the local level, political life centred on muncipalities was often active and sharply contested, reflecting a local sense of community and a belief that locals had the right to determine the affairs of their immediate locality. Moreover, colonials became more critical of, and ready to protest against, metropolitan government when, during the latter half of the eighteenth century, the Spanish and Portuguese crowns sought to impose closer economic and political controls. The reforms of Pombal in Brazil and of Charles III's ministers in Spanish America aroused opposition among creole elites and, in Spanish America, even triggered large-scale popular uprisings in the 'rebellion of the barrios' at Quito (1765), the Túpac Amaru rebellion in Peru (1780–2), and the Comuneros revolt in New Granada (1781).

While colonial grievances mounted, the influences of fresh ways of thinking drawn largely from the European Enlightenment broadened political horizons among the educated elites. Exposure to new ideas about science, political economy and education circulated through a small but burgeoning press, inspired creoles to perceive their societies and their positions in relation to the metropolitan powers in a different light, while the examples of the American and French revolutions showed that political change was possible, even desirable. Indeed, some creoles sought actively to follow these examples and to force the pace of political change. In Brazil, conspirators at Minas Gerais were arrested for plotting the overthrow of Portuguese government in 1788–9, and a group of blacks and mulattos were executed for demanding racial equality and a republic in 1798. In Spanish America, small and abortive revolutionary conspiracies also occurred in the 1790s, and some of their leaders – notably the Venezuelan Francisco de Miranda – became professional revolutionists who sought to persuade British governments to support their efforts to stir up rebellion against Spain. However, these outbreaks were of insufficient weight to challenge the colonial order. They were symptoms of an intensifying disaffection among small minorities within the educated classes, not the signs of anti-colonial or nationalist movements that had any substantial social base or serious prospect of overthrowing colonial rule.

The crisis of the colonial regimes came as a consequence of collapse at the centre rather than mounting pressure at the peripheries. Imperial crisis began in 1807–8, when Napoleon invaded Portugal and Spain, and plunged their governments into extraordinary crises. While the metropolitan countries were swept by war, colonial elites were forced to question the viability of the systems of governance which they had accepted for so long. This did not necessarily mean that they were eager to break with colonial rule. In Brazil, indeed, the creole elites were perfectly content to remain under Portuguese authority, albeit of a modified kind. For, when the French invaded Portugal in 1807, the Prince Regent Dom João, his family and the Portuguese court fled to Rio de Janeiro, set up government there and thus effectively converted Brazil into its own metropolis. The king's willingness to make concessions to the economic and political aspirations of the land- and slave-owning elites – such as free trade with Britain, aristocratic titles and posts in royal government – helped secure their loyalty, as did fears, natural to a slave society, that political disturbance might trigger slave rebellion (as it had in Haiti in the 1790s). Thus Portugal's crisis did not translate into Brazil's independence. This came only years later, in 1821, when Portugal's government sought to return Brazil to colonial dependence; it then took place smoothly, without serious disruption to the social order built on sugar and slavery.

In Spanish America, the repercussions of crisis at the centre were far more damaging. For, although only a small minority favoured independence, the crisis of the Spanish monarchy was less easily contained than that of the Portuguese. When Napoleon placed his brother Joseph on the Spanish throne in 1808 after deposing the Bourbon king, the Spanish empire was effectively decapitated. Most Spaniards refused to accept the French intruder and rallied in support of an emergency government which orchestrated military and political resistance to France in a war of national liberation that convulsed the Iberian peninsula. War in Spain brought political revolution too, when, to legitimize itself and solidify support, Spain's emergency government initiated a major change in the political system it inherited from the Bourbon monarchy. It proclaimed that, in the absence of the king, sovereignty had reverted to the 'people', and, in order to express the will of the Spanish nation, established representative institutions (starting with a Cortes or parliament). Thus began Spain's transition from absolutism to constitutional monarchy, with a liberal political system enshrined in the 1812 Constitution of Cadiz.

This political revolution aimed to preserve the empire by embracing peninsular and American Spaniards as co-equal citizens in a new constitutional regime, but it failed to have the intended effect. In some areas it was temporarily successful, particularly in Mexico and Peru where creoles feared that separation from Spain would encourage popular rebellion and race war, leading to social chaos. Elsewhere, however, creoles seized their chance to break with Spanish domination in 1810. Thus in Venezuela, Colombia, Argentina and Chile, colonial governments were toppled, royal officials expelled, and their places taken by creole leaders intent on self-government.

Their vision of political emancipation was, however, to prove difficult to achieve. The movement of new ideas, the enthusiasm for change, and a sense of distinctive 'American' identities had outpaced social change and did not reach far beyond the salons of educated Creoles. Affirmations of independence were not based in any widespread support, and, in their early stages, the movements towards independence reflected the character of societies dominated by white minorities. While their leaders claimed to represent the 'people', their concept of the 'nation' was rarely underpinned by any shared solidarities that crossed class and ethnic lines; indeed, the whites were themselves deeply divided on the political issues of the day. So, when Spain decided to repress the American rebellions by force, war against Spain was invariably interwoven with conflicts between regions and between social and ethnic groups.

Without a single, generally accepted symbol of authority, Spanish America broke up into many separate parts in 1810. Such division in turn brought disenchantment with creole governments and undermined their military effectiveness, allowing Spain to retake control of most of the empire following the restoration of Fernando VII in 1814. War was, however, to prove a powerful corrosive of colonial authority. Military mobilization, whether under leaders of revolutionary vision (such as Bolívar, Morelos or San Martín) or under local politicians and warlords with more parochial aims, brought new men into politics, fuelled patriotic sentiments, opened new avenues of social advance and undermined established patterns of wealth and power. It also destabilized the monarchy in Spain, leading to another deep political crisis in 1820 which, though it restored the constitutional regime established by the Cadiz Constitution, undermined Spain's authority and fighting capacity in America. Thus, although much still remained of the structures of the colonial past, Spain seemed an increasingly weak and unstable centre even to loyalists. In these circumstances, the balance of opinion and power shifted decisively towards the advocates of independence, and by the mid-1820s new states had replaced colonial governments throughout the American continents. Now entirely free of Iberian control, the countries of Latin America embarked on a future in which they could chart their own courses, albeit in cultural settings which long continued to bear the abiding marks of three centuries of Iberian rule.

Further reading

Anna, Timothy E., *Spain and the Loss of Empire*, Lincoln, NE and London, 1983

Boxer, Charles R., *The Golden Age of Brazil, 1695–1750*, Berkeley and Los Angeles, CA, 1964

Brading, D. A., *The First America: The Spanish Monarchy, Creole Patriots, and the Liberal State, 1492–1867*, Cambridge, 1991

The Cambridge History of Latin America, vols. I–II. Cambridge, 1984

The Cambridge History of the Native Peoples of the Americas, vols. II–III, Cambridge, 1999–2000

Cook, N. David, *Born to Die: Disease and New World Conquest, 1492–1650*, Cambridge, 1998

Gibson, Charles, *The Aztecs under Spanish Rule: A History of the Indians of the Valley of Mexico* Stanford, CA; London, 1964

Gruzinski, Serge, *The Conquest of Mexico: The Incorporation of Indian Societies into the Western World, 16th–18th Centuries*, Cambridge, 1993

Halperín-Donghi, Tulio, *Politics, Economics and Society in Argentina in the Revolutionary Period*, Cambridge, 1975

Hemming, John, *The Conquest of the Incas*, London, 1970

Lynch, John, *The Spanish American Revolutions, 1808–1826*, 2nd edn, Norton and London, 1986

McFarlane, Anthony, *Colombia before Independence: Economy, Society and Politics under Bourbon Rule*, Cambridge, 1993

McKinley, P. Michael, *Pre-Revolutionary Caracas: Politics, Economy and Society, 1777–1811*, Cambridge, 1985

MacLeod, Murdo J., *Spanish Central America: A Socioeconomic History: A Socioeconomic History, 1520–1720*, Berkeley, CA, 1973

Maxwell, Kenneth R., *Conflicts and Conspiracies: Brazil and Portugal 1750–1808*, Cambridge, 1973

Mills, Kenneth R., *Idolatry and its Enemies: Colonial Andean Religion and Extirpation, 1640–1750*, Princeton, NJ, 1997

Rodríguez O., Jaime E., *The Independence of Spanish America* (Cambridge University Press, Cambridge, 1998)

Schwartz, Stuart B., *Sovereignty and Society in Colonial Brazil*, Berkeley and Los Angeles, CA, 1973

Stern, Steve J., *Peru's Indian Peoples and the Challenge of Spanish Conquest: Huamanga to 1640*, Madison, WN, 1982

Thomas, Hugh, *The Conquest of Mexico*, London, 1993

2

Latin America since independence

Over the last two hundred years there have been continuous debates over the origins, development, identity and future of Latin America. Indeed, this term is itself a Parisian concoction of the 1860s that sought to bestow a terminological unity upon a region that seemed to lack cultural, political, economic and even geographical coherence, particularly to outsiders and especially to Anglo-Americans. Both at home and abroad the quest for a convincing explanation of the evolution of the American ex-colonies of Spain and Portugal has often descended into interpretations based on race or some 'Iberian tradition' or a ubiquitous economic 'dependency'. Whether optimist or fatalist in vision, such essentializing has usually taken on a providentialist spirit and combative tone, but it has rarely matched the assurance of the self-images and ideologies underpinning the popular culture of the United States from the 'manifest destiny' of the 1840s to the globalizing ambition of the post-Cold War era.

As much of the material in this *Companion* will show, that margin of comparison with 'the North' has provided a rich vein of cultural creativity so that even in conditions of economic inferiority and political disadvantage Latin Americans have retained a distinctive identity. By the end of the twentieth century this was also true inside the frontiers of the USA itself, where the expansion of the Hispanic population to over 30 million (roughly equivalent to that of Argentina) and the broader effects of globalization had further weakened the over-stressed notion of Anglo-Saxon supremacy, based on the ideology of Protestant supremacism, and the formal egalitarianism of the Founding Fathers, many of whom held slaves.

Until 1847 California – arguably the site and certainly the primary source of the twentieth century 'American dream' – was part of Mexico and thus 'Latin American'. This was also true of Texas until 1835, with all of Arizona and New Mexico as well as parts of Colorado, Utah and Nevada being ceded to Washington by the Treaty of Guadalupe Hidalgo that ended the Mexican-American War in February 1848. According to the US Bureau of Census, what it calls the 'Latino' population of the country is growing at such a rate that by 2050 it will be half that of the 'white' citizenry and double the number of African-Americans. At the turn of the century, Los Angeles is amongst the most important of the cities of Latin America, and Miami is best understood not just as a major conurbation of Florida (bought from Spain in 1819) nor even as a Caribbean entrepot but as a continental metropolis.

Nonetheless, 'Latin America' is still rarely treated as extending north of the Rio Grande, and this chapter will follow orthodox historiography in applying the term to those polities that derived from the possessions of Portugal (Brazil, declared independent in 1822 and a republic in 1889) and Spain (all the other mainland states bar Belize, Guyana and Suriname; the Dominican Republic; and Cuba and Puerto Rico, which remained colonies until 1898, after which the former was transformed into a republic and the latter into a commonwealth of the USA).

As can be seen from the table 2.1, the populations and economies of these countries remain very varied in size, and any idea of a Latin American commonality should always be qualified with respect for the region's diversity. Even at the start of the twentieth century, Brazil, only fifteen years a republic and the last state of the continent to abolish slavery, was justifiably behaving as a regional power with continental influence, and Argentina's flourishing agriculture had made it the seventh richest economy on the globe. At the same time, their shared neighbour Paraguay, invaded by both these states and Uruguay in the 1860s, was a tiny, impoverished backwater. Yet the retention of a buoyant Guaraní culture in Paraguay gave that country an indigenous vitality that had already been expunged from its large neighbours, which had emphatically embraced a course of Europeanizing 'civilization'. Bolivia, Peru, Ecuador, Guatemala and southern Mexico likewise possessed strong indigenous populations that had survived the conquests of the sixteenth century, adapted to Hispanic power over the subsequent two hundred years, and yet did not show much collective desire

Table 2.1 *Latin America: statistical profile*

	Size	Population (millions)				GDP per cap. (1970 US)			Life expectancy (years at birth)		Vehicles (per 000 population)		Illiteracy (% population 15+)	
	(1970 000 sq km)	1850	1900	1950	1995	1900	1950	1995	1930	1995	1940	1990	1940	1995
Argentina	2,777	1.1	4.7	17.1	34.6	439	773	1,402	53	72	30	178	18.3	3.8
Bolivia	1,099	1.4	1.6	2.7	7.4	–	261	310	33	60	3	40	72.1	16.9
Brazil	8,512	7.2	18.0	53.4	161.8	71	215	809	34	66	4	88	56.1	16.7
C. America*	499	1.8	3.0	8.8	32.5	–	310	559	32	70	6**	41	60.0	21.6
Costa Rica	51	0.1	0.4	0.8	3.4	–	371	880	42	77	6	87	26.8	5.2
Chile	575	1.4	3.0	6.1	14.2	283	576	1,392	35	75	10	82	27.1	4.8
Colombia	1,139	2.2	4.0	12.0	35.1	118	360	856	34	70	3	41	43.1	8.7
Cuba	115	1.2	1.6	5.5	11.0	272	380	480	42	76	10	47	23.7	3.5
Dominican Rep.	49	0.1	0.6	2.1	7.8	–	244	545	26	70	1	48	69.6	17.9
Ecuador	284	0.8	1.0	3.4	11.5	89	230	549	–	69	1	38	49.4	9.9
Mexico	1,973	7.6	13.6	27.7	91.1	261	458	1,090	34	72	7	119	53.9	10.4
Paraguay	407	0.4	0.6	1.4	5.0	–	295	559	38	69	2	45	40.7	7.9
Peru	1,285	2.0	3.8	6.9	21.6	104	370	562	–	67	4	31	57.6	11.3
Uruguay	187	0.1	0.9	2.2	3.2	–	864	1,351	–	73	32	139	18.7	2.7
Venezuela	912	1.5	2.5	5.1	21.8	106	974	1,248	32	72	10	105	58.0	8.9
Latin America	20,020	30.4	62.1	159.0	468.7	(194)	394	879	(36)	69	19	94	49.0	13.6
USA	9,373	23.2	76.0	150.7	255.4	1,478	3,299	7,742	59	76	–	–	4.2	1.0

* including Costa Rica and Panama

** Panama = 24.6

to adopt the paraphernalia of modernity which most official culture now automatically deemed to be progress. Thus, in addition to differences between countries, one must be sensitive to deep-seated social diversity within nation-states descended from colonies based upon military and sometimes social conquest.

The diversity of the region is perhaps most manifest in the fact that – in contrast to the thirteen Anglo-American colonies which declared independence in 1776 – the possessions of Spain and Portugal eschewed federalism and had by the start of the twentieth century mutated into some twenty separate republics. Indeed, they were only very cautiously embracing regional integration at the millennium despite a shared Iberian inheritance: absolutist rule through viceroys; all regions except Brazil administered in and dominated by the Spanish language; the liturgically and financially unchallenged sway of the Roman Catholic Church; common legal procedures and economic monopoly under the Habsburgs; common centralizing reforms under the Bourbon and Pombaline regimes in the late eighteenth century. This political separatism is generally accepted to be the result of strong regionalist sentiment, the massive natural obstacles to economic expansion and integration, and the weak commercial, industrial and social pressures to overcome those impediments.

For many scholars and commentators of the post-1945 era, such variety was merely parochial and folkloric in character precisely because until the late twentieth century nowhere – not even in Brazil or Argentina – was economic backwardness overcome, or the consistent political democracy associated with northern Europe achieved. Whether this is understood as an Hispanic lack of enterprise culture – 'underdevelopment as a state of mind' – or as a result of continued colonial institutional resistance to the accumulation of capital or as a consequence of a northern imperialist extraction of the surplus, Latin America was often perceived to be different within itself only in secondary ways and to inconsequential effect.

Since the 1970s, however, scholars have been much more sensitive in their treatment of colonial legacies or what has been called 'the problem of persistence', recognizing that many aspects of life did change, that by no means all change was progress or benefited the condition of humans alive at the time, and that the balance between continuity and rupture should not be viewed exclusively either from a northern-universalist standpoint or from a culturally relativist, particularist perspective.

Yet, despite its less judgemental and prescriptive approach, the new historiography of Latin America tends to emphasize continuity, the power of the past and the rhetorical or exceptional qualities of change. The prevailing fashion is to underplay the importance of political independence in the early nineteenth century, which is often depicted as the expression of traditional patriotism rather than modern nationalism, and to emphasize the political and socioeconomic ruptures of the 1920s and 1930s, which led to the massification of culture and production in the largest states, qualitatively widening the gap between them and the small republics.

The rest of this chapter is devoted to a survey of the region divided into chronological cycles: the challenge of independence, from 1800 to 1860; liberalism and modernity, from 1860 to 1930; populism, revolution and dictatorship, from 1930 to 1980; and neo-liberalism and globalization, from 1980 onwards. This periodization is only approximate, and it certainly does not apply equally to all countries or to every society within those countries. It is a rather traditional approach in that it perceives important political and economic shifts within the nineteenth century, and it adheres to the standard twentieth-century watersheds given by economic crises (the 1929 Crash and the 1982 debt crisis). On the other hand, it follows revisionist accounts in recognizing a bonding antagonism between the populist mobilizations of the 1940s and 1950s and the anti-communist dictatorships of the 1960s and 1970s.

Equally, such an approach should not be taken as seeing each period as the product of a comprehensive removal or transformation of the main features of the preceding epoch. Some aspects of life two hundred years ago – for instance, the prominent public role of the family or the importance of uniforms and public processions – remain intact and vibrant today. Others, such as merchant guilds or chapel-based charities, were eliminated or radically overhauled within a few years of the Patriot victories that ended European dominion. In Brazil, where independence amounted in one sense to the minor constitutional adjustments of 1807, 1815, 1822 and 1841 to monarchical rule, substantial economic developments were underway well before the establishment of the republic at the end of the century. At the same time, a strong case can be made for the notion that since the 1930s the Brazilian armed forces have occupied a quasi-monarchical role, and that a semi-continental state is as likely to require such a presence in 2000 as in 1800.

The challenge of independence, 1800–1860

There are at least two senses in which Latin American independence may legitimately be seen as part of the era of 'Atlantic revolutions' between 1760 and 1830. First, many of its avowed ideals and constitutional precepts were derived from the European enlightenment and the examples of the Anglo-American and French insurrections. Simón Bolívar's own education, outlook and practice illustrate this firmly, even as they also manifest complex counter-currents, Hispanic contradictions and the epoch's inevitable circumscriptions upon expressions of political universalism (the first popular vote for the president of the USA by adult white males was in 1824). Secondly, the loss of the American colonies of Spain and Portugal was a direct result of the Napoleonic wars. The French invasion of Iberia triggered a crisis in monarchical legitimacy, prompting the creation, diversion and destruction of armies, causing havoc with Atlantic trade and deepening the tensions caused by the reforms of the 1770s that had been designed precisely to increase the control of Madrid and Lisbon over their colonies.

Independence itself eventually yielded an unprecedented combination of practical authoritarianism and impractical constitutionalism. Nonetheless, the easy critique of its failed promise in terms of expanded liberty, economic development and the construction of coherent civil societies often ignores the shifting international context and the extraordinary rigours of a process which began within months of the French invasion of the Iberian peninsula in May 1808 and ended with the death of the last general loyal to the Spanish crown in April 1825. In that period the defeat of the Napoleonic empire enabled Spain to launch a renewed and particularly vicious struggle to regain its possessions in what are today Venezuela and Colombia, where a 'war to the death' was conducted until 1820. More than anywhere else, this campaign took on the qualities of a civil war as local creoles (Spaniards born in the continent) and mestizos (people of mixed race) strove to reconcile their convictions with past loyalties, the shifting balance of forces and the defence of family and property in cruel and unstable times. Unsurprisingly, many of those who supported the crown at the outset were leading the Patriot cause at the end.

In the seat of one viceroyalty, Mexico, early signs of popular enthusiasm for, and participation in, the struggle, together with the involvement of radical priests like Hidalgo, raised fears of some kind of social revolution, perhaps like that in Haiti in the 1790s, and so provoked a conservative military project within the rebel camp. This has usually been associated with the *caudillo* (warlord) Antonio López de Santa Anna, who would dominate the turbulent political life of the young republic until well into the 1850s. In Peru, the other viceregal seat of power, the experience of the chaos and destruction of the campaigns conducted over several years to its north (Bolívar and Sucre) and south (San Martín and O'Higgins) served to consolidate the reactionary disposition of the local elite, weakening support for a rupture with the metropolis so that in 1824 the Patriots had to all intents and purposes to invade the country.

The fact that even after their victory at the Battle of Junín in August 1824 Bolívar's forces had their horses stolen and were harassed by guerrillas drawn from the local Quechua people underscores the important point that the Patriots by no means enjoyed a monopoly upon popular support, and that the colonial regime was possessed of strong patriarchal attractions as well as the advantages of familiarity. Almost everywhere the cause of independence had threatened to impose sociopolitical novelty as well as causing huge material and personal destruction. Unsurprisingly, many Brazilians as well as relocated Portuguese members of the elite considered themselves fortunate to have escaped this pattern by virtue of the self-exile of the royal family – a move that was consolidated in 1822 by the refusal of the king's heir to return to Lisbon, a decision which led almost seamlessly to the declaration of Brazilian independence.

However consequential the divisions between Brazilian liberals and conservatives over the following thirty years, and whatever the limits on political freedoms and participation under the new empire, the achievement of sovereignty there was incomparably less violent and conflictive than in Spanish America. When the Emperor risked getting mixed up in a conflict of similar character by pursuing Brazilian claims on what is today Uruguay a combination of local opposition and British intervention forestalled deeper involvement. It was not until the 1860s and the war of the Triple Alliance against Paraguay that Brazil again ventured seriously into regional military conflict.

Independence cannot be fully understood without taking into account the roles of Great Britain and the USA, as well as those of Spain, Portugal and France. Whilst London formally stuck to a stance of non-intervention during the campaign, thousands of soldiers from the British Isles who had been demobilized after Waterloo went on to serve in the

Patriot forces, and the British merchant fleet, which had long experience of contraband as well as legal voyages in the Western hemisphere, continued to ply the most profitable trade almost regardless of the state of diplomatic relations with Madrid. Foreign Secretary George Canning boasted that he had 'brought the new world into being in order to redress the balance in the old', and there was a very real sense in which the British sought an advantageous 'balance of power' against the Spanish and French Catholic monarchies in addition to securing new allies more disposed to open their markets to cheap manufactures.

It was Canning's proposal of a joint approach to the independence struggle that led to the espousal of the Monroe Doctrine in 1823. Whilst this was subsequently interpreted as a declaration of opposition to any extension of European presence in the continent (and so also applicable to British possessions in the Caribbean), it began as a much narrower condemnation of colonialism and the monarchical form of government. Monroe sought, above all else, to signal the solidarity of the USA with the struggle of fellow republicans in the south. However, it would be another quarter of a century before Washington was able to act on its high-minded sentiments, and when it finally did so, through the Mexican-American war, this took the form of itself invading and annexing a neighbouring republic on grounds of expediency expressed as providence and without any European power being involved. Although the United States had nurtured a barely veiled desire for Cuba since Jefferson's presidency in the first decade of the nineteenth century, it made no direct move against the Royalist forces that retreated to the island after 1824, only invading it in the last months of the century. Indeed, although after the Mexican war Washington was able to force London to the bargaining table over Central America, it was not for nearly twenty years after the US Civil War (1861–5) and the closing of the western frontier that it seriously turned its mind to extending political and economic influence southwards.

Great Britain, in fact, never seriously sought to colonize the territories that it had wrested from 'Old Spain', even those zones of Nicaragua where for a while London maintained the fiction of having a kingdom on the Mosquito Coast. If the British had an imperialist design, it was one of 'free trade', occasionally – and much more occasionally than some of the literature suggests – bolstered by the force of the ships of the Royal Navy. Latin America became independent a decade after the establishment of the gold standard in 1815 and as the British cotton and textile industries were swamping existing markets at home and abroad. Over the next two decades falling textile prices and the gradual introduction of steamships had the effect of driving much small-scale and under-capitalized Latin American textile manufacturing enterprises out of business. Some goods, of course, were carried the other way – ships need ballast – but the trade was decidedly in Britain's favour, and it was not matched by significant investment in the region. Not only did the burgeoning railway industry at home offer a much better return and more secure guarantees to those holding capital, but those activities most enticing to speculators, such as silver mining, were amongst the most prejudiced by the wars, the most expensive to revive and located in some of the most inhospitable territory of the subcontinent. Many schemes collapsed in the years after independence whilst loans from Barclays and other banks incurred almost immediate default, wrecking the creditworthiness of the new states at a time of precarious financial stability.

The rapid collapse of expectations of an externally induced economic transformation of the old colonial structures is often elided with the widespread rule of *caudillos* (warlords) to depict a dark and retrograde age. Indeed, by the late 1830s liberals such as Domingo Faustino Sarmiento, the most vocal of the Argentine 'Generation of 1837', saw the state of the subcontinent as having regressed to a barbarism in stark contrast to European civilization, despite the fact that many features of the early political economy of independence were precisely Spanish in their origin. The real position, however, was never that bleak, and the orthodox image of mid-nineteenth-century Latin American political society as cleanly divided into conservatives (pro-Church; pro-military; centralist; defensive of corporate property and the merits of local traditions) and liberals (anti-clerical; pro-market; federalist; advocates of change and external models of civil society and industry) is unsustainable. So also is the view, eloquently expressed by Octavio Paz, that independence had achieved rupture from Spain but created nothing new, and so was a wholly vacuous if not negative experience. If a Latin American generation in the nineteenth century was fifteen years, we may say that three generations lived an existence of frugal sovereignty (including general food security), relative social stability, high political turnover, slight external intervention, and a broad notion – rather than sharp anxiety – that 'development' could be improved.

The achievement of sovereignty and the formalization of republican institutions were by no means inconsequential. After 1814 liberal forces in both Spain and Portugal themselves were weak, and the Iberian monarchies effectively restored reactionary authoritarianism without fomenting industrial progress. Moreover, whilst the Spanish monarchy resolutely defended slavery in its remaining colonies of Cuba and Puerto Rico, Portuguese merchants were prominent in the Brazilian slave trade, which, notwithstanding treaty agreements with Great Britain from 1816 to abolish it, continued and increased until 1850. Of course, as evidenced by the United States until 1861, slavery is perfectly compatible with the republican form of government, but in the independent republics of Latin America it flourished nowhere for long, was abolished everywhere by the 1850s.

The rights of citizenship as they are understood in the early twenty-first century scarcely prevailed in practice even within the small clusters of landlords, merchants, priests, judges and soldiers who comprised the local elites, regional oligarchies and national ruling classes. Nevertheless, the constant avowal of such liberties, their rhetorical deployment in factional disputes and their (often inaccurate) association with British supremacy and Anglo-American success both kept them in the popular purview and offered a mobilizing means of social control to supplement the rigours of conscription, the weight of custom and the dead hand of caste. When Europe underwent its brief and abortive revolutionary upsurge in the spring of 1848, the echoes in the Americas suggested that a select group of *puros* or idealist radicals were struggling alone against die-hard autocrats presiding over the conservative masses. However, the governments of the day were generally in the hands of men – often military officers – without a closed ideology and pragmatically inclined to an assortment of policies.

In some states, most prominently Mexico, this 'centre' was indeed flanked by a strong right and left, which defended sharp and coherent positions with respect to religious property and the centralization or federalization of power (together with the corresponding tax and militia systems). Furthermore, these civilian groups frequently resorted to military alliances, so that the first decades of independence in the most populous and historically most powerful of the old colonies were especially unstable. The Mexican Church had more property than any other and continued to be the country's main source of credit well into independence. It was a natural target for liberals, but attacking it did not automatically entail liberating capital tied up in inalienable corporate property, forgiving burdensome debt and promoting free thought or modern behaviour.

Many people, happy to be relieved of paying the tithe (effectively abolished in the 1830s), also rented property from the Church, borrowed at low rates of interest, sold their produce to it and drew solace not only from its strictures in a time of unnerving confusion but also from its rites, which reconfirmed the existence of community. From the 1850s, then, the Mexican Church would face effective liberal and secularist attacks on its privileges, wealth and doctrines, but, as during the Revolution sixty years later, it retained a remarkable popular loyalty, eventually surrendering the political platform of ultramontane conservatism in order better to uphold it in pastoral practice.

The independence wars had not been conducted with equal intensity throughout the region – no real fighting occurred in Central America – but once sovereignty was achieved a premium was everywhere placed upon stability. This was earliest and most emphatically achieved in Paraguay under the ascetic republican dictatorship of Dr Francia, one of the very few intellectuals to gain – let alone hold – political power. 'El Supremo' combined a populist manipulation of a peculiarly strong mestizo culture with ruthless treatment of enemies and an equally vigorous refusal to open the small and self-sufficient state to outsiders or to get involved in the conflicts of its feuding Platine neighbours. When Francia died in 1840, having ruled his pacified protectorate for three decades, much of his legacy was retained by Antonio López and then his son Francisco Solano López, but the latter drove it to destruction precisely by intervening in external affairs and so drawing the wrath of Brazil and Argentina down on what was depicted as a dangerous anachronism.

These two countries, Mexico (twenty-five governments in 34 years) and Paraguay (three governments in 60 years) – the most and least powerful sites of Spanish colonial power – stand at the extremes of the early republican experience. Most of the new countries witnessed a political and economic evolution that fell between the chaos driven by ideology and interest and autarkic stasis bred of aversion to the risks of change. Although he is popularly seen as an unbending tyrant, Juan Manuel Rosas, who, as governor of Buenos Aires, ruled most of what is today Argentina from 1833 to 1852, was quite capable of altering his positions on free trade or relations with Brazil and Europe. The Chilean governments that upheld the conservative legacy of the centralist dictator Portales after his death in 1836 retained an equally close alliance with the Catholic hierarchy and proved just as flexible on questions of trade. They, however, were more liberal on matters of education, not only permitting Andrés Bello, the diplomatic architect of independence, the space to experiment but also hiring the services of the very ideologues like Sarmiento and Alberdi who were struggling to overthrow Rosas in the name of civilization.

Whatever their particular ideological admixture or vulnerability to *caudillo* pretensions, all the new states suffered from the predictable post-colonial problem of uncertain administrative limits, materially and culturally contestable frontiers, and the escalation of localist sentiment into either federalism or, in some cases, international rivalry. Bolívar had continued to promote a federal solution even as he despaired of democratic governance of the type evolving in the United States. His final years were mired in conflict with Santander, whose championing of what today would be called a nationalist vision was no less refined and in many ways more practical and democratic. Once Gran Colombia had broken up into present-day Venezuela, Colombia and Ecuador the federal vision lost momentum. The Central American Confederation, enfeebled by clerical and popular antipathy and a phantom fiscal base, collapsed at the end of the 1830s, driving what had been a tranquil region into forty years of feuds, conspiracies and fighting that had strong inter-state as well as ideological and localist components. The effort by Andrés Santa Cruz in the same decade to combine Bolivia and Peru so threatened Chile and Argentina that both invaded the new polity and, together with the president's domestic rivals, soon succeeded in redividing states originally delineated by colonial jurisdictions and not yet possessing a cogent social basis for the personal ambitions and administrative jealousies that made up much of public life.

Rosas could invade Bolivia in 1838 in the name of Argentina, but Argentina did not exist as a formal polity until the 1860s. Provincial governments and identities extended well beyond survivalist obeisance to the local *caudillo*, making the construction of a nation-state a major politico-logistical as well as ideological challenge even for the most resourceful of leaders. Moreover, the broad settlement of inter-provincial feuds over the decade following Rosas's removal by the Unitarian forces did not of itself open up or pacify the southern frontier of Hispanic settlement and culture with Araucanian/Patagonian society. Just as the jurisdiction of the USA reached the Pacific long before its control – let alone law – was imposed on much of the intermediate territory, so most of the young Latin American states found themselves at mid-century with a serious imbalance between the formal and practical dominion they exercised.

On the other hand, the disturbing over-supply of soldiers bequeathed by the independence wars was dying off, the initial offensive on colonial institutions had cleared the institutional terrain, Spain had joined the major powers in recognizing their sovereign existence, and the political temper of the epoch required a sense of moral and material purpose rather than mere management of the status quo. The achievement of a more selective fellowship with the colonial past within the elite both allowed a wider recognition of the claims of the future and posed the challenge of pursuing modernity by eliminating 'barbarism'. Since this was in most cases associated with indigenous society and frontier culture, what the Argentine officer Lucio Mansilla called 'civilization without mercy' joined education, secularism, science and roads and railways in the symbolism of 'progress'. The attendant rupturing of social systems, suppression of ancient cultures and adoption of alien behaviour was indeed to produce unprecedented wealth, providing Latin America with a path of development coherent to outsiders and conducive to capitalist reproduction. However, for many of the subcontinent's 30 million people in 1860 the cost was so high as to make the post-independence years seem very far from a dark age.

Liberalism and modernity, 1860–1930

In the second half of the nineteenth century Latin America underwent rising economic growth driven largely by the export of agricultural products and minerals. At the same time the region as a whole – Argentina, Brazil and Mexico most particularly – began to acquire the attributes of capitalist modernity, including the emergence of banks; the development of both infrastructure and the state; and an incipient manufacturing sector with a few privileged workers receiving wages. A political universe that had moved from kings and viceroys to *caudillos* and essayists was further transformed with the appearance of political movements, still with strong personalist and 'social' attributes but now avowedly ideological in their pursuit of interest. The holding of elections was more common, although nowhere were women permitted to participate, and it was not until the 1916 poll in Argentina that a vote based on universal manhood suffrage was held. In addition to the restrictions imposed by property qualifications, most Latin American states excluded illiterates from the political nation until the 1950s (Peru and Brazil until the 1980s – see Table 2.1 for the contemporary rates). We may, then, only talk of the beginnings of a very distended and often-interrupted process.

It is only after 1860 that trade really takes off, improving in turn the conditions for investment, especially from Great Britain, which continued to rely on its sales of textiles into the region (half of UK textile exports in 1860; a third in 1900) and which increased imports from Latin America fourfold between 1860 and the First World War. This growth in commerce was focused in a few areas – Argentine beef, maize and wheat; Brazilian cotton, coffee and rubber; Chilean nitrates; Peruvian cotton – and the effect was almost always to concentrate capital, support services and political influence, these sectors becoming distinct productive successes rather than prompting a 'take-off' of the economy as a whole.

British investors increased their capital in the region from £81 million in 1860 to £1.2 billion in 1913, concentrating their stock in Argentina, Brazil, Chile and Mexico, and preferring government bonds and railways to any industrial activity. Capitalists as well as ideologues saw the Latin American future as one based on 'free trade', in which the region would exploit its natural resource endowment and comparative advantage of cheap, disciplined labour to sell competitively on the world market. This required a stable state to ensure social order and guarantee market transactions because credit and trade were trespassing beyond the bounds of parochial familiarity and personal trust. The institutionalization of the behaviour and the servants of the state, and alterations both to the horizon between public and private spheres and to the notion of property all had some local roots but were also part of a 'globalizing' trend and so involved the adoption of foreign models and values.

At the level of ideas and culture, this experience is treated extensively in the chapters that follow, but it should be noted here that the idealist liberalism of the early nineteenth century, derived from the Enlightenment and based on the rights of man, increasingly became subsumed and overtaken by a new strain founded on positivism and an almost mystical faith in the potential of science, and not just for the critical elimination of diseases such as yellow fever. It was also evident in the overhauling of the armies of the region by European experts, who 'professionalized' them not only with the latest weaponry (which opened up a technological gap between the military of the state and those of provincial *caudillos*) but also in logistical methods, strategic thinking and adhesion to corporate discipline. Revolts continued to occur and men continued to join armies for personal advancement and gain, but insurrections ceased to be the norm and were increasingly viewed as aberrant. Where the army did take power, it often did so on the grounds of establishing order so that the offices of the state could be returned to civilians.

The conduct of the military in the two major international wars of this period – the War of the Triple Alliance of 1866–71 (Paraguay against Argentina, Brazil and Uruguay) and the War of the Pacific of 1879–83 (Chile against Peru and Bolivia) – was a chaotic mix of old-style conscription, tactical bravado and strategic confusion with modern breech-loading weaponry of small and large calibre capable, as in the dreadful experience of Paraguay, of considerable slaughter. These conflicts showed up the need for reform and further modernization – the experience of the Brazilian officer corps helped to accelerate the end of the empire, and universal conscription was introduced in Argentina two decades before manhood suffrage (it was also the first of the region's systems to be abolished, in 1997). On the other hand, the wars marked a watershed between the era of local militias and a socialized military that could be led by virtually anyone with initiative and able to mount a horse (the basis of the Patriot forces at independence) and that of professional castes averse to many attributes of civil society and, by the 1960s, quite capable of taking state power without recourse to democratic justification as well as visiting horrible violence upon inhabitants now treated as security threats rather than citizens.

In the late nineteenth century the new military mission was precisely to create citizens and to secure the frontier and the orderly comportment of those who lived within it. In both cases that mission was driven by fierce new ideas about race and property. Even in the countries with strong autochthonous societies or widespread miscegenation – Mexico and Guatemala, the Andean states, Brazil and Paraguay – there was emphatic elite adoption of the popular European notions that humanity could be scientifically categorized into physical types, each of which manifested distinct behavioural attributes. This conviction, which carried little of the odium that racism was to acquire with the rise of Nazism in the next century, was readily compatible with the widening 'modernity gap' between Latin America and the USA, where the indigenous peoples were being driven from their traditional lands and forcibly removed to reservations as a consequence of white settlement based on farming and the development of railways that drove up land prices.

The fact that the USA was a country of recent European immigration – 4.5 million between 1840 and 1860 alone – encouraged the Brazilian oligarchy to seek a similar solution to what was expected to be a major crisis of labour supply with the abolition of slavery in the 1880s. In Argentina, where similar ideas about 'whiteness' subsisted with less intensity and in a smaller society with very few blacks, a comparable effort was made to recruit skilled workers from abroad, populate a pampa recently conquered from tribes driven back into Patagonia and 'improve' the racial stock of a people stigmatized by Sarmiento and for whom the schools he had set up when president were deemed a necessary but insufficient agent of civilization. Both countries registered some success – between 1880 and 1910, 2.8 million Europeans migrated to Argentina and 2.1 million to Brazil – but not to the degree that overhauled their demographic profile. Existing economic and social trends were accelerated rather than new ones established, and much of this flow of people can be explained by the fact that a Europe so often eulogized as the fount of progress and creativity created such progress at the cost of great poverty and under regimes often more autocratic and usually more aristocratic than those of the Americas.

The experience of the liberal years lies at the heart of subsequent ideologies about race and social identity in both Argentina and Brazil, with the elite of the latter simultaneously embracing a prescriptive 'whitening' and celebrating miscegenation in succession to the social death that was slavery. In Mexico, by contrast, the revolution of 1910–20 gave rise to the idea of a 'cosmic race' precisely in response to the social failures and the racial prejudice of the prolonged regime of Porfirio Díaz (1876–1910). The *porfiriato* is probably the best example of the mutation of regional liberalism from its early constitutionalist focus to the later emphasis on social engineering and the concentration of power, with modernization being given a much higher priority than democratic participation. The Díaz regime demonstrated that just as republics were compatible with slavery, so was liberalism with closed oligarchic rule and dictatorship.

Part of the explanation for this, of course, lies in the extended anarchy of the first sixty years of independence, which included not only the loss of much territory to the USA but also European invasion in the 1860s (notionally in support of the liberals but through the imposition of a monarch, the Emperor Maximilian). The nationalist and populist campaigns of the mestizo liberal leader Benito Juárez against Church wealth and conservative centralism in the 1850s and 1860s had linked him back to the independence heroes Guerrero and Hidalgo. Yet under Díaz, the democratic potential of that legacy was ruthlessly filleted, even the traditionally autonomous provincial elites being closely subjugated by a central state fortified as much by the new railways that could transport troops as by the infusions of US capital that enabled the raising of loans and paying off of political debts. For the first time in modern Mexican history, Anglo-American investment was welcomed, and it came willingly, drawn in by a labour regime which was cheap and which mixed contemporary European wage arrangements with rural debt-peonage systems that had prevailed four hundred years earlier. The repeating rifles of the *rurales* and the barbed wire of the new commercial ranches ensured a high degree of order in a countryside famed for banditry. Some enormous profits were returned, but one long-term outcome of the process was the unleashing of a revolution that would contain powerful social as well as political elements and that would – in the shape of Emiliano Zapata and the *Plan de Ayala* – forcibly reverse many of the changes in the legal status and practical usage of property introduced during the *porfiriato* under the rationale of economic liberalism.

The structure of land tenure and the pattern of productive and social activity in the Latin American countryside has always been complex, even when starkly inequitable in effect. In areas of dense indigenous settlement communal landholding often involved complicated arrangements for assigning its seasonal use to families of groups as well as differing customs of labour and distribution. Where the Europeans had settled and established farms – by no means everywhere that came under their administrative sway – there existed a range of methods for holding labour on the estates. Sometimes this was what many sociologists in the 1950s and 1960s considered the classic feudal device of *colonato* or the retention of a worker and his/her family on the manor in exchange for usufruct rights on a small plot. Just as often, though, large landlords or *hacendados* would rent out lands for a share of the crop or advance loans and deduct repayments (on unfavourable terms) from wages. Occasionally they would rely directly on wages, but until well into the twentieth century these would be largely in the form of kind and accommodation.

Until the expansion of export-led growth in the late 1900s, most peasant agriculture was for household subsistence with any surplus being offered for sale in village markets and most estate production was for regional commerce, being conducted as much to reproduce the social world of the *hacienda* (including the often conspicuous consumption and extremely leisured life of the owner's family) as it was to secure profit. Commercial accounting methods were used and labour sharply exploited but within a logic less of capitalist modernization than of hierarchical conservatism. There was also a stratum of small farmers and rich peasants – in Colombia they were responsible for much coffee production – but the fact that under the colony the Church was the region's largest landlord and remained the source of much agricultural credit into the early republic fortified the social and cultural obstacles to any economic transformation in the countryside. An often oppressive and unfair regime did not endure simply because of political power and state support: it would also be sustained by important elements of familiarity and negotiated social contracts based upon popular acquiescence.

Elements of this world may still be encountered in parts of Latin America at the start of the twenty-first century, and in some places, such as the central valley of Chile, this traditional system possessed formidable economic as well as social roots – as resilient in the face of the US-sponsored reforms of the 1960s as it was against the socialist challenge in the early 1970s or the neo-liberal market forces of the 1990s. However, in most regions, this system came under pressure from the late nineteenth century on both fronts, and whilst some landlords undoubtedly failed, the main social cost was borne by the rural poor. As commercial opportunities rose and profit in currency acquired increasing importance the terms of employment and tenancy on the hacienda and plantation tightened. Equally, it proved cheaper and easier to expand area in crop than increase yields, encouraging encroachment on peasant-worked lands. Where these were seen by those who lived and worked on them not simply as property and an economic asset but also as a birthright, the site of graves and religious places and the source of community, it proved exceptionally difficult to bring them to market. In the last decades of the century, then, it proved necessary to pass new laws 'unlinking' communal lands from their origins in inalienability. Much of this legislation identified private ownership as the principal source of progress, but often this virtue was achieved by outright trickery.

Subsequent patterns varied a great deal. What Zapata rebelled against in the Mexican state of Morelos after 1910 was quite similar to the experience of Guatemalan and Bolivian peasants, who won agrarian reform in the 1950s (very briefly in the former case). The social strains were also comparable to those suffered at the same time by squatters in Cuba whose access to lands was directly affected by movements in the world sugar price and so, too, the area planted in that crop or left free for them. Equally, the civil wars of Central America of the 1980s had important roots in a polarized rural system that lacked space for people either to move physically to a new frontier or to flourish on the basis of family production. Elsewhere – the south of Brazil, the Argentine pampa, parts of northern Mexico and the Venezuelan plains – population was light, production was pastoral rather than agricultural and the main challenges were those of establishing property right for the first time and securing a return from them by new methods of production and sale.

The long-range picture was one of a widening gap between commercial and subsistence agriculture, or between farming as a capitalist enterprise and as a family livelihood. Over the twentieth century the number of landless rural workers grew, as did migratory flows composed of these people – first inside countries, then within the region and then abroad, to the USA and beyond. Although the Latin American population was predominantly rural in settlement until 1960, the process of urbanization had in many places already consolidated the notion of land as property, challenging a life based on daily and seasonal cycles of nature as well as a parochial culture.

Nowhere was this process more acute than on the plantations established by US corporations from the late nineteenth century, primarily in the Caribbean area. Developments in the technology of shipping and refrigeration meant that it now became possible to base an export strategy on those perishable agricultural goods in which Latin America seemed to have a magnificent comparative advantage, particularly fruit and beef, as well as the staples such as coffee and cotton. The rise of the US fruit companies was, though, part of a general Anglo-American expansionism from the 1880s. By the time US troops invaded Cuba in 1898, many in the region feared and denounced this new 'imperialism'. In the case of Cuba, José Martí had long warned against 'exchanging one master for another', but elsewhere Spain had lost any political salience and – as in the famous essay of 1900 by the Uruguayan journalist José Enrique Rodó, *Ariel* – Spain persisted primarily as a cultural reference, now representing 'civilization' against the arrogant materialism and brutalist democracy of the USA. A few, such as the Peruvian Marxist José Carlos Mariátegui – who, like Martí, embraced US democratic culture – were able to strike a more nuanced image of Anglo-America in recognizing its emancipatory and reflective inheritance from the likes of Emerson, Thoreau and Whitman. Yet Mariátegui was also to the fore in championing 'Iberoamericanism' against the Pan-Americanism dictated by the United States.

Within five years of the overthrow of the last Spanish colonies in the Western hemisphere, President Theodore Roosevelt had added his 'corollary' to the Monroe Doctrine whereby the United States arraigned to itself the right to intervene in other regional states for the purpose of securing payments of debt, protecting the property and lives of foreigners and, in effect, sorting out governments of a contrary disposition. As with Monroe, the formal rationale was impeccably high-minded, but in distinction to Monroe, Roosevelt was able to implement his policy. In the first twenty years of the century, US troops were deployed in eight Latin American republics – on four occasions to help rebel forces – North American officials supervised half a dozen elections, refused to recognize ten governments and imposed explicitly political conditions on loans to six countries. Almost every case of this 'big stick' policy was in Central rather than South America, but if it proved more difficult to manipulate the larger and more distant states, they were scarcely less affected by the rise of US commerce and investment. By the outbreak of the First World War regional trade with the USA had overtaken that with Britain, and by 1938 – the last year of uninterrupted Atlantic trade before the Second World War – over a third of all the international commerce of the region was with the United States, double the level with Britain. Between the First World War and the Crash, US investment in Latin America tripled, with half the direct and portfolio capital in 1929 going to South America.

These levels of economic interaction meant that even convinced foreign policy idealists in the USA, such as Woodrow Wilson and William Jennings Bryan, could not evade a deep and perturbing involvement with their neighbours. Their 'dollar diplomacy' sought to reduce direct deployment of troops but achieved neither this nor the equitable Pan-American amity so often celebrated in official speeches north and south of the Rio Grande. To the contrary, the deployment of US forces in Mexico during the Revolution – and particularly their landing at Veracruz, where General Scott had caused such destruction in 1847 – not only revived a visceral anti-Americanism but gave it an increasingly ideological and 'anti-imperialist' quality. In the case of Mexico, this sorely tested bilateral relations between the capitals because, under the 1917 constitution, the possession of private property was circumscribed with regard to oil and mineral rights. The almost simultaneous victory of the Bolsheviks in Russia raised the prospect of US–Mexican relations being 'communized' when the real issues were nationalist sentiment, the institutionalization of common land (*ejidos*) and occasional state involvement in production.

In fact, the issue of public property would still complicate relations between the two countries at the end of the century, when the USSR had ceased to exist and the North American Free Trade Area (NAFTA) tied them together as commercial partners.

At the Pan-American conference held in Havana in 1927, the charge against US arrogance was led not by the Mexican delegation but by that from Argentina – the country most distant from and least affected by the USA. However, the substance of the criticism related to US activities in Central America, particularly Nicaragua, where the marines had been stationed for a number of years in support of an evidently unworkable policy of backing the dominion of the Conservative Party against the Liberals ousted with US support in 1909. When, in 1928, an obscure Liberal general named Augusto César Sandino refused on the grounds of sovereignty to sign a local pact brokered by the US, there began a low-level but vicious guerrilla war that would lock the US into a deeply unpopular sponsorship of a new constabulary – the National Guard, led throughout its fifty-year life by members of the Somoza family.

Sandino's anti-imperialism was of an eclectic nature that gave full expression to a number of important currents of Latin American thought including freemasonry, theosophy (belief in the trans-migration of souls), anarcho-syndicalism and communitarianism (but not communism). His embracing of a mysticism derived as much from the shrill streets of Buenos Aires as the squat baroque churches of Matagalpa, and his energetic proclamation of mestizo primacy made any bracketing of Sandino very problematic. Yet it was precisely this contradictory mixture of influences and voices that fired the Latin American radicalism of the 1920s, from the successful Mexican revolutionaries to the Peru-based APRA (American Popular Revolutionary Alliance) movement led by Haya de la Torre, who supported Sandino and outlived him by nearly fifty years but was never able to form a reformist government in Peru.

One of the central aspects of the APRA platform was the demand that the Panama Canal be placed under international ownership. The fact that Sandino supported this demand less than fifteen years after Washington's completion of a waterway that had been the principal objective of its support for Panama's 1903 secession from Colombia made the strategic issues at stake more salient than they might appear in retrospect. Certainly, the construction of a trans-isthmian canal route amounted to more than the achievement of an engineering project that had been promoted in various guises for more than half a century as the answer to the continent's bi-oceanic challenge. The legal annexation through tenancy of the land around the canal provided the USA with a powerful military base at the head of South America, thousands of kilometres from its own territory and well south of Mexico. From 1914 it was no longer possible to conceive of inter-American relations in terms of either an imbalance remediable by recourse to Europe or a denial of superior Anglo-American capacity.

In many respects the emergence of what is now termed a 'hegemony' on the part of the USA seemed compatible with the liberal project of modernization in the rest of the continent. Here was a more proximate and bountiful source of capital than had been Europe in the last century. Moreover, there was a significant degree of trade complementarity and institutional similarity even if the religious and cultural descent of the two Americas had been quite distinct. Yet, as we have seen, nationalist sentiment in the south had scarcely been sharper than at the end of the 1920s, when the US appeared to be set on a path of unparalleled affluence worthy of imitation and collaboration.

Populism, revolution and dictatorship, 1930–80

So extensively had Latin America embraced the strategy of export-led growth over the previous fifty years that it received the full impact of the Crash, only those sectors tied to domestic-use agriculture escaping a comprehensive fall in prices and contraction of markets, which diminished by the order of a quarter in the first half of the 1930s. It was very soon evident that this was not a cyclical slump of the type experienced in the 1890s and after the First World War. The markets had failed fundamentally and a market-driven ideology such as liberalism was put under such stress from the increasingly organized and vociferous working and middle classes of the cities that key sections of the elite and military opted to drop the pretensions and institutions of liberal democracy. By 1930 the Soviet Union had proved itself sufficiently durable to win the sympathy of knots of trade unionists in a region that shared several socioeconomic features with Russia, and although communist organizations never came to flourish in the continent except in Cuba after 1959, fear of them and the exploitation of anti-communism was henceforth a strong figure of populist as well as conservative politics.

The impact of the coups, failed popular resistance and uprisings was enhanced by the fact that it was – with a clutch of critical exceptions – region-wide in scope. The administration of F. D. Roosevelt, although itself the most progressive US government since Lincoln's, resolutely adhered to non-interference as part of a 'Good Neighbor' policy designed to avoid further international embarrassments such as the campaign against Sandino. Moreover, so comprehensive was the collapse of democratic institutions in the region that when this policy was introduced early in 1933, Colombia was arguably the only country upholding the rule of law and allowing free and fair elections. Had Washington cleaved to a policy of intervention in order to uphold liberal democracy, it would have had to invade the entire subcontinent. Those inclined to denounce the 'gringos' for their interference now had to confront the consequences of neglect.

The impact of the Crash and subsequent anti-liberal backlash was compounded by the fact that within a dozen years it was followed by another sharp externally induced shock, the Second World War. This intense and see-sawing period, in which both fascism and social democracy emerged as further ideological models for the subcontinent, provided the political education for a generation of civilian and military leaders who would dominate public life in the post-war epoch. Whether radicals or conservatives, their distrust of liberalism was founded in experience and in the opportunity to experiment with alternative policies and political cultures.

Neither Venezuela nor Cuba – countries that at the height of the Cold War in the 1970s stood as the regional exemplars for capitalist democracy and Communism – had experienced liberal politics in the 1920s. In Venezuela the dictatorship established by General Gómez in 1908 and fortified by the discovery of huge oil reserves was rocked by student opposition but held on until the death of the autocrat in 1935. The failure of the young reformists to unify around a programme that matched rhetoric and practice meant that after the war, anti-communism provided General Pérez Jiménez with local and international cover to install another authoritarian regime, which expanded the traditional system of favours to a graft and malfeasance fully comparable with those instituted by Generalissimo Trujillo in the Dominican Republic and General Somoza in Nicaragua since the early 1930s.

However, Venezuela's rapid modernization and oil wealth could no longer be sustained by such narrow, 'banana republic' means, and when, in 1958, the military struck in the name of institutionalized politics, the Social and Christian Democratic parties took care to keep their competition modulated, to exclude the Communists from the system and to secure a strong US alliance. At the same time, they regularized a form of 'machine' or network politics in which favours were exchanged on the basis of partisanship and depended largely upon electoral success. Over twenty years this system was sustained by oil income, but when the price fell it lost its vitality, and by the late 1980s it had been badly weakened by over-exploitation. Rather like Gómez's dictatorship, the 'partyocracy' was resilient enough to withstand the initial impact of economic crisis, and although it could not survive the sustained pressures that built up in the 1990s, it eventually fell not through a coup but at the ballot box.

Cuba almost matches Brazil in being an exception to most generalities about Latin America. Its revolution of 1959 remained throughout the Cold War a solitary American outpost of Communism – in Nicaragua the Sandinistas never seriously essayed the socialization of property – defying the United States throughout and, after 1991, also the logic of international relations when its reluctant sponsor, the USSR, collapsed. The Revolution had its origins both in the political failure to substitute the colonial regime with a stable liberal system and in the economic stresses derived from notionally successful indicators – high investment, high company integration, expanding production, intensive competition and work-rates – returned largely by US companies which dominated the sugar industry. In 1933 the particularly repressive Machado dictatorship collapsed before a revolt led by a sergeant named Batista, and the buoyant governments that followed claimed to have staged a 'revolution' although Batista always held control over the process, even when, as a result of the ideological alignments caused by the war, the Communists drafted a constitution and entered the administration.

As in Venezuela, the Cold War climate of the 1950s encouraged a descent into anti-communist dictatorship, but when Batista took that path in 1952 he sparked a much fiercer opposition, which would, in the shape of the Sierra Maestra guerrilla formed by Fidel Castro and Che Guevara, pick up more on the legacy of Sandino and Zapata than of Lenin. Confused as to how to react to the young bearded rulers of this small but highly strategic and wealthy island-state, the clumsy US political class did much to drive a not unwilling Havana into Moscow's arms. For decades Washington kept alive what was always an expensive and sometimes an embarrassing alliance for the Soviet Union by imposing on Cuba a punitive embargo, sustained well past the Cold War era largely because of the strong exile lobby in Florida. One central consequence was that

Cuban Communism was constantly revitalized by nationalist sentiment, Castro relying on far more than the ideological and cultural rigours of one-party rule to uphold an always personalist regime.

For a while Cuba did represent a genuine security threat to the USA, and so, with a grain of perversity, some source of Latin American pride. Castro picked up on Martí's hard-nosed romanticism, and for many on-lookers there was in the ethos of voluntary work, the sacrificial qualities of the guerrilla campaigns abroad, and in the formidable achievements in the field of health and education enough Spartan virtue if not to justify an autocratic government then at least to neutralize US attacks and exile invective. A renaissance in the 1990s of the musical and cinematic rich-ness released early in the Revolution further complicated the imposition of stereotypes drawn from the Eastern Bloc, but the reduction of the ques-tion of political leadership to the frailty of a single individual suggested that at least some aspects of the colonial past had not been overcome.

The Cuban Revolution was very much a generational phenomenon abroad as well as at home, and in the 1960s it was adopted as a model by many young people unpersuaded by Leninist orthodoxy, unattracted to Anglo-American materialism and unconvinced by liberal democracy, which, in its Christian form, stoked up more piety than could be accom-modated by a pusillanimous pragmatism, and in its social democratic form enunciated a rhetorical reform plainly beyond its practical capacity. In the wake of the Revolution, even the United States recognized that the socioeconomic and political structures of the region were in bad need of regeneration. Yet the virulent dictatorships of the following years owed their origin more to the exhaustion of political cycles begun with the Crash than to the Cuban Revolution itself.

After 1930 the pattern of Brazilian public life began to approxi-mate more closely to that in Spanish America. In that year a central-ist coup headed by Getúlio Vargas adopted and came to deserve the tag of 'revolution' by sweeping away the essence of the federal system sus-tained by provincial oligarchies under the 1891 constitution. Although the Depression made its costs clearer still, regional rivalry – not just be-tween São Paulo, Rio de Janeiro and Minas Gerais, but also in the impov-erished north-east – had weakened the 'Old Republic' on almost every front but especially in terms of international competition. It took Vargas half a dozen years to secure the institutionalization of a centralist regime in the *Estado Novo*. This 'pause' reflects the requirements of suppressing a resourceful movement of military radicals and the genuinely fascist

'Integralists' as well as those of constructing an alliance of officers, bureaucrats, ideologues and entrepreneurs able to sustain a corporatist project not dissimilar to those of Salazar and Franco in Portugal and Spain. The *Estado Novo*, though, was always 'American' – Brazilian troops fought in the Allied campaign in Italy – and it was far more focused on an industrialized future – the opening of the Volta Redonda steelworks at the end of the war was a key moment in the modernity of Latin America as a whole.

Brazil – a country of continental proportions – possessed both the underused capacity and the natural potential to exploit the ruptures in world trading caused by the Crash and the Second World War. Such an 'import-substituting industrialization' (ISI) involved increasing flows of foreign capital in the 1950s and 1960s but also a substantial intervention by the state since industrialization was seen by many in the military as a form of control of strategic resources necessary for national security. The dismantling of the *Estado Novo* in 1945 made inevitable by the international climate opened a twenty-year effort to combine its developmentalist impetus with a more open, competitive political life. But this, with almost equal inevitability, challenged both the unreformed structures of power and property in the countryside and the fragile social controls over an urban sector constantly being expanded by industrialization. Under the Kubitschek presidency in the 1950s, this strategy of liberal capitalism took on an impressive confidence, manifest in the construction of Brasilia as well as infrastructure on a positively North American scale. However, this was a shallow 'modernity' that over the next three decades would produce in the world's ninth largest economy the highest inequities of wealth to be found anywhere. Moreover, throughout the second half of the twentieth century there was no serious effort to reform a structure of land ownership which continued to spawn hunger and violence in the backlands even as production of crops like soya in the south was amongst the most modern and efficient in the world.

When, early in the 1960s, these burgeoning tendencies were joined by political agitation within the troops, the high command stepped in, imposing a regime that was to last for twenty-one years and resonate of the *Estado Novo*, not least because several of the corporatist measures from the 1930s were now given prominence. This was by far the longest of the modern military regimes of Latin America, in part because it possessed such strong antecedents as well as facing weak opposition. Largely resistant to personalism, it achieved stability through permitting a tightly restricted formal opposition and repressing all other. Moreover, once the 'oil shocks' of the 1970s had brought the 'miracle' levels of growth to a halt in a major oil-importing economy, the military embarked on a closely invigilated *abertura* (opening) predicated on the conviction that Brazilians were not 'ready' for 'full democracy'. This view ran quite counter to the evidence of a campaign for civil and human rights led in the early 1980s by the trade unions of the São Paulo industrial belt together with the Church – an alliance that mirrored the Solidarity movement in Poland, even if they also shared the attribute of having a more telling critique of the present than vision of the future.

The cycle of authoritarianism and populism in Argentina also began with a coup in 1930, and, like the *Estado Novo*, the government of Juan Domingo Perón (1946–55) combined strong nationalist and developmentalist motifs. However, the Argentine experience was much more emphatic at its ideological extremities, leading in 1976 to the imposition of a military regime more sanguinary and impious even than that of General Pinochet, whose 1973 coup in Chile provided a potent precedent. One key reason for both Perón's eager embracing of labour organisations in the 1940s and their repression in the 1970s by the junta was the deep tradition of trade unionism in Argentina. Thus, when the lodge of nationalist officers to which Perón belonged seized power in 1943, they could not readily take a middle course with respect to labour, which had been inefficiently held at bay since the 1930 coup by a mix of corruption, electoral fraud and police harassment. By October 1945, Perón had, as secretary of labour, won sufficient support to face down his conservative colleagues and establish a powerful movement which would directly and indirectly dominate the country for the rest of the century with its blend of nationalism and redistributionist rhetoric together with state interventionism and sponsorship of welfare and popular organization.

Unlike Vargas, Perón, who had decided sympathies with Germany and its allies, did not negotiate an early accommodation with the USA, which resulted in very frosty relations in the immediate post-war years although the president was plainly anti-communist. His administration also assumed a more confident style through the person of his wife, Eva Perón, in many ways its most charismatic figure and most truly modern politician in the projection of her personality. The fact that gold reserves built up during the war enabled the government both to nationalize British assets, especially the railways, and to preside over a post-bellum pay and consumer boom provided strong material foundations for the

Peronist project. These, though, were not prerequisites for a movement that responded keenly to a popular need for political incorporation and a bonding ideology with its *Justicialismo*, a notional 'third way' between capitalism and communism.

Perón's overthrow and exile in 1955, and his return in the early 1970s, formed part of a pattern of veto-politics whereby largely military regimes struggled to keep a mercurial labour movement in check as the economy stuttered and inflation fired up. Yet no social pact that excluded Peronism could be sustained, and even Perón's own return eventually proved to be of little avail, as extremists on both right and left claimed his imprimatur and colonized a disjointed organization. By March 1976, when the junta seized power from his third wife Isabel, Argentina had descended into a crisis that seemed to herald civil war.

In fact, the military declared war on a section of its own citizenry, inflating the subversive menace on the left out of all proportion, executing perhaps 15,000 people without formal process and usually after torture, before hiding their cadavers. The effect was to imbue a sophisticated and energetic civil society with a deep fear and sense of denial. However, the generals' conservative technocrats were not able to exploit the absence of the supposed problematic factor – unruly wage demands and lack of investor confidence – to stabilize an economy that was now registering the world recession as well as the aggregate effects of local mismanagement. Thus, the rather desperate decision in April 1982 to invade the Falkland Islands is best seen as a political gamble of an embattled and unpopular regime. Decisive defeat in that conflict made the military's subsequent efforts to secure impunity for the repression much more difficult than in Chile, particularly because they had been engaged in offering for adoption the children of their victims – a practice that even the most indulgent of civilian politicians could not overlook.

In Chile, Pinochet's coup in September 1973 against the constitutionally elected *Unidad Popular* alliance led by Salvador Allende was arguably an event comparable to the Mexican Revolution or Perón's taking of power in terms of marking a continental political moment. Certainly, the introduction from 1975 of an economic policy based on neoclassical doctrine by a team trained in the University of Chicago was to prefigure a programme adopted throughout the region a decade later. But in so violently destroying a party political system and civil contract of fifty years Pinochet was looking to a deeper past of hierarchical order. Even a decade after the dictator's departure in 1989 the effects could be clearly discerned. Amidst the Santiago smog and electricity cuts caused by a socially unconcerned, market-driven modernization, there prevailed a social caution, latent deference and a sense of community much more shallow than that in neighbouring states so often disparaged as primitive by the Chilean elite.

At the other end of the ideological spectrum, the Nicaraguan Revolution (1979–90) that overthrew the Somoza dictatorship may also be seen as closing rather than starting an epoch. Its derivations not only from Sandino but also Cuba, liberation theology and the cultural world of the 1960s virtually ensured US hostility, even from the Carter administration; and when Reagan took office eighteen months after the FSLN (the Sandinista National Liberation Front), there began a five-year campaign of public intimidation and covert subversion that was illegal under both US and international law and would have brought down regimes in much less ramshackle countries. The Sandinistas were better guerrillas than governors, and they frittered away immense goodwill, but the 'threat of a good example' that they posed for the rest of Central America was too sharp for Washington to tolerate at a time when a regional war seemed likely. As a result, Nicaragua was energetically embargoed and, under US sponsorship of the 'Contra' guerrillas, it began to experience the rural civil war that had already enveloped Guatemala and El Salvador.

By the early 1990s, when those countries had been pacified by internationally brokered truces, their small and dislocated economies had been notionally purified with stabilization plans and the impedimenta of constitutional democracy re-erected. The return of liberalism was, however, accompanied by little popular celebration since, beyond the exhaustion caused by war, the material condition of the poor was not significantly improved and their participation in public life had in some senses diminished.

Neo-liberalism and globalization

The neo-liberal economic cycle of the last two decades of the twentieth century began in Mexico, which in August 1982 threatened to default on a substantial debt built up through a combination of expansive state expenditure and the eagerness of the international banks to lend. Despite immediate and quite favourable treatment by the United States, the Mexican collapse had within a few months spread to the rest of the subcontinent, where a not dissimilar pattern of indebtedness and fiscal

over-reach prevailed. When a similar scenario of Mexican financial collapse occurred a dozen years later, the adoption in the interim of stabilization plans and structural adjustment under the aegis of the International Monetary Fund and World Bank provided somewhat greater
protection for the rest of the region, but the high level of interaction with
the rest of the world economy and the extent to which this was driven
by speculation over 'emerging markets' meant that the melt-down of
the Asian economies in 1997 rapidly threatened a Latin American slump.
Even with the fiscal discipline and stern exchange-rate regimes of the new
free-trade era, the large economies of Brazil, Mexico and Argentina remained exceptionally vulnerable to external shocks, and the small ones
that were dependent on trade with them and the USA were even more so.

One response to this was a revival of regional integration, which had
failed when attempted in the 1960s and 1970s on the basis of import-
substituting industrialization. Now given the form of free-trade areas
and economic communities, this process registered some advances in the
early 1990s, particularly in North America (NAFTA, including Canada,
the USA and Mexico) and the Southern Cone (Mercosur, including
Argentina, Brazil, Paraguay and Uruguay, with Bolivia and Chile as as-
sociates). Yet for all the ambition – including contemporary variants of
Bolívar's project for continental federalism – progress was tenuous and
ever prone to economic misadventure, not least a downturn in the US
economy, which performed very strongly in the 1990s. At the same time,
there was a limit to the potential for integration under a free-trade model;
whereas the liberals of the late nineteenth century had built railways, the
neo-liberals of the late twentieth century closed them down, destroying
the best means to secure physical integration with unanswerable arguments about short-term profit.

The rigours of the marketplace also increased international migration
in search of work, and they encouraged a tendency to the methods and
style of populist autocracy in order to calm rising discontent amongst
those millions for whom the obligatory promise of jam tomorrow accompanying the demands of austerity today was too predictable and at odds
with experience to be persuasive. Where dictatorship had produced murder and mayhem in the 1970s there was a much greater reluctance to follow this political course, a sharper appreciation of the value of even weak
and corrupt civilian institutions and greater caution in the face of calls
for deliverance from men of destiny. Yet even in Argentina, where President Menem upheld a neo-liberal programme throughout the 1990s,

elements of this style proved successful in harnessing Peronism to an economic platform with which it traditionally had little truck. In Peru and Venezuela, where economic crisis had been presided over by the traditional parties, Presidents Fujimori (who also defeated the Sendero Luminoso guerrilla) and Chávez (who borrowed promiscuously from Bolívar) were much more emphatic, closing down congresses, appealing directly to the people and relying on tight collaboration with the armed forces in what were effectively constitutional coups.

In Mexico the prospect for such a development was much slimmer despite the fact that the neo-liberal reforms began in 1982 and accelerated after 1989 had rolled back so many of the policies associated with the Revolution that popular discontent had broken into armed conflict in the southern states of Chiapas and Guerrero. The containment of these challenges obliged the PRI (the Institutional Revolutionary Party), which had ruled Mexico since 1929, to concede much greater space to the opposition, which was now allowed to win as well as contest elections, and which by 1998 was able to take control of the legislature and then, in 2000, the presidency. Equally, membership of NAFTA required the surrender of elements of sovereignty that had been jealously guarded from the time of the war of 1847, gaining constitutional status as well as ideological pre-eminence after 1917. The defence of the *ejido* was abandoned and the country's banking system now effectively depended on the US Federal Reserve Bank, where Mexico had no representative. In the same vein, as we have noted, millions of Mexicans not only lived in the USA but also travelled to and fro (legally as well as illegally) in pursuit of work.

Many such impoverished people there and further south faced the stark dilemma between the opportunities afforded by one of the most vibant economic sectors – the drugs industry, with Latin America the principal supplier and Anglo-America the leading consumer – and the violence and erosion of law and order that attended such an illicit and mafia-dominated trade. In Mexico the clans which dominated the cocaine trade made deep inroads into the state, particularly the police. In Colombia, which had suffered a civil conflict along party-political lines since the 1950s, they enjoyed less success in that objective and operated as autonomous cartels and then in league with some of the guerrilla and vigilante groups.

By the end of the century and despite repeated efforts to agree truces and organize amnesties, that conflict had escalated to levels similar to those in Central America during the 1980s, forcing hundreds of thousands of people to leave not just their homes but their countries. No amount of constitution writing and institutional tinkering – still less the supposed catharsis of legalizing drugs – seemed to offer the security necessary for ordinary daily life. Yet only politics provided the means by which a deeper social contract might be drafted and agreed. After a phase in which Washington toyed with the effective criminalization of the government of Colombia, it came to recognize more keenly both the international context and consequences of the problem and the necessity for it to be given a local solution. The tension between these two spheres was perhaps sharpest in Colombia at the end of the millennium, but everywhere the convergence between domestic life and global forces posed the primary challenge as well as the sharpest threat in the new century. Sure enough, less than three years into the millennium, the economy of Argentina suffered a comprehensive 'meltdown' following the failure of an overly ideological exchange-rate policy. The chaos and anomie that ensued involved remarkably little violence but offered a grim portent.

Further reading

Adelman, Jeremy (ed.), *Colonial Legacies: The Problem of Persistence in Latin America*, London, 1999

Bethell, Leslie (ed.), *The Cambridge History of Latin America*, vols. III–XI, Cambridge, 1985–95

Brading, David, *The First America: The Spanish Monarchy, Creole Patriots, and the Liberal State, 1492–1867*, Cambridge, 1991

Bulmer-Thomas, Victor, *The Economic History of Latin America Since Independence*, Cambridge, 2003

Chasteen, John Charles, *Born in Blood and Fire: A Concise History of Latin America*, New York, 2001

Dunkerley, James, *Americana: The Americas in the World Around 1850*, London, 2000

Dunkerley, James (ed.), *Studies in the Formation of the Nation-State in Latin America*, London, 2002

Fausto, Boris, *A Concise History of Brazil*, Cambridge, 1999

Halperin-Donghi, Tulio, *The Contemporary History of Latin America*, Durham, NC, 1993

Hamnett, Brian, *A Concise History of Mexico*, Cambridge, 1999

Lewis, Daniel K., *The History of Argentina*, Westport, CT, 2001

Lynch, John, *Latin America Between Colony and Nation. Selected Essays*, Basingstoke, 2001

Morse, Richard, *New World Soundings: Culture and Ideology in the Americas*, Baltimore, MD, 1989

O'Donnell, Guillermo, *Counterpoints: Selected Essays of Authoritarianism and Democratization*, South Bond, IN, 1999

3
_____

Spanish American narrative, 1810–1920

In an essay written in 1928, the Peruvian radical intellectual José Carlos Mariátegui reflected on literary nationalism:

> The flourishing of national literatures coincides, in Western history, with the political affirmation of the national idea . . . with the liberal revolution and capitalist order . . . 'Nationalism' in literary historiography is thus a phenomenon of the purest political extraction, foreign to the aesthetic concept of art . . . The nation itself is an abstraction, an allegory, a myth, that does not correspond to a constant and precise, scientifically determinable, reality.[1]

In recent decades the concept of the nation has been under scrutiny in ways similar to Mariátegui's critique. But in Spanish America, the creation of nations is inextricably intertwined with literary development, and no single historical narrative can account for the multiple developments in the literary sphere. National political projects shaped historiography as well as the history and concept of literature because, despite similarities of language and formation within the Spanish heritage, vast geographic extensions and striking cultural differences made Spanish America difficult to conceive without national categories. The dominance of the national framework did not, however, preclude other visions of the future. From the early years of the nineteenth century, independence leaders like Francisco de Miranda and Simón Bolívar envisioned a unified Spanish America joined together by a common linguistic and occidental cultural heritage. Some of the most notable writers of the century were passionately committed to a cultural unity that surpassed national borders, but invented and real national differences have inevitably marked our readings over a century later. A vision of unity remained constant, but throughout most of the century was overshadowed by the national programmes. Intellectual leaders like Andrés Bello (1781–1865), in his prologue to *Gramática de la lengua castellana* [Grammar of the Castilian Language] (1847), called for linguistic unification as an antidote to fragmentation and dispersal. Even though a coherent version of the Spanish language was maintained during the century, the early dream of a unified Spanish America gave way quickly to national and regional projects. Yet cultural and linguistic unity, at least on the level of the reading public, was far more successful than any of the political unification projects envisioned by early leaders. Simón Bolívar's own extensive writings, especially his poignant 'Jamaica Letter' reflect on the dreams and defeats of a politically unified Spanish America.

The written word was one of the tools that had bound together the Spanish empire in America. An extensive and labyrinthine network of official documents – letters, legal documents, inventories, scientific reports, chronicles, ecclesiastical writings – moved back and forth between Spain and the Americas through a complicated series of hierarchies. The successful independence movements of the early nineteenth century and the decline of Spain as a world power slowed down this exchange and opened new circuits for Spanish America with other parts of the world, particularly with Enlightenment ideals of individual rights. Debates about a secular view of the universe inaugurated a longstanding struggle with the state-supported Catholic Church in Spanish America, culminating in Mexico with the anticlerical reforms in 1859 under Benito Juárez. Of course, Spanish dominance in cultural affairs had been waning even before the independence wars. Even though Spain had jealously guarded its viceroyalties against Protestant reforms in northern Europe and republican stirrings, the colonials in America were not isolated from revolutionary currents sweeping the world. And Spain's weakened economic system with its overburdened bureaucracies was close to collapse. Half-hearted economic and administrative reforms had not appeased the empire's rebellious subjects, and over time Spain's grip on its colonies had grown shaky. Even the expulsion of the Jesuits in 1767 came far too late to extirpate many of the new currents of thought that had taken hold in America. From the beginning Spain had established major universities in the colonies, especially in the Caribbean, Mexico and Peru, which created a small class of intellectuals, some of whom were critical actors in formulating the ideals for the new republics.

Language politics

Despite the crumbling of its empire, with the exceptions of Cuba, Puerto Rico and the Philippines, which remained Spanish colonies until 1898, a linguistic empire held sway. Language itself was the enduring tool of empire, as predicted by Antonio Nebrija when he published, in 1492, the first grammar of Castilian Spanish. Despite enormous differences in culture, history, economy, and with vast geographic extensions as a block to unity, Spanish remained the common language for literature and the state. The linguistic unity of a great sector of the population led revolutionary leaders like Simón Bolívar to dream of a united Spanish America. Almost two centuries later, the dream of united republics still re-emerges from time to time, at least in limited affiliations like trade blocs or cultural projects. But there is no question that the Spanish language in itself has produced at least a limited cultural affiliation, even among countries that have waged wars against each other, such as the War of the Pacific (1879) or the War of the Triple Alliance (1864–70). While the internal unity of specific countries was weak given political, racial or even linguistic strife, a common language for the large majority of Spain's former dominions served as the platform on which to establish other organizing ideologies.

Ethnic and racial politics

In addition to linguistic coherence, the concept of *mestizaje* has been one of the most enduring and powerful ways employed to unify very different regions and cultures within Latin America. Primarily a concept formed in the twentieth century (even though its realities extend back to the first years of the conquest), *mestizaje* in the biological sense and transculturation in the cultural sense have been dominant forms for understanding Latin American cultures. Yet nineteenth-century Spanish America could not embrace *mestizaje* as a founding cultural principle, so the new republics sought other materials for their foundational stories. It is not until later in the century when thinkers like José Martí, most famously in his essay 'Nuestra América' (1891; 'Our America'), calls for the incorporation of the neglected branches of the American family tree, the indigenous and the African elements, within the symbolic tree of life.

Romanticism, at least in its emphasis on 'natural' man and individuality, was problematic for the nation-building and civilizing projects of the lettered *criollo* (those of Spanish descent born in America) elite who sought to build limited democracies without relinquishing their often tenuous hold on the social unity among diverse groups. The long wars of revolution had created unlikely alliances among *criollos* (with slaves, indigenous groups, urban and rural mestizos, traders, merchants and mercenary soldiers who stayed on after the wars). Throughout two continents the wars had left many regions impoverished and with decimated populations. Another legacy of the war period was the notable militarization of many societies, first as an instrument of democratization and then as a limitation to its extension.[2] Indian uprisings, especially in the Andean region (where the rebellions of Túpac Amaru were as recent as 1780), and in Mexico (the Caste Wars in Yucatan in 1849), also created an uneasy vigilance among the new leaders. How then could literature partake in Romanticism's exaltation of nature and individual rebellion if most writers belonged to a group dedicated to taming nature, especially human nature, and harnessing its energy for their own projects?

This dilemma – celebrating America's newness as a society and praising its unique characteristics while setting forth a plan for new and harmonious societies – has served as the energy for a literary production of great variety and dynamism. Carlos Alonso has identified Spanish America's commitment to the 'narrative of futurity' as an important factor that separates the region from other post-colonial situations. 'Since all formulations of national character are artificial abstractions – imagined communities – in any event, theoretically there were no compelling ethnic, linguistic, or demographic reasons preventing the Spanish American Creoles who defeated the Spaniards from constructing a narrative of national origins based on the indigenous past.' But the commitment to a narrative of the future condemned the indigenous past to 'historical and narrative invisibility'.[3] Invisibility is obviously an overstatement, but it does illustrate the overriding pattern of narrative development throughout the century. The critic Pedro Henríquez-Ureña puts it another way, showing how writers shaped local situations to European norms:

> For the romantics, if the colonial centuries were our Middle Ages, then the Indian past represented our Antiquity; the cult of the indigenous was now at its height. Two novels, *Cumandá* (1871) by Juan León Mera (1832–1894) and *Enriquillo* (1879–1882) by Manuel de Jesús Galván (1834–1910), the poems by José Joaquín Pérez (1845–1900)

entitled *Fantasías indígenas* (1877) . . . and the long poem *Tabaré* (1886) by Juan Zorrilla de San Martín (1857–1931) were the most outstanding works inspired by this cult.[4]

Discordant elements, like social strife, ethnic, gender and class division within the great patterns had to be dealt with in a number of ways. For indigenous groups, primary among these solutions was extinction or disenfranchisement. In artistic treatments, remaining indigenous elements were romanticized or treated as picturesque elements of national traditions. *Indigenismo* as an aesthetic or ethical stance would emerge late in the nineteenth century with writers such as Peru's Clorinda Matto de Turner and would be a dominant literary force in the twentieth century. Nonetheless, throughout most of the nineteenth century the important indigenous presence would be treated literarily within the constraints of a romanticized Indianism, as will be later discussed.

Narrative and hybrid forms

Contemporary literary categories are limited tools for understanding the complexities of literary production in nineteenth-century Latin America where the pre-eminent modern literary genre, the novel, made a late appearance. If we look only to the novel for evidence of a dynamic literature we will miss alternating currents of other genres. Indeed, many of the central narrative texts of the century are not novels: the treatises of Andrés Bello, Simón Bolívar's letters and essays, Esteban Echeverría's verse narrative *La cautiva* [The Captive] (1837) and his story 'El matadero' (1838; *The Slaughterhouse*), the autobiography of the Cuban slave Juan Francisco Manzano (1797–1853) *Autobiografía de un esclavo*, *Facundo* (1845) by Sarmiento, the verse narrative *Martín Fierro* (1872) by José Hernández, Ricardo Palma's *Tradiciones peruanas* [Peruvian Traditions] (1860), José Martí's essays and chronicles, José Enrique Rodó's *Ariel* (1900), to name just a few. Although there was a fairly steady production of novels in the decades after independence, other prose genres like histories, letters, treatises, biographies, memoirs, journalistic writings and speeches also occupied writers.

El periquillo sarniento (1816; *The Itching Parrot*), a satiric picaresque novel by Mexico's José Joaquín Fernández de Lizardi ('The Mexican Thinker'), was Spanish America's first contribution to the genre, where a marginal hero's travels and trials reflect on Mexican society of the moment. Many have argued that earlier narratives, such as Juan Rodriguez Freyle's *El Carnero* (1638; *The Conquest of New Granada*) or Alonso Carrió de la Vandera's *Lazarillo de ciegos caminantes* (1775; *El Lazarillo: A Guide for Inexperienced Travelers Between Buenos Aires and Lima*), could be claimed as early examples of the novel in Spanish America. Yet Lizardi's work, first published in serial form, is still generally considered the first of its genre in the region, in part because Lizardi was the first to proclaim his work a novel. Even its author's position was somewhat anomalous. An intellectual formed in Enlightenment ideals and a productive journalist, Lizardi was not part of the *criollo* elite, was precariously educated and lived on his slim earnings as a writer. Nor did he see himself as a shaper of the new Mexico, in the line of men of letters in other countries such as Andrés Bello, Simón Rodríguez, Esteban Echeverría and later Domingo F. Sarmiento. His adopted role was that of critic, satirist and counterweight to national leaders. He, like many other writers of the first part of the century, concentrated on other literary forms designed in the search for an audience, especially for periodical production.

The first historical novel, *Xicotencatl* (anon. 1826) did not establish a trend in the century's first decades. *Costumbrista* essays, an eclectic genre which included satiric, historical and social commentary, tended to serve the function of historical novels in other areas, such as those of James Fenimore Cooper in the US. These *costumbrista* essays, sometimes difficult to classify as fiction or non-fiction, constitute a steady stream of literary production throughout the century and may be a better indicator of cultural production than the better-known genres of novel and short story.[5] But the absence of novelistic production prior to independence does not signal a deficient literary heritage. Instead it turns our attention to other forms of literature and to a different process of post-colonial literary development. The novel's absence is fairly easy to explain on one level: Spain had forbidden the circulation and publication of novels in its colonies, owing to their dubious reputation and their open windows to temptation. But of course, like most prohibitions, this one was not very effective in keeping novels out of circulation, and studies show that novels like *Don Quijote* had their widest readership in the New World.

The end of Spanish domination did not open the floodgates of novelistic production. Literary hierarchies, printing facilities, reading publics and the very context of newly independent societies were not in step with reigning European trends. There were nations to be created, independence heroes to be celebrated, and often violent internal divisions to be fought over and solved. Other daunting goals included forging a citizenry from many interest groups and social classes, establishing educational systems in tune with American needs and even establishing an appropriate form of Spanish for the new nations.[6] In what registers could writers best express the enormous tasks and vast ideals before them? Poetry was still regarded as the pre-eminent form of creative expression, and it is in verse form that great military feats were immortalized, such as José Joaquín de Olmedo's 'Victoria de Junín, Canto a Bolívar' [The Victory at Junín, Song to Bolívar] (1825) and meditations on the tasks of post-war national and social reconstruction, as in the poetry and prose of Andrés Bello, especially his 'Alocución a la poesía' [Allocution to Poetry] (1823). Narrative poetry had a long life in Latin America and even dominated narrative prose during long periods, in contrast with literary development at the same time in many Western nations. Poetry of popular inspiration, such as the *cielitos* of Bartolomé Hidalgo in Argentina and the Mexican *corridos*, popular epic lyric poetry with origins around 1830, alongside the centuries-old traditions of popular song in verse form throughout Spanish America and Brazil (the *cordel*) occupied a central place in popular literature. One of the most important and popular literary works of the century, José Hernández's *Martín Fierro* (1872) was a verse narrative, based on traditional popular verse forms. But late in the century Zorrilla de San Martín's *Tabaré* (1886) marks an end to the prominence of verse narrative. With Rubén Darío's *Azul* [Blue] (1888) poetry begins to occupy another role in the literary sphere, largely abandoning its narrative function.

Many writers, with some exceptions like Lizardi, saw their roles as founders and shapers of new governments and societies, or at least veiled critics. Recent critical appraisals of nineteenth-century novels, especially *Foundational Fictions* (1991) by Doris Sommer, have pointed out how the romance plots and intrigues of many important novels of the periods can be read as allegories of national organization. While allegory may not always have been a prime intention, the national focus of nineteenth-century history inevitably helps to produce an allegorical reading. Of course, the very essence of fiction is its mimetic power, with novels resembling scientific reportage and journalistic essays hiding their fictional bases.[7] This sleight of hand between fiction and fact is compounded even further in situations of censorship or political liability, so contemporary readings of this fiction are enriched by a knowledge of the specific writing context.

Thematic trends

For general thematic trends, the search must become more specific, since regional issues often dominated literary production. To name a few broad trends, we could identify categories in both prose and poetry as: nation building (often figured in the form of domestic drama), Indianism (particularly in Mexico and the Andean region), anti-slavery literature (especially in the Caribbean), *costumbrismo* or an emphasis on specific local or regional customs and language, and the theme of exile. As the century advanced and modernization increasingly became the goal, both in technology and in the ideology of rational modernity, topics such as money and finance, medicine and heredity and the roles of women also became important subjects.

Modernity and the struggle between 'civilization and barbarism'

Just as in the literature of conquest and colonization, the dividing lines between fiction and non-fiction are not always clearly marked, as in Domingo F. Sarmiento's *Facundo* (1845). This fascinating 'biography' of an Argentine caudillo written by Sarmiento under the dictatorship of Juan Manuel Rosas (1835–1852) – whose full title is *Civilization and Barbarism. The Life of Juan Facundo de Quiroga* – is ostensibly a case-study in the evils of barbarism that attack the progress of civilization, as represented by Sarmiento's goals of an enlightened Argentina in the European mould. But Sarmiento's message is, like its generic form, a hybrid one. Facundo as a character is fascinating, and the extensive descriptions of life on the pampas convince us as much of its grandeur and uniqueness as of its barbarity. The hybrid nature of *Facundo* and its ambivalent spell are in some ways indicative of the paradoxes of nineteenth-century literature. For Sarmiento, the conflicts between civilization and barbarism do not easily conform to European prescriptions, especially in the context of the tenets of European Romanticism. Sarmiento himself, later president of Argentina and primary force in its future vision, illustrates better than any other figure the close alliances between writing and political action in the nineteenth century.

Modernity's paradigms, as promoted early on by Sarmiento, involved both technological advances and the implantation of an ideology that went against the grain of the legacy of the Spanish colonial system and against the Church. The onslaught of modernity, with its marvels and its devastations, like those later conjured in García Márquez's *One Hundred Years of Solitude*, was unevenly distributed, leading to a coexistence of multiple temporal levels, like those described in the Cuban Alejo Carpentier's 1940s essay on marvellous realism.[8] The spread of education and the creation of a new reading public, the expansion of printing and the flourishing of the periodical press and the extraordinary advances in transportation and communications throughout the century, especially the construction of a network of railroads, united Spanish America and its literature.

In a temporal scheme, it is clear that modernization's impact creates definite changes in literary production after the middle of the century.[9] Both the novel and the short story become increasingly dominant genres, and narrative poetry largely fades as a vehicle for public expression. The incorporation of new classes of readers, technological advances in printing and distribution and increased mobility widened the circuits of literary distribution. By the century's end, large cities boasted numerous periodical publications and were able to produce books for broad audiences at reasonable cost. Despite Lizardi's early example as a writer who earned his living as a writer for periodicals, it was not until the end of the century when a professional class of writers could sustain themselves economically solely by their writing.[10] Like many of the *modernista* poets at the turn of the century, writers supported themselves with all manners of writing assignments, from vignettes of daily life, *crónicas*, in newspapers, to short-story publications in serial magazines and dailies, and jobs as reporters (even Rubén Darío covered the racing track while working for *El Mercurio* in Valaparíso, Chile, around the time of the publication of *Azul*).

Science and travel

During the eighteenth century, travel expeditions, many of which were initiated as scientific and commercial explorations, began to exert a strong influence on philosophic and literary reflection in Europe. The three Pacific voyages by Captain James Cook for the Royal Society between 1768 and 1776 were especially important in igniting the European imagination. The fascination with voyages to distant lands was not new, of course, but the renewed interest in the sciences, especially the classifications of Linnaeus and Buffon, created a convergence of scientific and philosophical searches. Spain under Charles III (1759–88) commissioned teams of scientists from several countries to explore scientifically and commercially its American colonies, partly because of its project of trade liberalization among the colonies. One of the most important of these expeditions was the Botanical Expedition of New Granada, initiated in 1784 and led by the Spaniard José Celestino Mutis. In its thirty-three years of existence the team produced thousands of minutely detailed studies of the flora of the Colombian highlands, the expedition ending because of Bolívar's campaigns in the region.[11]

It is Alexander von Humboldt, however, along with Aimé Bonpland, whose scientific travels and prolific writings over thirty years 'laid down the lines for the ideological reinvention of South America that took place on both sides of the Atlantic during the momentous first decades of the nineteenth century'.[12] Beginning in 1799, von Humboldt produced writings and drawings which created an astonishing vision of South America as a vast reservoir of the grandeur of nature. Humboldt's reflections on South America produced three basic images – tropical forests, snow-capped mountains and vast interior plains – that came to signify metonymically 'South America' during the transition period of 1810–50.[13] These primal American scenes were incorporated into both European and American visions of nature and served as part of the fund of inspiration and imagery of Romanticism for writers of both continents. Roberto González-Echevarría in *Myth and Archive* has identified this tradition of scientific travel writing as the mediating form for Latin American writing of the nineteenth century:

> the most significant narratives, the ones that had a powerful impact on those that followed in the twentieth century, were not novels copied from European models, as Mármol's [*Amalia*] and Isaacs' [*María*] texts were, but issue from the relationship with the hegemonic discourse of the period, which was not literary, but scientific. This is so . . . in the case of some conventional Latin American novels, such as Cirilo Villaverde's *Cecilia Valdés* (Cuba, 1880), which owed much to reports on slavery . . . Sarmiento's *Facundo* (1845), Anselmo Suárez y Romero's *Francisco* (1880) and Euclides Da Cunha's *Rebellion in the Backlands* (1902) describe Latin American nature and society through the grid of nineteenth-century science. . . . This particular mediation prevails until the crisis of the 1920s and the so-called *novela de la tierra* or telluric novels.[14]

It is both in content – the gigantic scope of American natural marvels – and in form – the scientific report – that scientific and travel literature serves as part of the framework of both fiction and essay of the period.

Even though the degree of von Humboldt's influence on Spanish American fiction could be debated, given that many of his own descriptions mirror those of earlier chroniclers and poets of Latin America, if not in detail at least in the scale of gigantism, it is unarguable that the form of travel literature and scientific reportage, both in the natural and in the social sciences, had direct impact on literary formation during the period.

Vicente Pérez Rosales (1807–66) was marked by travel within and from his native Chile. Witness to the upheavals of the years following independence in Chile, he worked in many jobs from journalism to mining, and in 1848, attracted by discovery of gold in California, travelled there and wrote his first book, *Diario de un viaje a California* [Diary of a Voyage to California] (1850) whose adventures still captivate contemporary readers. Appointed by the government to encourage European immigration to Chile, he travelled to Germany where he recruited colonists there and in other countries. His other books, *Ensayo sobre Chile* [Essay on Chile] and *Recuerdos del pasado* [Memories of the Past], are memorable for his vitality of language and observation. Like Sarmiento, he saw European immigration as a constructive element for Latin America, yet unlike many of his contemporaries, he was not slavish in his admiration for all things European: 'Parents follow a bad course when they separate their children from their home and their country to study in Europe in perverse French or bad English, without first giving them elementary instruction that they can learn in Chile in correct Spanish.'[15]

Costumbrismo and travel

Here we must mention not just travel writing but also the immense production in the visual arts by travelling botanists, geographers, archaeologists and reporters, including von Humboldt and Bonpland, Johan Moritz Ruguendas, Frederick Catherhood, Jean Batiste Delbert, Claudio Gay and many others. Customs of dress, festivals, architecture, food, as well as visual studies of social relations, particularly of slavery and of 'picturesque' figures such as gauchos became staples of both visual arts and literature. The *costumbrista* school of writing, ranging from natural scientific observation to early anthropological reportage, developed into an enduring strain of Latin American cultural expression. It reflected both Indianist trends of nostalgic evocation of the Aztecs or Incas and in its more naturalistic expression, served as the basis of sociological exposé of social ills and marginal populations. It ranged from the glorification of local and national custom, as in Ricardo Palma's *tradiciones* which exalted colonial lore in fictional form, in contrast to more scathing denunciations of local deficiencies by others. 'El matadero' written in the 1830s by Esteban Echeverría is one of the central narratives of the century, and its vivid recreation of a Buenos Aires slaughterhouse under the Rosas dictatorship captures with vivid detail the butchery of that violent epoch. Echeverría's faintly veiled allegory of the defeat of liberal ideals is embodied in the form of the young Unitario (term for those who supported a strong central government against Rosas's federal policies) who fatally ventures into the barbaric realm of the slaughterhouse, populated by a cast of lower-class and bloodthirsty servants of the great Restorer. Echeverría's poetry and political writings make him one of the major figures of continental Romanticism, in both its political and its literary significance. He was recognized as leader of the young political idealists with whom he founded the Association of May (1838) and wrote its founding statement 'Dogma Socialista' which expressed their ideals of democratic liberalism. Exiled in Montevideo, he was a leader of the group that would eventually topple Rosas, although he died before he was able to return to Argentina.

Like the *costumbrista* art of the period, *costumbrista* writings preserve social landscapes and regional expression, often with an attention to descriptive detail that can seem tiresome to the contemporary reader, more accustomed to the terseness of the short-story convention as established by Edgar Allan Poe. One of the most notable *costumbristas*, the Chilean 'Jotabeche' (José Joaquín Vallejo, 1811–58), began publishing in satiric periodicals. His origins in northern Chile led him to portray mining activities and customs with both didactic and satirical intent, and he recorded a gallery of types, customs and landscapes of the time. Other *costumbristas* include Mexico's Guillermo Prieto (1818–97) who also was dedicated to journalism for many years. Under the pseudonym 'Fidel', he published weekly columns collected as *Los San Lunes de Fidel*, written between 1840 and 1881. His central topics were political economy, travel reporting and history. Like the *tradiciones* by Peruvian Ricardo Palma (1833–1919), part of Prieto's writings recreated Mexican viceroyal society, recasting historical legends into fiction.

Flora Tristán (France/Peru, 1803–44) presents to us another kind of travel writing, one mixed with autobiography. Her *Peregrinación de una paria* (1837; *Peregrinations of a Pariah*), written in French, recounts her experiences as a female traveller in the early nineteenth century, especially her voyage to Peru in 1833 to claim her paternal inheritance. Centring her observations on human beings rather than on landscape, Tristán identifies herself as an outsider in many ways, but also as a member of a Peruvian family. Politically active, Tristán has been reclaimed by French and Latin American traditions as a feminist and socialist pioneer.

Lucio Mansilla of Argentina published *Excursión a los indios ranqueles* (1870; *An Excursion to the Ranquel Indians*) as a result of his experiences on a military expedition of 'pacification' of Indians in southern Argentina during the 'Desert Campaign' which finally subdued Argentina's indigenous resistance late in the century. (In Chile the parallel military campaign was called 'Pacification of the Araucania' roughly during the same time period.) Written not long after Hernández's *Martín Fierro*, Mansilla's critical vision of the Indian is more like that of Hernández or Sarmiento, who condemned them as 'barbarians' in contrast to other more romanticized reconstructions of an Indian past. The late conquest of Indian territory in both Argentina and Chile (as in the US) can explain certain differences with literary Indianism in other parts of Latin America.

Much later in the century, writers like Fray Mocho, pseudonym of José S. Alvarez (1858–1903), cultivate a type of urban *costumbrismo*. Fray Mocho published countless articles in *Caras y Caretas*, the popular weekly magazine published in Buenos Aires, satirizing and celebrating the tumultuous growth and change of Buenos Aires as it absorbed waves of immigration. In particular, he contrasted rural life with the urban setting, most notably of gauchos displaced in the big city.

Indianism

By the middle of the nineteenth century, slavery was legally abolished in the new republics (although not until 1880 in Cuba and Puerto Rico, still colonies of Spain) and Indian servitude was eliminated at least legally, although not necessarily in practice. It is generally accepted that racism became stronger in the second half of the century, buttressed by the 'scientific racism' developed between 1850 and 1920, based on an appropriation of evolutionary theories to classify societies by their primitive or advanced characteristics. As noted by Alan Knight, this heyday of scientific racism corresponds with Mexico's phase of liberal state building and capitalist export-oriented economic development, culminating in the 'order and progress' dictatorship of Porfirio Díaz (1876–1911).[16] Yet prior to this period, another version of the Indian legacies had been woven into the fabric of national myths, not just in Mexico, but in many countries. An early indication is José Joaquín Olmedo's narrative poem *Victory at Junín. Song to Bolívar* (1825) where the Inca is resurrected as a prophet to presage the victory of the revolutionaries over Spain. With only decades separating Olmedo from the recent Indian rebellions in Peru, such an alliance is an unlikely one, but it serves as an illustration of the romanticization of the indigenous past as building blocks of national foundations. Especially favoured were idealized visions of vanquished heroes, like the Aztec Cuahtemoc or the Incan Atahualpa, whose evocation was safely distanced from contemporary ethnic divisions. Writers drew inspiration from standard romantic fare like Chateaubriand's far-fetched *Atalá*, historical novels by Sir Walter Scott or James Fenimore Cooper's novel *The Last of the Mohicans* (1826). Combining histories of Spanish conquest and the renewed archaeological interest in indigenous America, Spanish American writers retrieved rich narrative elements and cultural symbols to weave historical fictions and memorable narrative poems. Early examples were the novels *Netzula* (1832, Mexico) by José María Lafragua and *Cuauhtemoc, el último emperador de México* [Cuauhtemoc, the Last Emperor of Mexico] (1846) by Gertrudis Gómez de Avellaneda (Cuba), who also wrote one of the first anti-slavery novels, *Sab*. Other novels of the Indianist type include *Cumandá* by Ecuador's Juan Leon Mera, and *Enriquillo* (1882) by the Dominican Manuel Jesús Galván, in which the title character is based on the historical figure first related by Bartolomé de las Casas in the early sixteenth century. Other examples include: *Iguacaya* (1872) by Venezuelan José Ramón Yepes, Mexico's *Los mártires de Anáhuac* [The Martyrs of Anáhuac] by Eligio Ancona and *Nezahualpilli* by Juan Luis Tercero. In Argentina, Rosa Guerra published *Lucía Miranda* (1860) based on the legends of the American archetype of female captivity by Indians; in 1861 Eduarda Mansilla published another novel of the same name, and the legend has continued to inspire writers throughout the Americas.[17]

With Clorinda Matto de Turner's *Aves sin nido* (1889; *Torn from the Nest*), fiction based on Indian themes changes its focus. This novel, set in the region of Cuzco, is considered generally as the first *indigenista* novel because it shifts the emphasis to the poor social conditions of the

Indians themselves and their abuse by the Church and other powerful entities. Matto de Turner, like the indigenist tradition she founds, is not a revolutionary. The resolution of the drama lies in the positive influence that the civilization of Lima, bearer of the ideals of modern progress, can have on redeeming the backwardness of the interior of the country. Her compatriot Manuel González Prada (1844–1918) was more radical in approach. Iconoclastic and anticlerical, González Prada is known both for his fiery speeches on social and political topics, including socialism and anarchism, and for his *modernista* poetry. His famous essay, 'Our Indians' (1904), is an unsentimental indictment of Peru's policies toward the Indians.

In the first decades of the twentieth century the indigenous theme is developed in fiction, by writers such as Alcides Arguedas (Bolivia), Jorge Icaza (Ecuador), Gregorio López y Fuentes (Mexico) and Ciro Alegría (Peru), mixing naturalist denunciation of social conditions with paternalism. Alcides Arguedas was also influential as the author of *Pueblo enfermo* [A Sick People] (1909), a diagnostic of the ills of Bolivian society.[18] These first decades witnessed a heightened consciousness towards the Indian, especially because of the Mexican Revolution. *Los de abajo* (1915; *The Underdogs*), the classic novel of the Mexican Revolution by Mariano Azuela, while focused primarily on the dynamics of the Revolution, creates another sort of portrait of the indigenous protagonist which will be important in Mexican literature throughout the twentieth century.

Anti-slavery literature

Anti-slavery literature was, of course, most important in areas of large slave populations, Brazil, the US and the Caribbean. Because of the relatively late date (1880) of abolition in Cuba and Puerto Rico, this topic continued to be important throughout the century. And because of the pervasiveness of slavery throughout the Americas, the topic also served as a unifying factor among literatures in other ways quite different, including the US and Brazil. Cuba was central in this respect. It may help to remember that in 1850, Havana was the second largest city in Spanish America after Mexico City and considerably more populous than other cities and continued to be an important cultural centre. Some of the better-known anti-slavery novels include: *Cecilia Valdés* by Cirilo Villaverde; *Francisco* by Anselmo Suárez Romero; *Sab* by Gertrudis Gómez de Avellaneda; and *Romualdo, uno de tantos* [Romualdo: One of Many] by Francisco Calcagno. Like many nineteenth-century novels, sentimental romance is a major element of these works. But the question of race complicates romantic and social relations. In *Cecilia Valdés* (1839, expanded 1882), the beautiful mulatta Cecilia falls in love with Leonardo, son of a wealthy Spanish landowner, without knowing that they have the same father. Doomed to tragedy, the couple live out a racial drama, one of the many represented in various ways in the literature of the period. *Cecilia Valdés* especially has continued to be read also for its rich portrait of its time and place.

National romance

Some of the best-known novels of the century are shaped around the sentimental romance. Even when there are no racial questions involved, romantic unions are faced with obstacles in the form of political affiliations, exile and economic differences. As Doris Sommer has suggested, many of these novels can be read as allegories of national formation, where opposing factions and interests resolve their differences through matrimony, in effect a domestication of the often violent differences that threatened to pull the new nations apart. *Amalia* (1851) by Argentine José Mármol and *María* (1867) by Colombian Jorge Isaacs are considered classic novels of this category. Mármol's novel is more clearly politically motivated, and his protagonists, Amalia and Daniel, suffer the persecutions and intrigues of the political tumult of the times. *María* is set in the beautiful Valle del Cauca in Colombia. Its real hero is Efraín, whose Jewish father converted to Catholicism to marry his mother, and who has been in love with María since childhood. Modelled in part on the classic French romantic novel by Jacques-Henri Bernadin de Saint-Pierre (1788) *Paul et Virginie*, with the tragic death of its heroine and the suffering of its hero, the novel emphasizes the customs and the landscape of the region. Especially notable are Efraín's encounters with his friends at the hacienda through whom he is introduced to the story of Nay and Sinar, a slave narrative developed extensively in the novel, where the African past and cruel voyage of the slaving ship form a counterpoint to the idyllic existence within the hacienda.

Positivism and the belle époque

Positivist philosophy made an important impact, especially in late-nineteenth-century Mexico, Brazil, Uruguay and Argentina, although its influence was felt as well in other countries. Belief in technological progress, science and rationalism joined with economic expansion and increasing urbanization to produce transformed societies. Inevitably this rush towards progress produced an uneasiness among many intellectuals such as Martí, Rodó and Justo Sierra about the emphasis on materialism. Rodó's *Ariel* (1900), an extensive essay reclaiming for Latin America a specific 'Latinity' in opposition to the Anglo-Saxon ethic (specifically in the US) gave the name to a generation of young artists and intellectuals, the 'arielistas' who demanded a change of emphasis in public policy. In Mexico, some members of the group known as the Atheneum of Youth later became leading intellectuals and artists of the revolutionary governments of the twenties. More concerned with humanistic studies than with economics and science, some of their principles were incorporated into the early educational policies of revolutionary Mexico as designed by José Vasconcelos, author of *La raza cósmica* [The Cosmic Race] (1924).

The *modernista* (1888–1916) movement in poetry (and to a lesser extent in prose) can be seen in part as a reaction to positivist philosophy and practice. Its primary poet, the Nicaraguan Rubén Darío, was also known as a short-story writer – his landmark *Azul* (1888) contained short stories as well as poetry – and as a chronicler of urban life for major newspapers of the period, especially *La Nación* of Buenos Aires. Although many of the *modernista* poets, including Martí, José Asunción Silva, Amado Nervo, Manuel Gutiérrez Nájera, Leopoldo Lugones, also cultivated prose, the movement itself is primarily identified as a poetic movement. Lugones, nonetheless, is credited with being the first to practise the genre of the fantastic short story in Spanish America, a form that would have extraordinary success in the twentieth century. Horacio Quiroga (Uruguay) began his writing career as a *modernista* poet, but soon turned to the short story, becoming the master of the genre in the first decades of the twentieth century.

Money, medicine and the shaping influence of environment were not new themes in late-nineteenth-century literature, but their treatment, influenced by literary realism and naturalism, does show a change in practice. The novel *Martín Rivas*, by Alberto Blest-Gana, was published serially in Chile in 1862. Its title character, a modest provincial, goes to the capital and falls in love with a beautiful, aristocratic and wealthy young woman. A story of social ascension through hard work and virtue, the novel presents a portrait of the social customs of the times and accents the possibility of social ascension in a changing world, where business connections begin to replace bloodlines as the keys to success. Julián Martel's *La bolsa* [The Stock Market] (1891) is more explicit in its focus on the power of money in the social realm. The stock market of Buenos Aires becomes itself a character, as a distorting and dangerous force in social relations. Puerto Rico's Manuel Zeno Gandía, trained in medicine, focused naturalism's pessimistic focus on Puerto Rico's marginal rural population in *La granja: crónicas de un mundo enfermo* [The Farm: Chronicles of a Sick World] (1894), and in *El negocio* [The Business] (1922) on the corrosive power of money. In Peru, Mercedes Cabello de Carbonera combined topics of women's vulnerability with society's insistence on financial status. Prostitution, a staple of naturalist fiction, is the subject of Federico Gamboa's *Santa* (1902), set in Mexico City. Given heightened immigration to the cities, especially in Mexico and Buenos Aires, urban topics become a focus for many writers, and prostitution and urban poverty are themes developed in many writers of the period.

One of the most unusual novels of the period is *¡Tomóchic!* (1893) by Heriberto Frías. Set in Chihuahua, Mexico, the novel relates a story based on a factual event, the uprising of a Messianic cult against the government. The descriptions of the *soldaderas*, women who follow the military troops, foreshadow their representation in later novels of the Mexican Revolution, especially in Mariano Azuela's *Los de abajo*, and even in Elena Garro's *Los recuerdos del porvenir* (1963; *Recollections of Things to Come*), as well as Elena Poniatowska's memorable *Hasta no verte, Jesús mío* (1970; *Here's to You Jesusa!*).

Although naturalist-influenced novels abounded, perhaps the short-story form had the widest readership at the turn of the century. Given the expansion of the reading public and the proliferation of periodicals, the short-story form was widely distributed. Naturalist traits of social exposé and denunciation combine with specific local description to make many of these stories important historical documents as well. Juana Manuela Gorriti (Argentina/Peru), Javier de Viana of Uruguay, Baldomero Lillo and Augusto d'Halmar of Chile and Tomás Carrasquilla of Colombia are some of the most important short-story writers of the period. The Russian writers Tolstoy and Chekhov, as well as Edgar Allan Poe, were widely known and important in the development of the form in Latin America. It is with Horacio Quiroga, however, that the short story reaches its widest audience. His terse style, dramatic and often violent situations and his search for the extreme have made him a source for contemporary short-story writers.

Novelas de la tierra

Although, chronologically, the so-called 'novelas de la tierra' belong to the 1920s, their roots can be traced directly to events and fictions of the turn of the century. The processes of modernization and urbanization produced a fascination with provincial or natural origins. *Don Segundo Sombra*, by Ricardo Güiraldes, became a popular success from the moment of its publication in 1926. Its protagonist Fabio, under the tutelage of the titular gaucho, learns to face the challenges of nature through a masculine apprenticeship. Although nature in itself is not benevolent, the harsh life in the country is a school for character. The novel captured the imagination of an increasingly urban Argentine population and created a nostalgia for a way of life that had already almost disappeared. Nature is also the ruling force in *La vorágine* [The Vortex] (1924) by José Eustasio Rivera, where an expedition through the Colombian jungle pits its rather hapless hero against quicksands and dangers. Rómulo Gallegos, who also served as Venezuela's president, published *Doña Bárbara* in 1929, another classic novel where both nature and the title character herself present treacherous challenges. The three previously mentioned novels have continued to attract critical interest because of their telluric focus, but also because of their introduction of new techniques. They incorporate some vanguard techniques such as stream of consciousness, dream sequences and non-linear time in varying degrees.

Critical categories

The designation of thematic contextual categories, like those above, can help to structure an approach to nineteenth- and early-twentieth-century literature. Yet classification becomes more difficult if one searches for demarcations among literary movements, such as neoclassicism, romanticism, realism, and naturalism, complicated even further by mixes of genre. Spanish America has often been described in terms of the organic growth, or development, model, with the notion of infant societies – the new republics – making their first halting steps towards maturity. Such a history unfolds against a normative concept of social and economic development. Certain mistakes and flaws can be permitted, but constant tension or social upheaval will stunt healthy growth. The norm, in nineteenth-century terms, is inevitably Europe, especially France in cultural terms and England in economic ones. In literature, a critical tendency has tended to see the evolution of Spanish American literature against the patterns of French literature, especially the development of the novel, romantic poetry and later symbolist poetry. Unquestionably the French model was by far the most important, from the currents of Romanticism to the realist and naturalist novel, and toward the end of the century with the impact of symbolist poetry on the *modernistas*. French influences were mediated by Spanish, English and US influences (especially Edgar Allan Poe, James Fenimore Cooper, Herman Melville and Walt Whitman), with less penetration of the German influence except circuitously through Romanticism. Later in the century, especially with the naturalist novel and *modernista* poetry, writers make explicit their homage to writers like Zola, Verlaine and Laforgue. But if French and English societies saw the rise of the bourgeoisie, urbanism and industrialism early in the century as impetus to experiment with new tendencies and forms of fiction, particularly the realist novel, in Latin America the cause and effect could not be explained in the same way. The growth or development did not follow the same path, and waiting for eventual development in the same terms always casts Latin America in the role of deficient or as a case of retarded development. Antonio Cornejo-Polar's concept of heterogeneity is useful for understanding the impossibility of measuring Latin America in European terms, and gives us a way to understand vast internal differences within Latin America itself.[19] Heterogeneity in this sense means rejecting a single standard of measurement, allowing us to view regions and societies, sometimes coexisting side by side, as parallel and often separate situations. For example, in the Andean region there exist monolingual non-Spanish speakers with a distinct oral tradition, parts of which have been incorporated into the literature and popular culture in the Spanish of the region. And at the same time, a city like Lima could have a literary circle far more in tune with world capitals than with its regional ones. In the nineteenth century, with less communication and uncertain political boundaries, such heterogeneity was even more striking. At the same time we can build classificatory schemes, we must keep in mind the existence of multiple, heterogeneous and separate realities, like those noted by Carpentier in his encounter with Haiti in the middle of the twentieth century.

In literary histories of Spanish America non-hegemonic productions within lettered culture, such as women's writing, have often been ignored. Women's literary production, except for a few important figures like Gertrudis Gómez de Avellaneda (Cuba, 1814–73), Juana Manuela

Gorriti (Argentina/Peru, 1818–92) and Clorinda Matto de Turner (Peru, 1852–1909), did not readily fit most models for inclusion in the newly formed national canons. By refocusing the critical frame to include women's production, alternative prose forms – letters, diaries, periodical literature, short stories, didactic writings – emerge more clearly as an important form of literary production. Yet even though a history of nineteenth-century women's literature and culture has emerged recently to recast our notions of literary hierarchies, women's entry into lettered culture only followed the expansion of education for women, creating towards the end of the century a new group of writers. The expansion of education produced not just women writers but incorporated other social classes into lettered culture, creating an important new reading public.

The Colossus of the north

For much of the nineteenth century, the US was seen in its similarities as a new nation with distinctive energies, despite its apparent cultural, religious and linguistic differences. But later in the century, writers and intellectuals like José Martí, José Enrique Rodó and a younger generation of 'arielistas' reasserted the ideal of cultural unity for Latin America under the rubric of *latinidad*, the unity of societies linked to roots in Mediterranean cultures and Catholicism. This renewal of Bolívar's ideals in the cultural sphere arises in response to the growing dominance and threat of the United States. The United States was figured in Martí's essay 'Our America' (1893) and in Rodó's *Ariel* (1900), as the Colossus of the North, a mechanistic and materialistic economic and cultural system that would engulf and trample the Latin neighbours to the south like a giant in heavy boots. The US's annexation of almost half Mexico's territory in 1848, the Spanish-American War of 1898 and the colonization of Cuba, Puerto Rico and the Philippines, plus interventions in Mexico and Central America to ensure its financial investments, provoked a new consciousness at least among the cultural elite. Faced with the US's ascendance in economic and political realms from the late nineteenth century, Latin America reassessed its own cultural heritages and increasingly emphasized its differences.

Conclusions

One of the most notable characteristics of Spanish American literature in the nineteenth and early-twentieth-centuries is its wide range of genres and, despite the precariousness of existence for many writers, its sheer abundance. Writers did not confine themselves to one or two genres but instead integrated their writing into every aspect of public and private existence. Yet despite its abundance, a history of narrative of this period cannot be inclusive of all the spheres of artistic and intellectual life. Quite simply, until later in the nineteenth century, writing was not a tool available to the masses, and in some sectors, Spanish was not the common language. What a history of narrative does show us, however, are the lines of tension, conflict and dynamic creativity of societies in periods of enormous, often violent, change and transition. Readers must look for shifts of emphasis and genre, place of publication and historical context to begin to reconstruct a vision of nineteenth-century narrative. The former Spanish empire, transformed into a series of independent nations, sought to develop national histories, literatures, economies, mythic pasts and future projects. Some of the thematic categories mentioned earlier, such as *mestizaje*, anti-slavery, travel, modernization, journalism and scientific thought, can assist us in developing some guidelines for making connections among the literary productions of this diverse group of nations. Yet the history of narrative in this period is undergoing constant change. Definitions of literature and writing continue to change, and thus our sense of literary genres and thematics are also in constant transformation. Just as the very concept of the nation has been revised, and along with it national historiographies, so the concept of narrative itself and its links to nations and to regions is undergoing revision. Not just novels and stories but letters, memoirs, history and journalistic writing must be included to gain a realistic perspective of nineteenth- and early-twentieth-century narrative in Spanish America.

Notes

1. José Carlos Mariátegui, *Siete ensayos de interpretación de la realidad peruana* (Lima, 1963), p. 204. Translations are my own.
2. Tulio Halperin Donghi, *Historia contemporánea de América Latina* (Madrid, 1986), p. 151. Halperin Donghi also points out the increase in violence in daily life in post-revolutionary societies (pp. 148–59).
3. Carlos Alonso, *The Burden of Modernity: The Rhetoric of Cultural Discourse in Spanish America* (Oxford and New York, 1998), pp. 15–16.
4. Pedro Henríquez Ureña, *Las corrientes literarias en América Hispánica* (Mexico City, 1949), p. 153.
5. See Enrique Pupo-Walker's *La vocación literaria del pensamiento histórico en América. Desarrollo de la prosa de ficción: siglos XVI, XVII, XVIII y XIX* (Madrid, 1982) for a complete

tracing of this important literary form and its relationship with the chronicles of conquest and the development of other forms of fiction.

6. Angel Rama notes in *The Lettered City* (Durham NC, 1996) that three major figures of the republican period, Andrés Bello, Simón Rodríguez and Sarmiento, demonstrated an almost obsessive concern with spelling reform in their desire to facilitate access to writing.

7. Roberto González Echevarría, *Myth and Archive: A Theory of Latin American Narrative* (Durham NC, 1998), p. 8.

8. This essay served as a prologue to Carpentier's 1949 novel, *El reino de este mundo* (*The Kingdom of This World*).

9. In her valuable study on nineteenth-century literary historiography, *La historiografía literaria del liberalismo hispanoamericano del siglo XIX* (Havana, 1987), Beatriz González Stephan attributes new discursive formations (the regionalist or *criollist* novel, *costumbrista* sketches, poetic nativism and national literary histories) as efforts by intellectuals to reinforce nationalist sentiment when confronted with the invasion of English and French capital and European notions of progress (p. 37). Antonio Benítez Rojo, in 'The Nineteenth Century Spanish American Novel' (*The Cambridge History of Latin American Literature*, vol. 1, edited by R. González Echevarría and E. Pupo Walker, Cambridge, 1996), p. 435, makes this division circa 1870 in accord with the 'two great socioeconomic moments of the nineteenth century in Latin America'. Pedro Henríquez-Ureña's classic *Las corrientes literarias en la América Hispánica* (Mexico City, 1949) divides the nineteenth century in the following manner: 'The Declaration of Intellectual Independence (1800–1830)', 'Romanticism and Anarchy (1830–1860)', 'The Period of Organization (1860–1890)' and 'Pure Literature (1890–1920)'.

10. The classic study of the professionalization of the writer in Latin America is Angel Rama's *Rubén Darío y el modernismo. Circunstancias socio-económicas de un arte americano* (Caracas, 1970).

11. Stanton L. Catlin, 'Traveller-Reporter Artists and the Empirical Tradition in Post-Independence Art', in Dawn Ades (ed.), *Art in Latin America: The Modern Era 1820–1980* (New Haven and London, 1989), p. 43.

12. Mary Louise Pratt, *Imperial Eyes: Travel Writing and Transculturation* (New York, 1992), p. 113.

13. Ibid., p. 125.

14. Roberto González Echevarría, p. 12.

15. Quoted in Javier Pinedo Castro, 'Vicente Pérez Rosales', in L. I. Madrigal (ed.), *Historia de la literatura hispanoamericana*, vol. II (Madrid, 1992), p. 422.

16. Alan Knight, 'Racismo, Revolution and Indigenismo: Mexico 1910–1914', in Richard Graham (ed.), *The Idea of Race in Latin America, 1870–1940* (Austin TX, 1990), p. 78.

17. See Francine Masiello, *Between Civilization and Barbarism* (Lincoln, NE, 1992) for a study of women's writing in Argentina in the nineteenth century, and Fernando Opera, *Historias de la frontera: el cautiverio en la América hispánica* (Mexico City, 2001) for a study of the captivity theme in Latin America literature.

18. See Josefa Salmón, *El espejo indígena: el discurso indigenista en Bolivia, 1900–1956* (La Paz, 1997).

19. See his *Escribir en el aire* (Lima, 1994) and his first writings on the topic in 'El indigenismo y las literaturas heterogéneas: su doble estatuto socio-cultural' (*Sobre literatura y crítica literaria latinoamericanas*, Caracas, 1982), pp. 67–85.

Further reading

Brushwood, John, *Genteel Barbarism: Experiments in Analysis of Nineteenth Century Spanish American Novels*, Lincoln NE, 1981

Franco, Jean, *An Introduction to Spanish American Literature*, Cambridge, 1969

González, Aníbal, *Journalism and the Development of Spanish American Narrative*, New York, 1993

González Echevarría, Roberto and Enrique Pupo-Walker (eds.), *The Cambridge History of Latin American Literature,* vol. I, Cambridge, 1996

González-Echevarría, Roberto, *Myth and Archive: A Theory of Latin American Narrative*, Durham NC, 1998

Henríquez-Ureña, Pedro, *Literary Currents in Hispanic America*, Cambridge MA, 1945

Masiello, Francine, *Between Civilisation and Barbarism: Women, Nation and Literary Culture in Modern Argentina*, Lincoln NE and London, 1992

Meyer, Doris (ed.), *Rereading the Spanish American Essay: Translations of Nineteenth and Twentieth Century Women's Essays,* Austin TX, 1995

Molloy, Sylvia, *At Face Value: Autobiographical Writing in Spanish America*, Cambridge, 1991

Pratt, Mary Louise, *Imperial Eyes: Travel Writing and Transculturation*, New York, 1992

Ramos, Julio, *Divergent Modernities: Culture and Politics in Nineteenth Century Latin America,* tr. John D. Blanco, Durham NC, 1999

Sommer, Doris, *Foundational Fictions: The National Romances of Latin America*, Berkeley CA, 1991

4

Spanish American narrative, 1920–1970

Venezuelan critic Guillermo Sucre raised a crucial point about how the Spanish American novel's concern to name things in a 'new' world, its 'Adam-like passion', duplicated the foreign or exotic view of Latin America and led to exotic clichés about Latin America.[1] The writer most linked to this task of Adamic naming was the Cuban novelist Alejo Carpentier (1904–80). In his seminal essay-prologue 'De lo real maravilloso americano' [About American Marvellous Reality], Carpentier combined a compensatory theory called *lo real maravilloso* that located a natural surrealism in the excesses of Latin American history and geography (as opposed to an inner, dream-based surrealism emanating from the Paris he knew so well in the 1920s and 1930s) with a baroque intention to include everything in a novel, because the uniqueness of Latin American reality still had not been described. Behind this poetics lay a blueprint inherited from the great scientific travellers of the nineteenth century who attempted to categorize and list in European taxonomies all that was new to them, supplanting or ignoring the local indigenous ones, and aiming to surprise European readers with the novelties of an unimaginable reality. The mentor of later travellers was Alexander von Humboldt (1769–1859) whose five years wandering and exploring South America, Cuba and Mexico from 1799–1804 led to a self-referential tradition of scientific writing that established two paradigms; first, how to be as all-inclusive as possible in a written text; second, to expand the conventions of genre to allow everything to be included in what Charles Darwin called a 'miscellaneous' genre which appropriated narrative, essay, history and scientific discourses in order to capture and express an elusive reality.[2]

Humboldt's encyclopedic range and prose prompted Domingo Sarmiento (1811–88) to write hurriedly what became the hybrid master-text of an emerging Latin American awareness of the newly independent countries, the search for a tradition, for roots, for an identity not dependent on Spain, the ex-colonizer. The essay in question is *Civilización y barbarie: Vida de Juan Facundo Quiroga* (1845; *Life in the Argentine Republic in the Days of the Tyrants*), quoted from Humboldt in an epigraph. Humboldt offered Sarmiento theories about the link between land and character, about the pampas and the Russian steppes, about horses and culture and tyranny. Sarmiento's writing overlapped with autobiography, history, geography, narrative, denunciation and polemic, as if he were another European scientist surveying an unknown land (as indeed he was, because he had not travelled the pampas when he penned this essay in exile in Chile, having read about it through foreigners). Roberto González Echevarría has noted how the novel as a genre adopts previous discourses – 'truth-bearing documents' – that have attempted to mirror reality, and isolated the scientific travelogue in the nineteenth century and the anthropological text in the twentieth century as keys, allowing the novel to be read as more than 'fiction'.[3] Inherent in this palimpsest of texts where novels are written over travelogues is the attempt to single out what is unique to the Latin American experience, and here space and geography seemed to predominate.

Alejo Carpentier's claim that 'all great novels in our period began by making the reader cry out: "This is not a novel!"' was reaffirmed by González Echevarría who insisted that the novel always pretends not to be fiction, to be true, implicit in the very notion of realism.[4] If the novel competes with verifiable documents then one must define why it documents. Here we return to the problem of 'naming' in Latin America, justifying the novel's function as a variant of the classical Horatian definition of a work of art that it must please and be useful (*dulce et utile*). How useful could literature be? In fragile, emerging nations, stratified into a dominant class and the often indigenous masses, with small, urban middle classes, the Latin American writer could choose to write for the elite who read in his country, and then, with luck be read elsewhere in his own continent, even be published abroad through translation. Alternatively, writers could use their prestige as novelists to teach their elite readers about the country they lived in. This latter option implies treating their readers as foreigners in their own countries, with the writer as just another foreigner alerting readers to what they have not seen or understood. In the context of this Humboldtian tradition of foreigners naming Latin America, Octavio Paz compared Mexican fiction writers to D. H. Lawrence and found their descriptions of Mexican nature deficient;[5] Jorge Luis Borges claimed that only the English travellers had evoked Argentine countryside.[6] Foreign writers were listened to because the educated and literate elites in Latin America tended to turn outwards to France and Europe and the United States (and still do) to make sense of their realities and ignore their own hinterlands, their own histories and inheritances. Peruvian novelist Mario Vargas Llosa identified the limitations of a local readership in 1971: 'It is very hard to think of being a writer if one has been born in a country where almost nobody reads: the poor because they don't know how to or have the means to do so, and the rich because they do not feel like it. In such a society, to want to be a writer is not to opt for a profession but an act of madness.'[7] The distant possibility of becoming a professional writer is bound to a readership, as Rosario Castellanos noted in 1961, where the absence of a local readership meant that 'literature could not be exercised in an exclusively professional way'.[8] Once Latin American fiction is established as a genre that wants to catch and change this minority reader's perceptions, we can begin to describe the creation of a tradition of such writing that over the period 1920–70 slowly becomes self-referential, rather than always competing with foreign models through the disproportionately high number of translations read. The tradition thus established becomes that of Latin American readers beginning to read their own writers. An earlier version of what was meant by a tradition of Latin American writing would include Mario Vargas Llosa's war between 'primitives' and 'creators', his reworking of Sarmiento's over-cited opposition barbarism and civilization.[9] Emir Rodríguez Monegal promoted a tradition that saw a progression from rural novels to urban ones, setting up a collision between provincial or marginal and cosmopolitan and metropolitan.[10] But behind these attempts to explain Latin American fiction, I would argue that the reading public also defines the fiction as a continuity of endeavour that expands readership and where the continent's individual and social experiences become recreated as texts, an open Latin American tradition which privileges fiction, in Carpentier's words, the 'research tool'.[11]

The rise of the (semi-) professional writer in Latin America tied in with the rise of middle-class readers and book-buyers over the period

1920–70. In many ways the serious task of employing fiction to wake up the Latin American reader from false daydreams and alienation followed developments in Europe and the United States and only underlines the problem of whether to evaluate local fiction in local rather than comparative terms. The conflict between the unique subjectivity of a particular writer and the collective identification he or she might awaken in particular readers is also modified by intellectual fashions and perceptions, the most challenging in the first two-thirds of the twentieth century being 'surrealism', which offered theories about the effects of literature, the possibility of changing the reader and a potential tapping into deeper psychic zones of a self that might be universal. Surrealism found its critic in Jorge Luis Borges (1899–1986) who mocked the realist project of mapping a total reality (in his story 'El Aleph' the poet Carlos Argentino Daneri's claims to describe the planet, beginning with a few hectares in Queensland).

Before the novelists grappled with this problem of identifying their Latin American status, the Latin American poets had created their own awareness of a Latin American tradition. The cosmopolitan Nicaraguan poet Rubén Darío (1867–1916) was the founding figure, admired by later poets from the Peruvian poet César Vallejo (1892–1938) to the Chilean poet Enrique Lihn (1929–88). They, like their mentor Darío, absorbed foreign literatures and offered their digested version to native readers, inaugurating a tradition of appropriation that could be called transculturation. Thanks to the poets, Latin American-ness can be defined as a tradition of native writers who refer to previous Latin American writers so that what a Latin American reader can take from a Darío or a Vicente Huidobro or a Pablo Neruda (to name two influential Chilean poets) is not only a style, but a way of thinking the Latin American self. Victoria Ocampo once claimed that she did not set out to be Argentine, she just was. Borges in a seminal essay 'The Argentine Writer and Tradition' (1951) characterized Argentine culture as open to the world; the Argentine authors took what they liked from anywhere, that was what it meant to be an Argentine, a culture more open, more translational, than those limited by monolinguistic traditions like the French or the British. Such a version of being Latin American suggests an eclectic freedom from the constraints of tradition and continuity, and an openness to what is innovative. Alejo Carpentier reasserted this 'world vision far more open than the one held by certain European intellectuals'.[12]

A history of the Latin American novel confirms that fiction in Latin America is more serious than the escapist pleasure of reading. It assumes that a Latin American reader reads to discover his or her self, identifying with a novel's evaluation of national problems. Otherwise there would be no consensus, or even polemic, about a particular novel's personal and social importance. Most Latin American readers are urban, and obviously educated; however, in this specific Latin American absence of a novelistic tradition, this reader often looks abroad, literally importing, perhaps through translation, models of what fiction can achieve. In the 1920s and 1930s these models were a bizarre cross-fertilization between the nineteenth-century European realist novel and twentieth-century experimental writing.

Realist writing makes few demands on the reader; the reader absorbs the writing as if it conveys the real, with the craft and problems of the act of writing excluded from the text. The great nineteenth-century realists from Walter Scott to Dickens, Balzac and Galdós can be seen as chroniclers of new, mutating urban realities which the writer and reader share as confusions, and where plot functions as an ordering principle. That a writer can record more than the limitations of his or her subjective experience lies at the heart of the realist novel as chronicling contemporary history, exemplified in Galdós's series of novels recreating Spain's history, the *Episodios nacionales*. Argentina's first novel, José Mármol's *Amalia*, 1851 (novels had been banned during Spain's colonial control), defined itself as a 'contemporary chronicle'. If such historiographical realism is combined with a critical slant, aptly embodied by Emile Zola's pro-Dreyfus, open letter of 1898 'J'accuse', then we have a model of what Latin American writers and readers expected from the novel that both carefully records realities and denounces abuses.

The writer who best conforms to this nineteenth-century hybrid genre is the Venezuelan Rómulo Gallegos (1884–1969), who combined his part-time writing career with politics, briefly assuming the presidency of his country in 1947. What is clear with his realist project is the geographical mapping of a newish, ignored country, Venezuela (both for Venezuelans and for other Latin Americans and Spaniards), where Gallegos set, for example, *Doña Bárbara* (1929; *Doña Bárbara*) in the inhospitable *llanos*, and *Canaima* (1936; *Canaima*) in the Orinoco watershed. His novels offer realistic characters in plots barely saved from obvious symbolism (exemplifying E. M. Forster's lament of 'tyranny by the plot') by confusing moral qualities, where both characters and readers are taught lessons, are educated into nation-awareness. These novels can be easily read, and explain the Venezuelan predicament to natives living in the cities, to foreigners, including the Spaniards where *Doña Bárbara* was first published. Gallegos's short stories, published in Buenos Aires, were tellingly called *Cuentos venezolanos* (1949), signalling his country's specificities to other Latin American readers. Having lived in exile during Gómez's dictatorship, Gallegos was able to merge his political and writing career as an *explainer* of his country's woes in order to isolate its uniqueness. That his novels today may appear anachronistic, harking back to nineteenth-century models (*Doña Bárbara* echoes Galdós's *Doña Perfecta*) is due partly to Gallegos's *mission civilatrice*. Gallegos shrugged off experimental modernism (in the Anglo-American sense) and took his Latin American urban readers' ability to absorb realistic texts seriously.

Gallegos could stand as a model for a choice taken by the Latin American writer faced with an unknown but local readership and a didactic, patriotic responsibility that defined the role of the writer as educator (it is fitting that the writer who gave Latin Americans the explanatory concept of 'civilization or barbarity', Domingo Sarmiento, was primarily an educator). What literary critics have labelled the 'regional' or 'indigenous' or *costumbrista* or *criollista* or 'telluric' novel (this realistic fiction goes under various labels) groups together writers from many Latin American countries making the same aesthetic decisions. In Mexico, the novel that came to be the paradigmatic work on the confusions of the Mexican Revolution and Mexico's violent national self-discovery, Mariano Azuela's *Los de abajo* (*The Underdogs*), which, though written and first published in a newspaper in 1915, was not read in Mexico until 1925, articulates the same dilemmas as Gallegos's. Azuela (1873–1952) captured realistically the hinterlands and peasants of Northern Mexico in the middle of a civil war (later called the Revolution); he mocked the role of the elitist writer with his character, the ironically named coward Cervantes, who, instead of being the intellectual leading the masses, typically benefits from his opportunism, while his peasant hero dies pointlessly. Azuela adapted nineteenth-century realism, an evident debt in his other novels, while journalistic deadlines ironically enforced a modern, cinematic quality, capturing the novelty and violence of social change in Mexico.

In Colombia, José Eustacio Rivera's (1889–1928) travel-novel *La vorágine* (1924; *The Vortex*) pulls its first-person narrating rebel-poet and his pregnant mistress from Europeanized Bogotá on a journey into the heart of darkness, to the wild *llanos* and then jungle, confronting the lawless interior, far from public accountability, where rubber workers were cruelly exploited (an injustice reported on by Roger Casement), and where the narrator succumbs himself to the mindless violence inherent in tropical nature (no escapist paradise here). This novel revealed to Colombian urban readers uncomfortable experiences from their own backyard. That this local intention to reveal an injustice represented a continental problem accounts for the success of Rivera's sole novel. Rivera was read in Argentina by Horacio Quiroga (1878–1937) who turned his back on the comforts of a booming Buenos Aires to live in, and report on, the frontier in Misiones and the Chaco, where no respectable Argentines dreamt of travelling to, in aggressive short stories aimed at upsetting his urban readers' complacency. Quiroga boasted that he wrote badly, flouting the Spanish Academy's stress on good grammar; he captured the mind-frame of his illiterate pioneers, and their unpredictably violent lives, but wrote for urban middle-class readers. Quiroga was aware of European modernity, having travelled to Paris in 1900 and been sickened by the disparity between European literary models and his unexplored, un-named, local borderlands. Quiroga actually settled in San Ignacio, Misiones, as if the process of de-educating himself, of jettisoning his European veneer should rub off on his reader. When the Mexican education minister José Vasconcelos travelled to Argentina in 1922 he noted that Quiroga had brought Misiones into public consciousness ('It happens that a region does not exist until its singer appears') and praised Quiroga for what Gallegos, Rivera and others had sought, because 'in the interior of the Argentine province is where European varnish disappears to let one see the ethnic community in all its strength';[13] that is, in the interior, far off the tourist tracks, lay the 'real' Latin America.

As a realist project the angrier, more partisan so-called 'indigenist novel', represented by the Peruvian Ciro Alegría (1909–67), reported on the Andean hinterlands, on the enslaved Quechua-speaking 'serranos', who lived in Andean valleys and who were treated as foreigners in Lima, in Quito and other capitals; the realist novel form was not questioned and the detached perspective led to sentimentalizing the 'Indians'. This denunciatory realism would include writers from all the Andean countries, from the Ecuatorian Jorge Icaza (1906–78) to the Bolivian Alcides Arguedas (1879–1946), but despite ideological differences, most of these writers assumed they knew what these Indians were 'thinking', developed anthropological insights into their deprived lives and gave voice to the voiceless, a self-justifying role for writers that the Chilean poet Pablo Neruda had adopted from the anonymous builders of Macchu-Picchu in 1946: 'speak through my words and my blood'.[14]

It would be inappropriate to criticize the Latin American realist novel by arguing that urgent subject matter dominated the aesthetic quality of the texts, or that the attempt to forge a Latin American realist style ended up repeating, anachronistically, the European nineteenth-century novel. Rather, the 'regional' Latin American novel can be redefined as a critical response to Eurocentrism (i.e. the critical task is not to compare these novels with European developments in the 1920s), as well as an understanding of its peculiar readership. However, an awareness that fiction can question itself within the fiction is absent from realism, and it is inevitable to see the realist-regionalist works through Jorge Luis Borges's criticisms, not only that Quiroga rewrote Kipling badly, but that realist writing cannot capture the world, a defect inherent in all realism. Of the better-known writers who recreated rural life for city-readers, Ricardo Güiraldes's *Don Segundo Sombra* (1927; *Don Segundo Sombra: Shadows on the Pampas*) sought to merge the avant-garde of the 1920s, with its stress on daring metaphor and surprise (emphasized by Argentina's version of Spanish experimental writing called *ultraísmo*, out of which Borges himself had emerged) with explanatory realism about rural pampas life in a multilayered work that finally relegated the nineteenth-century gaucho to fiction. Güiraldes's (1886–1927) awareness of Parisian literary fashions came into conflict with the rural lifestyle that defined national life, and he tried to weld modern sophistication with rural backwardness aesthetically. But his work is not the same as the ghost stories told by the gaucho/guru Don Segundo to his disciple Fabio, the young orphan who discovers that he is a landowner; this novel is directed in its conscious explanation of rural details at a city-reader ignorant of *campo* reality.

The function of the Latin American novelists in the 1920s and 1930s appears to be contradictory; on the one hand they write to contain their modernizing countries in novels that criticize official and patriotic historiography; on the other hand, the realism of these novels aims at a manipulated and ignorant city-reader. That the writer *chronicled* what happened is a natural decision taken by many to overcome the contradiction between explaining and criticizing; that this writer aspired to a national voice (like a Balzac in France or a Galdós) is also crucial. The prolific Argentine writer Manuel Gálvez (1882–1962) confessed to a 'vast plan . . . I intend to reflect the multiple life of this complicated country of ours.'[15] He would be followed later by the Peruvian Mario Vargas Llosa (b. 1936), whose fiction maps out Peru culturally (focusing on the geography, the racial and class tensions, the recent history), or the Mexican Carlos Fuentes (b. 1928) who reorganized his novels into a meaningful sequence, 'La edad del tiempo', a *comédie humaine* or a Powellian 'Dance to the Music of Time', of not only Mexico, but Latin America and Spanish colonial expansion, where the independent, critical writer becomes the real historian, a position stressed as uniquely Latin American by many writer-critics.

However, the notion of a 'Latin American' literature is not necessarily implied in these national sagas, for Latin America is a term imposed on fragmentary and often hostile component countries (on-going border wars attest to this isolating and rampant nationalism). For a writer to cross a national frontier depends on a combination of factors from literary worth, critical support, personal contacts and publishing networks; even translation into French and English functions as a form of literary prestige, and thus export. In many cases there has been a snobbish tendency *not* to read national writers, as Héctor Yánover noted in his memoirs as a bookseller in Buenos Aires ('nobody read Argentine authors').[16] A proper, distributing publishing house did not begin to function in Mexico until 1933, and only the advent of bookselling and publishing skills from Spain after the collapse of the Republican cause in 1939 led to the dream of a continental publishing business, managed during Francoism by Mexico and Argentina, strategically both ends of the Spanish-speaking world (Losada, Sudamericana, Espasa-Calpe, Siglo XXI, etc.). Despite this, the Chilean writer Poli Délano learnt about Vargas Llosa's first novel after it had been translated into at least ten languages, and yet Chile and Peru share a border.[17]

In fact an explanation of the boom of Latin American writing in the 1960s can be sought in publishing houses, at least at four levels. The first concerns distribution. A good example is Gabriel García Márquez (b. 1928), a Colombian from the Caribbean-coastal culture whose fiction reports in a traditional sense on the Magdalena River watershed and banana plantations, correcting upland Bogotá's version of these ignored hinterlands. García Márquez was educated reading Argentine-published fiction, often translations, and sent his manuscript to the influential Argentine publisher Paco Porrúa of Editorial Sudamericana in Buenos Aires, which launched the 'Latin American' career of García

Márquez. A second level of Latin American awareness developed from the Cuban Revolution's continental aims: the magazine and literary prizes emanating from the Casa de Las Américas in La Habana (riding on the back of the enthusiasm generated in the early years of the 1959 Cuban Revolution). A third level was the role of Barcelona's publisher Carlos Barral, and his Premio Biblioteca Breve prizes in a culturally depressed Spain, with the prize-winners distributed to Spanish-speaking countries (winners of this prestigious prize included Vargas Llosa, Cabrera Infante, Haroldo Conti, Carlos Fuentes). A fourth level involved the colonialist prestige of being translated, which not only allowed Latin American writers to earn enough to think of themselves, at times, as professional writers, but also alerted different Latin American countries to read them, stamped with the seal of foreign approval. The obvious case is that of Jorge Luis Borges, a minority writer, who, after winning the Prix Formentor (sharing it famously with Samuel Beckett in 1961), was translated into English and French and began to be read outside local literary coteries.

Writers themselves are often good, practical critics, and influence taste. Although the Guatemalan Miguel Angel Asturias (1899–1974) eventually won the Nobel Prize in 1967, and knew and lived in the Paris of the surrealists, being translated and forewarded by Paul Valéry, it was being published by Losada in Buenos Aires (*Hombres de maíz*, 1949) that got the Argentine writer Julio Cortázar (1914–84) evaluating his work within his novel *Los premios* (1960). In fact, a Latin American tradition came into being in the 1960s that superseded the previous generational melange of foreign and national writer-models. Beatriz Guido noted this in 1968: 'something surprising has happened and it is that the Argentine book has reached the hands of the middle class that before solely read translations'.[18] Julio Cortázar's seminal experimental novel *Rayuela* (1963; *Hopscotch*) contains lists of recommended River Plate writers including Roberto Arlt, Juan Carlos Onetti and Leopoldo Marechal (whose rambling novel *Adán Buenosayres* (1948) replicates many of the 'bohemian' discussions on art and metaphysics of Cortázar's *Rayuela*), while Carlos Fuentes's essay 'La nueva novela hispanoamericana' (1969) functioned as a Manifesto promoting fellow Latin American writers, who often socialized together, but Fuentes goes back to the 1920s realists like Rivera and on to Carpentier, Borges, Vargas Llosa and García Márquez. So how a writer transcends national status and becomes 'Latin American' follows paths which converged in the 1960s boom of Latin American writing which became, in Philip Swanson's words, 'a sophisticated confection for a well-read liberal public'.[19]

One crucial text tells the story. Luis Harss's *Into the Mainstream* (1966) suggests, perhaps condescendingly, that Latin American writers had finally joined the club of fictional modernity, while the simultaneous Spanish version, published in Buenos Aires, was called *Los nuestros*, echoing the Cuban poet José Martí's 'nuestra América', and the sense that at last there was a Latin American literature that could compete with the canonical modernist texts.[20] These interviews and essays, packed with insights, are dedicated to Alejo Carpentier, Miguel Angel Asturias, Jorge Luis Borges, Juan Carlos Onetti, Juan Rulfo, Carlos Fuentes, Mario Vargas Llosa (the youngest there, aged 30), one Brazilian, Guimarães Rosa and, most presciently, Gabriel García Márquez, before *Cien años de soledad* was published.

Equally important in promoting this Latin American writing (no women there in Harss's list) was the literary magazine, *Mundo Nuevo*, founded by the Uruguayan critic and biographer Emir Rodríguez Monegal. Published in Paris, its first number of July 1966 opened with a long interview on Latin American literature with Carlos Fuentes (plus a story by the exiled Paraguayan writer Augusto Roa Bastos); the second number of August 1966 had a chapter from García Márquez's unpublished *Cien años de soledad*. As a critic and academic (especially at Yale) Rodríguez Monegal ceaselessly promoted the 'Latin American' novel.

What was new to this team of Latin American fiction writers, that could not be found elsewhere, was tentatively formulated by the Cuban novelist and musicologist Alejo Carpentier, who elaborated his (already referred to) compensatory theory about the uniqueness of Latin America as opposed to jaded, exhausted Europe (inevitable after the Second World War), along an inversion of surrealist values that found Latin American geography and history already, naturally, surrealist. Carpentier's 'The marvellously real' may have echoed the 'marvellous' that André Breton claimed to find inside the mind, but he put these perceptions into practice by juxtaposing the real, exuberant America, with pale, rational, European simulacrums, especially in his novel about the Haitian revolution, voodoo and the rise and fall of a black tyrant, *El reino de este mundo* (1949; *The Kingdom of this World*); and again in a later novel about the redemptive energies lying in the Orinoco jungle, *Los pasos perdidos* (1953; *The Lost Steps*), exaggerating stereotypes about exuberant, tropical Latin America. However, through a sterile South American musicologist who awakens to forgotten creativity, this novel questioned the function of the artist in Latin America, with a doomed sense of writers not belonging to the organic life of primitive and rural America, and obliged to be witnesses of contemporary anxieties.

Carpentier inaugurated a baroque style of writing that evaluated Latin American popular beliefs, magic and legend as being just as valid as the high art imported from Europe. By arguing that the Latin American novelist should name everything, like Adam, and include everything (Carpentier was a master of lists), he illustrated the baroque mode that defined the Caribbean basin, leading to novels by Guillermo Cabrera Infante (b. 1929) and by Luis Rafael Sánchez (b. 1936), based on spoken voices. Even García Márquez is more Caribbean than Colombian. This concept of tropical-baroque was developed more thoroughly by the Cuban writers José Lezama Lima (1910–76), and Severo Sarduy (1937–93). A journalistic term tagged on to this style of writing that refused to evaluate the Caribbean experience through rational, urban European values was 'magical realism'; the magical side was often seen as simply liberating, and enhancing the imagination, as this style coincided with the rise of 1960s drug culture, the New Age reading of Carlos Castaneda, Mervyn Peake and Tolkein. The realism part of the term is undeniable, as we shall see.

A counter-view to this slow emergence of the new Latin American novel was Mario Vargas Llosa's dismissal in 1968 of the earlier realist novels as 'primitive'. Commenting on Rivera's *La vorágine*, Vargas Llosa bandied terms like 'picturesque', dismissive phrases about country and landscape predominating over character, about content over form, about lack of objectivity, about the author interfering in the fiction with his or her opinions and so on: 'the technique is rudimentary, pre-Flaubertian' (Vargas Llosa published a monograph on Flaubert in 1986 and Flaubert is a cipher for conscious artistic craft).[21] However, much of the matter of the later, supposedly new Latin American novels can be seen as traditionally realist, including Vargas Llosa's own fiction, but catering for more sophisticated, urban readers.

According to critics like Rodríguez Monegal and Vargas Llosa the new Latin American novel could be equated with the urban novel and was born in 1939 with the Uruguayan Juan Carlos Onetti's (1909–94) short novella about urban alienation, *El pozo* (1939; *The Pit*) and his later creation of Santa María (an urban, River Plate dystopia) in a cycle of novels. That this choice of text was a partisan misunderstanding about the primacy of subject matter (urban anguish, itself a sign that the disease of modernity has reached Latin American cities) is obvious if the urban novel in Latin America is seen as having the same *function* as the rural novel. What links all Latin American fiction in the twentieth century is that the expanding Latin American cities were as unknown to their reading inhabitants as the countryside was earlier, as Carpentier predicted ('the great task of the American novel today is to inscribe the physiognomy of its cities into universal literature').[22] That is, cities like the Buenos Aires metropolitan area reaching over 2 million by 1914, or Mexico City with 1 million inhabitants by 1928, owing to differing sociological factors such as European immigration, rural migrations, industrialization, and made publicly vivid by the rise of the shanty town (*villa miseria, callampa, barriada, rancho,* variable national terms for this social phenomenon) defied the urban imagination. Nowhere was this refusal to imagine how cities changed more evident than in the hostile reception given the anthropologist Oscar Lewis in Mexico with his tape-recorded, but novelized anthropological story of Mexican slums, *Children of Sánchez* (1961). In 1966 Carlos Fuentes commented on Lewis's work: 'The fact is that behind the facade of gladioli and urban motorways, three million inhabitants of Mexico City live like pariahs. If we are irritated that it is a North American who reminds us, the fault is ours: the Mexican press, radio and television have been too busy with Gerber tins.'[23] Media manipulation massaging collective desires created a role for the critical writer, even more so today in the cities. The urban novel exposing violent social change did not begin with Onetti, not even if one shares Vargas Llosa's Flaubertian notion of novelistic craft, for we can point to Manuel Gálvez and Roberto Arlt in Argentina, or Martín Luis Guzmán in Mexico as writers narrating the new, unknown urban monsters.

Nevertheless, direct denunciatory realism no longer coped with the complexities of urban life, nor with the writer's or reader's own self-understanding. A substratum of realism continued to ground the novel in its task of creating verisimilitude, but mediated with mid-twentieth-century experimentalism from literary sources as wide-ranging as Faulkner, Dos Passos, Kafka and Sartre. A test of the disparity between writer, reader and the semi-illiterate masses would be to ask if the characters themselves of mid-twentieth-century Latin American fiction could read the novels they protagonized; the paradigmatic case would be Juan Rulfo's (1918–86) fiction. Rulfo's peasants from the state of Jalisco in Mexico, marginalized from mainstream civic participation, duped by revolutionary rhetoric (the revolution's promise of restoring land, the *ejidos*) and communicating through inarticulate violence, lie outside the tacit reading-agreement that ensures that Rulfo writes for an educated public. If his fiction is filtered through Faulkner and a vague notion of surrealist dream-aesthetics, his sole, baffling novel *Pedro Páramo* (1955; *Pedro Páramo*) offers the best image of how a writer tries to explain yet change a reader, however pessimistically. At one level, this is a novel about a cacique who controls the fate of all his subjects; his violence, his machismo and inner dreams of love are set in the arid Mexican desert (the *páramos*), itself a metaphor of values (no roots, no future, a T. S. Eliot *Waste Land*), but the novel demands a particular attention from the reader who has to make formal sense of what is fragmentary so that understanding becomes dream-like, with all laws of time subverted. The novel is both very *Mexican* (in terms of the geography, history, language), and yet universal, dealing with fate, illusions and myths of belonging. Rulfo's fusion of surrealist practice and social realism is seamless, while his control of voice makes a reader relate to orality (the working title had been *Los murmullos*). The Jaliscan peasants supporting the Cristero revolution of catholics and priests, the landless, mute and violent misfits in the hinterlands, make all Rulfo's fiction expressionist, at times absurdist. Gabriel García Márquez's tribute to *Pedro Páramo* was that he learnt the novel by heart. Rulfo taught many writers how to place their fictions and how to treat artistically this geographical marginalization, though often without Rulfo's laconic subtlety; the best Mexican follow-up being Elena Garro's (1920–) *Los recuerdos del porvenir* (1963; *Recollections of Things to Come*) set in Ixtepec, where time has stopped, and the reader struggles to make sense of what happens (making the reader work, or sharing uncertainty and ignorance with the reader, form part of mid-twentieth-century novelistic poetics).

But the writer who emerges from Rulfo's shadow to single-handedly represent 'Latin American' fiction outside Colombia is García Márquez and his creation of Macondo as a metaphor of unknown Latin America in *Cien años de soledad* (1967, *One Hundred Years of Solitude*). As already outlined, this novel snowballed from Paris through Buenos Aires (distributed by the publishing house Sudamericana, promoted by Tomás Eloy Martínez in the magazine *Primera Plana* and by Gregory Rabassa's translation into English in 1970), and then all over Latin America, where the belief system and oral history of coastal Colombia are inserted into the minds of several generations of Buendías in a sad family saga of the loss of a childlike, semi-westernized mentality, and the manipulation of memory by the official historians so berated by García Márquez. This novel seeds references to Rulfo, Borges and Carpentier in its text, while García Márquez's reading in an Argentine edition of the Uruguayan, surrealistic short-story writer Felisberto Hernández, suggests a Latin American inter-textuality that confirms the Latin Americanization of the continent's fiction tradition in the 1960s. Another sign of this continental inter-relatedness is Mario Vargas Llosa who wrote a long study of his friend García Márquez in 1971.[24]

Vargas Llosa's own prolific fiction plays with the urban reader's attention in subtle ways, while still maintaining the denunciatory function appropriate to the critical Latin American writer of the 1920s and 1930s. His first novel *La ciudad y los perros* (1963; *The Time of the Hero*) is set in a military academy in the outskirts of Lima. It deals with how 'macho' values are instilled in the boys, with bullying, betrayal, rape and murder. The boys represent a cross-section of Peruvian society. The novel is so immersed in a sense of place that a reader can follow the action on a map. The dialogue is vivid, especially an unidentified monologue that runs through the work (and that shocks the reader who discovers whose the voice is only at the end). Such was the power of the denunciation that a thousand copies were publicly burnt, while Vargas Llosa was accused of having a 'mente degenerada' (degenerate mind), and being in the pay of Peru's traditional enemy, Ecuador. Vargas Llosa's follow-up, *La casa verde* (1966; *The Green House*) referring to a brothel, moved the action to Piura in northern Peru and the Amazonian jungle, and again cleverly baffled the readers' realistic expectations by offering dual views of the same characters over time spans of some forty years, and fragmenting the story. Vargas Llosa's reader could as well be a sophisticated North American postgraduate student, aware of the French *nouveau roman*, as much as a Limeñan ignorant of her own hinterlands. His third novel, *Conversación en La Catedral* (1970; *Conversation in the Cathedral*), exhibited a greater narrative complexity and ambition. Referring again to a café/brothel, it demanded of its readers such attention to seamlessly crafted layers of meaning in a political novel set under the Odría military government, that it became an anatomy of an ignorant society which exactly evaded such interlocked complexities. 'Magical realism' could never be applied to Vargas Llosa, only 'realism', a functional use of language, a mirror critically reflecting life (in Stendhal's definition of a novel), and denouncing the reader (in terms of the inauthenticity analysed by Jean-Paul Sartre in the epigraph to Vargas Llosa's first novel). By gauging what Vargas Llosa demanded of his readers within his novels we can contrast his relationship with novelists from more continuous novelistic traditions, for his readers read not only for the kick of being aesthetically tricked, but to understand the predicament of their country, and thus perhaps define the Latin American novel.

The key to Latin American fiction from the 1940s to the 1970s is the realization that its readers are urban and urbane, can be native readers or foreigners, for the educated Latin American reader was in touch with what happened in Paris and New York, as much as, or more than, with what happened in Buenos Aires or Bogotá, or in his or her own backyard. A writer who dealt with this dilemma of who his readers might be was the Guatemalan Miguel Angel Asturias, who turned to the surrealism he knew first-hand from his decade in Paris (1923–33) to convey the experience of dictatorship in Central America in *El señor presidente* (1946; *The President*); his appeal to associative and mythical thinking grew in his masterpiece *Hombres de maíz* (1949; *Men of Maize*) where metaphorically dense opening chapters mimic the alien mentality of the distinctly 'other' of the legendary Maya, and where the novel ends on loss of rootedness, and in conventional, literary realism as the westernized style of this loss. Asturias, like Carpentier, assumed that there was a mythical depth in Latin America that differentiated it from the more rationalistic Europe, but his later works shifted into denunciatory realism closer to a Latin American reader's political expectations, or lapsed into tired pastiches of his earlier mythical works, to demand less of his readers' collaboration.

The Peruvian José María Arguedas (1911–69), the subject of a monograph by Vargas Llosa published in 1998, also sought from his anthropological studies, as much as from his personal upbringing, to enter the mind of the Quechua-speaking Peruvian peasants, especially in his haunting study of suffering *Los ríos profundos* (1958; *Deep Rivers*), where the boy Ernesto comes to understand his divided self and divided society. Arguedas was affected by the loss of belonging to this schizoid Peru; his untranslated, final, despairing novel, *El zorro de arriba y el zorro de abajo* (1969), has diary sections that defy fiction and continue his polemic with the cosmopolitan Latin Americanist writers like Carlos Fuentes and Julio Cortázar, as to who truly represents 'Latin America' and, in my terms, who they can claim as their readers. Arguedas sided with Juan Rulfo,

Juan Carlos Onetti and Augusto Roa Bastos, as writers who genuinely gave a voice to the silent mass of illiterate and barely literate Latin Americans (who in their turn could not read the novels about them). The paradox for these writers was that their readers came from bourgeois pockets in capital cities, or were foreigners who read the novels in translation.

By the 1950s it was not wild nature but unimaginable cities that preoccupied, and still preoccupy, writers (in 1998, the Colombian novelist R. H. Moreno-Durán attacked the 'Third World exoticism' of critics who see Latin America as rural).[25] The start was made in Buenos Aires, Babylon and Cosmopolis, by writers like Roberto Arlt (1900–42) who explored the seamy side of the burgeoning megalopolis, clearly situating his fiction (*El juguete rabioso*, 1926; *Los siete locos* [1929, *The Seven Madmen*]; *Los lanzallamas*, 1931 and *El amor brujo*, 1932) in the city, and focusing on vice (the white slave-trade), anarchism and immigration in a sprawling style mirrored in his chronicles of city life (*Aguafuertes porteñas*, 1933). His Buenos Aires was not the city that would attract investment or tourists, or flatter the social aspirations of the upwardly mobile amassing their fortunes. This chaotic, labyrinthine city was also the locus and theme of Leopoldo Marechal's (1900–70) long-in-gestation novel *Adán Buenosayres* (1948), where the marginalized suburb of Villa Crespo houses riff-raff and bohemians. The writer who most placed Buenos Aires on the cultural map was Ernesto Sábato (b. 1911), a scientist who turned his back on science to become a novelist, who learnt from the surrealists about chance encounters and who made the cafés and streets and underground (the *subte* or metro) the plot of his novels exploring unbalanced minds as reflections of urban mess in *El túnel* (1949; *The Tunnel*), *Sobre héroes y tumbas* (1961; *On Heroes and Tombs*) and *Abaddón, el exterminador* (1974; *The Angel of Darkness*). These writers exposed a 'secret' Buenos Aires in a baroque style owing as much to Dostoevsky as to surrealism, in an attempt to include everything. In Sábato's case he rewrote the history of the country, delineating the fall from grace of the landed oligarchy, the exclusion of immigrants and the status of art (Sábato is a great satirist). The writer who exemplified this textualized city is Julio Cortázar, who, in *Hopscotch* (1963), refused to mould his over-spilling material into realist plot and rounded character, and whose fictional city is as much an overlap between Paris and Buenos Aires as a clash between the New Jerusalem and Babylon, and a place of law that constrained desire. *Hopscotch* explicitly legitimated various readers in its schizoid attempt to satisfy both the escapist pleasure of getting lost in a text and the text as a mirror of an inner journey to an elusive national self.

The Mexico City of the 1950s was the explicit theme of Carlos Fuentes's first novel *La región más transparente* (1958; *Where the Air is Clear*). He deliberately meshed the different social classes and their desires; Fuentes's critical view of this megalopolis included the Mexican Revolution, fossilized by the 1950s by a manipulative, political rhetoric, to become the subject of what many still consider his best novel, *La muerte de Artemio Cruz* (1962; *The Death of Artemio Cruz*). His work continued the complex debate about the status of the modish present day, haunted by imminent, threatening pasts (both Aztec and Nazi) in *Cambio de piel* (1967; *A Change of Skin*). All Fuentes's impressive work of the 1960s, both novelistic and journalistic, explains and exposes Mexico as a confused problem that justifies the function of the writer as an independent guide and critic for the city-reader.

The Latin American novel of the 1960s is further unified by the shift, over the twentieth century, away from a literary language inherited from Spain, with its imperative of being *castizo* (pure) and grammatically correct, towards local spoken dialects and colloquial language. Popular culture and its parodies in the form of films, soaps, the radio, gossip and songs define specific Latin American speech-rhythms. The Cuban Guillermo Cabrera Infante's oral re-creation of Batista's Havana, *Tres tristes tigres* (1965; *Three Trapped Tigers*) was written in *habanero*, local city slang. The provincial Argentina in Manuel Puig's (1934–90) artfully fragmented novels, especially *Boquitas pintadas* (1969; *Heartbreak Tango; a Serial*), point to subversive distances from Castilian Spanish, and a joyful celebration of local lingos. Julio Cortázar's fiction can be placed as much by its *porteño* slang as by its physical descriptions, just as slang functions in most novels as a primal zone of self-identification (and thus realism) for the Latin American reader. As late as 1968 the novelist Beatriz Guido found the clue to what made the Latin American novel different: 'to dare to write as one speaks'.[26]

One last way of conceptualizing 'Latin American' literature is by way of its translatability, not only into another language, but also into the variants of Spanish (many novels of the 1920s to 1940s included glossaries). Latin American literature for European and North American readers is the history of individual works translated out of their national contexts in isolated ways (the Colombian writer José Eustacio Rivera was translated into English but not the novelists before and after him in Colombia). A Latin American writer, in order to be translated, must incorporate the problems of translatability into his or her work by not being too local. Countering this translational strategy, we can locate an equally Latin American position, *not* to be translated, to remain faithful to the local linguistic horizons and to reject the cosmopolitan possibilities of translational prestige. The nodal figures of Rulfo and Borges epitomize these creative dilemmas. Rulfo is revered as representing something uniquely Latin American from a complex Mexican angle, yet his work transcends referentiality (its re-creation of Jalisco and its peasants) because it is grounded on surrealist poetics, with Faulkner as mentor; further, Rulfo, uprooted from his native province, lived and worked in Mexico City, writing about his lost world, a world as foreign to contemporary urban Mexicans as to actual foreigners. In 1980 Rulfo wrote that 'in our village people are closed, yes, completely, one is a foreigner here'.[27] Translation does not dim this loss. Borges was early translated into French as a cosmopolitan writer of mind-puzzles by ignoring his deeply Argentine contexts, for he too had been uprooted (several crucial school years in Europe) and had to rediscover his cultural identity, as did his character Juan Dahlmann who in the story 'El sur' ironically encountered his 'South American destiny' in a dream knife fight with a gaucho.[28] The problems of translatability suggest that the Latin American writer has to resort to the foreigner's strategies of explaining in order to write about place and loss. The use of glossaries at the back of many realist novels, or the explanation of terms within the texts themselves, confirm that representing Latin American 'uniqueness' is a problem, and that writers cannot assume an obvious target audience in mind. The exiled Polish writer Witold Gombrowicz noted in his diary this problem of a self-conscious national destiny: 'Argentine literature will be born when its writers forget about Argentina.'[29]

The 1960s, then, saw the emergence of a genuine 'Latin American' fiction tradition, in the wake of an already established poetic tradition, with Jorge Luis Borges as the turning point, not only because of his stylistic and conceptual 'rigour', but also because of his self-consciousness as an eclectic writer. Clear pre- and post-Borges ways of envisioning the Latin American writer can be reformulated as the continuing clash in most Latin American novels between the demands of realism and the urgency of imaginative freedom, in terms of the exigencies of craft and a new professionalism dependent on inter-continental sales. In his

genres (including high and low culture), to a degree that future observers may find astonishing and bizarre. (This is one of the many reasons why Borges is such a crucial and emblematic figure, and not only in Latin America: the absence of meaning is one of his central themes.) It was, indeed, the 1960s that saw the beginnings of a curiously negative revolution – the 'deconstructive' turn – in literary studies and their gradual circumscription, undermining and appropriation by so-called 'cultural studies'. At the start of the era, popular culture was already beginning to take students and other young people away from the traditional high culture of the bourgeoisie; political, sexual and cultural revolution was in the air, along with feminism; yet literary criticism still mainly offered a basic Cold War alternative between a 'New-Critical' analysis of 'literature for its own sake' and, especially in Latin American oriented literary criticism, various forms of 'social' criticism loosely associated with old and new Marxisms. But the theories of Saussure, Lévi-Strauss and Barthes now inspired a new 'structuralist' approach to language and mythology, and Derrida, Althusser, Foucault and Lacan were writing the seminal texts which would, over the next two decades, elaborate and consolidate a 'post-structuralist' criticism which would, in a new 'post-modern' and indeed 'post-colonial' era, 'deconstruct' all previous approaches to language, society, culture and literature.

In the case of Latin American literature in particular, creative writing was henceforth inseparable from literary criticism. A leading member and propagandist of the Boom, Carlos Fuentes, published his 'structuralist' critique *La nueva novela hispanoamericana* [The New Spanish American Novel] in 1969 and Severo Sarduy, closely associated with the Parisian *Tel-Quel* group, produced his first theoretical essays on Latin America's supposedly distinctive 'neo-baroque' style in literature around the same time. Since the 1960s was the first period in which young scholars worldwide turned in large numbers to Latin American literature as a professional field of study, their rapid and large-scale adaptation to the new trends has meant that Latin American literature has been even more subject to new critical approaches during this period than other more established literatures.

It has also, at first sight, been much more diverse than before. Until the 1960s, when Latin America became definitively installed in global consciousness, it was normal, and by no means artificial, to view Latin American narrative in terms of a critical division between works oriented towards Latin America's own internal realities and works which, in one way or another, testified to Latin America's relationship with or differences from the wider international order, above all the European connection. Thus a plausible division could be established between a social realist or even Americanist narrative line which included *indigenista* literature, socialist realism and other politically committed movements and a developing 'magical realist' or 'transcultural' line which dealt in a more mythical and metaphorical way with the question of Latin American identity and the interaction of sophisticated 'First World' type intellectuals with illiterate or semi-literate 'Third World' type cultures.

No such simple divisions can be established in relation to Latin American narrative since 1970. On the one hand, admittedly, the Boom has continued to dominate the landscape through the hegemony of its principal protagonists, Gabriel García Márquez, Carlos Fuentes and Mario Vargas Llosa (the fourth member, Julio Cortázar, died in 1983), each of whom has gone on to create a grand œuvre comparable with the respective records of their predecessors Asturias, Borges and Carpentier. The achievements of Guillermo Cabrera Infante and José Donoso are not far behind. On the other hand, however, the new writers who have appeared on the scene since the end of the 1960s have opened up new avenues and created a narrative literature which, as mentioned, although now consciously more minor in key, is as innovative and diverse as any other regional equivalent in the world. It would therefore be impossible to maintain the old dualist analysis mentioned above, except perhaps in one important respect. Instead of such a division between a Latin Americanist and an internationalist mode it might be possible to suggest a newly accented division between those who continue to write, in a more or less traditional way, about the 'Other/s' and those who indulge in one of the many possible forms of what we could call 'Self-Writing'. This division was in reality inaugurated in the earliest moments of the New Novel in the 1920s, when Asturias wrote openly about himself as writer, explorer and anthropologist (the 'New Quetzalcoatl') in his *Leyendas de Guatemala* [Legends of Guatemala], and Borges, stimulated by the example of his compatriot Macedonio Fernández, began to talk about an eccentric character called 'Borges', henceforth the implicit protagonist of all his works. But such self-reflexive forms have proliferated irresistibly since the 1960s and even the old forms of social realism have transmuted into so-called *testimonio*, in which the old 'subaltern' protagonists – indigenous peoples, gauchos, blacks, proletarians, homosexuals, women – now speak with their own voices, even if the tape recorder and the questions are still put to them by academics and other intellectuals. Although writers take up widely differing positions in relation to this twin problematic, awareness of it is central to almost all writing currently appearing in the subcontinent.

In the interests of expository coherence, however, we will endeavour to expand the analysis here to reflect more fully the striking diversity of forms of narrative writing that have appeared on the Latin American scene these past thirty years. Critics have argued that the post-Boom narrative has exhibited many of the characteristics of so-called post-modern literature in general. It has been more everyday and less pretentious, less aestheticizing and rhetorical, more realistic and less rarefied, more debunkingly parodic and less loftily ironic, more humorous and less inclined to transcendent solemnities, more partial to everyday popular culture and less committed to the 'grand narratives of the West', less existentially pessimistic but also less ambitious, more interested in both love and eroticism and less interested in theories of any kind, whether political or philosophical. Above all it has been anti-canonical. (As for its much lauded optimism, it would be easy to argue that things are the opposite of what they appear: the Boom writers' apparent pessimism was merely a cold-eyed appraisal of the past at a moment when Latin Americans and Latin American writers were actually more optimistic than ever before; whereas Latin America's history since 1970 has been so black and disappointing that writers feel obliged to look for hope in even the most ordinary and unpromising places.)

This general panorama has led some critics to assert that the move to a more accessible form of writing, to the 'traditional' virtues of literary storytelling, is the predominant phenomenon of the post-Boom era and therefore of post-Boom narrative, a phenomenon which, accordingly, chimes with one of the predominant aesthetic characteristics of the whole postmodern era. And certainly a number of writers have had considerable success with such apparently old-fashioned and transparent narrative methods. Among the best-known examples would be the Chileans Antonio Skármeta (b. 1940) and Isabel Allende (see below), and the Argentinian Mempo Giardinelli (b. 1949), each of whom achieved their literary success from exile, another central phenomenon and theme of the 1970s and 1980s. Skármeta's works, all to a greater or lesser extent politically (though not programmatically) committed, include *Soñé que la nieve ardía* (1975; *I Dreamt the Snow Was Burning*), set in the period prior to the overthrow of Salvador Allende's Unidad Popular government in 1973,

La insurrección (1982; *The Insurrection*), on the triumph of the Sandinista Revolution in Nicaragua and *Ardiente paciencia* (1985; *Burning Patience*), a novel about a young Chilean fisherman whose political consciousness is opened by his contact with Pablo Neruda and his poetry, again during the period prior to the overthrow of Unidad Popular. (This novel was adapted into the internationally successful movie, *Il Postino*.) Giardinelli's works include *Por qué prohibieron el circo?* [Why Did They Ban the Circus] (1976), *La revolución en bicicleta* [Revolution by Bicycle] (1980) and *El cielo con las manos* [To Heaven With Our Hands] (1982), all freshly written, reader-friendly books with high entertainment value. A more surprising phenomenon, perhaps, has been the huge international success of a different kind of post-modern narrative, reminiscent of Conrad and Greene but flatter and less melodramatic, in the work of Alvaro Mutis (b. Colombia, 1923), previously known as a poet but author now in old age of a stream of novels about the wandering seaman Maqroll the Lookout, including *La nieve del almirante* (1986; *The Snow of the Admiral*), *La última escala del tramp steamer* (1988; *The Tramp Steamer's Last Port of Call*) and *Abdul Bashur, soñador de navíos* (1991; *Abdul Bashur, Dreamer of Ships*).

On the other hand, however, and contrary to the facile generalizations of some critics, other writers have taken the opposite approach by writing some of the most bristlingly experimental and opaque prose seen in Latin America since the period of the 1920s avant-garde, writing which, in this sense, must be considered an extension of some of the exploratory gestures of the Boom itself. And this literary lineage, which has convinced some critics that Latin America continues to be the privileged home of the baroque (or 'neo-baroque'), may be thought to be more characteristic of Latin American writing as a whole than the more diaphanous forms which García Márquez promised on the first page of *Cien años de soledad* but then, perfidiously, denied. Among the leading examples of such writerliness, which returned to Western literature above all through the 1950s *Nouveau Roman*, would be the Cuban Severo Sarduy (1937–92), himself a member of the later *Tel-Quel* group, author of dazzling experimental tours de force like *Gestos* [Gestures] (1963), *Cobra* (1975; *Cobra*), *Colibrí* [Hummingbird] (1982) and the autobiographical *Los pájaros en la playa* (1992; *The Beach*); another Cuban, the dissident Reinaldo Arenas (1943–92), with *Arturo, la estrella más brillante* [Arturo, the Brightest Star] (1984); the Mexican Salvador Elizondo (b. 1932), who, like Sarduy, repeatedly stages the dramas of writing itself in works like the sadistic classic *Farabeuf* (1965; *Farabeuf*), the obsessional

El grafógrafo [The Graphographer] (1972) and other works; and the Chilean Diamela Eltit, mentioned below, whose writing is aggressively alienating and ferociously impenetrable. Another Cuban, Eliseo Alberto (b. 1951), began his now highly successful professional career with a similarly avant-gardist text, *La eternidad por fin comienza un lunes* [Eternity Begins at Last One Monday] (1992).

Of course the Boom writers themselves wrote both in transparent mode (the most characteristic works of García Márquez before *El otoño del patriarca*) and in opaque mode (much of Cortázar). What mainly characterizes the work of their successors is not, as some commentators have rather superficially suggested, a stylistic or technical turn (accessible or inaccessible, readerly or writerly), because the writers of both tendencies (and many writers in any case belong to both tendencies) are much more aware than most pre-Boom authors of the nature and challenges of writing itself. What really separates the post-Boom from the Boom is, rather, as mentioned above, the absence of a grand narrative, which, in the case of Latin America, used to mean above all the various two-hundred-year searches for a national identity circumscribed by the five-hundred-year search for a continental identity. These epic metaphorical searches had led, in the case of the New Latin American Novel and its climax the Boom, to what writers themselves called 'totalizing' works, Cervantine or Joycean books which allegorized or mythologized an entire country or continent or, indeed, the world and human life themselves. This sort of ambition, ironically, was dissolved at precisely the moment that Latin America approached its own five hundredth anniversary, and by 1992 itself the main response to the problem was the development of what were called 'new historical novels' (somewhat surprisingly given the almost complete absence of an 'old' historical novel in the continent), works which mainly questioned the coherence of Latin American historical development and indeed the meaning of history itself.

In Latin America, as elsewhere, the most visible change in the literary panorama is surely in the number of women writers who have emerged and the impact they have made. This goes far beyond matters of sociology to matters of world-view and reader expectations. It is indeed a phenomenon of world-historical importance. Some women choose to write in a 'typically feminine', apparently delicate and intuitive way; others confound such stereotypical exigencies and declare implicitly that women, like men, can write however they like. Prior to 1970 there were many excellent women writers in the continent (the Chilean María Luisa Bombal and the Uruguayan Armonía Somers are just two examples of shamefully neglected authors) but it was difficult for them to make an impact; now there are many more and several of them must be counted among the most important of all Spanish American writers. We should mention the great pathbreaker, Clarice Lispector (1925–77), even though she is Brazilian, because of the vast influence she has had on women writers all over Latin America and beyond. Her most important novels are *A paixão segundo G.H.* (1964; *The Passion According to G.H.*) and *A hora da estrela* (1977; *The Hour of the Star*). Elena Poniatowska (b. Mexico, 1933) is best known for her documentary works, and her novel *Hasta no verte Jesús mío* (1969; *Here's to You Jesus!*), about the life of a working-class woman in Mexico City, is an astonishing example of the fusion of genres. The best-known Latin American woman writer of the twentieth century is, of course, Chile's Isabel Allende (b. 1942), author of *La casa de los espíritus* (1982; *The House of the Spirits*), *Eva Luna* (1987; *Eva Luna*) and the recent bestseller *Hija de la fortuna* (1999; *Daughter of Fortune*). Still not embraced by many serious literary critics, Allende is a deceptively artless narrator whose trajectory is, in a sense, although belated, similar to that of the Boom novelists rather than their successors. More of a cult writer, but undoubtedly profoundly original and adventurous, is another Chilean, Diamela Eltit (b. 1949), author of *Lumpérica* (1983; *E.Luminata*), *Cuarto mundo* [The Fourth World] (1988), *Vaca sagrada* (1992; *Sacred Cow*) and *Los vigilantes* [The Watchers] (1994), all focused on the interface between writing, gender, ideology and the body. Other important women writers are Cristina Peri Rossi (b. Uruguay, 1941), author of *La nave de los locos* (1984; *The Ship of Fools*) and *Solitario de amor* (1988; *Solitaire of Love*); Luisa Valenzuela (b. Argentina, 1938), whose most influential work is the chilling political allegory *Cola de lagartija* (1983; *The Lizard's Tail*); Angeles Mastretta (b. Mexico, 1949), best known for easy-read melodramas like *Arráncame la vida* (1985; *Tear This Heart Out*); Laura Esquivel (b. Mexico, 1950), writer of the international bestselling 'cooking novel' *Como agua para chocolate* (1989; *Like Water for Chocolate*); and Gioconda Belli (b. Nicaragua, 1948), author of *La mujer habitada* (1988; *The Inhabited Woman*), a feminist view of the Sandinista Revolution.

Women authors have been largely responsible for the continuing popularity worldwide of 'magical realism', the brand-name for the best-known mode of Latin American writing, which has been successfully exported to all corners of the planet, though most particularly other regions of the so-called 'Third World'. The technique fathered by Miguel Angel Asturias and the Gabriel García Márquez of *Cien años de soledad* has, however, been superseded by the mode patented by the former in his *El espejo de Lida Sal* (1969; *The Mirror of Lida Sal*) and the latter in his stories entitled *La increíble y triste historia de la cándida Eréndira y de su abuela desalmada* (1972; *Innocent Eréndira*). This variant often degenerates into mere style, usually of a rather cloying variety suggestive of the verbal equivalent of a second-rate Disney cartoon. However, many 'Latina' novels in the United States have taken up this anti-pragmatic style to great acclaim, and Spanish American authors like Laura Esquivel and Isabel Allende are occasionally guilty of its worst excesses – like *Eréndira*, both *La casa de los espíritus* and *Como agua para chocolate* were turned into popular 'magical realist' movies.

By contrast, overtly committed political writing, of the kind whose genealogy could be traced all the way back to the 1920s, was going the way of 'grand narratives' and falling rapidly out of fashion by the time of the Boom. Certainly, writers from Puig to Eltit have been exhaustively exploring what we might call the 'politics within': parodies and/or critiques of the media and their impact, through 'mass' and 'popular' culture, on consciousness and ideology; the complex problematic of sexuality, gender and eroticism; and pastiches of pulp fiction, soap operas, pop music and other popular forms (see below). But old-style social and socialist realism were out of fashion and favour long before the fall of the Berlin Wall in 1989. Curiously, this noticeable shift away from party politics and heart-on-sleeve commitment took place at a moment – the 1960s to the 1990s – when real politics was as brutal and tragic as at any time in Latin America's history. A harsh view might conclude that various forms of middle-class rights took precedence over the old proletarian causes and campaigns and that United States definitions have replaced Soviet ones. In communist Cuba literature has, of course, continued to be political, which is why relatively few novels – the novel being the most self-revealing and declaratory of all literary genres – have been published. Carpentier's officialist *La consagración de la primavera* (1978; *Rite of Spring*) has been almost universally panned. Reinaldo Arenas's *Otra vez el mar* (1982; *Farewell to the Sea*) was an almost equally unsuccessful *anti*-revolutionary novel. One of the few works which have summed up the contradictions and complexities of the Revolution is Jesús Díaz's (1941–2002) anguished *Las iniciales de la terra* [The Initials of the Earth] (1987). His *Las palabras iniciales* [The Initial Words] (1992) then negated such revolutionary idealism as he had managed to salvage in the earlier work. Mexican narrative between 1968 and the early 1990s produced a whole series of novels on the 1968 student movement, none of them as successful or influential as *La noche de Tlatelolco* (1971; *Massacre in Mexico*) by Elena Poniatowska, author of other similar works like the magnificent *Hasta no verte Jesús mío* (1969), already mentioned, *Nada, nadie* (1988; *Nothing, Nobody*), about the major 1986 earthquake in Mexico City and *Tinísima* (1993; *Tinisima*), a fictionalized biography of the revolutionary photographer Tina Modotti. These 'documentary' narratives by a leading middle-class journalist and novelist are closely related to so-called *testimonio*, a form consecrated in the 1960s by the cultural institutions of the Cuban Revolution. The first major Latin American exponent of this form, a close cousin of Oscar Lewis's *Children of Sánchez*, was the Cuban Miguel Barnet, whose *Biografía de un cimarrón* (*Biography of a Runaway Slave*) was published in 1966. The best-known *testimonios*, without doubt, are those of Domitila Barrios de Chungara, *Si me permiten hablar* (1977; *Let Me Speak*), about the Bolivian mining proletariat, and the world-famous autobiography by a Guatemalan Indian woman, *Me llamo Rigoberta Menchú* (1985; *I, Rigoberta Menchú*), a touchstone of so-called 'political correctness' outside Latin America. Where novelists continued to deal with politics, it was in a more oblique, anguished and self-reflexive fashion, as in *Respiración artificial* (1980; *Artificial Respiration*) by Ricardo Piglia (b. Argentina, 1941) and his later *La ciudad ausente* (1992; *The Absent City*).

The treatment of popular urban culture itself, another topic inaugurated by the Boom, varies from implied critique to apolitical parody and pastiche. Among the first exponents were the young writers of the Mexican *Onda* or 'New Wave', José Agustín (b. 1944), Parménides García Saldaña and Gustavo Sainz (b. 1940), all heavily influenced by rock-and-roll and 1960s psychodelia. Agustín's *La tumba* [The Tomb] (1964), *De perfil* [In Profile] (1966) and *Se está haciendo tarde* [It's Getting Late] (1973) were early paradigms and Gustavo Sainz's, *La princesa del Palacio de Hierro* (1974; *The Princess of the Iron Palace*) was one of the high points of the movement. Both writers moved later to more traditionally respectable and responsible fiction. Without doubt, however, the most successful and influential exponent of narrative involving the simultaneous exaltation, pastiche and critique of popular culture was Argentina's Manuel Puig (1932–90), one of the most important writers of the entire era. *La traición de Rita Hayworth* (1969; *Betrayed by Rita Hayworth*) illustrated the importance of Hollywood glamour and ideology in Latin America's small unglamorous towns, whilst *El beso de la mujer araña* (1976; *The Kiss of the Spider Woman*) counterpointed questions of revolutionary politics and private morality in a wholly novel fashion. Other significant works in this vein are Guillermo Cabrera Infante's *Tres tristes tigres* (1965; *Three Trapped Tigers*) and *La Habana para un infante difunto* (1979; *Infante's Inferno*), Severo Sarduy's *De dónde son los cantantes* (1967; *From Cuba With a Song*), Vargas Llosa's hilarious *La tía Julia y el escribidor* (1977; *Aunt Julia and the Script Writer*), and two novels by Luis Rafael Sánchez (b. Puerto Rico, 1936), *La guaracha del macho Camacho* (1980; *Macho Camacho's Beat*) and *La importancia de llamarse Daniel Santos* [The Importance of Being Called Daniel Santos] (1989), both of which assert the importance of popular music in forging identity and resistance in Latin America.

Yet another area opened up by the Boom was the question of sexuality and eroticism (often perceived, in Latin America at least, as the positive other side of torture and repression). All the Boom writers joined the 1960s sexual revolution by examining these issues and Latin American narrative has continued to feature them centrally ever since. The body has come to the forefront of ideological attention at the same time as the text has come to the forefront of literary inquiry. Sarduy, in all his work but particularly *Cobra* (1972), *Maitreya* (1978; *Maitreya*) and *Colibrí* (1984), has explored the intersection of cultural and sexual ambiguity; Manuel Puig's *El beso de la mujera araña*, mentioned above, is one of the best-known works about the interface of the homosexual and hetero-sexual worlds; Luis Zapata (b. Mexico, 1951) caused a sensation with his pathbreaking *El vampiro de la Colonia Roma* [The Vampire of the Colonia Roma] (1979) about gay hustlers in Mexico City; Fernando Vallejo (b. Colombia, 1942) has recently produced, in *La virgen de los sicarios* (1994; *Our Lady of the Assassins*), a novel about gay hit-men in Medellín; and the Chilean Pedro Lemebel has written an extraordinary series of texts entitled *Loco afán: crónicas de Sidario* [Crazy Desires: Chronicles of the Aids Days] (1996). Women writers have been equally energetic: Reina Roffé (b. Argentina, 1951) has authored several texts with an erotic and particu-larly a lesbian problematic, most notably *El monte de Venus* (1976; *Mount Venus*), whilst *Canon de alcoba* [Canon of the Bedroom] (1988) by Tununa Mercado (b. Argentina, 1939) offers every form of sexual orientation imaginable in what has to be one of the most compelling and seductive of all Spanish American erotic books. Other works on sex and sexuality by women writers include Diamela Eltit's extraordinary *Vaca sagrada* (1991;

Sacred Cow), Cristina Peri Rossi's Solitario de amor (1988; Solitaire of Love) and El amor es una droga dura [Love is a Hard Drug] (1999), Apariciones (1996; Apparitions) by Mexican Margo Glantz (b. 1930), La nada cotidiana [Nothing Every Day] (1995) by Cuban dissident Zoe Valdés (b. 1959), which she has followed with a stream of similarly erotic bestsellers (in Spain, not Cuba). Naturally the men have wished to prove, perhaps vainly, that they can go further. Mario Vargas Llosa, provocateur extraordinaire, has gleefully joined the fray with two pornographic novels, Elogio de la madrastra (1988; In Praise of the Stepmother) and Los cuadernos de don Rigoberto (1997; The Notebooks of Don Rigoberto); the Venezuelan Denzil Romero's La esposa del doctor Thorne [Doctor Thorne's Wife] (1988) is an equally scandalous pornographic novel about one of Latin America's female icons, Manuelita Sáenz; and Argentina's Federico Andahazi (b. 1963) has written an internationally notorious work El anatomista (1997; The Anatomist) implicitly comparing the discovery of the clitoris with the colonization and conquest of the New World.

In a panorama where radical political change seems not to be on the agenda, lesser forms of resistance and subversion become more important. As well as popular culture and erotic provocation, other kinds of transgression are to be found in works connected with detection and crime; these range from relatively innocent, almost bloodless English-style whodunnits to American-style hard-boiled noirist novels, often with a perverse or subversive edge. The Boom writers have all explored the genre in various ways – Fuentes's La cabeza de la hidra (1978; The Hydra Head), García Márquez's Crónica de una muerte anunciada (1981; Chronicle of a Death Foretold), Vargas Llosa's Quién mató a Palomino Molero? (1986; Who Killed Palomino Molero?), but other writers have produced more interesting experiments: Jorge Ibarguengoitia (Mexico, 1928–83), with Las muertas (1977; The Dead Girls) and Dos crímenes (1979; Two Crimes); Mempo Giardinelli with the bolero-like Luna caliente (1983; Sultry Moon) and Qué solos se quedan los muertos (1985; The Dead Remain Alone); Alberto Fuguet (b. Chile, 1964) with Tinta roja [Red Ink]; (1996) and Ricardo Piglia with Plata quemada [Money to Burn] (1997), a novel which, characteristic of the new Latin American epoch, both multicultural and multi-thematic, fuses the problematics of crime, politics and homosexuality.

As soon as the momentum of the Boom began to fail, in the early 1970s, and particularly after the great political and literary parting of the ways marked by the Cuban Padilla Affair in 1971, serious fictive revisions of Latin American history began to take place, initiated at first by Boom writers and even pre-Boom writers. Thus 1974–5 saw the publication of three novels about dictatorship – *Yo el Supremo* (*I the Supreme*) by Augusto Roa Bastos (b. Paraguay, 1917), *El recurso del método* (*Reasons of State*) by Alejo Carpentier (Cuba, 1904–80) and *El otoño del patriarca* (*The Autumn of the Patriarch*) by Gabriel García Márquez (b. 1927) – and a novel about authoritarianism more generally on an even wider Hispanic canvas in the shape of *Terra nostra* by Carlos Fuentes. Each of these works radically questioned earlier versions of Latin American history but Fuentes's novel shamelessly and unapologetically refashioned it, thereby setting a trend that has continued right through the Spanish American and Brazilian half-millennium celebrations and up to the present. Fuentes has written several other historical novels, *Gringo viejo* (1985; *Old Gringo*), about Ambrose Bierce and the Mexican Revolution, *Cristóbal Nonato* (1987; *Christopher Unborn*), about the implications of 1992, *La campaña* (1990; *The Campaign*), about Spanish American independence, and *Los años con Laura Díaz* (1999; *The Years With Laura Díaz*), a mural of twentieth-century Mexican history. Three of Mario Vargas Llosa's novels, *La guerra del fin del mundo* (1981; *The War of the End of the World*), *Historia de Mayta* (1984; *The Real Life of Alejandro Mayta*) and *La fiesta del chivo* (2000; *The Feast of the Goat*) are also historical in orientation. *La fiesta del chivo* is an extraordinary account of the Trujillo dictatorship and its aftermath in the Dominican Republic. Likewise three of García Márquez's novels, *El amor en los tiempos del cólera* (1985; *Love in the Time of Cholera*), *El general en su laberinto* (1989; *The General in his Labyrinth*) and *Del amor y otros demonios* (1994; *Of Love and Other Demons*) can also be classed as historical novels, whilst *Noticia de un secuestro* (1996; *News of a Kidnapping*) could be called a narrative of current history. Most of these novels, however, with the exceptions of Fuentes's *Terra nostra* and *Cristóbal nonato* (Fuentes, characteristically, tries to have it both ways), are really rather traditional historical novels, as if the Boom novelists are still wishing to set Latin America's history straight. By contrast, works like *Los perros del paraíso* (1983; *The Dogs of Paradise*) by Abel Posse (b. Argentina, 1936), a hilarious and outrageous rewriting of Columbus's exploits, or the less flashy *Noticias del Imperio* [News from the Empire] (1987) by Fernando del Paso (b. Mexico, 1935), about the aftermath of the French invasion of Mexico in the 1860s, or *Santa Evita* (1995; *Saint Evita*) by Tomás Eloy Martínez (b. Argentina, 1934), attempt a more radical and subversive reordering of the continent's traditional histories and myths.

The historic quest for identity appears to be over. In the endless dialectic between the individual subject and society, the balance in Latin

American narrative seems to have shifted, for the time being, to the individual. Thus Latin America's fictions no longer appear as wilfully Latin American as they used to seem up to and including the Boom. Now it is language and writing, the body and sexuality, the subject and ideology, consciousness and the media, which seem to be the main objects of concern in Latin American fiction. And yet, unmistakably, the novels and short stories of the post-Boom have gradually begun to develop the outline of another continental identity, perhaps an even more tenacious one, at the level of writing itself. It is this new identity that, however tentatively, this brief essay has sought to suggest.

Further reading

Franco, Jean, *The Decline and Fall of the Lettered City: Latin America in the Cold War*, Cambridge, MA, 2002

Martin, Gerald, *Journeys Through the Labyrinth: Latin American Fiction in the Twentieth Century*, London, 1989

Shaw, Donald L., *The Post-Boom in Spanish American Fiction*, Albany NY, 1998

Sklodowska, Elzbieta, *La parodia en la nueva novela hispanoamericana*, Amsterdam, 1991
    Testimonio hispanoamericano: historia, teoría, poética, New York, 1992

Swanson, Philip, *The New Novel in Latin America: Politics and Popular Culture after the Boom*, Manchester, 1995

Williams, Raymond L., *The Postmodern Novel in Latin America: Politics, Culture and the Crisis of Truth*, New York, 1995

6

Brazilian narrative

Brazil's literary narrative began to emerge only after the country's formal independence from Portugal in 1822, and it gained full force only in the second half of the nineteenth century. While generally accompanying the Western literary tradition's major trends and transformations, it has developed its own voice and matured into an important part of a rich and diverse national literature. It has not always received the international acclaim that has been accorded Spanish American literature, but that perhaps has less to do with quality than with the facts that it is written in Portuguese rather than Spanish and that translations have been rather slow in coming. It was not until the 1950s, for example, that turn-of-the-century writer Machado de Assis, whom Susan Sontag has described as 'the greatest author ever produced in Latin America',[1] was translated into English.

Brazil is a continent-sized country with tremendous disparities in wealth and education. Given the country's historically high rate of illiteracy and relatively small reading public, fictional narrative has largely been a form of expression produced by and for a privileged minority of Brazilians. In absolute terms the number of people with the cultural disposition and cultural capital necessary to consume literary works has grown progressively over time, as access to public education and literacy has expanded, but it continues to be limited in relation to the country's total population. Even at the dawn of the twenty-first century, it is not uncommon for a novel's initial print run to be no more than three thousand copies. Consequently, it has been difficult for writers to subsist on literature alone, and they have often been economically dependent on such occupations as teaching, journalism and particularly government service.

Literary categorizations of any sort run the risk of oversimplification and generalization, but they can also be broadly useful for presenting a framework in which to understand and to extract a certain commonality from widely diverse works published in different historical circumstances. Critics have attempted to account for the major characteristics of Brazilian literary production in a number of ways. In relation to the nineteenth century, for example, some have focused on period styles (e.g. Romanticism), while others prefer to emphasize thematic tendencies (e.g. the 'Indianist' novel) that played a significant role in the development of Brazilian fiction.

To account for the historical dynamics of literary practice in Brazil, critic Antonio Candido has more productively suggested that Brazilian literature has developed through the dialectics of localism and cosmopolitanism.[2] Writers have attempted to express or describe the local – that which is unique about Brazilian culture and society – while at the same time working within cosmopolitan or European literary conventions. At different moments, they may stress one or the other, although in reality the two seldom exist in isolation.

Brazilian narrative's localist focus has generated multiple works concerned with the country's national identity, constituting a major trend within Brazilian narrative almost from its beginnings. This trend has found expression in such important modes or genres as literary regionalism, the historical novel and the Indianist novel, with its search for national symbols and myths. It has also frequently assumed the form of social criticism through fiction, generating myriad denunciations of the violence, inequality and injustice of the country's social relations, whether in rural or urban settings, particularly in the post-1930 period. These currents transcend period styles to constitute discourses that pervade Brazilian narrative throughout its historical development. An Indianist discourse, for example, can be traced from José de Alencar (1829–77) in the middle of the nineteenth century, through the modernists of the 1920s, to the more recent neo-Indianism of Antônio Callado (1917–97) and Darcy Ribeiro (1922–97). The same may be said of regionalist fiction – at least from the late nineteenth century until the 1950s – and the historical novel, both of which have long and rich traditions in Brazil.

The cosmopolitan thrust has led, on the one hand, to psychological or philosophical explorations of language, self and the human condition, and, on the other, to vibrant experimental or vanguardist currents that dialogue with universal forms of expression. Machado de Assis, for example, quite consciously inserted his mature work into the Western literary tradition, explicitly rejecting the picturesque nationalist concerns of his predecessors. His focus, rather, was on human nature and broad philosophical questions, leading some critics to suggest, quite incorrectly, that his fiction was somehow 'un-Brazilian'. In the 1920s, modernists such as Oswald de Andrade (1890–1954) drank heavily from the achievements of the early-twentieth-century European avant-garde, while in subsequent decades novelists such as Lúcio Cardoso (1913–68) and Clarice Lispector (1925–77) explored religious, existential and philosophical concerns having little to do with cultural nationalism. In reality, the local/universal dichotomy is a false one, since few works are exclusively on one side or the other, although it is broadly useful as an analytical tool.

Brazilian narrative in the nineteenth century

When the roots of Brazilian narrative began to take hold in the 1830s and 1840s, the country had only recently freed itself from Portuguese colonial rule. Despite the nation's independence in 1822, the prevailing structures of power, based on large slave-holding estates and an essentially agricultural economy, were not immediately transformed. Early writers of fiction tended to be the sons of wealthy, landed families who had the opportunity to study law or medicine, either abroad or in one of the country's few institutions of higher education. At the time of Brazil's independence, only some 20,000 people might have had the cultural disposition to participate in the new nation's cultural life even as active consumers, much less as potential producers. The country's first press was established in 1808; the first newspapers were published in 1813. The incipient cultural field, in short, was decidedly underdeveloped, and quality narrative was slow to emerge.

Foreign works nourished the small reading public that did in fact exist, as translations of French and English narratives were published as early as the second decade of the century. Although numerous classical European writers (Cervantes, Swift, Fielding) were available, many more popular or popularesque tales of lesser quality also found their way into Portuguese, with a perhaps nefarious influence. Alfredo Bosi has suggested that French sub-literature, either in the original or in poor translations, served as the model for what many consider to be the first Brazilian novel, *O filho do pescador* [The Fisherman's Son] (1843), by Antônio Gonçalves Teixeira e Sousa (1812–61).[3]

It was common for works of this period, both foreign and domestic, to appear initially in newspapers. Through much of the nineteenth century, a very close relationship existed between fiction and the press, since many novels were first published in serial form as *folhetins* (*feuilletons*). This mode of publication obviously has implications for literary structure, which often tended towards the episodic, not unlike today's popular *telenovelas* or soap operas. Many short narratives, as well as some of the most important Brazilian novels of the century, first appeared as *folhetins*, including José de Alencar's *O guarani* [The Guarani] (1857) and Machado de Assis's *Memórias póstumas de Brás Cubas* (1881; *Epitaph of a Small Winner; Posthumous Memoirs of Bras Cubas*). The close association between literary production and the press would also generate what has become an important Brazilian literary genre, the *crônica* or sketch, a short narrative that typically attempts to give the reader a glimpse into different aspects of everyday life in the country. Such writers as Carlos Drummond de Andrade (1902–87), Rubem Braga (1913–90), Fernando Sabino (b. 1923) and Affonso Romano de Sant'Anna (b. 1937) have assiduously cultivated the *crônica* as a literary genre and form of cultural expression.

Brazil's first popular novelist of the Romantic period was Joaquim Manuel de Macedo (1820–82), who wrote some twenty novels between 1844 and 1876, as well as works of drama, poetry and other genres. Macedo's 1844 novel, *A moreninha* [The Little Brunette], is widely considered to be the first important Brazilian work in the genre. Although he explored diverse thematic areas, Macedo is best known for his sentimental novels that, although limited in ambition and literary quality, offer a valuable portrait of well-to-do human types and social relations of nineteenth-century Rio de Janeiro. The sentimental novel, with its focus on amorous intrigues, marital strategies and family relationships, would become a major current of nineteenth-century Brazilian literature, with practitioners including such notables as José de Alencar, Aluísio Azevedo and Machado de Assis.

A decade after Macedo's debut, Manuel Antônio de Almeida (1831–61) published his only novel, *Memórias de um sargento de milícias* (1854; *Memoirs of a Militia Sergeant*), a precursor of Brazil's realist novel. Initially appearing in serial form in 1852–3, Almeida's novel traces the misadventures of the young rogue Leonardo in his encounters with diverse popular social types in the first decade of the century in Rio de Janeiro. The novel

Particularly important are Oswald de Andrade's two avant-garde novels, *Memórias sentimentais de João Miramar* (1924; *Sentimental Memoirs of John Seaborne*) and *Serafim Ponte Grande* (1933; *Seraphim Grosse Pointe*), and Mário de Andrade's *Macunaíma* (1928; *Macunaíma*).

Oswald de Andrade was perhaps the most iconoclastic of the Brazilian modernists. Known primarily for his free spirit and polemical bent – evident in his manifestoes 'Manifesto da Poesia Pau-Brasil' [Brazil Wood Poetry Manifesto] (1924) and 'Manifesto Antropófago' [Anthropophagite Manifesto] (1928) – he wrote a number of novels, including the trilogy titled *Os condenados* [The condemned] (1922–34) and the two social novels that together form *Marco zero* (1943–5). His most important narrative works are the two avant-garde novels, *João Miramar* and *Serafim Ponte Grande*. The former, often referred to as a 'cubist' novel, is a semi-autobiographical account of the narrator's travels in Europe and the Middle East. The latter, apparently initiated in 1926 but published only in 1933, a 'great non-book composed of fragments of books', in the estimation of critic Haroldo de Campos, is a literary tour de force of parody and satire.[5]

The most important narrative of Brazilian modernism is *Macunaíma*, by Mário de Andrade (1893–1945). Subtitled *O herói sem nenhum caráter*, or *The Hero without a Character*, Andrade's novel is an allegorical discussion of the nature of Brazilian civilization and the national psyche. Characterized by its author as a 'rhapsody', it orchestrates popular and folk motifs in Rabelaisian fashion around a structural core formed by indigenous legends. Through the combination of such disparate elements *Macunaíma* develops an allegorical synthesis of Brazil. Although clearly nationalist in intent, the novel takes the discussion to a higher and more complex level than most of the author's contemporaries. *Macunaíma* critically dissects reigning myths of nationalism that resonated in the debates of the 1920s. More importantly, it provides a model for creating a national literature. Through its satire and parody of Brazilian society, language and culture and its radical recasting of literary language based on the incorporation of popular elements – what in the novel is called a *fala impura* or 'impure speech' – *Macunaíma* reaffirms the critical, regenerative value of literary invention.

The return of realism

By 1930, the vanguardist impulse of the initial phase of modernism had largely dissipated, although works such as Oswald de Andrade's *Serafim*

Ponte Grande, Plínio Salgado's *O esperado* [The Expected One] (1931) and Patrícia (Pagu) Galvão's *Parque industrial* (1933; *Industrial Park*) attempted to keep it alive, now with a decidedly ideological slant on either the extreme right (Salgado) or left (Andrade and Galvão). At the same time, the modernist inclination towards the literary discovery of Brazil bore fruit in such important interpretations of Brazilian society and culture as Gilberto Freyre's *Casa grande e senzala* (1933; *The Masters and the Slaves*) and Sérgio Buarque de Hollanda's *Raízes do Brasil* [Roots of Brazil] (1936). After 1930, a year marked politically by a revolution that swept Getúlio Vargas to power, the novel replaced poetry as the most important literary genre in Brazil, with realist narrative, whether social or psychological, replacing experimental or avant-garde prose as the dominant aesthetic choice. A number of factors help explain this shift. First, access to public education increased, leading to the growth of the reading public; second, the country's publishing industry expanded, contributing to an increase in the number of works published; and, third, a new generation of writers from different regions of the country emerged with great force.

The most important of the new writers were from Brazil's impoverished North-east, which was the focus of their writing. Writer-politician José Américo de Almeida initiated what has since come to be know as the 'novel of the North-east' in 1928 with his *A bagaceira* (*Trash*). Shortly thereafter, Rachel de Queiroz, Brazil's first important female novelist, Jorge Amado, José Lins do Rego and Graciliano Ramos all debuted with novels of remarkable force. Working within a regionalist and socially conscious framework, each of these novelists developed a significant body of work that has assured them an important position in Brazil's literary canon.

From the state of Ceará, Rachel de Queiroz (b. 1910) wrote her first novel, *O quinze*, at the age of nineteen. Set during the drought of 1915 (thus the numerical title), the novel focuses on the experiences of a young woman against the backdrop of climatic and social devastation. Other novels of the period, all of which have a social bent and express a concern with women's position in society, include *João Miguel* (1932), *As três Marias* (1936; *The Three Marias*) and *Caminho de pedras* [Road of Stones] (1937). Born in Paraíba, José Lins do Rego (1901–57) was one of the most popular novelists of the 1930s. His 'Sugar Cane Cycle', comprising the novels *Menino de engenho* (1932; *Plantation Boy*), *Doidinho* (1933; *Doidinho*), *Bangüê* (1934; *Bangüê*), *O moleque Ricardo* [The Boy Ricardo] (1935) and *Fogo morto* [Dead Flame] (1943), paints a broad portrait of the transformation and decadence of the north-eastern sugar plantation, frequently with a memorialistic tinge.

The most complex of the north-eastern novelists was Graciliano Ramos (1892–1953), whose fiction combines social critique and psychological analysis. The first-person narrator of *São Bernardo* (1934; *São Bernardo*) draws a portrait of self-destruction based on egotism, brutality and greed, creating an allegory of Brazil's process of capitalist modernization. The ramblings of the tortured narrator of *Angústia* (1936; *Anguish*) create a Dostoevksy-like atmosphere of crime, guilt and existential anguish. In *Vidas secas* (1938; *Barren Lives*), Ramos shifts from the first person to the third in a portrayal of the plight of a peasant family forced to flee their homeland because of a drought. Through the use of indirect free discourse, Ramos gives voice to the inarticulate and the dispossessed who are brutalized by the climate and the social structure. *Memórias do cárcere* [Prison Memoirs] (1953), in which Ramos recounts his experiences in an Estado Novo prison in 1936–7, is one of the most important anti-authoritarian documents yet written in Brazil.

The most popular and widely translated of the North-eastern novelists is undoubtedly Jorge Amado (1912–2001), who chronicles the lives of popular classes in his native Bahia in such works as *Jubiabá* (1935; *Jubiabá*) and, much later, *Tenda dos milagres* (1969; *Tent of Miracles*), a novel which offers unbridled praise of popular culture and miscegenation. Other works such as *Terras do sem-fim* (1942; *The Violent Land*) and *São Jorge dos Ilhéus* [São Jorge of Ilhéus] (1944) focus on struggles for control of land in the cacao region of southern Bahia. Since the 1958 *Gabriela, cravo e canela* (*Gabriela, Clove and Cinnamon*), Amado has published a series of novels of manners, often with a female protagonist, as in *Dona Flor e seus dois maridos* (*Dona Flor and Her Two Husbands*) and *Tereza Batista, cansada de guerra* (1972; *Tereza Batista, Home from the Wars*).

In aesthetic – and at times political – opposition to the social realism of the North-eastern novelists, a significant psychological current also emerged in Brazilian narrative in the 1930s. In 1937 Octávio de Faria (1908–90) published *Mundos mortos* [Dead Worlds], the first of fifteen volumes of the *Tragédia burguesa* [Bourgeois Tragedy] (1937–79), a *roman-fleuve* that focuses on the spiritual failure of a generation that grew up in Rio de Janeiro between the wars. Lúcio Cardoso (1913–68) explores the human psyche in such novels as *Luz no subsolo* [Light in the Basement] (1936) and *Crônica da casa assassinada* [Chronicle of the Murdered House]

(1959). Rio Grande do Sul's Érico Veríssimo (1905–75) staked out his own terrain in the 1930s with a series of novels dealing with the dilemmas of young, middle-class, urban characters (e.g. *Caminhos cruzados* (1935; *Crossroads*)). Influenced by Aldous Huxley and other British writers, Veríssimo frequently used counterpoint techniques and cultivated the novel of ideas. His epic trilogy *O tempo e o vento* [Time and the wind] (1949–52) provides a panorama of the social and political development of his home state between 1745 and 1945.

Post-war narrative

The regionalism that emerged with such force in Brazilian narrative in the 1930s began to lose ground in the following decade. The writer who perhaps did more than anyone else to hasten its decline was João Guimarães Rosa (1908–67), whose first published work, the volume of short stories titled *Sagarana* (*Sagarana*), appeared in 1946. Rosa wrote brilliant and sometimes unusual narratives that transcended regionalism with their linguistic experimentation and their emphasis on philosophical questions. His 600-page *Grande sertão: veredas* (1956; *Devil to Pay in the Backlands*) recounts epic tales of struggle and revenge in an extended first-person monologue and a Faustian framework. Rosa's linguistic innovations – which include syntactic inversions, creative use of oral forms of narration, neologisms and borrowings from ancient and modern languages – and his metaphysical explorations have led critics to refer to his work as constituting a 'great divide' in modern Brazilian narrative. Rosa's philosophical questioning, psychological insights and linguistic innovations are also present in the shorter narratives included in such works as *Corpo de baile* (1956) and *Primeiras estórias* (1962; *The Third Bank of the River and Other Stories*).

Novelist Clarice Lispector (1925–77) joins Rosa as one of the great innovators of Brazilian prose in the post-war period, and like Rosa, she is widely recognized as one of the world's most important modern writers. Born in the Ukraine, her family immigrated to Brazil when she was two months old. Lispector published her first novel, *Perto do coração selvagem* (*Near to the Wild Heart*) in 1944. The dense, introspective and poetic prose of her deeply philosophical novels and short stories explores issues of self, consciousness and language. *A maçã no escuro* (1961; *The Apple in the Dark*) is representative of Lispector's longer prose in its depiction of the protagonist's struggles to create an authentic personal self. *A hora da estrela* (1977; *The Hour of the Star*) combines social awareness and psychological analysis with reflections on the role of the writer in modern society. Lispector's short fiction often describes moments of epiphany in which her protagonists gain some sort of unexpected insight. *Laços de família* (1960; *Family Ties*) includes some of her most critically acclaimed work in the genre.

In addition to Rosa and Lispector, the post-war period witnessed the emergence of a new generation of writers no longer bound either to the avant-garde experimentation of the modernists or to the rather conventional realism of the 1930s' regionalists. Although normally set in his home state of Bahia, the fiction of Adonias Filho (1915–90) melds, in a densely poetic, elliptical style, the social concerns of the regionalist novel with psychological and existential introspection (e.g. *Memórias de Lázaro* (1952; *Memories of Lazarus*)). In short stories such as 'O ex-mágico' and 'Os dragões' (1947; 'The Ex-Magician' and 'The Dragons' in *The Ex-Magician and Other Stories*), Murilo Rubião (b. 1916) weaves fantasy, science fiction and magic into sometimes enigmatically symbolic tales. Lygia Fagundes Telles (b. 1923), who published her first book of short stories, *Praia viva* [Living Shore], in 1944, is one of a growing number of significant women writers that began to appear in the 1940s, today constituting a major body of work within modern Brazilian narrative. Perhaps best known for her novel *As meninas* (1973; *The Girl in the Photograph*), her fiction often focuses on the limitations imposed on women by social conventions. Frequently working with allegory and diverse forms of literary experimentation, Osman Lins (1924–78) explores the nature of literature, love, moral choices and fate in the short narratives of *Nove, novena* [Nine, Novena] (1966) and the novel *Avalovara* (1973; *Avalovara*).

Recent trends

The military coup d'état of 1964 that initiated twenty-one years of dictatorial rule obviously had a major impact on Brazilian literature and culture. Numerous works of fiction have explored the impact and ramifications of authoritarianism as well as the resistance movement that rose up against it. Exemplary in this regard is the work of Antônio Callado (1917–97), whose *Quarup* (1967; *Quarup*) is perhaps the high point of the novel of resistance in the 1960s. A complex mosaic of the Brazilian nation in a moment of crisis, *Quarup* is epic in scope and design. Set in part against the backdrop of the peasant leagues in the country's North-east, the novel relates the progressive politicization of a Catholic priest whose initial desire is to civilize indigenous peoples, perhaps as a means of escaping his own sexuality, and who ultimately chooses to take up arms against the government. Callado offers a much more critical perspective on the armed resistance in two later novels, *Bar Don Juan* (1971; *Bar Don Juan*) and *Reflexos do baile* [Reflections of the Ball] (1978), revealing it to be tragically self-destructive. Among other significant fictional narratives dealing explicitly with repression and resistance in the post-1964 period are Carlos Heitor Cony's *Pessach: a travessia* [Pessach: The Crossing] (1967), Ivan Ângelo's *A festa* (1976; *The Celebration*) Renato Tapajó's *Em câmara lenta* [In Slow Motion] (1977), Márcio Souza's *Operação silêncio* [Operation Silence] (1979) and Ana Maria Miranda's *Tropical sol da liberdade* [Tropical Sun of Freedom] (1988).

Themes of social justice are not limited to narratives about the dictatorship. They also shape the neo-Indianism of Darcy Ribeiro (1922–97; *Maíra*, 1976; *Maíra*), the historical vision of João Ubaldo Ribeiro (b. 1940; *Viva o povo brasileiro*, 1984; *An Invincible Memory*); Rubem Fonseca's (b. 1925) bleak and often violent portraits of urban society (*A grande arte*, 1983; *High Art*); the political satire of Márcio Souza (b. 1946; *Galvez, Imperador do Acre*, 1976; *The Emperor of the Amazon*); the allegorical fiction of Ignácio de Loyola Brandão (b. 1936; *Zero*, 1975; *Zero*); and the pop narratives of Roberto Drummond (1937–2002), with their carnival-like atmosphere (*Sangue de Coca-Cola* [Coca Cola Blood], 1981), as well as the work of many other contemporary writers.

In the post-1964 period, the concern with national identity that had long characterized Brazilian narrative has often been framed in terms of more localized identities based on race, gender, sexual preference, ethnicity or religion. The emergence of a black consciousness movement included a growing number of writers concerned with questions related to being black in a country that has long denied the ultimately undeniable existence of racial discrimination. Associated with the literary review *Cadernos negros* [Black Notebooks], which was founded in 1978, writers such as Cuti (Luiz Silva), Miriam Alves, Márcio Barbosa and Esmeralda Ribeiro are slowly making their way into a literary field that only very reluctantly accepts race as a legitimate matter for aesthetic exploration. While their work clearly represents an affirmation of black identity, it is just as clearly concerned with issues of social justice in a stratified and rigidly hierarchical society.

With novels such as *O centauro no jardim* (1980; *The Centaur in the Garden*) and *A estranha nação de Rafael Mendes* (1983; *The Strange Nation of Rafael Mendes*), Moacyr Scliar explores multiple aspects of the Jewish experience in Brazil, often using a magical or fantastic discourse. Writers such as

Caio Fernando Abreu (b. 1948; *Morangos mofados* [Mouldy Strawberries], (1982), João Silvério Trevisan (b. 1944; *Testamento de Jônatas deixado a David* [The Will Jonas Left David], (1976) and Silviano Santiago (b. 1936; *Stella Manhattan*, 1985; *Stella Manhattan*) have offered diverse perspectives on gay life.

Although the number of significant women writers had been growing since the 1930s, it was only after 1960 that women began to constitute a major force within Brazilian narrative. Today, numerous outstanding female writers explore social, psychological and existential themes, often using highly poetic and experimental literary forms. In the semi-auto-biographical *A república dos sonhos* (1984; *The Republic of Dreams*), Nélida Piñon (b. 1936) traces several generations of a Galician immigrant family, while the short stories in *O calor das coisas* [The Warmth of Things] (1980) offer a harshly critical look at Brazil under military rule. In her micro-stories (e.g. *Contos de amor rasgados* [Tales of Torn Love], 1986), Marina Colasanti (b. 1937) explores multiple aspects of love, emotion and modern urban society. Sônia Coutinho (b. 1939) deals with women's situation in contemporary Brazil in *Uma certa felicidade* [A Certain Happiness] (1976), while the stories of *Os jogos de Ifá* [The Games of Ifá] (1980) focus on Afro-Brazilian culture in her native state of Bahia. More recently, Ana Miranda (b. 1951) has written a series of historical novels and works dealing with important Brazilian literary figures such as Gregório de Mattos (*Boca de Inferno*, 1989; *Bay of All Saints and Every Conceivable Sin*) and Augusto dos Anjos (*A última quimera* [The Last Chimera], 1995). Among other important women writers are Maria Alice Barroso (b. 1926; *Um Nome para matar* [A Name to Kill], 1967); Edna van Steen (b. 1936; *Cio* [Heat], 1965); Lya Luft (b. 1938; *Reunião de família* [Family Reunion], 1982); Tânia Jamardo Faillace (b. 1939; *Fuga* [Flight], 1964); Ana Maria Machado (b. 1941; *Alice e Ulisses* [Alice and Ulysses], 1983); and Marilene Felinto (b. 1957; *As mulheres de Tijucopapo*, 1982; *The Women of Tijucopapo*).

Writers such as Silviano Santiago, Haroldo Maranhão, Sérgio Sant'Anna and João Gilberto Noll exemplify what some might call a postmodern narrative in Brazilian prose, with their fragmented, sceptical and self-reflexive narratives, their frequent use of pastiche and their recycling of previous literary styles and discourses. In his tour de force *Em liberdade* [In Freedom] (1981), Santiago recreates the style of Graciliano Ramos in a fictional intimate diary of the days immediately following Ramos's release from prison in 1937, thus exploring the role of the writer in an authoritarian society. *Memorial do fim: A morte de Machado de Assis* [The Death of Machado de Assis] (1991), by Haroldo Maranhão (b. 1927), is a metafictional, biographical tale of the last days of the greatest of all Brazilian writers, using multiple citations from Machado in its construction. In works such as *Amazona* (1986), Sérgio Sant'Anna (b. 1941) uses parody and satire to explore dilemmas of contemporary Brazilian literature and society. João Gilberto Noll (b. 1947) narrates the anomie of existence in a fragmented and decadent world in such works as *A fúria do corpo* [The Fury of the Body] (1981) and *Harmada* (1993). The protagonist of Noll's *Hotel Atlântico* (1989; *Hotel Atlântico*), for example, narrates a journey from Copacabana to Southern Brazil that is characterized by his own physical mutilation and disintegration.

This essay has offered only the broad contours of a rich narrative tradition. The omissions are many, particularly since the emphasis has been on prose fiction. A thorough discussion would need to expand the scope and depth of focus to include other genres, media, and modes of expression. Brazilian literary narrative enters the twenty-first century with the knowledge that it is no longer the cultural standard-bearer that it once was. In many ways it has been displaced by narratives of mass culture – particularly the popular *telenovela* – and pressured by the neo-liberal marketplace, which favours accessibility over complexity (e.g. the 'new age' narratives of Paulo Coelho). These factors do not prefigure the end of Brazilian fiction. Rather, they represent new challenges for new generations of writers to meet.

Notes

1. Susan Sontag, 'Foreword', in Machado de Assis, *Epitaph of a Small Winner* (New York, 1990), p. xix.
2. Antonio Candido, *Literatura e sociedade: estudos de teoria e história literária* (São Paulo, 1975), p. 109.
3. Alfredo Bosi, *História concisa da literatura brasileira*, 2nd edn., (São Paulo, 1972), p. 112.
4. Ibid., p. 151.
5. Haroldo de Campos, '*Serafim*: Um grande não-livro', in Oswald de Andrade, *Obras completas 2. Memórias sentimentais de João Miramar e Serafim Ponte Grande* (Rio de Janeiro, 1971), p. 107.

Further reading

Bueno, Eva Paulino, *Resisting Boundaries: The Subject of Naturalism in Brazil*, New York, 1995
Ellison, Fred P., *Brazil's New Novel: Four Northeastern Masters*, Berkeley CA, 1954

The creation of the city, and of the poem, as the binding of time in lasting splendour, are not enough. Nothing less than an alteration of the language, of the relation of words and things in the binding of time, which is the history of flesh, would be enough.

For these reasons it is an intensely Latin American poem and may be compared, for example, with Peruvian César Vallejo's concern with the future of the language in *España, aparta de mí este cáliz* (*Spain, Take This Cup From Me*) or with Chilean Raúl Zurita's action in *Canto a su amor desaparecido* [Song to His/Her/Their Disappeared Love] which creates in the language a place – a ground and surface where words may be inscribed – where the disappeared can be buried. One of the most important factors in the architecture of Neruda's poem is the tone. Section X begins with an invocation ('Piedra en la piedra') and is organized around recurrent vocatives (for example, 'The poor hand, the foot, the poor life'; 'Hunger, coral of man') whose content takes us away from admiration or invocation, to shock, grief and strong tenderness. Invocations are the common stuff of epic (the *Iliad* begins with one: 'Sing, Goddess, of the cursed wrath of Achilles') but Neruda turns them in a new direction: narratives of splendour are interrogated, so too the grand mythology of nature rising to culture. Strong tenderness seems the right description because it holds a principle of sociability: the mutuality of tenderness as basis of the social. This is a long way from some of the most influential twentieth-century poetry in English. In T. S. Eliot, for example, tender feelings do not lead to social solidarity but pull in the opposite direction, towards isolation and paralysis, as in 'The Love Song of J. Alfred Prufrock'; tenderness in Neruda, on the other hand, includes anger and capacity for action.[5]

If Neruda, in 'Alturas', abandons the certainties of human progress, which is itself one of the main narratives of modernity, this is not the case with the rest of the book *Canto general*, which relies recurrently upon confidence in liberation from the effects of conquest, colonialism and neo-colonialism. The accounts of long continuities of struggle for liberation are presented, for example, through symbols of the resurgence of nature, for example as a tree, out of seeds, after the death of the individual. Neruda was at that time close to the Communist Party, whose version of inevitable progress towards socialism becomes entwined in his work with the mythology of nature as resurrection. Some of his poetry of the 1950s moves close to socialist realism, but his talent was too great to become entangled either long or deeply in such a reductive programme for art.

Confidence, rigidified, produces belief-structures. The greatest on-slaught against belief-structures in modern Latin American poetry came from the avant-gardes which flourished between 1920 and 1940. The title poem of the Argentine poet Oliverio Girondo's (1891–1967) *Espantapájaros* [Scarecrow] (1932) has the typographical shape of a scarecrow whose head consists in

> Yo   no   sé   nada
> Tú   no   sabes   nada
> Ud.   no   sabe   nada
> Él   no   sabe   nada
> Ellos no saben nada
> Ellas no saben nada
> Uds. no saben nada
> Nosotros no sabemos nada

> I   know   nothing
> You   know   nothing
> You   know   nothing
> He   knows   nothing
> They know nothing
> They know nothing
> You   know   nothing
> We   know   nothing

Girondo's renunciation of knowledge is part of a consistent abandon-ment of fixities which runs throughout his work. His methods include a deliberate entry into religious areas, such as confession and guilt, which he turns inside out, so that what he should have done and did not do is:

> No lamí la rompiente,
> la sombra de las vacas,
> las espinas,
> la lluvia[6]

> I did not lick the breakers on the beach,
> the shadow of cows,
> thorns,
> the rain

which is a non-selective adoration of everything: no room here for a god.

Abandonment of belief-structures involves Girondo, for example in the poem 'Derrumbe' [Collapse] in the imagination of a body without skeleton, and even without memory. A similar state of extreme fluidity, with minimum of past, can be found in the first book published by the Peruvian poet, Emilio Adolfo Westphalen (b. 1911), 'Las ínsulas extrañas' [Strange Islands] (1933):

La mañana alza el río la cabellera
Después la niebla la noche
El cielo los ojos
Me miran los ojos el cielo
Despertar sin vértebras sin estructura
La piel está en su eternidad
Se suaviza hasta perderse en la memoria[7]

Morning offers river hair
Then mist night
Sky eyes
Gaze at me eyes sky
To wake without vertebrae without structure
Skin in its eternity
Softens until lost in memory

Here also there is the imagination of a body without bones, resistant to capture by fixities of any kind, as a relationship with language. This facilitates the use of poetry for exploring the plasticities of the language, reducing pre-selection to a minimum. Just as a rigid body limits the capacity to dance, so, inverseley, the poem's abandonment of rigidities increases the capacity for unselectedness, another word for which is chaos.[8] Avant-garde poets experimented with the release of words from instrumental discourses into the play of sound, the most extreme example of which is Huidobro's (1893–1948) *Altazor* (1931; *Altazor*), which ends with pure sounds without 'meaning', to the discomfort of those for whom a poem must repeat recognizable, and therefore already existing, meanings. Yet sound patterns, because they affect the body, are meaning, and a poem situates words, or sounds, as occurring between human beings. As Bakhtin's disciple Voloshinov points out, there is no such thing as the stable, inherent meaning of a word, but only meaning as 'the effect of interaction between speaker and listener produced via the material of a particular sound complex'.[9]

Nevertheless, there are limits to the possibilities of experimental writing, which are displayed, for example, in César Vallejo's (1892–1938) book *Trilce* (1922). Its use of invented words and of rare and specialized vocabulary and its sometimes extreme breaking of any line of association take it over the edge, occasionally, into the unreadable. There has to be a degree of common ground, of shared inherited cultural orientations, or of the shared responses of the body to sound pattern, for a reader to want to continue. Vallejo's prime concern when writing *Trilce* was the degree of freedom that could be achieved before it became 'libertinaje', in other words permissiveness.[10]

A particular drive of the avant-gardes is the freeing of words from Literature, as in Vallejo, Neruda, Huidobro, Manuel Bandeira, Oswald de Andrade, to mention some of the Latin Americans, who tend to get left out of international anthologies, just as much as in European and US avant-gardists such as James Joyce, William Carlos Williams, Pierre Reverdy, Kurt Schwitters.[11] In Latin America this freeing of language also meant opening poetry to what had previously been excluded: popular, regional and ethnic cultures, and the rhythms and intonation of everyday speech. As Oswald de Andrade (1890–1954) puts it in his *Manifesto da Poesia Pau-Brasil* [Brazil Wood Poetry Manifesto] (1924), the issue was to combine the forest with the school: to bring together what was 'primitive' in Brazil with what Western tradition could teach:

> Poetry exists in facts. The saffron and ochre shacks in the greens of the shanty-town, beneath the Cabraline blue, are aesthetic facts.
> Carnival in Rio is the religious happening of the race. Brazil-wood. Wagner sinks beneath the samba parades of Botafogo. Barbarous and ours. Rich ethnic background. Vegetable wealth. Minerals. Cooking. The vatapá stew gold and dance.[12]

Or, as Williams puts it, 'The primitives are not back in some remote age – they are not BEHIND experience.'[13] The Brazilian cultural historian Nicolau Sevcenko argues that the non-Western world, far from being peripheral to modernism, is actually central to it.[14] Citing the French poets Max Jacob and Guillaume Apollinaire, and Brazilian modernism, he proposes that their fascination with cannibalism as a way of absorbing the other, is a representation of the relationships generated by the new technologies of the twentieth century, which 'all concurred to involve the whole world in a tight network': 'Each part simultaneously incorporates as well as reviles the other's culture, . . . with an effect of decontextualization. . . . Cultures existing so far as separated traditions now see their legacies as being suddenly discontinued when they are intersected by one another, causing a series of short-circuits worldwide.'

In Brazil, cannibalism functioned as a central metaphor for an active and inventive, as opposed to mimetic and subordinate, relationship with Western culture: to devour and thus incorporate the other, in an act which had always been the ultimate horror for Western travellers such as Columbus and Robinson Crusoe, but which for native practitioners could be a form of respect. Oswald, in his *Cannibalist Manifesto* of 1928, takes cannibalism as a universal relationship between human beings, though the prime reference of the idea is to the notion of changing the relationship between modern and 'pre'-modern cultures away from colonial domination, so that primitive thought and twentieth-century technology could work together. Mário de Andrade's novel *Macunaíma* and José María Arguedas's poems and novels, such as 'LLamado a algunos doctores' [A Call to Certain Doctors] and *El zorro de arriba y el zorro de abajo* [The Fox From Up Above and the Fox From Down Below], to name just two, show some of what can be done, but the challenge still stands.

The expansion of poetry to include new cultural forms and materials would take considerable space to chart properly. Here only a few key examples can be mentioned. In Peru, Alejandro Peralta (1899–1973) and Galamiel Churata (1897–1969), both of them natives of the highland town of Puno, experimented with native Andean scenarios in avant-garde forms, though the possibilities of that type of cross-cultural work continued to emerge in the 1950s and later, say in the poetry of the Bolivian Jaime Saenz (1921–86) and the Peruvian José María Arguedas (1911–69). In Puerto Rico, in the work of Luis Palés Matos (1898–1958),[15] and elsewhere in the Caribbean, consciousness of *négritude* was brought into poetry. Again, that was a beginning or a process which has continued in later writers, such as the young black Brazilian poet Edimilson de Almeida Pereira, whose poems transmit the black spirituality of North-east Brazil not as folklore but as a particular aesthetic territory. For the Brazilian avant-garde, Amazonia – the vast region of the rainforest, less degraded then than now – became a mythic area, offering fictions of participation in nature and of resistance to wage-labour discipline, in the context of the corporatist social programmes, based on family and patriotism, of the Getulio Vargas regime.[16] In 'Evocação do Recife' [Evocation of Recife] (1930), which traces the formation of his sensibility to childhood in the

North-east, Manuel Bandeira (1886–1968) sums up the problem of re-shaping the language of poetry:

> A vida não me chegava pelos jornais nem pelos livros
> Vinha da boca do povo na lingua errada do povo
> lingua certa do povo
> Porque êle é que fala gostoso o português do Brasil
>   ao passo que nós
>   o que fazemos
>   é macaquear
>   a sintaxe lusíada[17]

> Life didn't come to me in newspapers or books
> It came from the mouth of the people the incorrect language of the
> people
> the correct language of the people
> Because they are the ones that savour the Portuguese of Brazil
>   meanwhile we
>   what we do
>   is ape
>   the syntax of the Portuguese of Europe

Here the inheritance of correct and educated writing brought from Europe, whose high culture supplies the received definition of Literature, is counterposed with the freer shapes of the actual spoken language of Brazil.

Brazilian modernism assembled a coherent set of objectives, which proposed ways of combining artistic experimentation with exploring popular speech and with ethnographic research into the cultures of the interior. The Spanish American avant-gardes tended to be less successful in resolving the difficulty of articulating a modernist sensibility with the conditions of a peripheral modernity. As Peter Elmore puts it in a study of modernity in the Peruvian novel,

> The tragedy of peripheral societies has to do with their historical disharmony, with the curse of anachronism: in them there coexist, in convulsive synchrony, stages which were successive in the metropolitan centre.... Nevertheless, in order to articulate their experience,... intellectuals from societies like ours have had no other paradigm than the modern, and they have tried to translate its imperatives into the specific conditions of their own environment.[18]

Thus the manifestoes of the Spanish American avant-gardes read more like a utopian novel than like statements of coherent artistic practices.[19] Vallejo drew attention to the problem in an essay of 1930, where he argues that what matters is 'la poesía nueva a base de sensibilidad nueva' (poetry that's new on the basis of a new sensibility):

> In genuinely new poetry new images may be lacking – they are a function of ingenuity not of genius – but the creator of this type of poetry enjoys or suffers a life in which the new relationships and rhythms of things and men have become blood, cell, something in other words which has been vitally and organically incorporated into the sensibility.[20]

His examples are cinema, airplane, jazz band, motor and radio, and it is not difficult to find others. The contradictions of modernism without modernity were particularly acute in a city like Lima, which was provincial and cosmopolitan at the same time, and where power was still in the hands of an upper class which had inherited its power from colonial times. The work of the Peruvian poet Martín Adán (1908–85) confronts this situation:

> Nada me basta, ni siquiera la muerte; quiero medida, perfección,
>   satisfacción, deleite.
> ¿Cómo he venido a parar en este cinema perdido y humoso?[21]

> Nothing is enough for me, not even death; I want measure,
>   perfection, satisfaction, delight.
> How did I end up in this godforsaken smoky cinema?

By the end of the 1930s the avant-gardes had lost their impetus as specific intellectual and artistic projects. After the rise of Stalinism and Nazism and the defeat of the Left in the Spanish Civil War, it was difficult to sustain the identity of artistic innovation and social revolution. Vallejo's last poems, *Poemas humanos* (*Human Poems*) and *España, aparta de mí este cáliz* (*Spain, Take This Cup From Me*), written in the late 1930s, delineate that crisis better than any others. Unlike the Right or the Left, who placed their confidence in the grand continuities of heroic sacrifice for Empire or Progress, Vallejo ends up (in poem XIV) entrusting the whole process of artistic and social creativity, which includes the language, to the children of the world:

> Niños del mundo,
> si cae España – digo, es un decir –
> [...]
> ¡Cómo vais a bajar las gradas del alfabeto
> hasta la letra en que nació la pena²²

> Children of the world,
> if Spain falls – I say: it's a saying –
> [...]
> How are you going to go down the steps of the alphabet
> to the letter in which pain was born!

Another poem from *España* refuses any continuity after death unless it include the everyday things of a semi-literate combatant's life, even the spoon he carried in his jacket. Vallejo and Neruda coincide in defining human beings by their common needs (everyone needs a spoon) and in rejecting the selective continuity which dominates Western ideas of history in so far as they exclude the conquered and the marginalized as 'failures'.

The shock of the 1930s, after the avant-gardist optimism of the previous decade, was particularly acute in Brazil. Poets found themselves caught between the rigid ideology of the Communist Party and the uselessness of individual isolation, in a situation where an oppressive state machine was seeking to take over all aspects of life. Carlos Drummond de Andrade's (1902–87) response to these conditions is particularly powerful because it is an unblinking one. In 'Elegia 1938' [Elegy 1938], he writes:

> amas a noite pelo poder de aniquilamento que encerra e sabes
>   que, dormindo, os problemas te dispensam de morrer.
> Mas o terrível despertar prova a existência da Grande Máquina
>   e te repõe, pequeninho, em face de indecifráveis palmeiras.²³

> you love the night for its power to annihilate and you know that with
>   sleep problems don't require you to die.
> But the terrible awakening proves the Great Machine exists and puts
>   you back like a child in front of indecipherable palm trees.

Not even nature can guarantee meaning: a situation as terrible, though in different terms, as the one Neruda confronts in 'Alturas'. But in his later book, *A rosa do povo* [The Rose of the People] (1945), Drummond comes through to a sense of attachment to the forms of free collective life, which have been 'obscured by the darkness of alienation':²⁴

Essa viagem é mortal, e começá-la.
Saber que há tudo. E mover-se em meio
a milhões de formas raras,
secretas, duras. Eis aí meu canto.

Ele é tão baixo que sequer o escuta
ouvido rente ao chão. Mas é tão alto
que as pedras o absorvem. Está na mesa
aberta en livros, cartas e remédios.
Na parede infiltrou-se. O bonde, a rua,
o uniforme de colégio se transformam,
são ondas de carinho te envolvendo.[25]

This voyage is mortal, and to begin it.
To know that there is everything. And to move in the midst
of millions of rare, secret, hard
forms. That is my song.

It is so low that not even an ear close to the ground
will hear it. But it is so high
that the stones absorb it. It is on the table
open in books, letters and medicines.
It has permeated the wall. The tram, the street,
the school uniform are transformed,
they are waves of tenderness enveloping you.

Oliverio Girondo, suspicious of any programme, nevertheless stated that it was crucial to have 'fe [,] en nuestra fonética, desde que fuimos nosotros, los americanos, quienes hemos oxigenado el castellano, haciéndolo un idioma respirable' (faith in our phonetics, since it was us Americans who have put some oxygen into Spanish, making it a breathable language).[26] Latin American poetry, in the sense that it can be called that, was built upon the differential intonation and rhythm of the Spanish and Portuguese of the subcontinent. Intonation includes both tone (the characteristic of a particular utterance) and accent (characteristic of a region or social group): the Latin root of accent is *canere*, to sing. Intonation is also, as Bakhtin points out, what gives the relationship between any language action and that which is outside it, that is, between language and the social environment. Hence what the Word is capable of, which poetry tests, involves the plasticity of the language as spoken.

In this sense, the formation of Latin American poetry can be traced to two types of process: the creation of cities where it was possible to live in contemporaneous contact with international modernism despite the continuing coloniality of the societies, and the invention of forms of expression capable of transmitting the specificities of the local. The first set of conditions date from around 1880 and have to do with economic modernization. The second set of changes cannot be charted so quickly or clearly. For a start, they do not coincide fully with the first. For example, Gauchesque poetry, which dates from 1816 to 1880, brought the oral poetry of the mestizo peasants of the River Plate area into written form: it showed for the first time the possibility of making poetry out of the spoken language.[27] One of the key conditions for its emergence was the fact that Buenos Aires was the area where Spanish colonial institutions had least weight: the Spanish had not brought much more than their language, and they could not control that. The best-known poem of the Gauchesque, which closes the cycle, is José Hernández's *Martín Fierro* (1872–1879).

A second difficulty, when it comes to tracing where and how specifically Latin American poetic forms arise, has to do with the confused debate about Spanish American *modernismo*. The term is used to refer to poets writing between approximately 1880 and 1910, who broke away from the vocabulary, rhythms and sensibility of the neoclassicism that was prevalent in poetry in Spanish. The debate hangs on the idea that the cultural referents of *modernismo*, particularly at the beginning, had little or nothing to do with Latin America. The kind of evidence invoked is the fact that a poem such as 'Divagación' [Digression], by Rubén Darío (1867–1916), uses settings from Italy (medieval), Germany, Spain, China, Japan, India and Jewish tradition, and apparently says nothing about Latin America. A more careful version of that idea can be found in Angel Rama's proposal that Darío and other *modernistas* needed to appropriate 'the instruments, forms, and literary resources of the literature created in the heat of the European economic universe', but that, because they were dazzled by European modernity, they tended towards servile imitation of it.[28] Nevertheless, the argument ultimately rests upon the demand that poetry should be nationalist, which, as Borges had humorously pointed out, is like saying that the Koran is not an Arab book because there are no camels in it.[29] The lack of cultural references to Latin America points if anything to an incomplete modernity, not to artistic failure.

A careful reading of Darío shows that even in poems like 'Divagación' there is nothing servile. The materials may not be local, but they are actively placed together in a vision of sufficient density so that the poem achieves its own artistic autonomy. Crucially, Darío and other *modernistas* invented a new language for poetry in Spanish, of more subtle and varied

The Cuban José Martí, in a lucid essay on Walt Whitman published in 1887, wrote:

> Rhyme or accentuation? Oh no! His rhythm is in the stanzas which are joined together, in the midst of that apparent chaos of convulsive superimposed phrases, by a wise method of composition which assembles ideas in vast musical groupings, which is the natural poetic form for a people who build not stone by stone but in enormous blocks.[35]

The proposal is for the necessity of a language adequate to the new speeds of the modern city. As a poet, Martí himself did not write like that. He preferred simple, regular measures, like the ballad, which was the most common form of popular poetry. In this sense, his decisions as a poet point to the need to work through the territory of Romanticism, as a foundational basis, which meant breaking with classical conventions of poetic language and finding forms of expression for particular and personal feeling. This happens especially with regard to the relationship between personal emotion and place, a necessity heightened by his exile from Cuba and his deep involvement in its liberation from Spain, for which he died in 1895.

Unlike Spanish America, Brazil produced a Romantic poetry in the strong, historical, sense of the word. For example, Castro Alves (1847–71) gave a Brazilian location to the Romantic project of liberation by identifying the poet's voice with the African slaves which were the deep contradiction at the core of Brazilian liberalism. His poem 'O navio negreiro' [The Slave Ship] dramatizes the horrors of the slave trade and his shame at Brazil's involvement in it:

> Era un sonho dantesco . . . o tombadilho,
> Que das luzernas avermelha o brilho,
>   Em sangue a se banhar.
> Tinir de ferros . . . estalar de açoite . . .
> Legiões de homems negros como a noite,
>   Horrendos a dançar . . .[36]

> It was a Dantean dream . . . the deck
> Shone red in the stars' bright light,
>   Awash with blood.
> Clanking of irons . . . snapping of whips
> Legions of black men black as night,
>   In horrible dance.

After the abolition of slavery in 1888, the poets known as Parnassians attempted a more modern tone and language. Raimundo Correia, for example, achieves a fine musicality in poems like 'Plenilúnio' [Full Moon]:

> Quantos à noite, de alva sereia
> O falar canto na febre a ouvir,
> No argênteo fluxo da lua cheia,
> Alucinados se deixam ir . . .[37]

> How many drift hallucinated
> And hear in fever the singing
> Speech of serene dawn
> In the argent stream of full moon . . .

Nevertheless, as Manuel Bandeira pointed out, the Parnassians never abandoned their 'conformity to Portuguese grammar'.[38]

Mário de Andrade's book of 1922, *Paulicéia desvairada* [Hallucinated City], is not concerned with correct grammar but with the assemblage of words and phrases without narrative in response to an urban environment which places heterogeneous elements together. Thus the poem 'O domador' [The Tamer] rapidly composes the landscape of São Paulo, tracing its cosmopolitan elements:

> Alturas da Avenida. Bonde 3.
> Asfaltos. Vastos, altos repuxos de poeira
> Sob el arlequinal do céu ouro-rosa-verde . . .
> As sujidades implexas do urbanismo.
> *Filets* de manuelino. Calvícies de Pensilvânia.[39]

> At the Avenue. No. 3 Street Car.
> Asphalt. High, vast spurts of dust
> Against the gold-rose-green harlequin sky . . .
> The filth built into cities.
> Manuelino fillet steaks. Pennsylvania bald heads.

Mário's city also includes migrations from the rural and the past. He is particularly attentive to the visual and calls the book 'clearly impressionist',[40] a remark that points to a certain limitation in its composition, which is his tendency to throw together disparate elements, without careful articulation of their relationships. Manuel Bandeira's *O ritmo dissoluto* [The Dissolute Rhythm] written at approximately the same time, is similarly concerned with breaking the moulds of regular verse and normative grammar. As well as ordinary speech, it includes song, and from time to time creates a dance of words. The different types of voicing are beautifully varied, with effects that can be delicate and tender, as in the poem 'Noite morta' [Dead Night], or in these lines: 'Uma pequenina aranha urde no peitoril da janela a teiazinha levísima. / Tenho vontade de beijar esta aranhazinha' (A tiny spider spins its delicate web on the windowsill. / I feel like kissing that little spider).

The usefulness of a chronological scheme is to show similarities and differences. But it is limited in the case of a poet like Manuela Bandeira by the fact that the coherence of his work stretches across chronological divisions: his first poems were written before Brazilian *modernism*, and at the end of his life he was writing in the *concretista* mode. The standard chronological presentation can similarly fall short with the work of women poets, because its terms are derived from concerns that they did not necessarily share. Thus the work of Gabriela Mistral (1889–1957), Alfonsina Storni (1892–1938), Delmira Agustini (1886–1914), Juana de Ibarbourou (1892–1979) and other women poets writing between approximately 1910 and 1940 could be called, variously, Romantic, *modernista*, *postmodernista*, and *vanguardista*. What needs to be considered are the ways in which their priorities were different from what those labels are able to indicate. For example, Storni's sense of the language available to her had to do with popular traditions of theatre and other types of verbal performance, which she uses to expose the moulding of a woman's body by force of law and custom in a highly conservative environment. The Venezuelan poet Enriqueta Terán (b. 1918) used Spanish renaissance forms and diction in her first books, then moved to a post-avant-garde mode in which she explores how the 'oficios' or trades specific to women shape the senses and mould gesture and word. In 'Circunstancias del nombre' [Circumstances of the Name], a poem that dramatizes the making of her own sensibility, she writes:

> La joven construye su casa
> ... nombrando renglones dulces, experiencias de hilo muy fino
> torcido sobre el muslo, hilo y mano, figura entera en el umbral,
> figura que recuerda cuanto esperó, cuantas lluvias, techos de lluvia
>   sobre el desamparo.
> Nombrando piedras[41]

> The young woman builds her house
> . . . naming sweet lines, experiences of very fine thread
> twisted over the thigh, thread and hand, whole figure on the
>   threshold,
> figure that recalls how much she waited, how many rains, roofs of rain
>   over abandonment.
> Naming stones

Terán's late work shows one of the new directions in poetics since 1950. Once one moves to the second half of the century, there is less agreement among critics about what is important, or even about what to call the new types of poetry: there is a lack of a useful map. Part of the difficulty has to do with attempting to classify without clarifying the actual components and processes of composition. Terms like 'voice', 'conversational' and 'documentary' have been used, but they do not define modes of composition, because they do not indicate the components of verbal art a poet is using. Intonation is prior to voice, rhetoric to conversation and place of enunciation to document.

Another part of the difficulty in delineating what has been happening since 1950 is that the avant-gardes had laid down a vast project of innovation, and it was difficult to know what could be done after that. Octavio Paz (Mexico, 1914–98), in his work of the 1950s, combines avant-garde language (surrealist in orientation) with mythical narratives of cyclical renewal, for example in the poem 'El cántaro roto' [The Broken Water Jar]. The strategy is similar to that of his long essay 'El laberinto de la soledad' ('The Labyrinth of Solitude'), where a modernist perception of self as mask is interwoven with narratives of return to mythic origins. Later, in *Blanco* (1969; *White*), Paz experiments with degrees of combinatory freedom which allow the words on the page to be read in various different orders, without mythological programmatics.

The major innovator in the Spanish language of the second half of the century is probably Nicanor Parra (1914), in the sense of being the most radical and far-reaching. He began by attempting to write in an epic vein, an ambition which owed more than a little to the epic scale of Neruda's work. But the heroic characters he needed 'began to fall apart and the hero imperceptibly changed into an antihero'. Parra turns the situation inside out: what is alive and valuable must be whatever is outside and cannot get in: 'a character who was trying to get into the poem, and this was the antihero'.[42] His notion of the 'anti-poem' arose from there. An example is 'La trampa' [The Trap], where the speaker is invaded by uncontrollable

tombstones ('lápidas'), imaginary in the sense a book is, in order to be read: the tombstones are the land, history, and the language, embedded in each other, in all directions and without fixed order. His two most recent books, *Anteparaíso* [Anteparadise] and *La vida nueva* [The New Life] trace literal events of writing on the sky (with smoke from an aeroplane over New York) or on the Atacama desert (with heavy earth-moving equipment). These writings are not expressions of a voice, and therefore not assimilable to any ideological statement, or even to an idea, but take one back into what in the language is prior to voice – called 'murmurings' by Juan Rulfo (Mexico, 1918–86), whose work, despite being short stories and a novel, goes further than that of any other Mexican writer of this century in exploring the plasticity of the spoken language.

The extraordinary Brazilian poet João Cabral de Melo Neto (b. 1920) is similarly concerned with the physicality of the Word. His early book, *O engenheiro* [The Engineer] (1945), explores the making of lived spaces, including cities, buildings, dance, objects upon a table, as an action coterminous with poetic composition:

> A luz, o sol, o ar livre
> envolvem o sonho do engenheiro.
> O engenheiro sonha coisas claras:
> superfícies, tênis, un copo de água.
>
> O lápis, o esquadro, o papel;
> o desenho, o projeto, o número:
> o engenheiro pensa o mundo justo,
> mundo que nenhum véu encobre.[51]

> Light, sun, the open air
> wrap the engineer's dream.
> The engineer dreams of clear things:
> surfaces, tennis, a glass of water.
>
> The pencil, the T square, the paper;
> the drawing, the project, the number:
> the engineer thinks a just world,
> a world no veil covers.

His sense of form as spatial construction comes via Mallarmé and cubism but also from a particular Brazilian experience of the creation of new urban spaces and new architectural forms. Form arises for Cabral through slow, rigorous attention; it is not found in nature, like a shell, or by leaping into the invisible:

Não a forma encontrada
como una concha [. . .]

não a forma obtida
en lance santo ou raro,
tiro nas lebres de vidro
do invisível;

mas a forma atingida
como a ponto do novêlo
que a atenção, lenta,
desenrola,

aranha . . .[52]

Not the form found
like a shell [. . .]

not the form obtained
through sacred or extraordinary leap,
shooting at the glass hares
of the invisible;

but form obtained
like the end of a ball of thread
which attention slowly
unrolls,

like a spider . . .

The Word is neither the empirical object out there in the world nor an
idea, but self-embedded, as in Neruda's 'Alturas':

(Te escrevo:
flor! Não *uma*
flor, nem aquela
flor-virtude – em
disfarçados urinóis.)

Flor é a palavra
flor, verso inscrito
no verso, como as
manhãs no tempo.[53]

(I write you
flower! Not *a*
flower, not that
flower-of-virtue – inside veiled
urinals.)

Flower is the word
flower, verse inscribed
in verse, like
mornings in time.

This poem is entitled 'Antiode (contra a poesia dita profunda)' [Antiode (Against Poetry That's Called Profound)]: composition for Cabral is the careful placing of surfaces, in a process of inscription. The surfaces are at once verbal, visual and mineral – the last of these being a term he uses to define the written word (his first book was called *Pedra do sono* [Stone of Sleep]) but which also relates to the spoken word in the speech of North-eastern Brazil, the area where he grew up: 'o sertanejo fala pouco: / as palavras de pedra ulceram a bôca' (the man of the backlands speaks little: / words of stone ulcerate his mouth).[54]

The capacity to work with the fluidity and inventiveness of the spoken language is part of the challenge of the twentieth-century avant-gardes to bring into literature what was previously excluded, in other words, the total environment. Brazilian *concretismo*, founded in the 1950s by Haroldo de Campos (b. 1929), Augusto de Campos (b. 1931) and Décio Pignatari (b. 1927), takes up that challenge and extends the work of the earlier avant-gardes. Their main inspirations include the early twentieth-century European avant gardes, and Oswald de Andrade. Their method of working with these transmissions is neither neoclassical nor post-modernist: like Pound and Oswald (in his cannibalist proposal), their approach to inheritance is to make it contemporary – to assimilate it and do something new and vital with it. Their 'transcreations' – a term which compounds translation with creation – offer an exemplary method: to find or invent in the Brazilian language those equivalents by which texts from other times/places can live. Their choices are strategic (Li-Po, Ecclesiastes, Mayakovsky, Villon, Mallarmé, Dante, Homer, etc.) and amount to the making of a set of resources, which has little to do with any idea of there being a fixed canon of 'great authors' which everyone has to study.

Their 'Plano piloto para poesia concreta' [Pilot Plan for Concrete Poetry] speaks of 'total realism' as a way of achieving 'total responsibility towards language'. It comprises all patterning of language (verbi-visi-voco, in Joyce's phrase), as writing, visual pattern, voice, in all its relationships with the outside, which include advertising and politics and at the same time the range of pre-conscious effects of the objects we call words. As against what they call 'the poetry of expression', they propose Concrete Poetry as 'tension of words-things in space-time',[55] arising out of a method of composition based in a 'direct' rather than 'logico-discursive' juxtaposition of elements, which involves, in particular, attention to the ideographic aspect of the written word. The manifestoes need to be read not as a prescription but as a starting point for experiment. Their own work is highly varied, and includes, for example, Haroldo de Campos's magnificent *Signantia quasi coelum/Signância quase céu*, [Signage Almost Sky][56] a long poem-voyage through the spaces, typographic and cosmic, that exist between and inside words, or Augusto's 'TVGRAMA 1 (tombeau de mallarmé)', a visual text which rewrites Mallarmé's famous statement that the world exists so as to end up in a book as '†udo†††exis†e / †††††††††††††† / praacabarem†v' (every†hingexis†††s / †††††††††††††† / †oendupin†v).

Neo-baroque poetry in the Spanish-speaking countries shares concerns and inspirations with *concretismo*, particularly in the decision not to reduce sense to the logico-discursive dimension of language. Thus the Argentinian Néstor Perlongher's (1949–92) major poem, 'Cadáveres' [Corpses], explores the interstices of the language, its smallest everyday gestures, as the place where the corpses – the disappeared – of recent Argentinian history can be located:

> En eso que empuja
> lo que se atraganta,
> En eso que traga
> lo que emputarra.
> En eso que amputa
> lo que empala.
> En eso que ¡puta!
> Hay cadáveres.[57]

> In the thing that pushes
> that sticks in the throat,
> In what swallows
> what prostitutes.
> In what amputates
> what impales.
> In what whores
> There are corpses.

The poem enters areas of the language where there is no clear meaning, where nothing is being expressed, but where there is complicity with the violent facts; for that purpose, Perlongher recombines sounds, tones and the different historical and social layers of Argentine Spanish, always moving towards the outside of the uttered, to the web of unacknowledged social violences that infiltrate it. He preferred the term 'neobarroso' (neomuddy) to neobarroco, since it was closer to the actual muddy waters of the River Plate.

The recent anthology *Medusario*[58] collects together twenty-two poets, with work dating from approximately 1970, who can loosely be called neo-baroque. The Cuban poet José Lezama Lima (1910–76) is included as their main precursor. Lezama, in various important essays, sees the baroque as the primary design and sensibility in Latin American poetics. There is a crucial acknowledgement here of transmissions from Spain and their recombination with Latin American inheritances. For the Peruvian Martín Adán – mentioned above – the Spanish baroque, prolonged in the language of colonial Peru and its poets, is still the major inheritance for a Peruvian poet in the middle of the twentieth century.[59] The same could not be said of other Latin American countries, except perhaps Mexico. Peru and Mexico were the main centres of Spanish colonial power, and where cultural transfer from Europe was strongest. In the early colonial period, for example, there were poets writing in Latin in the Peruvian altiplano. A great deal of erudite, as well as popular poetry was produced in the Spanish colonies (narrative fiction was banned), but there tended to be a rigid division between the two. It is in the seventeenth century that a sense of locality starts to emerge in erudite poetry, as in the satirical work of the Peruvian poet Juan del Valle Caviedes (1652–99) against unscrupulous doctors and other abusive figures of colonial society. A creole consciousness begins to emerge in Caviedes's poems, such as 'Lo que son riquezas del Perú', which characterizes Peruvian history as 'robos, tiranías y injusticias' (robberies, tyrannies and injusticies).

The most important of all poets of the colonial period is the Mexican woman Sor Juana Inés de la Cruz (1651–95), author of a wide range of poems in both popular and erudite genres. Her most complex poetry is the long poem 'Primero sueño'. It is an astonishing intellectual achievement, re-thinking Plato's notion of eternal forms and Aristotle's concept of categories (which marked the pre-modern styles of thought that dominated in the Spanish colonies) in a movement from dream to waking, subjective and historical at the same time, which anticipates the Enlightenment's confidence in reason. The almost thousand-line poem ends with a return from night to day, which is also an assertion of confidence in the senses and in being a woman:

> mientras nuestro hemisferio la dorada
> ilustraba del sol madeja hermosa,
> que con luz judiciosa
> de orden distributivo, repartiendo
> a las cosas visibles sus colores
> iba, y restituyendo
> entera a los sentidos exteriores
> su operación, quedando a luz más cierta
> el mundo iluminado y yo despierta.[60]

> While the sun's beautiful golden
> skein illuminated our hemisphere,
> moving with judicious light
> in distributive order, giving
> to each visible thing its colour,
> restoring their full
> operation to the external senses,
> and leaving the world revealed
> in more certain light and myself awake.

The journey traced in this late-seventeenth-century poem is historical as well as personal, from a shadow-world into the light of reason, and, with its confidence in sense-data, towards the modernism that was then yet to come and which is still able to challenge us.

A major dynamic of modern Latin American poetry has been the opening of the field to territories previously excluded from the poem, and these include, very importantly, poetries written in, or influenced by, native and African languages. This is an area which a brief general essay cannot do justice to, since genres and transmissions are radically different from those of written poetry in Spanish and Portuguese. There was a vast range of verbal art throughout the subcontinent before the arrival of the Europeans. Surviving examples, i.e. ones that have been transcribed and translated, belong mainly to Mexican and Andean civilizations.[61] During the colonial period, there was a considerable body of poetry composed in the native languages, most of it 'anonymous' in the sense that the notion of authorship in the Western sense did not exist among native groups. A fine example of this poetry is the elegy to the death of Atawallpa ('Apu Inka Atawallpaman' [Elegy on the Death of Atawallpa]), which is likely to have been written in the eighteenth century, though its materials go back much further. 'Authored' poetry in Quechua – which had become the main native language in the Andes – begins during the period of emancipation from Spain (the early nineteenth century) and one of its key figures is Wallparrimachi. Wallparrimachi may in fact have been a composite figure, put together by native singer-poets, in order precisely to satisfy Western concepts of author.[62] Over the past fifty years, there has been a large number of poets writing in or out of native languages – Nahuatl, Maya, Quechua, Aymara, Mapuche and Guaraní are the main, but not the only ones. Among the best known poets working in that way have been José María Arguedas (mentioned above), who composed first in Quechua and then translated his poems into Spanish, and Jaime Saenz, the Bolivian poet whose work, written in Spanish, is strongly marked by the native Andean imagination. The intersection of twentieth-century poetics with Afro-Brazilian sensibility and spirituality can be seen in the work of Edimilson de Almeida Pereira (b. 1963), born in Minas Gerais, whose book *O homem da orelha furada* [The Man with a Perforated Ear] takes the spoken word of ritual and oral tradition as a basis for renewed exploration of the power of the Word:

> Dançar o nome com o braço na palavra: como em sua casa um
> maconde.
> Dançar o nome pai dos deuses que pode todo neste mundo e suportar
> o lagarto querendo ser bispo na sombra.
> Dançar o nome miséria, estrepe e tripa que a folha do livro é. E se
> entender dono das letras em sua cozinha.[63]

> Dance the Deity with your arm shaping the word: like a session in
> your own home.
> Dance the Deity Top of the Gods who can do anything whatever in
> this world and invest the lizard who asks to be a bishop of dark.
> Dance the Diety of Ill-Influence, the stick and stretch of the printed
> page. Declare yourself proprietor of all the writing in the kitchen.

The question remains, as Vallejo wrote,

> ¡Y si después de tantas palabras,
> no sobrevive la palabra![64]

> And if after so many words,
> the word itself does not survive!

* * *

Note: I am grateful to Raquel Rivas Rojas for help with bibliographical aspects of this essay.

Notes

1. Pablo Neruda, *Canto General* (Buenos Aires, 1955), p. 26. The roman numerals in parentheses refer to the section numbers of the poem.
2. Neruda spells Pichu, 'Picchu'.
3. As Gordon Brotherston points out, Neruda exaggerates the disappearance of Inca culture, ignoring specific material continuities that archaeology and anthropology point to. Nevertheless, the poem stands as an interrogation of history. (See G. Brotherston, *Latin American Poetry: Origins and Presence*, Cambridge, 1975, especially 42–6.)
4. William Carlos Williams, *Imaginations* (New York, 1970), p. 160.
5. T. S. Eliot, *Collected Poems* (London, 1947), p. 25.
6. Oliverio Girondo, *Obras: Poesía* (Buenos Aires, 1968), p. 304.
7. Emilio Adolfo Westphalen, *Otra imagen deleznable* (México, 1980), p. 16.
8. See Charles Olson, *Collected Prose*, Berkeley, 1997, 160, and D. H. Lawrence, 'Chaos in Poetry', in *Selected Literary Criticism* (London 1956).
9. V. Volosinov, *Marxism and the Philosophy of Language* (New York, 1973), pp. 102–3.
10. See Américo Ferrari (ed.), *César Vallejo: Obra poética* (Colección Archivos, Madrid, 1988), p. 163.
11. See, for example, V. Kolocotroni et al. (eds.), *Modernism: An Anthology of Sources and Documents* (Edinburgh, 1998). Note that J. Rothenberg and P. Joris's *Poems for the Millenium* (Los Angeles CA, 1966) is an exception.
12. 'Manifesto da poesia Pau-Brasil', in Gilberto Mendonça Teles, *Vanguarda Européia e Modernismo Brasileiro: Apresentação e crítica dos principais manifestos, prefácios e conferências vanguardistas, de 1857 até hoje* (Rio, 1972), pp. 203–8. Translation by Mike Gonzalez and David Treece.
13. William Carlos Williams, *Imaginations* (1970), p. 134.
14. In a talk given at the Centre for Latin American Cultural Studies, King's College London, 3rd March 1999.
15. The Biblioteca Ayacucho has published Palés Matos's *Poesía completa y prosa selecta* (Caracas, 1978).
16. See Mário de Andrade, 'Rito do irmão pequeno' (1931).
17. Manuel Bandeira, *Testamento de Pasárgada* (Rio, 1980), p. 26.
18. Peter Elmore, *Los muros invisibles: Lima y la modernidad en la novela del siglo XX* (Lima, 1993), p. 39.
19. I am grateful to Raquel Rivas Rojas for this point. The best collection of avant-garde manifestoes is Nelson Osorio's *Manifiestos, proclamas y polémicas de la vanguardia literaria hispanoamericana* (Caracas, 1988).
20. César Vallejo, *El arte y la revolución* (Lima, 1973), p. 101.
21. *La casa de cartón* (Lima, 1971 [1928]), p. 59. The quotation is from a poem included in this novel.
22. César Vallejo, *Obras completas*, ed. R. González Vigil (Lima, 1991), p. 808.

23. Carlos Drummond de Andrade, 'Sentimento do mundo', in *Sentimento do mundo* (1935–1940), in *Obra completa* (Rio, 1967), p. 101.

24. I take this phrase from Mike González and David Treece, *The Gathering of Voices: The Twentieth-Century Poetry of Latin America* (London, 1992), p. 182.

25. Drummond, 'Consideração do poema', in *A Rosa do Povo* (1943–1945), *Obra completa*, p. 137. Translation by Mike Gonzalez and David Treece.

26. Girondo, *Obras: Poesía*, p. 59.

27. I am drawing here on an unpublished study of Latin American poetry by Hugo Gola.

28. Angel Rama, *Rubén Darío y el Modernismo* (Caracas, 1985), pp. 124–5.

29. Jorge Luis Borges, 'El escritor argentino y la tradición', in *Discusión* (Buenos Aires, 1957).

30. Rubén Darío, *Prosas profanas* (1896).

31. Darío, in *Cantos de vida y esperanza* (1905).

32. The idea is developed in Georges Bataille's essay 'William Blake', in his *Literature and Evil* (London, 1983).

33. Manuel González Prada, 'Notas acerca del idioma', in *Páginas libres* (Lima, 1966), pp. 245, 246, 255, 257.

34. Andrés Bello, *Obras completas* (Caracas, 1952), Vol. 1, p. 46.

35. José Martí, *The America of José Martí: Selected Writings* (New York, 1953), p. 254 (translation modified).

36. Antônio de Castro Alves, 'O navio negreiro', in his *Os escravos* (São Paulo, 1972), pp. 177–8.

37. Raimundo Correia, 'Plenilúnio', in his *Poesías* (Rio, 1976), p. 93.

38. Manuel Bandeira, *Apresentação da poesia brasileira* (Río, 1957), p. 92.

39. Mário de Andrade, *Poesias completas* (São Paulo, 1987), p. 92.

40. Ibid., p. 60.

41. Enriqueta Terán, *Casa de hablas* (Caracas, 1991), p. 211. A bilingual edition has recently been published: Ana Enriqueta Terán, *The Poetess Counts to 100 and Bows Out*, translated by Marcel Smith (Princeton, 2003).

42. Leonidas Morales, *La poesía de Nicanor Parra* (Santiago, 1972), p. 193.

43. Ibid., pp. 125–6.

44. *Cántico cósmico* (Managua, 1989), Cantiga X.

45. *Barricada*, 10th March 1980.

46. Gonzalo Rojas, *Oscuro* (Caracas, 1977), p. 179.

47. Ibid., 165.

48. Juan L Ortiz, *Obra completa* (Santa Fe, 1996), pp. 667–8.

49. Jorge Eduardo Eielson, *Poesía escrita* (Lima, 1976), p. 276.

50. Raúl Zurita, *Purgatorio* (Santiago, 1979), p. 47.

51. João Cabral de Melo Neto, *Antologia poetica* (Rio, 1967), p. 262.

52. Ibid., p. 251.

53. Ibid., p. 257.

54. Cabral, 'O sertanejo falando', in *Antologia poetica*, p. 8.

55. In Mendonça Teles, *Vanguarda Européia e Modernismo Brasileiro*, pp. 251–2.

56. Haroldo de Campos, *Signantia quasicoelum* (São Paulo, 1978).

57. *Alambres* (Buenos Aires, 1987), p. 54. The whole poem is published in translation in *Travesia* 1, 2 (1992): 185–98.

58. México, 1996. See also, Horácio Costa (ed.), *A palavra poética na América Latina: Avaliação de una geração* (São Paulo, 1992).

59. Martín Adán (Rafael de la Fuente Banavides), *De lo barroco en el Perú* (Lima, 1968), pp. 376–7.

60. Sor Juana Inés de la Cruz, *Obras Completas* (Mexico, 1951), vol. 1, p. 359.

61. Among the most useful collections are Edmundo Bendezú's, *Literatura quechua* (Caracas, 1980) and Miguel León-Portilla's *Cantos y crónicas del México antiguo* (Madrid, Historia 16, 1986). The best single book on this literature is Gordon Brotherston's *Book of the Fourth World: Reading the Native Americas Through Their Literature* (Cambridge, 1992).

62. This point has been made forcefully by Julio Noriega, to whose book, *Buscando una tradición poética quechua en el Perú* (University of Miami, 1995), the reader is directed.

63. 'Orelha furada', in *O homem da orelha furada* (Juiz de Fora, 1995), p. 11. Translation by Bill Griffiths.

64. The poem which begins with these two lines and takes its title from the first is in César Vallejo's *Poemas humanos* and was written in approximately 1936 (first published in Paris, 1939).

Further reading

Brotherston, Gordon, *Latin American Poetry: Origins and Presence*, Cambridge, 1975

Rowe, William, *Contemporary Poets of Latin America: History and the Inner Life*, Oxford, 2000

Running, Thorpe, *The Critical Poem: Borges, Paz, and Other Language-Centered Poets in Latin*, Lewisburg, 1996

Tapscott, Stephen, *Twentieth-Century Latin American Poetry: A Bilingual Anthology*, Austin TX, 1996

Treece, David and Mike Gonzalez, *The Gathering of Voices: The Twentieth-Century Poetry of Latin America*, London, 1992

8

Popular culture in Latin America

Popular culture is a term used to refer to a very broad and diverse array of forms and practices such as salsa, samba, religious ritual and magic, carnivals, *telenovelas* (television soaps), masks, pottery, weaving, alternative theatre, radio, video and oral narrative as well as the 'whole way of life', the language, dress and political culture of subordinate classes and ethnic groups. It covers a whole spectrum of cultural practices, which are seen as lying outside the institutionalized and canonized forms of knowledge and aesthetic production generally defined as 'high' culture. These practices have in turn been studied within different disciplinary frameworks and variously defined as 'folk culture', 'mass culture', 'the culture industry' and 'working-class culture'. To gain an understanding of popular culture in Latin America is therefore a challenge to our sociological imagination: it entails examining particular cultural manifestations while simultaneously being aware of how the very object of study, and hence our knowledge of it, is framed in a certain way by a given intellectual tradition or disciplinary framework.

Popular culture as folklore

The term 'folklore' was first coined in 1846 by J. Thomas, a member of the British Society of Antiquaries, an institution that was dedicated to the collection of what was then regarded by intellectuals as 'popular antiquaries', the curious and irrational customs and beliefs of the uneducated 'common people' or folk. A pejorative connotation was attached to this notion of folklore: it was seen as the residue of a pre-scientific and pre-industrial era. In Germany, in the context of the Romantic reaction against the Enlightenment and classicism, the idea of the culture of the people as a distinct sphere that differed from elaborate forms of knowledge disseminated through learned institutions, acquired new and positive political connotations. According to Herder (1744–1803) the non-institutionalized cultural traditions of a people manifested in stories, songs, customs, rituals and language formed a unique collective consciousness, through which a specific identity, spirit or *Volksgeist* was expressed. This notion was invoked by the national liberation movements of mid-nineteenth-century Europe that were struggling against the domination of France and the Austro-Hungarian Empire, as a way of claiming the right of nations – in which the 'spirit of a people' was expressed – to govern themselves according to their own customs. Thus, the notion of popular culture became interwoven with the search for and affirmation of national identity. At the same time, the term 'popular culture', as it was used by critics of capitalism and industrialization, became a metaphor for a mode of being which was disappearing as a result of the mechanization of work and the prevalence of commodity exchange. In the shared customs of pre-industrial societies, it was argued, a sense of community, now lost in the soulless association of people, had been preserved. Popular culture thus came to be associated not only with the traditional customs of a people but also with the peasantry, who, in contrast to the individualized and more cosmopolitan culture of letters also created collectively and anonymously. The prototype for this form of creation was oral culture. It is from this intellectual tradition of popular culture as folklore that we have inherited two important theoretical tools for the study of popular culture: the idea that popular culture is, on the one hand, a 'whole way of life' or a lived culture consisting of particular customs, rituals and festivities and, on the other, that this 'way of life' produces symbolic forms – music, language, artefacts – which can generically be defined and studied as 'texts'.[1]

This conception of folklore is clearly articulated by Marion Oettinger, curator of Folk Art and Latin American Art at the San Antonio Museum. According to Oettinger, Latin American folk art is characterized by its ties with family and community tradition.

As a chronicle of the life of the community that produced it, the aesthetic and thematic boundaries of folk art are defined by local artistic and social values, which speak with a communal voice through the materials of traditional aesthetic expression. With its roots in the world of the peasantry and the urban poor, far 'removed from the centres of power, wealth and formal learning in Latin America', this art is 'at the service of the society from which it springs'.[2] In this conception, culture is produced by the people and for the people.

One particularly rich form of folk culture in Latin America studied by both folklorists and anthropologists is the rituals, festivities, belief systems and artefacts connected to popular Catholicism and more broadly to the syncretic religious forms and practices which have emerged in the encounter between European, Native American and African cultures. In contrast to official Catholicism with its hierarchy, elaborate doctrinal system and conception of the priest as a mediator between god and man, popular Catholicism is characterized by a sense of the effective presence of the divine or numinous in the visible world. Mysterious beings, devils, souls of the dead and in particular saints and the Virgin, who are syncretically amalgamated with Native American and African deities inhabit the sphere of everyday life. The blurring of boundaries between the real and the imaginary makes reality extraordinary and a place therefore in which miracles can occur.

Of core significance in the practices of popular Catholicism are the fiestas and pilgrimages in honour of a patron saint or virgin whose divine intervention is sought to solve difficulties in life. Followers can show gratitude for a favour obtained by making pilgrimages to a sacred city and leaving ex-votos and *retablos* in churches dedicated to a patron saint or the Virgin. Most of the *ex-votos* represent parts of the body that have been healed: heads, arms, legs and hands made of wood or more recently of polystyrene. Other offerings include objects related to specific situations of the pilgrim such as photographs, bridal and baptismal gowns, candles, crosses, crutches, wheelchairs, a radio, a hoe, a strand of hair. *Retablos* are small paintings, frequently of individual saints or of the difficult circumstance for which help is sought, which are placed behind the altar (*retro tabula*) as a testament to the efficacy of the saint's or Virgin's supernatural powers.

Another significant aspect of popular Catholicism can be found in the various forms of popular drama that emerged in the course of the encounter between Europe and Native America in the sixteenth century. Introduced by Franciscan and Dominican friars in the colonial period in order to convert the indigenous population to Christianity, these forms of popular drama or morality plays (*autos sacramentales*) enacted lively dramatizations of the life of Christ, the prophets and the saints, their revelations and martyrdoms. In order to facilitate the process of conversion, native pagan dances and masquerades were incorporated into Catholic practices on holy days, thus fostering the development of original native theatrical forms. Examples of these in the Brazilian context that have retained their vitality are the *Pastoris*, *Congadas* and *Reisados* which have been defined by the Brazilian folklorist Mario de Andrade as dance-dramas (*danças dramaticas*). Like the majority of dance-dramas, the *Pastoris* are performed during Christmas festivities. Children and young people dressed in the white attire of shepherds and carrying baskets full of fruit, eggs and other offerings, dance and sing a variety of hymns, waltzes and sambas against the backdrop of the manger at Bethlehem. In the course of the play in which a lost shepherdess is tempted by Satan, a multitude of allegorical figures including angels, the fours seasons, the Sun, Moon and Earth, human virtues such as Faith and Hope, as well as an array of animals, appear in order to proclaim the birth of Christ. The *Congadas*, performed in small towns and villages in rural areas as well as in the poor outskirts of major urban centres, re-enact the coronation of the kings of Africa, narrated through song and dance combined with devotional songs to Our Lady of the Rosary, Saint Bendict and the Divine Spirit. The term *Reisado* refers to the performance of a theme, contained in popular song, on the eve of the Epiphany.

One of the richest and most elaborate dance-dramas in Brazil, performed as a *Reisado* or during the festivities of Saint John in June, centres on the death and resurrection of a dancing *boi* or ox. Entitled *Bumba-meu-Boi*, this form of popular theatre, which in some regions can last a number of days, links a variety of disparate songs, poems, choreographic elements and characters from everyday life as well as a host of animal and supernatural creatures.

In the Andean region, in Guatemala and Mexico, plays recreating the Spanish conquest are performed in ways that reinterpret and resist the European interpretation of this event. In the Conquest play in the city of Oruro in Bolivia, for example, the dramatic action ends with the appearance of the Spanish king who punishes the ruthless Conquistador Pizarro for killing Atahuallpa, the legitimate Inca monarch. Prior to his final defeat and death, Atahuallpa makes his son promise to return to the valley of Vilcabamba, the site of final Inca resistance to the Spanish Conquest in 1572.

Although it is difficult to generalize, many of the expressions of popular religiosity are characterized by a love of theatricality and decoration, suggesting a deeper historical connection with an indigenous baroque style going back to the seventeenth century which, in its unfettered imagination and extravagance, has frequently been seen as an aesthetic form particularly attuned to the Ibero-American conception of the world.

A more extended discussion of the syncretic interactions between the Iberian, Native American and African elements and of the meanings attributed to the sacred in popular Catholicism goes beyond the scope of this overview, in particular since they vary considerably depending on the regional context and historical period. However, to give an indication of the different layers of meaning that can be attached to certain sacred symbols, we will examine briefly the figure of the devil and of the Virgin of Guadalupe.

In their efforts to christianize the 'New World', the Spanish superimposed the notion or figure of the devil onto Native American deities and metaphysical systems. As many scholars have pointed out, in the subsequent process of incorporating the devil as a figure in popular religiosity, the characteristics and meaning of the devil were refashioned, since in the Native American and in the African worlds the Manicheistic division between Good and Evil, Heaven and Hell seems to have been absent. Instead, for example, the figure of the devil has been appropriated in different contexts as a symbol that gives expression to the threats posed to the independence of the peasant mode of existence by capitalism and more generally by modernity. Thus, according to the North American anthropologist Michael Taussig, the image of the *tio* or uncle in the form of statues or devil figures in the tin mines of Oruro in Bolivia, to whom the miners carry out rites of sacrifice in order to ensure the productivity of the mine, is a way of giving imaginative form to their experience of becoming proletarianized wage-labourers dependent for their livelihood on the world market price of tin. As peasants, their relations with each other and with nature were governed by the principle of reciprocity; however, with their loss of control over the means of production, the devil comes to represent 'the radically different concepts of creation, life and growth through which the new material conditions and social relations are defined'.[3] Similarly, in the *literatura de cordel*, booklets of poems written by rural migrants from the North-east in São Paulo, Satan appears as the 'administrator of the modern world' either in the form of the destructive force of nuclear energy plants or, more moralistically, as the demonic presence which teaches children to disregard their parents' advice and women to transgress their prescribed gender roles of wife and mother.

The Virgin of Guadalupe is said to have first appeared to the christianized Indian Juan Diego early one morning in 1531 in Tepeyac, near what is now Mexico City, asking him to build a temple in her honour. The shrine to her was erected over that of Tonantzin, an Aztec divinity whose name means 'our mother'. Since then the dark-skinned Virgin of Guadalupe, syncretized with Tonantzin has been claimed as the protector of the oppressed in their hopes for a better world. Creole nationalists carried her image into battle in their struggle for liberation from Spain and similarly, the peasant leader, Emiliano Zapata, almost a century later, claimed her as the protector of the peasantry seeking 'land and liberty' while today she is revered by the Zapatista Army of National Liberation. She is also the venerated icon of Mexican-American women for whom, in their subordinate position as women and as Mexicans in the USA, she is 'consoler, mother, healer, intercessor and woman', a source of strength on which to draw.[4]

In 1995 she appeared to a janitor mopping up water from a burst pipe in Mexico City's Hidalgo metro station where she now has her own shrine. Sightings of her by poor people have become increasingly widespread as economic insecurity for the poor in Mexico has grown with the imposition of neo-liberal economic policies; she has been sighted at other metro stations and her image is imprinted on T-shirts, pens and watches. According to the lottery-ticket vendor Juventina Cerda, who has her tickets blessed by Our Lady of the Metro, the fact that, 'the Virgin appeared here means there is going to be a change for the humble people'.[5]

In Latin America, for historical reasons, the idea of popular culture as folklore has remained salient despite criticisms of its underlying assumptions. In the twentieth century, under the aegis of populism and in the context of nation building and the processes of modernization, hitherto regionally or ethnically specific cultural traditions were frequently drawn on to construct a national identity. The cases of Brazil and Mexico are particularly illustrative of the connections that have been established in Latin America between popular culture and the nation. In the 1930s, samba, the music and dance of poor Afro-Brazilians living in Rio de Janeiro was, as we shall see, transformed by the state from an ethnically specific and marginalized cultural practice into a symbol of national identity. In post-revolutionary Mexico, the promotion of indigenous culture became part of state-sponsored official indigenism, a cornerstone in what the archaeologist Manuel Gamio, who carried out the first pilot study of the ancient site of Teotihuacan on behalf of the government, defined as 'forging the Nation'.

In these and other instances in which popular culture is used to 'invent' a national tradition, a contradiction is apparent in that the popular cultures which are being used to represent the nation in its progress towards modernity are simultaneously transformed or eliminated by the very process of nation building and modernization. At the same time, the idea of popular culture as folklore has been used as a point of reference by intellectual and political currents critical of capitalism and Western modernity. In the work of radical folklorists such as José María Arguedas and Mario de Andrade, the cultures of the Andean region and the pre-capitalist ways of life of the popular classes in Brazil offer alternative visions of the social. Indeed, the connection with the past maintained by the rituals and oral forms of culture practised by rural communities – in other words, their important role as the upholders of a collective memory – has been highlighted by artists and writers concerned with creating original and uniquely Latin American forms of literary and artistic expression. In comparison to Europe, in Latin America the concept of folklore thus connects to richer and more complex layers of meaning. Beyond the concern with the disappearance and preservation of specific artefacts and traditions, it has been a source, since the early twentieth century, of alternative conceptions of the social order, of identity and development. However, in order to understand why folklore and indeed other conceptions of popular culture connote such a rich variety of meanings, it is important to consider key formative processes in the history of Latin American societies.

Two major and interconnected factors would seem particularly relevant to any attempt to grasp the significance and place of popular culture in Latin America: the colonial legacy and the uneven processes of development, the combination and simultaneity of different economic structures and ways of life which characterize Latin American societies.

The conquest and colonization of Latin America brought about the encounter between Native America, Europe and Africa creating in the process a mestizo society. However, the mixture, or *mestizaje*, which took place, was simultaneously marked by violence and the subordination of the Native American and African peoples. The literary critic Martin notes: 'Mestizo America' was not 'a complementarity but a conflict, an opposition, the variable sign for a real contradiction that determines many others'.[6] The popular cultures of Latin America could be considered as sites in which this conflictive *mestizaje* occurs, involving in different contexts and historical moments greater or lesser processes of acculturation, that is the substitution of the native by the European or transculturation, the transformation of the European by the native American and African. Similarly, at different historical moments, depending on the particular relations between elite and popular cultures, the latter might be held in low esteem or, alternatively, might be positively re-evaluated. Thus, for example, in the nineteenth century, elite aspirations for Latin America involved uncritical imitation of France and Britain, considered as the most advanced civilizations while the pre-capitalist Iberian, indigenous and African worlds were by contrast repudiated and defined as 'barbaric' and 'backward'. In the twentieth century, on the other hand, in the wake of the Mexican Revolution in 1910, as Latin American political and cultural elites sought to construct national identities grounded in Latin America's own unique and original characteristics, popular cultures were assigned positive value since it was here that Latin America's uniqueness was seen to lie. Popular cultures would play an important role in formulating alternative conceptions of the social order, particularly in the various populist, socialist and anti-imperialist attempts to reform or radically transform Latin America since the 1920s.

Uneven development is a term which political economists and sociologists use to refer to the combination or 'articulation' of pre-capitalist and capitalist economic and social formations in Latin America, in other words, to the coexistence and interpenetration of 'tradition' and 'modernity' and Latin America's marked economic, social and cultural heterogeneity. These terms, and the social reality to which they refer, are of relevance in the study of popular cultures for they illuminate why, in contrast to Europe and the USA, where the process of capitalist development and modernization has been more complete, folk cultures, and in particular a collective indigenous memory, still persist. They are also useful in elucidating how very different forms of 'popular culture', whether understood as folk culture, as mass culture or as expressions of ideological resistance to the social order, exist as distinct, but also interconnecting, spheres.

Nevertheless, despite the density of meanings associated with the term folklore and its continued widespread use, its validity has been subject to criticism. The cultural theorist Néstor García Canclini, author of several major studies of popular culture in Latin America, has challenged the assumption that traditional popular cultures are inevitably being swept aside by modernity. In his view, the idea that the expansion of capitalism in Mexico is bringing about the gradual disappearance of handicraft production (*artesanía*) by indigenous peasants, as well as the ways of life that sustain this production, is too simplistic. To some extent, this affirmation is true in that the presence of television, cars and mass-produced utensils and clothing is increasingly evident in indigenous communities; similarly, there is a growing tendency for designs with a mythical and religious significance to be adapted to the tastes of a national and international consumer market.

In his study of Tarascan *artesanía* in Michoacán, for example, Canclini argues that economic and political factors have contributed to the flourishing of *artesanía*, albeit in a new form. Since the 1920s, following the Mexican Revolution, Mexico's indigenous heritage has been promoted by the Mexican state as a source of national identity and cohesion, essential for the development of state-led capitalism. Furthermore, *artesanía* has also been promoted by the Mexican state as a source of income to supplement insufficient agricultural livelihoods and thus hold back the tide of rural-urban migration.[7]

In another instance quoted by Canclini, it is involvement with the forces of modernity that has fostered the growth of a tradition of handicraft production. In Ocumicho the production of clay devil figures, made primarily by women, only became a local tradition from the 1960s. Exhibited in Mexico City and New York and marketed by the national government, this form of *artesanía* in turn gave rise to a strong sense of local tradition and ethnic identity. In the handicrafts themselves, the growing involvement of folk art with urban modernity is expressed in the hybrid amalgamation of traditional and modern, sacred and profane imagery where devils appear as irreverent spirits in a variety of biblical scenes, flying aeroplanes, holding telephones and sitting astride buses heading towards the United States.[8] This example illustrates that tradition and modernity do not necessarily stand in opposition to each other and that increasingly, with the 'ruralization' of the cities owing to migration from the countryside and the impact of transnational cultural flows, self-enclosed rural communities, as originally conceived by folklorists, are subject to a multitude of new cultural and economic pressures. As Canclini observes: 'In the last decades Latin America has changed from being a society with millions of dispersed peasant communities with traditional cultures that were local, homogenous, frequently indigenous and quite isolated, into a largely urban society with a heterogeneous symbolic world in which the local constantly interacts with the national and transnational.'[9]

The interpenetration of the local and the global is clearly exemplified in the work of Zapotec weavers in Teotitlán del Valle in the Mexican state of Oaxaca studied by L. Stephen. She traces the ways in which handicrafts entered the national market in the 1940s, circulating increasingly since the 1980s in the world market to satisfy global consumer demand for 'traditional' goods, which have apparently retained their non-mechanical aura.[10] Exporters involved in the sale of Mexican, Indian and Persian rugs, who mediate between local producers and foreign department stores, exercise pressure on the weavers to produce the design which is most in demand on the world market, independent of its social or religious meaning, thus removing designs from their local context. In this process of inclusion in the broader world market, the notions of 'local tradition' and 'ethnic identity' become negotiating tools used by local indigenous handicraft workers in order to control the new relations of production in which they have become involved. On the one hand, indigenous merchants use claims to local tradition and ethnicity as a means of obtaining higher prices and asserting control over their products. On the other hand, weavers who are tied to the merchants through kinship but whose economic position is weaker, use claims to local tradition and ethnic unity to reinforce relations of reciprocity with the aim of ensuring that the money obtained by the merchant class is invested in the community: in land, food, and in the festivities and rituals through which kinship relations are articulated and 'tradition' is maintained.

This example demonstrates that the collective local traditions that are the object of folklorist studies are not necessarily a collection of fixed cultural traits but rather a contested space and that, as in the case of the producers of devil figures in Ocumicho, involvement in the global economy, and the struggle to retain control over handicraft products, can lead to a strengthening rather than a weakening of local identity.

The studies discussed above are useful in that they offer valid critiques of the assumption within folklore studies that popular cultural traditions tend inevitably to disappear with the advance of modernity and industrialization according to a linear evolutionary pattern. They draw attention to the complex, contradictory and surprising relationships between tradition and modernity, local identity and global forces. Nevertheless, there is a danger of overstating the case in the sense that with the advance of industrialization and agribusiness since the 1950s, there is also a countervailing tendency for communities to lose cohesion and access to their collective memory, as weavers, potters, singers and storytellers are either displaced by new technologies or incorporated into broader and more differentiated commercial circuits including the tourist trade, radio and the music industry.

Popular culture as 'mass' culture

In the second major disciplinary framework through which popular culture has been constructed as an object of study, it is referred to as a product of mass culture: radio, cinema, recorded music, comics, *fotonovelas* and, above all, television. Here, the popular refers to a cultural form that is 'popular' not necessarily because it is made 'by the people for the people' – the people in this case referring to the peasantry, the rural workers and the urban poor – but because it is consumed on a mass scale. Popular culture in this sense has frequently been opposed to the idea of folklore. In contrast to the latter, which, it is assumed, is only authentically popular when it emerges from the creative impulse of the people, mass cultural products are defined by the need to make profits. In this view, cultural forms become standardized in the process of being transformed into commodities, thus reducing the consumer's ability to think critically or engage in experiences which are not adapted to, or cannot transcend, the prevailing definition of reality.

According to the anthropologist Jorge de Carvalho, with the imposition of mass cultural production, popular culture or folklore suffers a similar fate to high culture. The classical tradition of high culture and popular culture are in his view the two halves of a sphere that has come apart. Drawing on the work of the Frankfurt School, on the concept of the 'culture industry' developed by Theodor Adorno and Max Horkheimer, he argues that while both high and popular culture maintain a collective memory, the mass media merely create momentary stimulation, fragmentation and amnesia: 'Both high and popular culture are linked to tradition and contribute to the creation of a collective memory. In contrast, what defines the culture industry is that it produces amnesia: it offers the illusion of complete participation and instantaneous communication between producer and consumer, but without the capacity to accumulate.'[11]

In the 1960s and 1970s, during the height of populist and anti-imperialist sentiment in Latin America, this contrast between popular culture as folklore and mass culture was fairly widespread. The critique of mass culture is made in trenchant fashion in Ariel Dorfman and Armand Mattelart's 1973 book *How to Read Donald Duck*, an analysis of the imperialist assumptions to be found in Disney comics.[12] It can also be seen in the work of the Popular Culture Centres (CPCs) established in Brazil between 1962 and 1964, which aimed to promote class-consciousness among the popular sectors. This was to be achieved through the establishment of adult literacy programmes, the performance of plays and films, the publication of stories and the organization of song and music festivals. The manifesto of the CPCs states: 'the structure and composition of popular culture is determined by the aim which is its *raison d'être*: it only exists if it acts as a cultural force with the purpose of making the masses aware of their historical situation . . . popular culture only exists where the process of transformation of an alienated consciousness into revolutionary consciousness, actively involved in political struggle, is emerging'.[13]

In these approaches, which contrast the mass media and popular culture, certain assumptions about the effects of the mass media, which have since been questioned and reformulated, are implicit, in particular the idea that the recipients of media messages passively absorb the ideological contents of media products. This view overlooks the fact that the products of the culture industry are decoded differently depending on the cultural traditions, discourses and political loyalties of cultural consumers. It is also a view in which insufficient account is taken of the specific historical contexts in which the media develop in any given society. This qualification is of particular relevance to Latin America for two reasons. First, given the incomplete secularization of popular memory and the widespread prevalence of magical and religious practices originating in indigenous and African traditions, in popular Catholicism and spiritism, the messages contained in the media are not necessarily those which viewers create in the process of reception. The messages are, as it were, resignified. Second, owing to the historical context in which the media have emerged in Latin America, namely as a crucial element in the broader process of nation building in the twentieth century, they have had an important role in the formation of national identities and in shaping the contours of a specifically Latin American modernity.

In carrying out this role, the media – cinema, radio and television – have drawn on earlier forms of popular culture associated with folklore, such as oral narrative as well as popular theatre, the serialized novel or *folletin* and the circus. At the same time their development has been closely linked to key political formations in Latin America, in particular populism in the 1950s and 1960s and the military regimes of the 1970s and 1980s. In each of these periods the media have, in diverse and often contrasting ways, been instrumental in projecting and constituting a notion of 'the people' as the basis of the nation. As the cultural critic Jesús Martín Barbero has pointed out in his work on popular and mass culture, it is necessary to conceive of the media more subtly. Their role and the cultural goods they produce cannot simply be understood by reference to the logic of the capitalist market or the class interests of those who own and control media institutions, although these are important elements.[14] Rather, in the context of Latin America's heterogeneity and uneven forms of development, the media have acted as 'mediators' between the state and the masses, between the rural and urban, tradition and modernity. Thus, for historical reasons, a clear separation between popular culture understood as folklore and mass culture is difficult to sustain even though they are distinct phenomena. The mass and the folk meld with each other in a variety of ways, depending on the specific cultural form and historical context.

The ways in which the process of mediation operates becomes clearer if we consider the social and economic contexts in which radio, cinema and television emerged. Radio and cinema developed first, between the 1930s and 1950s, during the period in which many Latin American countries were characterized by populist regimes attempting to launch the process of industrialization through import-substitution. With the spread of radio throughout the national territories, listeners in regions that had hitherto remained enclosed within their own boundaries were increasingly drawn into feeling part of a shared national culture. As R. Pareja points out with respect to Colombia: 'Before the emergence and dissemination of radio, the country was a puzzle of regions separate from each other. Before 1940 Colombia was a country with countries within it rather than a nation. The diffusion of radio allowed for the experience of a visible national unity, a cultural identity shared simultaneously by the people from the coast, from the interior, from Pasto and

Santander.'[15] Samba in Brazil and the tango in Argentina, both forms of cultural expression specific to particular groups – to Afro-Brazilians and to rural migrants in the city of Buenos Aires – became symbols of national identity through radio. A qualification needs to be added here, for as R. Ortiz notes, despite the efforts at centralization and national unification of the Vargas governments in Brazil following the revolution of 1930, the obstacles to the development of capitalism and with it the ability to create a fully developed culture industry, were still limited.[16] This would be fully realised only much later in the 1970s, with television acting as the key mediator in the process of cultural integration. Nevertheless, during this period, populist governments, particularly in Argentina, Brazil and Mexico, sought legitimacy by employing a style of charismatic, patrimonial and personalist politics, addressing the new working and middle classes in an almost Messianic way as 'the People-Nation' whose vocation it was to create the modern, developed nation. As the Brazilian sociologist F. Weffort observes, with populism as a form of political organization 'the ghost of the people' enters on the stage of history as the most important source of legitimation.[17]

In this context, despite the limitations pointed out by Ortiz, radio acts as a mediator of the processes of social transformation by representing the novel entity of 'the people'. In the *radio-novelas*, the many audience-participation and musical programmes in which folkloric popular cultural elements were incorporated, in the broadcasting of football championships and news programmes that used styles of enunciation which harked back to the narrative styles of oral culture and the melodramatic structure of popular theatre, 'the people' were offered an image of themselves with which they could identify.

Cinema, in particular Mexican cinema, was also instrumental in creating images of 'the people' as repositories of national identity. In the films *Insurrección en México* [Insurrection in Mexico] (1911) and *Revolución orozquista* [The Orozco Revolution] (1912), which record on the battlefield the struggle between the troops of Huerta and Orozco, the Revolution itself is transformed into a filmic event of epic proportions.[18] With the advent of sound after the First World War, films drew on the popular music already available to a mass audience through the radio, in particular rural country music such as the *canción ranchera*, which became an essential ingredient of a nationalist film industry and its evocation of a rather stereotypical and sentimental 'Mexicanness' based on singing crooners or *charros*, the ranch or hacienda, the innocence of rural life, alongside comics and musical sketches taken from variety shows. In the work of film makers such as Emilio Fernández and cinematographer Gabriel Figueroa, however, the lyrical evocation of the Mexican landscape, and the virtues and qualities of its people acquire a new, deeper and more sophisticated dimension. According to Barbero, Mexican cinema, despite its possible reactionary or formulaic qualities, became a medium which constituted a new popular urban subjectivity, satisfying 'the hunger of the masses to make themselves socially visible . . . in a sequence of images which rather than ideas offers them gestures, faces, ways of speaking, and walking, landscapes, colours'.[19]

In the verbal and corporeal language of the legendary comedian Cantinflas, the transformation of an earlier popular form, the circus, into a form which articulates a new urban, popular subjectivity via the mass media is clearly illustrated. Cantinflas, alias Mariano Moreno, began his career as a comedian, dancer and acrobat in the 1920s in the vaudeville acts of the *carpas* (tents) on the poor outskirts (*arrabales*) of Mexico City. Mexican critic Carlos Monsivais' eloquent description of the *arrabal* evokes not only the outskirts of Mexico City but also those of many contemporary Latin American cities:

> The word *arrabal* – with its suggestion of pool halls, dens, taco stands, neighbourhoods, dust, hungry dogs, children with a supplicatory look – describes and invents what it names, an instant catalogue of realities and illusions: the Way of the Cross (poverty), shared purgatory (the neighbourhood), tradition (religious imagery decorating the rundown), irresistible sordidness (the Cabaret), redemption (family love and neighbourly solidarity), fallen angels (prostitutes), real men and real women, the born-to-lose and innocence-in-the mud. It connotes, however, one benefit, rootedness – which paradoxically, accompanies a forgetting of one's own origins. Heaven and Hell, a reality that is equally distant from reality and conventional 'illusion', bars, tents, dance halls, cornerstalls, improvised football pitches and wrestling, boxing rings all fall within the circumference of the *arrabal*.[20]

By the 1940s, through his genial embodiment of a popular type, the film character Cantinflas – the irreverent and pathetic outcast, a clown excelling in the art of improvisation, a fool and man with a heart – Mariano Moreno had become a national myth and a film icon. This use of the absurd and the picaresque, which, according to Monsiváis, is demonstrated in the nonsense language of *cantinflinismo*, is echoed in other popular trickster figures throughout Latin America and could be seen, in conjunction with the popular religiosity and baroque imaginary present in folk culture, as significant elements of popular sensibility.

A further instance of the ways in which the mass media incorporate earlier forms of popular culture can be found in television and more specifically in the *telenovela*, which perhaps more than any other genre in Latin America has been instrumental in creating a unified national market for cultural goods and in providing the narratives and images through which the 'imagined community' of the nation can become lived experience. The expansion of television as the cornerstone of a modern culture industry is also a revealing example of how the national and the global interact and how this interaction itself has given the *telenovela*, which draws on earlier popular and often regional forms, such a central role in shaping the national imagination. The processes by which the popular, the national and the global have become intertwined can be explored by briefly tracing the key steps in the formation of Brazilian television.

The first television channel, TV Tupi, was launched in the early 1950s by a wealthy businessman, Assis Chateaubriand, a man inspired not only by commercial interests but also by the notion that television was essential to the formation of a modern nation. However, since at this stage the process of industrialization was still incipient, television relied on North American companies for technical assistance and sponsorship. Television stations were predominantly regional, and despite the importation of programmes from the US, they mainly reflected regional cultures. Moreover, since only a small percentage of the population owned television, programming concentrated on theatre, dance and music. It was at this stage a vehicle for 'high culture' rather than a popular mass medium or indeed a culture industry as conceived by Adorno and Horkheimer.

Gradually, as a consequence of the developmentalist policies of President Kubitsheck (1956–61), who claimed he could squeeze fifty years of industrialization and modernization into five, television sets were produced in greater quantities and more cheaply. Television thus became a vehicle to reach large audiences, integrated into the new capitalist urban-industrial society through advertising and political mobilization in favour of the developmentalist project. Programming was increasingly concentrated in the capital Rio de Janeiro and São Paulo, the industrial heartland of Brazil, while the broadcasting of programmes nationally led to greater homogeneity and a weakening of the former regionalism, with São Paulo and Rio represented as the modern face of Brazil.

However, it was only in the 1970s, during the height of the right-wing military government that the whole of Brazil was integrated into a national communications network through the establishment of 'Embratel', the Brazilian Enterprise for Telecommunications. Paradoxically, it is during this period, characterized by Brazil's greater integration in the world economy and the massive entry of foreign capital, that the media corporation TV Globo became a national institution, symbolizing the status of Brazil as a modern nation. With US financial and technical assistance, TV Globo was able to set up a sophisticated and efficient television structure through which it obtained a virtual monopoly of the national television market, enabling it to create a popular television culture no longer dependent on foreign and particularly US imported programmes. A key factor in establishing its cultural hegemony was the *telenovela*: TV Globo screens different serials in prime time six times a week and exports its products to over 112 countries outside Brazil.[21] This stands in marked contrast to the programming of soap operas in the US which takes place in the daytime and is directed primarily at 'homemakers'.[22] Moreover, the US soap operas by no means occupy the same pivotal place in the national culture as the *telenovelas* in Latin America, where politicians have been known to request videotaping of the latest instalment in order not to miss the next narrative development while sitting in Congress or the Senate. What distinctive economic, social and cultural processes account for this phenomenon?

In attempting to explain the extraordinary popularity and influence of the *telenovela* in Latin American culture two elements have been highlighted. First, that they portray issues which address the experience of a large proportion of the population: the conflicts and divisions between rich and poor, the rural and urban, tradition and modernity, men and women. Thus, for example, in *telenovelas* such as *Pantanal* [The Swamp] (1990) *Renascer* [Born Again] (1994) and *Patria Minha* [Fatherland] (1994) the environment, political corruption, agrarian reform, the current nationwide campaign against hunger led by the sociologist 'Betinho' and the issue of confidence in Brazil's future were incorporated into the plot. Similarly, in the Venezuelan serial *Por Estas Calles* [Through These Streets] (1992) the social and economic crisis in the late 1980s was vividly exposed.

Second, the aesthetic devices through which the broader themes are transformed into plots are almost invariably in the form of the emotional life of the family, which in Latin America, with its personalist and family traditions, is a primary form of sociality. Using the conventions of melodrama as a genre to transform the larger issues – the abstract time of the nation and history – into private passions, the *telenovela*'s success in establishing itself as a prime televisual genre is connected to the centrality of this form of sociality, in particular for the popular classes living in the poor neighbourhoods of the cities, for whom it functions as a strategy of survival and a form of resistance. The melodrama as aesthetic genre here functions again as a form of mediation between pre-modern folk narratives, the transitional genres of the serialized novel, the popular theatre of the nineteenth century and contemporary urban mass culture.[23]

Incorporated into the themes and structure of the *telenovela*, thus anchoring it in popular memory, is the struggle between Good and Evil of oral narrative, the emphasis on the gestural language of the body, the emotional excess of popular melodrama and the openness to the extra-fictional world of current events which characterized the nineteenth-century serialized novel. The blurring of boundaries between reality and fiction is clearly illustrated in two examples. In 1992 the *telenovela Anos Rebeldes* [Rebellious Years] recounting the history of the student movement and its resistance to the right-wing military government in the 1960s and 1970s was shown on Brazilian television. The transmission of this *telenovela* coincided with revelations of the corrupt practices of the current president Fernando Collor, evoking widespread public outrage. Informed by the turbulent events shown in *Rebellious Years*, students and subsequently broad sectors of civil society demonstrated on the streets wearing black to convey their state of mourning at the lack of ethics in Brazilian political life. In the same year, one of the main actresses of the *telenovela De Corpo e Alma* [Body and Soul], Daniella Perez, was murdered. Spectators were puzzled as to whether she had died in reality or in fiction. Subsequently, Gloria Perez, the murdered actress's mother and renowned author of *telenovelas*, initiated a campaign to revise the country's Penal Code which culminated in her handing over 1.3 million signatures in support of revisions to the law in front of a crowd of 70,000 people gathered in the Pacamebú football stadium in São Paulo. This was followed by a minute of silence in homage to Daniella Perez and by the musical theme of the *telenovela* in which she acted.[24]

What seems particularly worthy of note in examining the role of *telenovelas* in Latin America is the way in which they function as points of convergence, or sites of *mestizaje*, between the popular, the national and the transnational, between pre-capitalist and capitalist elements. In other words, it is primarily the success of the *telenovela* that has enabled national culture industries, as emblems of the nation and modernity, to grow and become established. The very success of the *telenovela* itself, however, is predicated upon the aesthetic devices used, which are embedded in earlier local popular forms, and their use in addressing contemporary themes affecting society, thus promoting not only national integration but also the 'sentimental integration of the different Latin American countries – a standardization of ways of feeling and expressing, of gestures and sounds, dance rhythms, and narrative cadences'.[25] Simultaneously, with the large-scale export of *telenovelas* and the need to take undifferentiated audiences provided by the global market into account, there is a marked tendency to create increasingly stereotypical and 'exoticized' images of Latin America. There is thus a similarity between the fate of *artesanía* and the *telenovela*. Indeed, this raises questions relating to the ideological content rather than the form of the *telenovela* and of popular culture in general.

For a genre that is designed to achieve high ratings and attract advertising money, a considerable number of the *telenovelas* such as, for example, *Malu Mulher* [The Woman 'Malu'] and *Roque Santeiro* [Roque the Saint Carver] in Brazil and *Por Estas Calles* in Venezuela have been both aesthetically innovative and politically radical. This is related to the fact that, given the weakness of the film industry and the financial difficulties encountered by movie houses, many scriptwriters and playwrights with radical leanings find employment in the major television channels.

Nevertheless, although the obstacles to greater social justice and personal happiness are dramatically portrayed in ways that address the trials and tribulations of social life, the *telenovelas* also tend to present the problems of the protagonists as surmountable through individual effort, regardless of the structural constraints experienced by the individual in her or his social context, and to favour readings of the very real issues addressed in ways which confirm rather than question dominant commonsense prejudices. Moreover, since they are also sites for major national and transnational advertisers, extolling the virtues of consuming Nike or Reebok, the *telenovelas* function as a key link in the expansion of capitalism and the ideology of consumption.

The complex interrelationship between the structure of ownership of the media, the ideological content of the *telenovelas*, the aesthetic form and the viewers' circumstances and codes of reception raises issues which are central in the analysis of popular culture, namely the link between popular culture and the social relations of power. This brings us to the third disciplinary framework within which popular culture has been studied and which is defined by the importance given to ideological conflict, resistance, domination and hegemony within the sphere of popular culture.

Popular culture and power relations

Approaching popular culture from this angle can be traced back to the history of socialism, in particular the Marxist tradition, in which the concept of popular culture has been used to mount a critique of the effects of capitalism, in particular the dehumanization and oppression of the working classes. Thus the concept of popular culture was intimately linked to the development of class-consciousness and the notion of emancipation; popular culture was seen as a form of resistance or oppositional culture prefiguring a new social order no longer characterized by alienation and human exploitation. The concept of hegemony as outlined by the Italian radical Antonio Gramsci is of central importance in this approach for it emphasizes that the acceptance by oppressed or subaltern social groups of belief systems which bind them to the existing power structure are important in the maintenance of the social order. Ruling groups, according to this analysis, gain the consent of the popular sectors in the cultural sphere to the values, aspirations and meanings that underpin the prevailing social order, even though these may not be in their own interests.[26]

Popular culture in the Gramscian sense, rather than simply being derived crudely from the interests or experiences of subordinate social groups that exist in a state of purity, is the site in which the struggle for cultural power between dominant and subaltern groups takes place, in which hegemonic and counter-hegemonic forces and impulses negotiate and enter into relationship with each other. This Gramscian approach to popular culture gradually came to replace the somewhat more simple model prevalent in the 1960s and 1970s, in the heyday of theories of dependency and critiques of US cultural imperialism, which tended to equate the study of popular culture in Latin America with an analysis of the ideological domination to which the popular classes were subjected.

The *telenovela* is a good illustrative example of how the sphere of popular culture can be seen as a site of conflict between hegemonic and counter-hegemonic forces. In the Venezuelan *telenovela Por Estas Calles* [Through These Streets] the police, the medical profession and business interests are caricatured and debunked in a melodramatic sentimental plot mixed with current news items. This was a heady mixture which galvanized the nation and occasioned protests from the Ministry of Communications and the Metropolitan Police amongst others, who feared its subversive and potentially counter-hegemonic power. At the same time, the genre as a whole and its importance as a vehicle for advertising is an integral element of the expansion of a capitalist society and culture, which in Latin America has been characterized by extreme inequalities in wealth and power. It could thus be considered an important means through which adherence to belief systems and perceptions that validate, or at least do not question, the social order is upheld.

As noted above, for historical reasons specific to Latin America, the 'popular' is imbued with a particularly rich array of meanings and practices, within which the struggle for hegemony is fought. This struggle is well illustrated in the history of carnival festivities in Brazil and in the associated development of samba as a popular form of music and dance.

Samba gradually developed into a specific popular cultural practice in the early twentieth century in the wake of the abolition of slavery (1888) and the eviction of the poor from the city centre of Rio de Janeiro, parts of which were being demolished under the direction of the urban planner Pereira Passos in order to give way to a 'modern' city with wide boulevards and lighted shopping arcades modelled on Paris. Migrants to the city, in search of work in the new wage labour market and forced to live on the hillsides or *morros* of Rio de Janeiro, found refuge from racial discrimination and unemployment in the Afro-Brazilian religious temples, which became the cradle from which samba emerged.

Coexisting with samba were other carnival festivities: masked balls imitating the European carnivals of Venice and Paris and sumptuous parades with allegorical floats. While these forms of carnivalesque merriment were organized and frequented mainly by the new middle classes, the 'popular classes' composed of workers, artisans, small businessmen and semi- or unemployed people, also claimed the streets in the form of groups of costumed blacks dancing to the syncopated rhythm

of samba – the *blocos* and *cordões*, and an alternative parade of *ranchos* –
processions of dancers whose origin goes back to the celebrations of the
nativity in the north-east of Brazil during the twelve days of Christmas.
These associations, articulating a new black subculture, that invaded the
urban landscape during carnival, transgressing class and geographical
boundaries, formed *Escolas de Samba* or Samba Schools, whose parades
gradually became the predominant form of street carnival. In the mid-
1930s, during the populist regime of Getulio Vargas, these groups,
that had initially been persecuted by the authorities and seen as a
threat to Brazil's self-image as essentially white and European, were
officially sanctioned by the state. The carnival processions came to be
organized by the state authorities in the form of a competition for a cash
prize. Concerned with nation building and the creation of a national
consciousness, the state made use of the new technologies of radio broadcasting and recording, through which popular song and music were
becoming increasingly accessible to a national audience, appropriating
samba in order to promote a specifically patriotic national consciousness.[27] From being the disreputable expression of a subaltern group,
samba was metamorphosed into a symbol of national identity.

Since the 1930s the Samba Schools have changed considerably. They
have grown in size with some comprising as many as four thousand
members. They have become official national tourist attractions financed
partly by the state tourism agency Riotour, by transnational companies as
well as by the illegal lottery game known as *jogo do bicho* (the animal game)
and the drug trade. The carnival parade has become a nationally televised
spectacle generating considerable revenue for television companies and
Riotour as well as a vehicle for the self-promotion of media celebrities
who adorn the floats in positions of prominence.

It is beyond the scope of this chapter to outline the trajectory of samba
and the transformations in the associated carnival festivities in their
full complexity and detail. It will suffice to highlight some of the more
important dimensions within samba and carnival in which the struggle
for power and hegemony is played out.

Muniz Sodré, in his inspiring and perceptive writings on samba
has, for example, highlighted the importance of the body and the
musical/dance form of samba as one such site in which the struggle for
power is fought. He emphasizes that in the 1920s, during the early period
of its development, sambas were composed collectively according to a
syncopated rhythm, which in the Candomblé religious ritual functions

as the transmitter of *axé* – the divine and vital energy which underlies existence. Rhythm and syncopation, however, is not an abstraction but a physical force affecting all the organs of the body while also defining consciousness, and, in the case of samba, a form of cultural resistance against slavery and its dehumanization of the slave's body. Sodré, moreover, points to a further element of resistance: in contrast to Western music, African syncopated rhythm is characterized by a sequence that always returns to the beginning in a cyclical movement which is endlessly repeated. This, he argues, acts as an affirmation of life in which 'to sing, to dance, to enter into the rhythm is like listening to one's heartbeat – it is to feel life without allowing for the symbolic inscription of death'. In addition, he points out that samba constitutes a reappropriation from below, a form of *transculturation*, by Afro-Brazilians of the European culture imposed on them, in that it fuses European melodic structures and African rhythms generating a synthesis which revealed 'the way in which blacks made use of the European tonal system while simultaneously destabilising it rhythmically through syncopation'.[28]

The counter-hegemonic potential of samba is also highlighted in further debates on the significance of the symbolic forms and changed social relations which characterize the period of carnival. The early twentieth-century Russian critic Mikhail Bakhtin argued that carnival allows for the temporary emergence of a world without the customary social divisions and hierarchy, in which individuals divested of their habitual social roles and disguised as princes, devils, as death and fools relate to each other in a free, familiar and expressive manner. Reinforced by the atmosphere of collective joy and communion, which stands in contrast to the suffering of everyday life, carnival announces in Bakhtin's terms, the 'gay relativity of prevailing truths and authorities' enacting a form of ritual dethroning and rethroning.[29] The absolute is relativized, the sacred and serious is profaned through laughter, and, as Bakhtin points out, the 'lower' sphere of the body, its forbidden impulses and desires, displaces the 'higher' sphere of moral decorum while the street is transformed into a site in which pleasure and irreverence replace toil and worry. Beyond the brief period of carnival, however, the mode of existence characteristic of carnival is seen as constituting the ethos of the world of samba itself as well as specific genres of samba music, in particular the *samba malandro*. Surviving on the margins of society through trickery and privileging the orphic and pleasurable world of music and dance, the sambista dethrones the sacred petty-bourgeois values of thrift and hard work. Formally, the carnivalesque ambiguity and relativization of values is expressed in the lyrics of the *samba malandro* with its bittersweet eulogy of life on the margins, its irony and love of paradox. While in both the above examples we can see elements of counter-hegemonic resistance at work, social forces aiming at its containment are also seen as present. Sodré and other cultural historians point to the ways in which the expansion of the culture industry, the media and state appropriation of carnival have divested samba of its oppositional qualities in terms of both its production and consumption. As composers become professional musicians, samba loses its improvisatory character introducing a rift between producers and consumers, severing the links between the composer and the musical community. Similarly, with the official organization of the carnival parade by the state, the originally intricate and playful steps of samba tend to be replaced by acrobatic and stereotypically erotic performances, which draw on the body language of commercial advertising. In her analysis of the fate of samba under the regime of Getulio Vargas, D. Shaw traces the ways in which the *samba malandro* became the object of censorship and attempts to foster popular song which uncritically praises the nation. In a different vein, which departs from the mainstream Bakhtinian discourse on carnival as an oppositional expression of popular culture, anthropologists have pointed to the ways in which prevailing gender, race and class hierarchies are reproduced rather than inverted during the festive rituals of carnival. As N. Scheper-Hughes points out: 'Male cross-dressing *blocos* are a central component of *carnaval* play . . . Women rarely, if ever, cross-dress in *carnaval*. The role of those women who do participate in *carnaval* is to undress not to cross-dress . . . Moreover, the representation of female gender and sexuality . . . is a projection of male fantasies. It offers only a travesty of female gender and sexuality.'[30]

The debate on the relations of cultural power involved in the creation of samba as a popular cultural form acquired a further level of complexity as a result of the thesis put forward by Hermano Vianna that samba and its privileged place in Brazilian culture needs to be understood as a product of the relationships established between black musicians such as Pixinguinha and Sînho, and elite intellectuals and artists such as the composer Villa Lobos, the French poet Blaise Cendrars and the anthropologist Gilberto Freyre.[31] From this point of view, the development of samba was not simply the product of the musical community of poor blacks in Rio but was co-created by members of other classes and nations in their interactions with the creators of samba. Thus, for example, according to Vianna, Gilberto Freyre's highly influential theory that Brazil's unique identity and its claim to a place amongst modern nations lay in the 'impurity' of its racial and cultural mixture, the Brazilian modernist's and Blaise Cendrar's 'discovery' of black and popular Brazilian music contributed significantly to the development of samba as a specific genre of popular music. Vianna's work, then, raises important questions regarding popular culture: to what extent is the popular a 'hybrid' product which makes use of influences and symbols pertaining to other social classes and nations and to what extent is it an identifiable practice of a subordinate class which contests the domination of other classes? With specific respect to the development of samba: was it primarily the product of the processes of 'cultural mediation' that Vianna describes or rather an expression of the black population's evolving history?

An overview of the meanings and expressions of popular culture in Latin America in relation to notions of power and ideological conflict would be incomplete without an examination of the role of popular education and its connection to social movements and grass-roots organizations which have emerged in the region since the 1970s around demands for land, work, wages, housing and issues such as gender inequalities, human rights abuses, indigenous peoples and community development.

Organizationally, the practitioners, centres and networks of popular education in Latin America as a whole are brought together by the Latin American Centre for Adult Education (CEAAL).[32] Ideologically, the popular culture movement is grounded in an eclectic variety of intellectual approaches. It is informed partly by the work of the Peruvian thinker José Carlos Mariátegui, known for his attempt to combine Marxism with indigenous traditions, by the socialist education movements in Chile and Argentina in the early twentieth century, the socialist experiments in Cuba and Nicaragua as well as the notion espoused by the radical wing of the Catholic Church, that the purpose of popular education consists in helping 'the popular classes' to overcome oppression and injustice at different levels, economic, political and spiritual. It is also crucially informed by the work of the Brazilian pedagogue Paulo Freire for whom the process of emancipation from oppression was a political-pedagogical practice entailing analysis of the causes of oppression, transformative action as well as a continuous process of reflection, or *conscientizaçao*, on the ways in which external forms of oppression have been psychologically internalized. It is concerned with the relationship between the objective and subjective dimensions of oppression and emancipation and the relationship between practice and theory. As Freire notes, the precondition for the creation of a more just social order and the development of a counter-hegemonic culture is that 'Culture as an interiorised product which in turn conditions men's subsequent acts must become the object of men's knowledge so that they can perceive its conditioning power.'[33]

Methodologically, the popular education movement has made use of a broad variety of exciting and innovative techniques including the development of alternative media such as video and community radio networks and drama as tools to promote *conscientización*. Of particular importance to the popular education movement has been the work of the Brazilian dramatist Augusto Boal, author of the *Theatre of the Oppressed* who uses theatre as a way of enacting the social and existential problems experienced by the popular classes, while simultaneously creating, through drama, a vision of their transcendence.

Developing in parallel with the popular education movement in Latin America and informed by a conception of popular culture as emancipation from oppression, as the repository of the utopia of a more just and rehumanized world and as a counter-hegemonic practice is the particular genre of Latin American cinema which emerged in the 1950s and 1960s and gradually developed into a continental movement defined as New Latin American Cinema. Its approach, tenets and aesthetic devices have since been taken up outside the immediate context of Latin America and defined generically as a form of 'Third Cinema'. In this form of cinema 'the popular' exists in a different mode to the cinematic productions of the 1930s discussed above, that is, as a commitment to use cinema as a form of consciousness raising. It aimed to reveal through a realist and critical aesthetics the deformations and scars in the social fabric of Latin America brought about by underdevelopment, colonialism and imperialism, to depict the dreams, aspirations and sufferings of its people as expressed in the vitality and energy of its national and popular cultures, and in the unique features of Latin America as a continent.

The aim of *conscientización* was to be achieved, as the Cuban filmmaker Tomás Gutiérrez Alea stated, through the creation of a cinema in which the spectator 'ceases to be a spectator in the real world and that confronts reality not as a given but as a process in which one can have an active role'.[34] The utopian and counter-hegemonic conception of the social role of the New Cinema in Brazil is formulated in a particularly trenchant and succinct way by the Brazilian film maker Glauber Rocha when he comments on the 'aesthetics of hunger' through which he sought to bring to light the reality of underdevelopment in his films: 'We know – since we made these sad, ugly films, these screaming, desperate films where reason does not always prevail, that this hunger will not be cured by moderate governmental reforms and that the cloak of technicolor cannot hide, but only aggravate its tumours. Therefore, only a culture of hunger, weakening its own structures can surpass itself qualitatively.'[35]

The contemporary status of the popular

In recent years, critics have begun to examine how the structural changes brought about by processes of globalization have affected some of the key material and symbolic determinants of 'the popular'. They focus on the increasingly fragile status of 'the nation' as a political and economic reality and as a symbolic referent, as Latin America suffers the impact of cultural and economic globalizing forces.

According to Jean Franco, with the disembedding of social relations and cultures from their place of origin as a result of globalization, it is no longer clear where the popular as a distinctive practice of the popular classes, as a genre or as a form of political and cultural resistance is located: 'Migrations, the mixing of high-tech and "primitive", of mass-mediated and oral culture, the scrambling of languages as they cross borders, the scrambling of social classes who can no longer be securely stratified except through taste – all this has seriously compromised any notion of an undiluted popular culture "made by the people themselves".'[36]

In a similar vein, Ortiz argues that with the growth of an increasingly homogenous and international popular-mass culture connected primarily to the world of consumption, of fast food, Levis jeans, Disney and fashion, popular culture, whether as folklore or other forms of culture 'produced by the people' no longer plays the same pivotal role in defining national identity. According to Canclini, to the extent that globalization is occurring under the sign of neo-liberalism, politics and civic life are becoming a spectacle mediated by a commercialized transnational culture industry and the electronic media.[37]

It would seem, however, that, valid as the observations of Franco, Ortiz and Canclini may be, the tendencies which they highlight provide a significant although partial image of how contemporary change is affecting 'the popular', since globalization has also generated new local and transnational groupings within Latin America which remain tied to the idea of 'the popular' as a form of emancipation from relations of domination and as the affirmation of localized tradition.

Examples of such groupings are the growing trans-American indigenist movements in Latin America, which demand land, credit and access to basic services such as health and education as well as recognition of their local cultural identity and difference, the trans-Latin American popular education movement discussed above and Afro-American groupings which combine reference to a global experience of the black diaspora with an affirmation of local histories. The Landless Movement in Brazil offers another significant example of popular protest: it is a group seeking land reform which reconstitutes 'traditional' forms of mutual assistance based on reciprocity on the plots which they have been granted by the state. However, it has to be kept in mind that this reaffirmation of the 'local' does not necessarily entail a reinstatement of 'purer' earlier local forms of popular culture since they are increasingly mediated by their willing or unwilling insertion in the very global processes to which they are a response. A good illustration of this process of mediation is the language and tactics used by the Zapatista National Liberation Army in Mexico in its struggle for indigenous rights and its critique of the effect of neo-liberal economic policies on indigenous life. The denunciation of corporate global capitalism and its destructive effects on the local economy and culture of the indigenous peoples in southern Mexico is formulated by making use of concepts from economics and the social sciences and by disseminating their messages globally through the Internet. Their message however is couched in the lyrical mytho-poetic language of the indigenous culture that the Zapatistas defend.

The use of indigenous myth by the Zapatistas, as they struggle for their rights and local identity in the context of neo-liberal globalization, reveals the continuing contemporary relevance of popular culture conceived as 'folklore'. The specificity of popular culture in Latin America in this sense, lies in the fact that folk traditions persist and develop as part of the daily life and memory of poor urban and rural communities. In contrast to the European tendency to view 'folkore' as made up of practices of mere aesthetic and museological interest, 'folklore' in Latin America still exists as a means for the construction of identities: Afro, indigenous, gender, migrant. It also endures as a reference point and material for elite art and literature, and as I have tried to show, as a repository of themes, images and forms of communication used by 'mass culture'.

The intimate link with traditions of folklore has also contributed to shaping the very specific character of mass culture in Latin America: radio, television and popular music distributed by the culture industries have drawn extensively on 'folklore', and in particular on oral cultural traditions. As we saw, the character and national significance of the Latin American *telenovela* lies in the fact that, in contrast to US 'soaps', its themes relate to issues of overall national concern and that, as in oral narrative, these themes are woven into plots which change with reference to current events, blurring the boundaries between reality and fiction. Similarly, radio announcers use the cadences and verbal rhythms of oral culture while the popular music that is sold on the global market as 'world music' is steeped in 'folkloric' musical tradition. Popular culture understood as the struggle for hegemony, resistance and emancipation, has also been informed by urban and rural forms of 'folklore'. For example, the popular education movement, spanning a large part of the Latin American continent, and the very concept of *concientización* itself, are grounded in the assumption that popular forms of art, knowledge and ways of life contain a potential reservoir of emancipatory energies which a progressive political-pedagogic practice can transform into movements of resistance against oppression. The emancipatory role attributed to popular culture has also perhaps been greater than in the European context, since the structures and agents of oppression which the Cuban or Nicaraguan revolutions were aimed at, were not only contemporary and local but also imperialist and part of Latin America's colonial legacy. While in eighteenth- and nineteenth-century Europe the revolutionary bourgeoisie assumed the role of creating a democratic polity of citizens, in Latin America, in the absence of a strong bourgeoisie with an emancipatory ideology, social and grass-roots movements, such as the popular education movement, have seen the creation of a genuinely democratic public space as part of their role.

The three dimensions of popular culture established above for analytical purposes cannot therefore in reality be separated into three distinct genres. With the impact of globalizing forces, they are becoming increasingly interconnected, creating hybridized forms which at times reveal the homogenizing and diluting effect of mass culture, and at other times show the inventive retrieval of folk traditions and the creation of new forms of popular and high cultural forms. To follow these changes and to witness their vitality and utopian energies makes the study of the sphere of popular culture in Latin America a complex and rich field of inquiry.

Notes

1. See Raymond Williams, *Culture* (Glasgow, 1981).
2. M. Oettinger, *The Folk Art of Latin America* (New York, 1992), pp. 3–4.
3. M. Taussig, *The Devil and Commodity Fetichism in South America* (Chapel Hill NC, 1980), p. 17.
4. J. Rodríguez, *Our Lady of Guadalupe* (Austin TX 1994), p. 86.
5. J. Ross, 'The Virgin of the Metro Endorses Cárdenas', *Latin American Press* (24 September 1998), pp. 3–4.
6. Gerald Martin, *Journeys Through the Labyrinth* (London, 1989), p. 11.
7. N. García Canclini, *As culturas populares no capitalismo*, ed. brasiliense (São Paulo, 1983).
8. N. García Canclini, *Culturas híbridas* (Mexico, 1989).
9. Ibid., p. 265.
10. See L. Stephen, 'Weaving in the Fast Lane: Class, Ethnicity and Gender in Zapotec Craft Commercialisation', in J. Nash (ed.), *Crafts in the Modern World*, Buffalo NY, 1993, pp. 25–52.
11. J. de Carvalho, 'Notas para una revisión del concepto de cultura popular tradicional', paper given at a conference at the Institute of Folkloric Studies, Rio de Janeiro, September 1988, p. 6.
12. Ariel Dorfman and Armand Mattelart, *How to Read Donald Duck: Imperialist Ideology in the Disney Comic* (New York, 1975).
13. C. E. Martins, 'A questão da cultura popular', in O. Favero, *Cultura popular, educacão popular* (Rio de Janeiro, 1983), p. 39.
14. J. M Barbero, *De los medios a las mediaciones* (Barcelona, 1987).
15. R. Pareja, *Historia de la radio en Colombia* (Bogotá, 1987), p. 184.
16. See R Ortiz, *A Moderna Tradição Brasileira*, ed. brasiliense (São Paulo, 1988).
17. F. Weffort, *O populismo na política brasileira* (Rio de Janeiro, 1978), p. 71.
18. A. López, '"A Train of Shadows": Early Cinema and Modernity in Latin America', in V. Schelling (ed.), *Through the Kaleidoscope: The Experience of Modernity in Latin America* (London, 2000), pp. 148–76.
19. Barbero, *De los medios*, p. 181.
20. C. Monsiváis, *Mexican Postcards* (London, 1997), p. 89.
21. R. Mader, 'Globo Village, Television in Brazil', in T. Dowmunt, *Channels of Resistance, Global Television and Local Empowerment* (London, 1993), pp. 67–90.
22. A. López, 'Our Welcomed Guests: *Telenovelas* in Latin America', in Robert Allen (ed.), *To be Continued: Soap Operas Around the World* (London, 1995), pp. 256–75.
23. See Barbero, *De los medios*.
24. See T. Tufte, 'Living with the Rubbish Queen', PhD dissertation, University of Copenhagen, 1994.
25. Barbero, *De los medios*.

26. See A. Gramsci, *Selections from the Prison Notebooks* (London, 1971).

27. See D. Shaw, *The Social History of Brazilian Samba* (London, 1999).

28. M. Sodre, *Samba, o Dono do Corpo*, ed. Codecri (Rio de Janeiro, 1989), pp. 24 and 26.

29. M. Bakhtin, *Rabelais and His World* (Bloomington IN, 1984).

30. N. Scheper-Hughes, *Death Without Weeping* (Berkely CA, 1992), p. 502.

31. H. Vianna, *O Misterio do Samba* (Rio de Janeiro, 1995).

32. See L. Kane, *Popular Education and Social Change in Latin America* (Nottingham, 2001).

33. P. Freire, *Cultural Action for Freedom* (Harmondsworth, 1975), p. 35.

34. T. Gutiérrez Alea, *Dialéctica del espectador* (Mexico, 1983), p. 57.

35. Glauber Rocha, 'An Aesthetic of Hunger', in M. Martin (ed.), *New Latin American Cinema*, vol.I (Detroit MI, 1997), p. 246.

36. J. Franco, 'Globalization and the Crisis of the Popular' in T. Salman (ed.), *The Legacy of the Disinherited* (Amsterdam, 1996), pp. 263–79.

37. N. García Canclini, 'Contradictory Modernities and Globalization in Latin America', in V. Schelling (ed.), *Through the Kaleidoscope*, pp. 37–52.

Further reading

W. H. Beezley, and L. A. Curcio-Nagy, *Latin American Popular Culture*, Wilmington DE, 2000

E. P. Bueno, and T. Ceasar, *Imagination Beyond Nation: Latin American Popular Culture*, Pittsburgh PA, 1998

W. Rowe. and V. Schelling, *Memory and Modernity: Popular Culture in Latin America*, London and New York, 1991

T. Salman (ed.), *The Legacy of the Disinherited, Popular Culture in Latin America: Modernity, Globalization, Hybridity, Authenticity*, Amsterdam, 1996

Studies in Latin American Popular Culture, ed. Department of Modern Languages, University of Arizona, Tucson, 1985–

9

Art and architecture in Latin America

In the 1920s a group of Brazilian intellectuals produced an 'Anthropophagite Manifesto', arguing that they should devour the arts of Europe in order to nourish themselves and to produce a new Brazilian culture, vital and powerful. This image is a helpful way of articulating much of Latin American culture in the twentieth century, as artists and intellectuals have actively sought ways of affirming their strength and autonomy while still acknowledging Europe as an important source of ideas. The cannibal metaphor is also a useful way of approaching the art of earlier centuries: much of the best of colonial art and architecture is not a weak and belated echo of European innovations, as conventional notions of centre and periphery would have it, but a translation or transformation of imported ideas to suit a different context. This chapter will argue that the art and architecture of Latin America are interesting for their selective appropriations and manipulations, for their originality rather than for their dependence.

Colonial architecture: introducing Latinity

During the colonial period the dominant manifestation of European culture was architecture. Within a hundred years of Columbus's landfall in the Caribbean the Spanish settlers had superimposed a recognizably European imprint on the landscape from Mexico to Chile, burying the vast religious and urban complexes of the indigenous inhabitants, especially the Aztec and Inca, beneath uniform grid-plan towns, straight streets and arcaded squares, stone-fronted government buildings, palaces and town houses and, above all, religious foundations: churches and monasteries with generous dimensions, and imposing facades and bell-towers. Another hundred years on and allowing for local and regional differences, especially in the Portuguese territories of Brazil, this approximately Mediterranean pattern extended from California to Patagonia. Even in the countryside, where the land itself was still largely shaped by traditional native American agricultural practices, the cupolas and bell-towers of the parish churches effectively 'Latinized' the landscape.[1]

This apparently European appearance is not a copy of contemporary European practice, however. The ubiquitous grid-plan town is an adaptation of theoretical notions of city planning, ultimately Roman in origin, and the resulting urban regularity conveniently served to demonstrate the new colonial order, both to the settlers themselves and to their native subjects. The architecture, too, exhibits features appropriate to the specific requirements of Latin America. The missionary church, for example, was typically a single nave structure fronting a large walled atrium organized as, in effect, a second church in the open air: an open chapel served as both high altar and pulpit and, in the corners of the atrium, small open-sided pavilions called *posas* could be used as lateral shrines or altars.[2] This open-air church provided a training ground for the indigenous peoples, an intermediate space between paganism and Christianity. The open-air church found its grandest expression in Mexico but versions recur throughout Spanish territories in America, from New Mexico to Chile and Argentina, and is without European precedent. In stylistic terms, the architecture of the early colonial period tended to be plain and functional, even austere, with the emphasis on the underlying grammar of the esoteric language of classical architecture. Again this is closer to the European *idea* of architecture than it is to contemporary practice. In particular, the prevalence of the Doric, traditionally characterized as the oldest of the classical orders, suggests a need to iterate the underlying foundations of Mediterranean civilization in its New World manifestations.

Another striking innovation in Spanish American architecture is the development of a clear visual code to denote function: on entering a church one passes beneath an arch, while with a secular building, even the palace of a viceroy, the entrance is lintelled. In Europe these two forms of entrance were applied arbitrarily to either religious or secular buildings. In Spanish America the consistent use of the arched portal on religious foundations serves to set the church apart from all other buildings, both Spanish and indigenous, and framed with a set of orthodox classical mouldings it would have been recognized by Europeans as a reworking of a Roman triumphal arch. The parallels between Spain's American enterprise and Roman imperial expansion were not lost on contemporaries, and the use of the classical motif of military victory on the facade of the Christian church brought together the ideas of secular and religious control in a peculiarly apposite way. On the other hand, all the early colonial churches of Spanish America were built using indigenous labour and close attention to detail can reveal evidence of the way native craftsmen manipulated and adapted these buildings in order to accommodate them to their own spiritual universe. Recent research has revealed that the orientation of rural churches repeatedly takes into account the local geography, placing each within a traditional network of sacred mountain peaks; occasional stones with cryptic carvings placed high on a bell-tower or on a plain expanse of wall are precisely aligned to certain movements of the sun or stars; and even the carving on the main portal can incorporate ancient calendrical and cosmological knowledge.[3] But identifying such elements requires detailed scholarship and understanding of native culture and does not undermine a broader view of early colonial architecture as essentially European in form and function. In the seventeenth century the rather stern bookishness of the architecture of the early colonial period gives way to expressive exuberance. Or rather, the underlying structures remain largely unchanged beneath the new highly ornamented overlay. Typically, the church facade becomes the focus of ever-increasing elaboration in the style of a multistorey altarpiece, with a profusion of niches, statuary and richly decorative shallow-relief carving. In church interiors the decoration breaks out of the confines of the altarpiece to spread up the walls and over the ceiling.

Brazilian colonial architecture differs from that of Spanish America. It is interesting that despite the great distances between the various regional centres (Recife, Salvador, Rio de Janeiro, Minas Gerais) they have more in common with each other, architecturally speaking, than they do with the Spanish colonies. The roots of Brazil's distinctive architecture lie in the period 1580 to 1640, when Portugal was under Spanish domination and its resentment found expression in a strongly nationalist cultural identity.[4] During this period, developments in Portugal included a marked secular quality to religious buildings and this in turn was to become one of the most striking aspects of Brazilian architecture. Exterior walls are broken by numerous windows, galleries and verandas, making them appear more like palaces than churches. In plan, too, Brazil's churches are very different. In Spanish America the prevailing tendency is for a very simple longitudinal plan that focuses attention up a long nave to the high altar and chancel. Architecturally the chancel marks the climax of the design: it is as wide as the nave, and often higher, better lit, with more elaborate vaulting, and with a polygonal apse. In Brazil the inverse is true. The nave is generally a more centralized, well-lit, multidirectional space, and the volumes tend to close down rather than expand around the high altar. The Brazilian interest in undulating walls, curved facades, round towers and elliptical naves is almost entirely absent in Spanish America where the solid rectangular ground plans of the sixteenth century persist, and exterior walls tend to be flat and plain, and unrelated to the decoration of the facade, unlike in Brazil where church design is much more unified. Typically, a Brazilian church will be held together visually by a succession of giant-order pilasters and an encircling pedestal and entablature, the stone work contrasting with the whitewashed wall surfaces between. In Brazil the architectural decoration of the exterior is restrained and largely abstract rather than iconographic. Lavish decorative detail is concentrated on the interior.

Colonial art: emerging diversity

Even allowing for the differences between Brazil and elsewhere, however, the architecture of the whole of colonial Latin America can be characterized as relatively homogeneous: grid-plan urban centres around a central square; the larger buildings with stone mouldings at least around the doors and windows; churches distinguishable from a distance by their bell-towers; the widespread use of whitewash, tiled roofs, metal window grilles and wooden shutters. This relative homogeneity reflects the nature of architectural patronage: founding towns and constructing major buildings was inevitably in the hands of the small colonial elite, Europeans and high-ranking creoles, usually holding high office in government or religious institutions, who were themselves relatively homogeneous. Painting, sculpture and other forms of artistic production are more complex, however, and it can be helpful to think of these in terms of three main overlapping categories: a layer (sometimes very superficial) of European introductions, which affects and is affected by regional and also by local considerations. European introductions include artistic categories (easel paintings, altarpieces, sculptures), materials (oil on canvas, polychrome wood) and imagery, above all the imagery of the Christian church, all of which were without direct precedent in Native American culture. Once in Latin America the regional factors which condition this superimposed art include the existence of indigenous skills and techniques (featherwork and stone carving in Mexico, for example, and tapestry weaving in the Andes), very different visual languages (the pictographic texts of Mexico, the geometric masonry of Peru) and alternative ideologies (Native American, African and, over time, distinctive American perspectives amongst the creole elite). Local factors – the impact of an individual or group of individuals, a particular local circumstance or belief – produce, in turn, pockets of distinctive, geographically circumscribed artistic production. The iconography of Christianity, for example, filters down from the European models, and is progressively adapted and transformed according to regional or local needs. So, too, an iconography both from and of the Americas, both real and imagined, permeates the imported European art and culture at all levels.

Catholic Christianity provided a common visual currency, introducing European styles and techniques of painting and sculpture (as of architecture) and a standardized core of Christian iconography: the Crucified Christ, the Virgin and Child, and selected saints and angels. The visual arts imported to Latin America were not Spanish, nor Portuguese, nor Iberian so much as European, a mix from many different European countries. Artists arrived from Spain, Italy, Germany and the Netherlands, and enterprising merchants imported paintings, sculptures and especially engravings. From the middle of the seventeenth century the influence of Zurbarán, who together with his assistants produced numerous paintings for the American market, was felt throughout the Spanish territories; even more important were the numerous engravings after works by Rubens which circulated far and wide, reinforcing the strong Flemish influence on colonial art.[5] French and Flemish engravings provided the source material for a distinctive feature of Brazilian colonial art: the blue and white tile paintings imported from Portugal representing religious and mythological scenes that decorate the interiors of churches and cloisters along the coast.

There is no clean break between this imported Euro-Christian imagery and the emergence of regional styles and categories of art, more a sort of sliding scale.[6] At one extreme there are works which achieve great originality while working entirely within a European frame of reference, as in Cristóbal de Villalpando's tremendous 1685 painting of *The Triumph of the Eucharist* in the Sacristy of Mexico City, which draws on but does not copy from engravings after Rubens.[7] Another powerfully original artist was the Brazilian sculptor known as Aleijadinho, the 'Little Cripple', whose tour de force is the sculptures (1800–5) lining the ceremonial approach to the church in Congonhas do Campo, Minas Gerais, a series of inspired transformations of Flemish engravings.[8]

Accurate copying from European models is more common and copyists were sometimes so proficient that a regional accent is not apparent. Indigenous artists Juan Gerson in Mexico in the sixteenth century and Diego Quispe Tito in Peru in the seventeenth both transformed Flemish engravings into paintings with complete assurance and understanding of European representational conventions. For others these conventions were less important, especially the various devices developed in Renaissance Europe to achieve a convincing representation of space on a two-dimensional surface (single-point perspective, foreshortening, shading, scale). In the Cusco school of painting, for example, flat patterns of gold are applied over the contours of the figures to create highly decorative images where the two-dimensional concerns of fabric and the three-dimensional concerns of European representation are held in tense juxtaposition. This points to a more general characteristic of Andean colonial painting: the careful attention given to different types of fabric testifies to the persistent significance of textiles, so highly valued in Inca times. The introduction of native flora and fauna, of local geographical features and local costume details all serves to distance colonial production from European prototypes.

As well as the modification of existing traditions, new categories of art evolve. In Mexico these include the famous caste paintings which categorize the different racial types resulting from the mixing of Spanish, African and Indian blood, the *biombos*, painted wooden screens, and the *enconchados*, painted wooden panels inlaid with mother-of-pearl, the last two often including narrative scenes of the Spanish conquest of Mexico. In their various ways these manifest the growing pride of the creole elite in their specifically Mexican, rather than European, roots. In the Andes, too, there were new subjects of regional relevance, most famously the numerous paintings of angels with guns, swords or pikes. When in their traditional location, on either side of the nave of a church, these richly dressed figures provided a military guard of honour for the high altar.[9] These, like the Mexican examples, have no direct European iconographic precedent but respond to particular Andean circumstances: the taste for expensive textiles, military parades and spectacle, and the persistent indigenous belief in spirit beings that can mediate between the celestial and earthly spheres. The figure of Santiago became popular in the Andes for similar reasons: for the Europeans, he represented the triumph of Christianity over first the Moors and then the Indians; for the Indians, Santiago galloping across the sky with his flashing thunderbolt overlapped with the indigenous Illapa, god of lightning, who, although dangerous, presages the rains on which the fertility of the crops depends.[10]

As well as such regional manifestations of colonial art, there are also very local initiatives that again can come from any one of the many different sectors of colonial society. At the end of the sixteenth century in Tunja in Colombia, for example, the houses of the colonial nobility were decorated with intricate allegories made up of emblematic plants, animals and Christian symbols. The different elements can be traced to a variety of sources – French, Flemish, German and Spanish – but the combinations are unique, suggesting that the patrons were highly cultured intellectuals who imported the most up-to-date books and prints from Europe, and who enjoyed devising their own complex religious programmes.[11] In Bolivia the mountain of silver of Potosí was the object of local devotion, and artists represented it thinly disguised as the Virgin Mary, a head and hands added to the triangular peak, so visually conflating the Christian mother of god with the Andean earth mother Pachamama.[12] Throughout Latin America, regional and local concerns could condition the iconography of a church. Santa Efigênia in Ouro Preto, Brazil, for example, was built by a black brotherhood of slaves and freed slaves. The richly painted and gilded carving of the interior includes marine imagery such as cowrie shells and lobsters, and this, together with the choice of saint on each of the altars, suggests links with the Africo-Brazilian cult of the *orixas*.[13]

The different levels of local, regional and European are not, of course, mutually exclusive and over time there has been considerable exchange between them. Aspects of Euro-Christian culture are taken up and incorporated into local production. A successful local development can attract wider interest, and there are famous cases where what began as a very local phenomenon grew into a symbol of international significance. Devotion to the miraculous image of the Virgin of Guadalupe in Mexico is a case in point. It began as an entirely local cult – tradition holds that the Virgin revealed herself to the Indian Juan Diego in 1531 on the hill of Tepeyac – but has grown into one of the most popular pilgrimage destinations, and one of the most famous Christian images, in the world. Her Mexican identity was confirmed when she was invoked against the Spaniards during the battle for independence in the early nineteenth century, and her standard was carried by Zapata's troops during the revolution of 1910. Throughout the twentieth century she has been endlessly incorporated into works of high and popular art across the Americas to become an icon of Latin American identity. But this is to get ahead of ourselves.

Nineteenth-century transitions

Towards the end of the eighteenth century there was a widespread shift away from baroque and rococo extravagance in favour of the plainer neoclassical style of art and architecture, a style which implied – as in France – a degree of moral and political regeneration and helped to provide the climate for political change. The independence movements were informed by European ideas, by the philosophy of the Enlightenment and the politics of the French Revolution, so that in looking for models on which to base their new countries the creole and mestizo elites of Latin America looked to Europe and above all to France for guidance. In Spanish America, therefore, the struggle for independence from Spain produced – somewhat ironically – a new and more focused dependence on Europe in the field of the visual arts, and specifically on France, as the newly defined territories tried to build the cultural and institutional infrastructure of independent nations.[14]

But as well as looking outwards to Europe, Latin Americans also began to look afresh at their own countries. So, for example, the new sense of nationhood created a demand for portraits of the heroes of the independence movement, and a new interest in the land and landscape over which they themselves now had control. The young national governments sought to improve the cultural and educational levels of their countries: as well as universities and national museums, they founded art institutions modelled on the French Academy, they imported French artists and architects to teach in them and they provided grants for students to study in Paris. In the nineteenth century the urgent need to record and celebrate the events of recent history coincided with and contributed to the renewed interest in contemporary artistic practice in

Europe, especially France. Just as in France David adapted the grand style of academic history painting to commemorate events from the French Revolution, so in Latin America artists began to extend the traditional range of subject matter to include aspects of their own recent history. Important examples include the Colombian José María Espinosa (1796–1883), who fought in the campaign for independence and painted landscapes and scenes of the battles in which he had participated, and Uruguayan Juan Manuel Blanes (1830–1901), who captured the dusty vastness of the pampa, the lonely life of the gaucho and the pain as well as the glory of the war of the Triple Alliance.

The independence movements were largely headed by the creole elite. In rejecting Spanish political control this elite did not immediately reject Spain's role in the conquest and settlement of the New World because to do so would be to reject the role that their own forebears had played in this process. In art, therefore, the recuperation of history included reclaiming – and mythologizing – the achievements of the first conquerors. In Peru, Ignacio Merino (1817–76) produced grandiose paintings celebrating Columbus, a theme which Juan Cordero (1824–84), and José María Obregón (1832–1902) also popularized in Mexico. This was gradually extended to include subjects from pre-Columbian history, and eventually, by the end of the century, Mexican artists such as Felix Parra (1845–1919) and Leandro Izaguirre (1867–1941) could paint large history paintings that were firmly rooted in the European academic tradition but which criticized the brutality of the conquering Spaniards and their destruction of indigenous culture. The other important recuperation was that of the landscape. The finest example is that of José María Velasco (1840–1912) whose Mexican landscapes are imbued with a sense of history, but are also full of promise for the future.

In architecture the nineteenth century was a period of eclecticism. The neoclassical style remained the choice for government buildings, and capital cities everywhere sprouted pedimented porticoes and columniated facades to project a cosmopolitan image and to bolster their government's self-confidence. The architects were frequently foreigners: Paraguay's Government House in Asunción, dating from the middle of the century, was built by the Italian Alejandro Ravizza; Chile's National Congress building of 1848 in Santiago is by the French L. A. Hénault; the Capitol in Bogotá, begun in 1847, is by the English architect Thomas Reed. The last decades of the century saw the construction of numerous theatres for which a rather more decorated *beaux-arts* style was felt appropriate (the Teatro Colon in Buenos Aires begun in 1889, the Teatro Guzman Blanco in Caracas of 1881 and the Opera House in Manaus opened in 1896), while neo-Gothic was the choice for churches.

Twentieth-century art: pioneers and cannibals

Until about 1920 much of Latin America remained locked into the traditions of academic figure and landscape painting. Impressionism had a limited impact: it arrived late – while European artists were already busy dismembering the relationship between perception and representation to produce cubism (Picasso, Braque) and abstraction (Kandinsky, Mondrian) – and it remained an almost exclusively decorative style rather than a challenge to the old order. From the 1920s, however, as the economies grew and horizons expanded, so the hope and excitement which modernization was generating in cultural circles in Europe began to spread. Latin America was very receptive to modernity. The possibility of building a new, modern nation that could take its place on the international stage on equal terms with the countries of the Old World was very attractive. During the 1930s and 1940s, a number of the wealthier countries of Latin America embraced the new forms of art and new styles and techniques of architecture, because modernity was widely equated with industrialization and economic development, and also from a sense of social responsibility: a modern nation was one with a healthy, educated people and hygienic standards of living. Modern art and architecture could help to achieve these.

The first major modern movement in art in Latin America was Mexican muralism. One of the most persistent strands in Latin American art in the last eighty years has been an engagement with political and social issues, and the struggle for social justice. This in turn has gone hand in hand with a desire for authentic forms of self-expression and freedom from cultural dependency. These preoccupations have taken many different forms but Mexican muralism was the first, and its influence was the most far-reaching.[15] Muralism flourished in Mexico in the years immediately following the Revolution as a result of a combination of circumstances: a climate of revolutionary optimism and cultural experimentation that challenged traditional Eurocentricism; a small but strong group of relatively mature artists of energy, ideas and ability; and a visionary minister of education, José Vasconcelos. Vasconcelos believed that Mexico was destined to play a central role on the international stage. He understood that ideas could be more quickly assimilated through images than any other medium, and he had the courage to allocate the funds, and the walls of public buildings, to the artists to do with as they saw fit. The muralists shared a belief in the power of art to transform society for the better, to challenge social, political, economic and cultural stereotypes, and to enrich the intellectual life of their country, and during the 1920s and 1930s, they covered miles of wall with paintings representing aspects of Mexico's past and present and the future to which all aspired.[16] Although it is representational and often narrative in form, it is important to recognize Mexican muralism as a *modern* movement. It was modernizing in intent, in that it challenged the old order – culturally, socially and politically. By definition, it was a public, accessible form of art: it was not a commodity that could be bought and sold by a wealthy elite. Its purpose was to educate, inform, enlighten, politicize and so empower the general public, in particular the working classes.

The muralist movement was not a unified force, however. The three leaders took different directions and did not always see eye to eye. Diego Rivera (1886–1957) sought to promote a pluralistic vision of Mexican society by drawing on the rich heritage of the pre-Columbian past and contemporary popular culture, and he investigated pre-Columbian styles and techniques in an effort to create an aesthetic language that was new and Mexican.[17] He was deeply influenced by native pictographic traditions of communication and sought to develop a modern equivalent, a visual language that could be read like a book. The art of José Clemente Orozco (1883–1949) is less optimistic: he saw both the pre-Columbian past and the revolutionary present in a more negative light, the former as barbarous, the latter often tarnished by corruption and cruelty.[18] He offers no comforting narratives and his expressive, aggressive technique serves as a metaphor of Mexico's harsh, contradictory reality. David Alfaro Siqueiros (1898–1976) was much the most politically active of the three, and an internationalist both ideologically and artistically. In his art he deliberately avoided traditional materials and methods, preferring to use modern industrial paints and spray guns.[19] He looks forward to a fully socialist future where the workers will have won the right to the benefits of the modern industrial era, and his often fragmented and complex imagery does not patronize or make concessions to his audience.

Figure 1 David Alfaro Siqueiros, 'From the University to the People and the People to the University', 1952, Rectorate Building, UNAM campus, Mexico City.

The Mexican muralist movement is undoubtedly one of the most important manifestations of twentieth-century Latin American culture. Its impact elsewhere in the region, as well as in the US and Europe, has been enormous. The work of Rivera, Orozco and Siqueiros in New York, Detroit, Los Angeles and San Francisco triggered a home-grown muralist movement in the US.[20] The influence of the Mexicans on Picasso's first mural and almost his only major explicitly propagandistic work of art – his famous *Guernica* of 1937 – is unmistakable even though the artist himself would have denied it. In Latin America Mexican-influenced muralism has recurred whenever artists have felt the need to make a clear, public statement in a language that has not been borrowed from outside. It surfaced in Ecuador and Colombia in the 1930s, in Venezuela and Peru in the 1940s and in Bolivia in the 1950s. It reappeared in revitalized form before and during Allende's Chile, and after the coup exiled Chilean artists reintroduced their new brand of muralism to the US and Europe, and, most vigorously, to Central America. Muralism is alive and well in Chiapas in southern Mexico. Sometimes the influence of Mexican muralism's bold figurative style and tendency to social content can be sensed in the work of artists who are not primarily muralists: in Ecuador in the social realism of Eduardo Kingman (1914–98) and Osvaldo

Guayasamín (1919–99), for example, and in Colombia in the pneumatic figures that people the canvases of Fernando Botero (b. 1932) or the anthropomorphic gourds of Ramiro Arango (b. 1946).

In Brazil muralism enjoyed some popularity in the 1930s but found a distinctively nationalist voice when Cândido Portinari (1903–62) took the idea of a public mural art and translated it from painting into the more traditional Brazilian medium of blue and white tiles. Unlike Mexico, where the muralists' most important early commissions were for walls of existing buildings and where commissions for new buildings have resulted in a rather awkward relationship between mural and architecture, Portinari's tile murals are satisfyingly integrated into modern structures. His whimsical work for Niemeyer's equally whimsical church of São Francisco in Pampulha, Minas Gerais, of 1942, is a good example.[21]

Generally speaking, however, from at least 1920, Brazil followed its own trajectory. The 1920s saw the emergence of an influential group of avant-garde intellectuals who developed the theory of anthropophagy as a strategy for addressing the unavoidable influence of European culture. In the famous Anthropophagite Manifesto of 1928, Oswald de Andrade argued that the way forward was for Brazilians to be cultural cannibals, to feed on foreign imports and ingest them, and in this way to produce art that was entirely their own. The work of Tarsila do Amaral (1886–1973) and Anita Malfatti (1889–1964) of the earlier 1920s had in effect already been doing just this: internalizing aspects of European modern movements such as Fauvism and cubism, but transforming them into paintings that are Brazilian in form, colour, content and intention. Amaral's paintings of strange figures seated in tropical landscapes are versions of the monsters of the medieval imagination, which Europeans believed they would encounter in their explorations into the unknown, but the European originals have been reborn as powerful new native myths.[22]

This reflexivity, this deliberate distancing from the modern movements of Europe, characterizes much of the best of twentieth-century Latin American art, but it takes many different forms. Joaquín Torres-García (1874–1949) returned to his native Uruguay in 1934 after over forty years abroad. His aim was to establish an autonomous artistic tradition in South America by bringing together the ancient geometric and abstract tendencies of pre-Columbian Andean art with the aesthetic theories of Piet Mondrian and Theo van Doesburg of the Dutch *De Stijl* movement, while also embracing the public, pedagogical responsibilities of art as articulated by the Mexican muralists. His *Cosmic Monument* of 1939 in the Parque Rodó in Montevideo synthesizes ideas and art forms: this piece – a stone wall carved in shallow relief with a repertoire of what Torres-García considered universal symbols – is sculpture, mural and architecture as well as a glyphic text. It has its roots firmly in both ancient Inca masonry and contemporary European abstraction but the result is something new and different. In 1943 Torres-García founded a school where he disseminated his ideas, and his wider importance lies in the way in which he validated abstraction as an authentically Latin American mode of expression for future generations, especially in Uruguay and Argentina.[23]

From the mid-1940s Argentina had a flourishing artistic avant-garde. Members of the *Madí* movement founded in 1945, including in particular Gyula Kosice (b. 1924), produced works that were deliberately difficult to classify. Neither pictures nor sculpture, they are often made of moveable sections, so encouraging the intervention of the spectator and diminishing the traditional role of the artist as autonomous creative genius.[24] Military regimes are notoriously conservative in cultural terms and so the very existence of Madí and its rival movement *Arte Concreto-Invención* under Perón was in itself radical. In fact, abstraction has often flourished under repressive political regimes in Latin America, regimes that would not tolerate the explicitly political purposes and content of the social realist tradition of Mexican muralism and its followers. In the 1950s, under the dictatorship of Pérez Jiménez, Venezuela produced autochthonous avant-garde movements – constructivism and kineticism – with overlapping interests in the optical vibrations produced by juxtaposed colours and lines in both two and three dimensions. The work of Alejandro Otero (b. 1921), Jesus Rafael Soto (b. 1923), Gego (b. 1914) and Carlos Cruz-Diez (b. 1923) destabilizes the sense of sight and prefigures Op-art movements elsewhere. The exceptional position enjoyed by abstract art in Venezuela owes a great deal to the architect Carlos Raúl Villanueva (1900–75) who in the early 1950s persuaded the military government to provide funds for a range of artists of predominantly abstract tendencies from Europe, the US and Venezuela to contribute to the new University City in Caracas. The results blend in with the architecture to such an extent that it would be artificial to try and classify them as one or other. Alexander Calder's cloud-like stabiles in the ceiling of the Aula Magna function as acoustic shields, Alejandro Otero's stained glass is both abstract mural and structural wall, and the protective grilles on air-conditioning vents are metal sculptures by Victor Vasarély.[25]

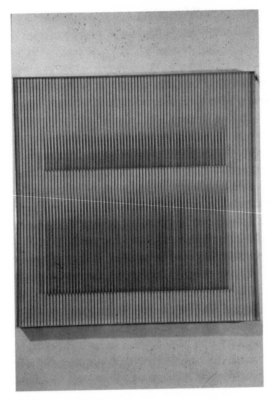

Figure 2   Carlos Cruz-Diez, 'Physichromie No. 1270', Mixed Media, 1990.

In Brazil, under the military dictatorship of the later 1960s, the neo-concretists experimented with interactive forms of art in all manner of more or less subversive ways. Lygia Clark (1920–88) exploited sensations of touch, first with manipulable sculptures that acquired a life of their own under the hands of the participant spectator, and later with devices like interlinked garments that required people to explore each others' bodies. Hélio Oiticica (1937–80) worked with people from the Rio *favelas*, creating ephemeral art works and carnival-like events in the streets, or introducing fragile shantytown-like structures into Rio's art galleries.[26] The influence of the neo-concretists is evident in the work of artists of the younger generation in Brazil. Ernesto Neto's (b. 1964) penetrable sculptures of translucent lycra can be seen as direct descendants of the work of Clark and Oiticica.

Figure 3 Amilcar de Castro, Untitled, 1980.

Latin American abstraction has taken many forms and, as elsewhere, has often been both a celebration of and a challenge to ideas of progress and modernity. The neo-concretists' preoccupation with physical engagement with works of art can be seen as one response to the limitations of a machine-driven world. The work of Sérgio Camargo (b. 1930) represents another: although the complex geometry of his pure white constructivist reliefs suggests the use of modern industrial materials, they are in fact of wood and Carrara marble. Like a latter-day Torres-García, he often creates sculptures that suggest architecture: walls that go no-where and support nothing. Fellow Brazilian Amilcar de Castro (1920–2002) does something similar but using a more modern material. He takes immensely thick sheets of solid iron and cuts and bends them to shape as if they were of thin card. The material has lost its function and gained grace. Colombian Edgar Negret (b. 1920) also uses iron, bolting together a series of similar-shaped pieces to create organic forms out of inorganic matter. From the older generation in Argentina Lúcio Fontana (1899–1968) produced slashed and pierced canvases that offer a multiplicity of readings. From the traditional perspective of representational art, the illusion of space here becomes reality; from the modernist perspective, the cerebral calm of the uninterrupted flat surface has become the locus of physical violence.

Not surprisingly, the existence of these two vigorous branches of modern art in Latin America – muralism on the one hand and abstraction on the other – has generated creative tensions between the two. Part of this can be attributed to the involvement of the US. During the 1940s and 1950s contemporary US art was promoted in Latin America via the touring shows organized by the Museum of Modern Art of New York as part of the Cold War propaganda offensive. These exhibitions sought to promote US art and to make a strict division between figurative and abstract art (US abstract expressionism in particular) or, as the US authorities saw it, between politically motivated social realism, and politically neutral abstraction, which was in turn presented as a choice between the old-fashioned and the modern.[27] Their prime target was Mexican muralism and its many offshoots around the region (including in the US itself), but Latin America has strongly resisted any such simple polarization. Intellectuals devised various strategies for countering cultural dependency, whether real or perceived, while cultural exchange – much of it fruitful – inevitably continued and its impact was considerable but, as ever, the borrowings were not passive. In Latin America, works that suggest a debt to abstract expressionism often incorporate a figurative element, and also, vice versa, representation is often reduced to the pure essentials. Artists have used the sheer sensuality of large areas of pure colour to draw the spectator into a narrative content that is often powerfully painful and disturbing. The attraction of delicious paintwork can make the observer feel uncomfortably complicit in a scene of horrific political repression, for example. In recent years Guillermo Kuitca (b. 1961) of Argentina, Jacopo Borges (b. 1931) of Venezuela, José Balmés (b. 1927) of Chile and the Brazilian Sirón Franco (b. 1947) have all exploited this effect in different ways.

Another recurrent element in the modern art of Latin America is that of surrealism. In the 1930s the surrealists, and André Breton in particular, had been drawn to Latin America precisely because of its otherness – the ancient pre-Columbian past, and the Native American and African contributions to the dynamic popular culture of the present – and the ways these non-Western artistic manifestations contradicted and subverted the more conventional norms of European art or Eurocentric art in Latin America. In the earlier twentieth century, surrealism helped to validate these alternative, authentically Latin American elements in the Latin American artist's world and its influence has continued to be felt by the younger generation. Cubans Wifredo Lam (1902–82)

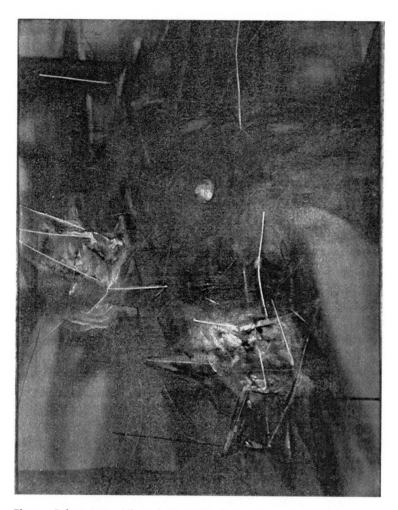

Figure 4 Roberto Matta, 'The End of Everything', 1942.

and José Bédia (b. 1959) draw on Afro-Cuban culture, Mexicans
Rufino Tamayo (1899–1991) and Francisco Toledo (b. 1940) on ancient
Mesoamerica, Brazilians Tunga (b. 1952) and Roberto Evangelista
(b. 1946) on Amazonian iconography, to suggest or reinvent different
mythical or spiritual constructs. Chilean Roberto Matta (1911–2002)
creates complex multidimensional spaces that seem to offer a window
into the thought-processes of the brain. Often a surrealist element is
combined with elements from a different tradition. Fernando de Szyszlo

(b. 1925) in Peru, for example, is stylistically indebted to abstract expressionism but his content is closer to surrealism, evoking the psychologically unsettling world of ghostly, vaguely malevolent spirits from the pre-Columbian past. The other 'other' – woman – is exemplified by Frida Kahlo (1907–55), who investigates herself, her own body and her personal relationship with Mexico with an agonizing frankness that is deliberately closer to the untrained productions of popular artists (also dear to the surrealists) than to the knowing sophistication of so much of European modernism.[28] For Kahlo and others, popular art has been an attractive source of inspiration: produced by the people, for the people, it offers an authentic alternative to the grand narratives both of European art and of the Mexican muralists. Intimate in scale and of local or personal import, popular art was traditionally produced to meet a particular practical or spiritual need and so had an urgency and rationale that many felt to be lacking in 'high' art. From the 1920s to the present, numerous other Latin American women have pursued parallel paths, exploring the overlapping worlds of the body, the home, the Church and popular art: from Maria Izquierdo (1902–55) to Rocío Maldonado (b. 1951) in Mexico, from Amelia Pelaez (1897–1968) to Ana Mendieta (1948–85) in Cuba, from Anita Malfatti (1889–1964) to Katie van Scherpenberg (b. 1940) in Brazil.[29]

The post-modern era in Latin America, as elsewhere, has resulted in a fragmentation of the traditional languages, ever-greater diversity of expression and increasing attention to issues of globalization. Artists throughout the region have found ways of addressing (exploiting, exposing, negotiating, subverting, accommodating) the issues of global capitalism and international finance, the international art market, the homogenization of culture, the loneliness of the Internet, the ever-changing nature of identity, the increasing isolation of individuals and the consequent focus on the nature of self. All these are placed under the artistic microscope in different ways: Alfredo Jaar (b. Chile, 1956) has addressed the rape of Latin America's natural resources, Eugenio Dittborn (b. Chile, 1943) the continuing political repression, Cuban American Coco Fusco (b. 1960) the persistent arrogance and prejudice of the 'First' world towards Latin and Native America.[30] The pervasive influence of the US in Latin America is a recurrent theme. In Colombia in 1976, Antonio Caro (1950) produced a print with the single word *Colombia* in the distinctive cursive lettering of Coca-Cola, while more recently, Nadín Ospina (b. 1960) has taken characters from Disney and

Figure 5   Nadin Ospína, 'Idol with doll', 2000.

transformed them into stone 'idols' in the manner of the ancient pre-Columbian culture of San Agustín. Brazilian Cildo Meireles (b. 1948) forged zero dollar bills and added subversive slogans to Coca-Cola bottles before putting them back into circulation. The self-portraits in video and in crayon on paper of Eduardo Padilha (1964) also from Brazil, are painful explorations of self-abuse, self-effacement, self-delusion. Digital art disseminated via the Internet is increasingly popular as a way of reaching new audiences, and on equal terms with other artists around the globe.

Twentieth-century architecture: constructing modernity

Architecture has always been used by ambitious governments as a way of demonstrating their power and their success, and nowhere more so than in Latin America in the twentieth century.[31] The English-speaking world has tended to forget that in the middle decades of the century Latin America was held in high regard, especially in the United States, for the quantity, quality and diversity of its new architecture. Governments of quite different persuasions sponsored networks of public schools and hospitals, extensive housing schemes and university cities, and dared to do so in an uncompromisingly modern language. Numerous books and articles of the 1960s and 1970s celebrated Latin America's adventurous architectural spirit, and in particular the way it achieved a distinctively national or continental flavour by using local materials or motifs, or by incorporating murals, mosaics or sculptures into the composition.[32] During the twentieth century, the problem of a style that could be both modern and national preoccupied architects and critics from Finland to Japan, and Latin America provided some imaginative answers.

The issue of national identity in relation to architecture arises at the beginning of the century. For most countries, the French *beaux-arts* tradition that had been so popular in the late nineteenth century, especially with dictators like Mexico's Porfirio Díaz and Venezuela's Guzmán Blanco, was replaced by various reworkings of colonial architecture. This was a remarkably Pan-American phenomenon and included cross-fertilization from the Californian mission style (itself based on the architecture of Mexico and New Mexico) and the Iberian Renaissance and *mudéjar* traditions.[33] The neo-colonial style served various purposes. Schools lent themselves particularly well to colonial-inspired designs that are part monastery, part hacienda: the Escuela Benito Juárez in Mexico City of 1923 and the Escola Normal of Rio de Janeiro of 1928, for example, both make use of enclosed arcaded courtyards, arched doors and elliptical windows with stone detailing, and free-standing facades with ogival profiles decorated with stone finials.

The neo-colonial style also provided a way for countries to construct an architectural heritage to match their colonial importance, so in Lima, for example, where repeated earthquakes left the city centre with little evidence of its earlier political and economic significance, the Plaza de Armas was reinvented in a grand colonial mould: the Archbishop's Palace, complete with wooden balconies and richly carved stone portal, dates from 1924, and the Government Palace from 1937, while the cathedral facade was somewhat generously reconstructed in the 1940s. Guatemala City has little genuine colonial architecture (the original capital of the region had to be abandoned following an earthquake in 1773), but during the 1930s and 1940s several neo-colonial public buildings, including the National Palace, the Police Headquarters and the Post and Telecommunications building, helped to fill the gap. Chile and Argentina, which could not lay claim to a colonial tradition on the scale of that of neighbouring Peru or Bolivia, borrowed from the Andean baroque and the Spanish Renaissance. Venezuela's colonial architecture was similarly limited but architects made good use of a local type of squat, pot-bellied *panzuda* column to create a distinctively national version of the neo-colonial style. Carlos Raúl Villanueva (1900–75), one of the most important Latin American architects of the century, used it to good effect in his El Silencio housing development in Caracas of 1941-3.[34] This, the first major slum-clearance and urban regeneration scheme in Latin America, rehoused between three and four thousand people into seven low-rise blocks, and in doing so, created for Caracas an elegant old colonial barrio of a type it had never had, with arcaded street facades, stone *panzuda* columns and baroque portals, blue-painted woodwork and whitewashed walls.

When the attraction of the neo-colonial style faded – and it faded sooner in some countries than in others – there were two main stylistic routes available, one decorative, the other severely plain. The first was provided by art deco, which offered two advantages: in rejecting the classical architectural language that underpinned both the American neo-colonial and European neoclassical/*beaux-arts* styles, it was visibly modern and progressive; and in allowing absolute freedom of content in terms of the decorative detail, it encouraged the incorporation of regional and national motifs into a modern design. The second was the anti-decorative route of a more avant-garde architecture variously termed functionalism, rationalism, the International Style or simply the Modern Movement, a style that made explicit use of modern materials and derived from Le Corbusier and the Bauhaus. Generally speaking, after widespread popularity during the 1920s and 1930s art deco was edged aside by the rhetoric of the much more radical modernism of steel, glass and, above all, reinforced concrete.

Mexico is a good example.[35] After a brief flirtation with neo-colonial ideas, it is not surprising that the revolutionary government was one

Figure 6 Juan O'Gorman, studio house of Diego Rivera and Frida Kahlo, 1931–2, Mexico City.

of the first in Latin America to find its conservative resonances unacceptable. For a while art deco provided a suitable alternative for state-funded projects, as it could be simultaneously grand, modern and Mexican. The Ministry of Health building, begun by Carlos Obregón Santacilia (1896–1961) in 1926 is faced in stone and with sculptural details carved in a sort of deco-Aztec mode, including the Mexico-Tenochtitlan emblem of the eagle and the cactus emblazoned over the main entrance, and the Palacio de Bellas Artes, begun in an extravagant sort of *beaux-arts* baroque under the Porfiriato, was completed in 1932 with exquisite deco-Maya internal decor in metal and marble. One of the first examples of the more radical modernist architecture was the house that Juan O'Gorman (1905–82) built for the artists Diego Rivera and Frida Kahlo in the San Angel district of Mexico City of 1929. The two separate houses (reflecting their semi-detached modern marriage) are of reinforced concrete with simple cubic volumes and large areas of steel-framed window, they are raised off the ground on stilts or *pilotis*, and apart from the brightly-painted walls they are without any form of ornament or superfluous decoration. In other words, they conform closely to Le Corbusier's radical proposals for a new architecture of 1923, an architecture which he argued was 'style-less' and so safe from the whims of fashion.[36]

On the strength of the Rivera–Kahlo house, O'Gorman was commissioned by the minister of education to build some thirty schools and colleges. This he did with speed and efficiency between 1932 and 1935, so establishing a functionalist architectural style in Mexico that was eminently acceptable to the government: it was associated with radical social and cultural reform, and it was cheap and fast to build. O'Gorman's schools were followed by equally functionalist hospitals and clinics by José Villagrán García (1901–92) and large-scale high-rise housing developments by Mario Pani (1911–93), so that by the 1950s the Mexican government could pride itself that its nation was a visibly modern one.

The functionalist style was widely associated with social reform and was embraced, for example, by Uruguay's liberalizing democracy from the late 1920s on, as in the Clinical Hospital in Montevideo of 1928 by Carlos A. Surraco (1896–1976) and the subsequent work of Julio Vilamajó (1894–1948).[37] In Brazil, the government of President Getulio Vargas similarly recognized modernist architecture as an effective signifier of a nation that was modernizing in both social and economic terms. The Ministry of Education and Health building of 1936 was designed by a team of young Brazilians under Lúcio Costa (1902–98) and in consultation with Le Corbusier. This building, the first modern slab-block high-rise in the world, uses a strongly Le Corbusian language (*pilotis*, curtain walls of glass, roof gardens, modern materials) but combines it with an unmistakable regional accent (the selective use of blue and white glazed tiles and local pink granite, heavy sun-screening, native Brazilian plants in the gardens), a combination which has been termed 'regional modernism'.[38]

Commentators on the regional characteristics of earlier twentieth-century Latin American architecture have often drawn attention to the tendency towards 'plastic integration', the incorporation of painting and sculpture and also of local flora and even the local topography into the architectural designs.[39] In Mexico, the first major foray into this field was the University City begun in 1950. This was intended as much as a showpiece for the cultural and intellectual achievements of modern Mexico as for the bold originality of its architecture. This project involves a tension between the modern and the Mexican. On the one hand, much of it is in the International Style – rectilinear volumes, long ranges of glass and extensive use of *pilotis*. On the other hand, there were efforts to make reference to Mexico's layers of history, from the pre-Columbian and colonial periods through independence to the twentieth century, all of which are embedded into its landscape. The landscape finds its counterpart in the stadium: shaped like a volcanic crater, it binds the University City into the valley of Mexico and to the volcanoes that encircle it. Some buildings make deliberate use of local materials. Several buildings incorporate reliefs in the black and red volcanic rock continuously popular from the pre-Columbian era, so, for example, rooting the glass, steel and concrete central tower of the Rectorate into place and time. The Frontón Courts echo the geometric severity of Aztec pyramids. Covered walkways and patios are reminiscent of the private courtyards of colonial architecture, as the great open terraced plazas are of pre-Columbian ceremonial centres. Murals are used periodically throughout the University City, although the most obvious are not always the most comfortable examples of plastic integration. Rivera produced a large relief for the stadium, which works well, but the more complex, allegorical murals and mosaics elsewhere, such as Siqueiros's bizarre work for the Rectorate, are sometimes more confrontational than integrated. In his design for the university library, Juan O'Gorman abandoned his functional 'style-less' style for an architecture that was explicitly Mexican. The building, a simple cubic block, is not so much architecture as the setting for his own intricate mosaics representing in semi-pictographic form the history and cosmology of Mexico, ancient and modern.

Venezuela is dominated by the figure of Villanueva, architect of El Silencio, but more importantly of the Caracas University City of the 1940s and 1950s where, as in Mexico, the campus was designed as a celebration of culture and learning and is a model of how modern art can be integrated into architecture. A galaxy of artists from Venezuela, Europe and North America were invited to contribute and the result is an exceptionally coherent whole, perhaps because Villanueva was very much the guiding hand, and because the main core was constructed within a relatively short space of time. This is a very different sort of spatial organization from that in Mexico – intimate rather than monumental, colourful walls, tropical plants, lattice-work screens suggestive of colonial domestic architecture, shady walkways, colonnades and quiet patios reminiscent of the monastery and perhaps of Old World universities. Beyond the central area, architecture reasserts its autonomy in the monumental cantilevered concrete ribs of the university's Olympic stadium and swimming pool, also by Villanueva.[40]

The Caracas Metro, begun in the 1970s, represents the way the ideas of artistic and intellectual integration explored in the University City have born fruit on a bigger urban scale. The metro was designed to address some of the many problems of a city that had grown uncontrollably, where there was no regulated transport system, and with extremes of rich and poor that fragmented the city into separate and often hostile barrios. It was explicitly an exercise in social and urban integration, and its construction was accompanied by an extensive education programme to encourage the citizens to take responsibility for their transport system and their locality. Each station has an identity that relates to the barrio, each has public space around and within it, with works of art, gardens, seats, kiosks and cafes. Some have spaces for temporary exhibitions, or a little amphitheatre, integrating art into the urban environment. In other words, each station acts as a sort of local community centre. At the same time there is an overriding 'metro style' which helps to provide visual links between the different regions of the city, so that travelling around is less threatening. The project has certainly achieved some of its aims: because there is a sense of local pride and responsibility, the spaces within the orbit of the metro are largely self-regulating so that even in the rougher parts of the city the graffiti, rubbish and other side-effects of poverty tend to remain outside the limits of the metro's public space. The dream of integration is of course limited by the constraints of reality.

Brazilian modernist architecture is full of imaginative leaps.[41] The possibilities offered by reinforced concrete stimulated Affonso Eduardo Reidy (1909–64) to develop the curvaceous main block of the Pedregulho residential complex in Rio de Janeiro of 1947, and the frame of cantilevered concrete ribs from which the Museum of Modern Art is suspended (begun 1954, also in Rio). Lina Bo Bardi (1914–92) reworked this idea in the São Paulo Museum of Art (1968) hanging the all-glass gallery from two huge concrete arches, while the Exhibitions Palace in Salvador of Glauco Campelo (b. 1945) is an extravagant cross between a portion of a suspension bridge and a two-legged dinosaur. These buildings all use Le Corbusian *pilotis* which allow for a public concourse area or garden below the buildings themselves, a feature common to much modern Latin American architecture. In Brazil the 'integrating impulse' is most strongly apparent in the relationship between architecture and gardens. Just as the metro has provided Caracas with at least a degree of integration, so in Rio de Janeiro it is the gardens. The gardens by Roberto Burle Marx (1909–94) for the MES building marked the beginning of a long and influential career during which he designed both public and private gardens throughout the city as well as those all along the famous Flamengo, Gloria and Copacabana beaches. Others followed suit so that it is hard to imagine modern Brazilian architecture without its complement of luscious tropical vegetation.[42]

And then, of course, there is Brasília.[43] Brasília must be one of the most overlooked achievements of the twentieth century – it is barely acknowledged in recent surveys of modern architecture – but to plan, lay out, build and inaugurate a city on this scale in under four years (1956–60) takes extraordinary courage, and it deserves to take its place among the greatest urban and architectural achievements of all time. Driven by President Jucelino Kubitschek and designed by Lúcio Costa, the original vision was of a utopian administrative centre that was to be radically different from other Brazilian cities, a symbol of modernity and the associated values of order, prosperity and hygiene. Brasília was laid out along Le Corbusian lines, zoned according to function, with generous allocations for parks and gardens, and linked by an efficient network of highways and service roads. The most important government buildings were designed by Oscar Niemeyer (b. 1907) who combines cubic profiles and arching, inverted colonnades in a way that is modern and international, but which also has echoes of Brazilian baroque. In the self-consciously monumental disposition of the different buildings and the use of white marble cladding for the central governmental complex there are broader echoes too, of Washington, of course, but also of classical antiquity. Like other fiat capital cities (Canberra, Washington, Chandigarh) Brasília has a certain air of artificiality, but it is mellowing. It has often been criticized for failing to provide cheap housing for the workers, and while this is true, to have done so would have been to have built in the social disparities which the city was intended to transcend. Nowadays the original (inevitable) shantytowns are themselves high-rise cities with their own outlying shantytowns, and while Brasília has its social problems, they are certainly no worse that those of many other cities.

Brasília was planned to be both modern and Brazilian, a reconciliation between two apparently different traditions. This debate, between national and international, between local and modern, lies behind the tremendous diversity of architecture in Latin America. At one extreme there are the International Style steel and glass towers of business and

Figure 7   Oscar Niemeyer, Itamaratí Palace, 1962, Brasília.

commerce that could be anywhere in the world, and at the other are the many experiments with local materials and traditional techniques. In the former category, the Torre Latinoamericano of 1950–2 in Mexico by Augusto Álvarez (1914–95) and the Edificio Polar in Caracas by Martín Vegas Pacheco (b. 1920) and José Miguel Galia (b. 1919) of 1953–4 were among the first and the most interesting.[44] As such buildings multiplied, however, they became increasingly banal, and most cities now have their share of glossy mirror-glass prisms and post-modern shrines to global capital: plenty of conspicuous consumption and shock value. The Simón Bolívar building by Mario Paredes (b. 1936) in Santiago of 1989–92 is a rather unsubtle skyscraper-temple to the new gods of high finance. The 1990s Banco de Crédito in Lima's La Molina district is an even more extreme example: designed by the Miami-based Arquitectónica group, the extravagant use of steel, glass, space, air-conditioning and, above all, water for the internal gardens and fountains contrasts painfully with the adjacent squatters' settlements where the most acute shortage in the barren terrain is that of water.

On the other hand, the regionalist tendencies of Latin American architecture were not, or certainly were not at first, a matter of choice but were the result of the particular conditions of the region. Because Latin America lacked the industrial development on which the European modern movement was predicated, the first exponents of modern architecture had to adapt the theory to their own reality. There were no factories to mass-produce new building materials but there was no shortage of labour. Rural migrants to the cities brought with them a range of traditional artisanal skills that architects learned to exploit to good advantage. It is not an accident that the building material par excellence of twentieth-century architecture in Latin America has been reinforced concrete. The technique involved is close to that of traditional *tapia*, walls made of mud and stones using wooden formwork, a technique that has been used continuously throughout the region for generations. This traditional skill, adapted to a material that is vastly stronger and more versatile, has allowed architects to experiment with all manner of shapes and forms that would be unthinkable in any other medium. Reinforced concrete could create curves, arches and undulating canopies, ribs and vaults. In the 1950s in Mexico the engineer Felix Candela (1910–98) was using it to produce exquisitely thin shell-like vaults. During the same decade, Villanueva was using it for the giant, curving external ribs of several of the University City buildings in Caracas. The Buenos Aires Bank of London and South America of 1966 by Clorindo Testa (b. 1923) is enclosed within a massive concrete exoskeleton that suggests steel girders, an appropriate blend of sophistication and security. Brazilian modern architecture is famed for its inventive use of curvilinear concrete forms, particularly as designed by Oscar Niemeyer and executed by the engineer Joachim Cardozo (1897–1978).

Concrete in Latin America is more than just a means to an end, however. Le Corbusier claimed that he was the first person to exploit the aesthetic effect of exposed concrete – in his Unité d'Habitation in Marseilles in 1947 – but in Latin America it appears much earlier, and what may have begun as a matter of expediency was quickly taken up as an appropriate and authentic expression of Latin American modernity. It seems probable that the Uruguayan architect Julio Vilamajó was already exploiting the visual interest of rough-cast concrete in the 1930s. Brazilians were experimenting with it in the 1940s, and by the 1950s it is ubiquitous. The solid prismic towers by Mathias Goeritz (1915–90) at the entrance to Satellite City in Mexico City of 1957 exemplify the particular aesthetic of concrete. They may look like pure geometry from a distance but, as one gets nearer, the imprint of the wooden formwork announces the very manual process by which they were constructed. This explicit contrast between tradition and modernity, between the traces of very traditional methods of construction on the surfaces of buildings of modern design and modern materials is found everywhere. The contrast is most striking where it is least expected: on the exposed concrete surfaces on the interior of Testa's elegant Bank of London and South America in Buenos Aires, for example, or the serene vaults of Candela's church of the Medalla Milagrosa in Mexico City of 1954. The hand prints in the cement blocks of Emilio Duhart's (b. 1918) United Nations building in Santiago de Chile (1966) emphasize the humanitarian aims of the institution as well as acknowledging the human involvement in its construction. Elsewhere architects have made extensive use of brick, again drawing on traditions of craftsmanship that were not so readily available in the US: Eladio Dieste (b. 1917) in Uruguay, Rogelio Salmona (b. 1929) in Colombia, Fernando Castillo (b. 1918) in Chile, Ricardo Porro (b. 1925) in Cuba. Other ways in which architects have sought to locate their work within the region include the widespread use of colour-washed walls and gardens, roofs and patios planted with indigenous flora. And throughout Latin America, architects have experimented with different ways of providing ventilation and sun protection – sunscreens and blinds, airbricks, louvres and lattice-work, which may be of concrete or metal, clay or cement, wood, reed or bamboo – and which also create patterns of light and shade that move and change throughout the day.

Behind these general tendencies lie many local styles. In Mexico, the thick, colour-washed walls, small windows and cubic forms developed by Luis Barragán (1902–88) in the 1940s and pursued by his followers, particularly Ricardo Legorreta (b. 1931), are a reworking in concrete and cement of the aesthetic of popular adobe construction. In Brazil, Severiano Porto (b. 1930) has returned to the traditional techniques and materials – wood and thatch – of the Amazonian region. Fruto Vivas (b. 1928) in Venezuela, uses a variety of materials but with an eye to the ingenious ways in which the shanty-town dwellers adapt their houses to the steep terrain. Similarly, the beach houses of Peruvian Juvenal Barraco (b. 1940) are constructed along traditional lines – rough-finished walls and patios shaded by split bamboo – to suggest the informality of camping on the beach as well as the home-made feel of the houses of rural migrants to the outskirts of Lima. In many ways the plurality of styles that followed the crisis of modernity in Europe and the US has always been a part of Latin American architecture and this has remained one of its great strengths.

Urban futures

Latin America remains in many ways profoundly different from Europe or North America. In the 1950s no one predicted the torrent of rural migration that would overwhelm so many cities in Latin America in subsequent decades. Mexico City and São Paulo are famous examples but most major cities have grown far faster than town-planning departments could possibly cope with. This has created problems unlike anything faced in the developed world but, as in the case of the Caracas Metro, the impulse to create an urban environment where the buildings and intervening spaces relate to one another and work together to promote the collective values of the society that inhabits them still survives. Throughout Latin America public space remains an important arena for creative endeavour: town squares, pedestrian precincts, parks and zoos everywhere have involved architects, urban planners and artists in interesting experiments using various combinations of tiles, mosaic pavements, murals, reliefs, sculptures, covered walks, canopied spaces, street furniture, trees, gardens and water. Niemeyer's 1954 Ibirapuera Park in São Paulo, home of the famous Bienal, is an early example where the water and the sinuous covered walks complement the rectilinear pavilions to create a modernist environment. We have already mentioned Rio de Janeiro's southerly waterfronts, so imaginatively landscaped in the 1970s with Burle Marx's distinctive black and white mosaic pavements, clusters of shady trees and gardens to create space not just for strollers but for café tables, kiosks, joggers and temporary art installations. The visitor to Caracas is welcomed by Carlos Cruz-Diez's vibrant coloured patterns, first on the floor of La Guaira airport, then on walls and grain silos along the route into the city centre, and then on a sculptural monument in public squares, in banks and businesses, and as an installation in a gallery or a stage set in a theatre. As well as his many architectural projects in Córdoba, Argentina, Miguel Angel Roca (b. 1940) has designed parks and plazas, and his witty use of patterned pavements in the colonial city centre (1979–80) gives a quirky post-modern unity to the eclectic architecture. There are also many interventions into the city of a much more ephemeral nature. Very recently (2001) the Zócalo in Mexico City provided the setting for an opera with works of art in the form of light projections on to the surrounding buildings by another Argentinian artist, Jorge Orta (b. 1953).

The relative informality of Latin American city planning and government leaves room for architectural and artistic experimentation within the urban environment. There are still endless opportunities for relatively cheap, small-scale interventions which can nevertheless have a real impact. The changes wrought by the European conquerors in the sixteenth century created a new culture that came to have its own history and cultural evolution. The impact of modernity and post-modernity has not been dissimilar. Latin America, like everywhere else, is exposed to and imposed on by external forces but it continues to generate new ideas, new solutions. History's grand attempts to mould the region into homogeneity have resulted only in ever-greater diversity.

Notes

1. V. Fraser, *The Architecture of Conquest: Building in the Viceroyalty of Peru* (Cambridge, 1990).
2. J. MacAndrew, *The Open-Air Churches of Sixteenth-Century Mexico* (Cambridge, 1965), was the first full-length study of this phenomenon in Mexico.
3. E. Wake, 'Setting the new cosmic stage: some observations on native landscape painting in Sixteenth-Century Mexico', in V. Fraser (ed.), *Illegitimate Arts: Studies in the Iconography of Colonial Latin America* (Nashville, forthcoming).
4. G. Kubler and M. Soria, *Art and Architecture of Spain and Portugal and their American Dominions, 1500–1800* (Harmondsworth, 1959).
5. Kubler and Soria, *Art and Architecture*; D. Bayón, *Historia del arte hispanoamericano*, vol. II (Madrid, 1987).
6. The exhibition catalogue, D. Fane, *Converging Cultures: Art and Identity in Spanish America* (New York, 1996), has good examples.
7. F. de la Maza, *El pintor Cristóbal de Villalpando* (Mexico, 1964), pp. 66–7.
8. S. Sebastián, *El Barroco Iberoamericano: Mensaje iconográfico* (Madrid, 1990), p. 126.
9. R. Mujica Pinilla, *Angeles apócrifos en la América virreinal* (Lima, 1992).
10. *America, Bride of the Sun: 500 Years, Latin America and the Low Countries* (Antwerp, 1992), pp. 189–96.
11. Sebastián, *El Barroco*, pp. 94–106.
12. T. Gisbert, *Iconografía y mitos indígenas en el arte* (La Paz, 1980), p. 20.
13. M. Bonnet, 'Cultural Cross-Roads in Colonial Brazil: The Church of Santa Efigenia', in Fraser, *Illegitimate Arts* (forthcoming).
14. D. Ades, *Art in Latin America* (London, 1989).
15. O. Baddeley and V. Fraser, *Drawing the Line: Art and Cultural Identity in Contemporary Latin America* (London, 1989).
16. J. Charlot, *The Mexican Mural Renaissance* (London, 1963).
17. D. Rochfort, *The Murals of Diego Rivera* (London, 1987); D.Craven, *Diego Rivera as Epic Modernist* (London, 1997).
18. *¡Orozco!* Catalogue, Museum of Modern Art (Oxford, 1980).

19. P. Stein, *Siqueiros, His Life and Works* (New York, 1994).
20. L. Hurlburt, *The Mexican Muralists in the United States* (Albuquerque, NM, 1989).
21. D. Underwood, *Oscar Niemeyer and the Architecture of Brazil* (New York, 1994).
22. A. Amaral, *Tarsila: Sua obra e seu tempo* (São Paulo, 1975).
23. M. C. Ramírez, *El Taller Torres-García: The School of the South and its Legacy* (Austin TX, 1992).
24. Ades, *Art in Latin America.*
25. *Obras de Arte de la Ciudad Universitaria de Caracas* (Caracas, 1991).
26. *Modernidade: art brésilien de 20e siecle* (Paris, 1988).
27. E. Cockcroft, 'Abstract Expressionism, Weapon of the Cold War', *Artforum* 12 (10 June, 1974), pp. 39–41.
28. H. Herrera, *Frida: A Biography of Frida Kahlo* (New York, 1983).
29. *Latin American Women Artists 1915–1995,* curated Geraldine P Biller, Milwaukee Art Museum 1995.
30. G. Brett, *Transcontinental: Nine Latin American Artists* (London, 1990).
31. V. Fraser, *Building the New World: Studies in the Modern Architecture of Latin America 1930–1960* (London, 2000).
32. P. Damaz, *Art in Latin American Architecture,* New York, 1965; F. Bullrich, *New Directions in Latin American Architecture* (London, 1969); G. Chase, *Contemporary Art in Latin America* (New York, 1970); C. Bamford Smith, *Builders in the Sun: Five Mexican Architects* (New York, 1967).
33. A. Amaral (ed.), *Arquitectura neo-colonial: América Latina, Caribe, Estados Unidos* (São Paulo, 1994), includes essays on neo-colonial architecture throughout the Americas.
34. S. Moholy-Nagy, *Carlos Raúl Villanueva and the Architecture of Venezuela* (New York, 1964).
35. F. González Gortázar, co-ord., *La arquitectura mexicana del siglo XX,* (Mexico, 1994); E. Burian (ed.), *Modernity and the Architecture of Mexico* (Austin TX, 1997).
36. Le Corbusier, *Vers une Architecture* (Paris, 1923).
37. M. Arana and L. Garabelli, *Arquitectura renovadora en Montevideo, 1915–1940* (Montevideo, 1995); A. Lucchini, *Julio Vilamajo: Su arquitectura* (Montevideo, 1970).
38. Underwood, *Oscar Niemeyer.*
39. Damaz, *Art.*
40. Moholy-Nagy, *Carlos Raúl Villanueva.*
41. Y. Bruand, *Arquitectura contemporanea no Brasil* (São Paulo, 1981).
42. S. Eliovson, *The Gardens of Burle Marx* (Portland OR, 1990).
43. W. Staübli, *Brasília* (New York, 1966); J. Holston, *The Modernist City: An Anthropological Critique of Brasília* (Chicago IL, 1989).
44. H. R. Hitchcock, *Latin American Architecture since 1945* (New York, 1955).

Further reading

Ades, D., *Art in Latin America,* London, 1989
Baddeley, O. and V. Fraser, *Drawing the Line: Art and Cultural Identity in Contemporary Latin America,* London, 1989
Barnitz, J., *Twentieth-Century Art of Latin America,* Austin TX, 2001
Bayón, D., *Historia del arte hispanoamericano,* 3 vols., Madrid, 1987–8

Bayón, D. and M. Marx, *History of South American Colonial Art and Architecture: Spanish South America and Brazil*, New York, 1992

Brett, G., *Transcontinental: Nine Latin American Artists*, London, 1990

Craven, D., *Art and Revolution in Latin America 1910–1990*, London, 2002

Fraser, V., *Building the New World: Studies in the Modern Architecture of Latin America, 1930–1960*, London, 2000

Gruzinski, S., *Painting the Conquest: Mexican Indians and the European Renaissance*, Paris, 1992

Mosquera, G. (ed.), *Beyond the Fantastic: Contemporary Art Criticism from Latin America*, London, 1995

Sullivan, E. J., *Latin American Art in the Twentieth Century*, London, 1996

Traba, M., *Art of Latin America, 1900–1980*, Washington DC, 1994

Turner, J. (ed.), *Encyclopedia of Latin American and Caribbean Art*, London, 2000

10

Tradition and transformation in Latin American music

Cuban author and musicologist Alejo Carpentier wrote that Latin American music is a phenomenon like an explosion whose history and evolution, unlike the history of European music, cannot be traced in a linear or coherent pattern. According to Carpentier, Latin American music arises from nowhere as a series of accidents, unplanned events and startling surprises. One might argue that all culture is an accident, but Carpentier's point is intended to emphasize the arbitrary and even violent roots of Latin American music. The music now associated with the countries and regions of Latin America originated from three cultural formations: indigenous American, European and African, but the genealogies of the many products of these sources are not easily traced. Once the Europeans had arrived in the Americas, followed later by the Africans they brought as slaves, the three traditions began to mix and alter, so that it was no longer possible to speak in terms of pure forms, whether European, African or indigenous.

The history of Latin American music is therefore a complicated affair. There are conflicting versions of the origins of many forms, often the result of calculated speculation from uncertain evidence or the consequence of a particular politics of identity. Some musicologists have sought the origins of Argentinian tango in English country dancing of the mid-seventeenth century and have offered a genealogy that passes through the Cuban dance forms, the *habanera* and *contradanza*. Their genealogy exemplifies the accidental transformations likely to be undergone by any genre, but overlooks important local phenomena, including the wave of European immigration to South America in the late nineteenth century and the earlier significant presence of black communities in the River Plate republics where tango first appeared.

It also reflects a tendency, of varying importance in different places and moments of history, to attribute greater cultural value to products of European origin by diminishing or negating contributions of other sources.

Indigenous and African origins

Scholars have found it difficult to recreate pre-Columbian music, although archaeology, colonial texts and the study of traditional music of regions where large populations of indigenous peoples remain have provided some understanding. More is known of the pre-Columbian music of Peru and Bolivia than of Mexico, where native music was more actively repressed by colonial authorities. In the same vein, very little is known about the music of Caribbean peoples, who were extinguished within one hundred years of the Conquest. The oldest native accounts of the Spanish Conquest are the *icnocuicatl*, songs of sorrow describing the fall of Tenochtitlán, composed by surviving Nahuatl poets in about 1523, some four years after Hernán Cortés landed on Mexican shores. Spanish chroniclers acknowledged at the time the importance of music in indigenous societies and wrote of performances of singing and dancing by the people of the Caribbean. The pre-Columbian codices of Mesoamerica contain pictorial representations of musical instruments, and in texts such as Felipe Huamán Poma de Ayala's account of Inca society before and after the Conquest, there are lyrics of popular pre-Conquest songs.

The degree of survival of indigenous musical practices, however, has depended on variable factors. They have not fared well in areas with an early high concentration of Europeans, but in the remoter jungle and mountain regions, traditions remained untouched or closer to their roots for longer periods. Moreover, the process of assimilation to which indigenous peoples were submitted included active policies of destruction of instruments, the extirpation of local musical practices and the conscription of indigenous musicians and music to the service of the new colonial society. Thus, the colonial Church both prohibited the use of indigenous instruments for non-ecclesiastical purposes while, at the same time, using them in church music. As noted by Bernal Díaz del Castillo, one of the conquistadors who accompanied Cortés to Mexico and later wrote of his experiences, the Aztec king, Moctezuma, was 'very fond of music and entertainment'. This fondness for music was something about the New World that the colonizers both appreciated and exploited. Soon after they established the first of their colonial outposts, they began to use music and musical instruction in a wider programme of domination and control, especially in the context of religious conversion.

The character of pre-Columbian music owed much to the wind and percussion instruments that predominated throughout indigenous America, although with considerable local variation and widely differing nomenclature. The shell of a marine snail was used in Mexico and conches were common to many regions. Vertical flutes, pan-pipes and *ocarinas* were made of baked clay in Mexico, and in the Maya-Quiché regions of Central America, the wind instruments also included the *chirimía*, a general name for a clarinet-like instrument. In the Andean region, wind instruments were customarily made from reeds, palm leaves and tree bark. The most common was the *quena*, a reed flute that has become more widely known through modern recordings of Andean-style music and the presence of South American musical groups in many North American and European cities as a result of the Latin American diaspora of the twentieth century. The drums and shakers of South America were less varied than in the North, although an early-nineteenth-century traveller to the jungles of Paraguay returned with stories of pan-pipes and scrapers fashioned from the bones of slaughtered missionaries. Animal bones were certainly used to make instruments in South America, including llama skulls as drums in Peru, and instruments of human bone are known from other parts of Latin America, particularly Mexico. The drums of pre-Cortesian Mexico, however, were conventionally made of other materials. The *huehuetl* was a vertical drum made in different sizes from hollowed sections of a tree with the opening at one end covered with animal hide. Similarly, the *teponaxtle*, a sacred instrument used for ceremonial occasions, was also made from a tree, although sometimes from stone. It was placed horizontally and struck to the left or right of an opening cut into the wall of the drum so that the pitch varied according to where it was struck.

The sacred meanings attached to instruments, to the music and to the occasion of performance were among the reasons why the Europeans sought to prohibit and control them. Prohibition might have been prompted by perceptions of primitivism or by evangelization and a programme of cultural assimilation, but was also a form of political control, since music could readily become the focus around which the beleaguered cultures of the conquered people or transported African slaves could rally. In Cuba, for example, measures were adopted to prohibit the manufacture of the large *conga* drums and in Peru, in 1614, the Archbishop of Lima ordered all indigenous instruments destroyed.

Although music in the neo-African tradition predominates in Latin America where Afro-Americans are concentrated, principally Brazil and the Caribbean, including Venezuela and Colombia, its influence is not limited to this area. Music throughout the continent is indebted to the polyrhythmic structures and the syncopated 2/4 time of neo-African traditions. Afro-American music differs significantly from the principal indigenous traditions with their monotonous rhythms and elegiac or melancholic tones. But neither indigenous nor Afro-American music should be simplistically categorized. The syncopated music of Latin America is generally of African origin, but there are differences. Syncopation in Brazil, for example, is far less complex than in Cuba. Slaves were brought from different parts of Africa, including Senegal, the Ivory Coast, Dahomey (present-day Benin), Angola, Mozambique and Sudan. They had not necessarily had any previous contact with each other and were not a homogenous group. For this reason and the relative isolation of each group of Africans from others in the Americas, many different song and dance forms have evolved: *merengue* in the Dominican Republic and Haiti, *conga* and *rumba* in Cuba, *cumbia* in Panamá and Colombia, *samba* in Brazil, not to mention variations on each of these and the many other forms practised more locally. Similarly, the music of indigenous America varies greatly from one region to another, not just between an Aztec-Maya-Quiché tradition in the North and the Inca tradition in the South, but more locally and among groups living in relative proximity to each other. Whereas the melodic structure of indigenous music was predominantly based on a pentatonic scale, the musical practices in Amazonia seemed to have depended only on three or four notes, seldom exploiting the full potential of the scale, while the traditions of the Mapuche, now located in southern Chile at the other end of the continent, are not exclusively pentatonic and are evidence of similar possible variations before the Conquest. Regardless of its structural variations, however, music had important social and ceremonial functions throughout the continent at the time of the arrival of the Europeans, a condition which undoubtedly made indigenous people amenable to participation in the rituals of the colonial Church, and it also had more intimate purposes, as in the melodic forms of the Andean *huayno, vidala* and *yaravi* still practised in contemporary South America, which would have made it equally receptive to the forms of popular secular music brought from Europe.

Colonial music

In contrast to the indigenous and African traditions, which may have left only residual traces in some regions or may never have gained a foothold in others, there are no places in the Americas where European musical traditions have not reached and where they do not flourish in some form. Moreover, European influence has been both continuous and changing during the five centuries of history since the first ships arrived. Whereas the number of indigenous people declined rapidly immediately after first contact and then grew slowly back to pre-Conquest levels, and the importation of Africans ceased in the nineteenth century, the European population has not only expanded constantly but has repeatedly renewed its traditions through new waves of immigration.

In this context, indigenous music became a kind of substratum, a layer of cultural practices upon which European musical forms were imposed and into which African traditions were also drawn. Against this background, the traditions of the colonial period evolved along two main lines: the music of the Church, which would merge into art music after independence, and music in a more popular vein, which engaged in a more energetic mix of forms than the school music of the ecclesiastical tradition and developed the context from which popular music of the nineteenth and twentieth centuries would evolve. Each region, even in colonial times, has its own musical history, of course, but it is nonetheless possible to generalize about Latin America as a whole, even to detect certain similarities between Brazil and Spanish America.

The great cathedrals of the Spanish colonial cities such as Havana, Mexico, Puebla, Cuzco, Lima, Sucre and Santafé de Bogotá were the headquarters, so to speak, of a rapid process of cultural *mestizaje* and uneven exchange. Musical directors, or chapel masters (*maestros de capilla*), were important colonial administrators, as well as artistic leaders, appointed by the crown and responsible for the musical life of the colonies. Hernando Franco (1532–85), for example, was a major colonial composer, who served in this capacity at the cathedral in Mexico City from 1575 to 1585. Among his tasks as *maestro de capilla* was to ensure that adequate numbers of trained musicians and singers were available to perform in cathedral choirs and orchestras. Although not specifically involved in the training of musicians, as in the later Jesuit missions in South America, cathedral choirs and orchestras often relied on native musicians and singers. The first mestizo to be appointed *maestro de capilla* in New Spain was Gonzalo García Zorro, son of an indigenous woman and a Spanish captain, who was sent to Spain for a letter of legitimacy before he could take up his duties as musical director in Santafé de Bogotá in 1575.

Cathedral orchestras included instruments such as the organ, harp, flageolet, bassoon, different types of horns and, later on, violins and other stringed instruments, as well as flutes. The choirs sang polyphonic harmony and Gregorian chant. Musicians and singers were paid employees of the cathedral who at times had to be disciplined. A study of the cathedral of Santafé de Bogotá by Robert Stevenson tells us that in 1586, seminarians at the cathedral went on strike after an order from the archbishop to sing the canonical hours every day in the cathedral. Spanish, Italian, as well as mestizo and indigenous musicians and composers wrote and performed masses, *magnificats, salve reginas*, requiems and other genres of sacred music, following the patterns of musical composition and performance prevalent in Europe at the time. As was to be expected, musical accomplishments were measured against European standards, initiating a long-standing tradition of colonial insecurity vis-à-vis artistic production in the metropolis. From our perspective, however, the most fascinating aspect of early colonial music is the way in which the indigenous substratum pokes through the measured European scales. Although sacred music of the period made no attempt to incorporate native stylistic elements, which were considered inappropriate for religious worship, there are traces of pre-Colombian culture in numerous compositions, as, for example, in the Andean wind instruments that accompany *Hanacpachap cussincuini*, an anonymous composition in Quechua from seventeenth-century Cuzco.

In Brazil, churches were also a focus of musical performance and creation, although the Portuguese were generally slower than the Spanish to establish a network of cultural institutions at a level where it could support musical activity as rich and varied as that found in some of the major Spanish colonial cities. As the colonial capital, Salvador enjoyed an ecclesiastical infrastructure commensurate with its status. The position of chapel master was maintained in its cathedral from 1559, but similar appointments were often also made in parishes. A comparable situation obtained in the state of Pernambuco, whose history of musical institutions dates from the sixteenth century. However, the hub of institutionalized musical activity in Brazil did not remain fixed in one place during colonial times, but moved as the economy and politics dictated. The new-found wealth of Minas Gerais resulting from the mining of gold and precious stones beginning in the second half of the seventeenth century fostered the development of a musical culture throughout the state rather than concentrating it in one cathedral city, and the organization of musicians in brotherhoods (*ermandades*), a practice equally common in other parts of Brazil, gave greater control over their profession to the musicians themselves. More significantly, perhaps, the movement of the capital to Rio de Janeiro in 1763 resulted in the economic and cultural decline of Salvador and the corresponding rise of Rio de Janeiro as the musical centre of the country, especially after 1808 when the Portuguese royal family arrived in Brazil, fleeing Napoleon's army in Europe. This period is associated in particular with the work of José Maurício Nunes Garcia (1767–1830), whose compositions of mainly sacred music, written in the European styles of the day, for their number (over 200) and quality, make him the most significant figure of Brazilian music of the colonial period.

In addition to the church music they brought with them or composed in the new lands, the colonists also brought a vast repertoire of popular dances and songs to all parts of the Americas – *romances, villancicos, alabados, cantos infantiles, cantos navideños, pregones, tonadillos* to the Spanish colonies, *modinhas* and *toadas* to Brazil – and soon began to add to them with verses that spoke of local conditions and events, and music that drew on familiar European traditions as well as more local forms. Notable examples may be found in the work of Sor Juana Inés de la Cruz (1648/51–95), one of Mexico's most celebrated colonial poets, who composed *villancicos* set to music by Antonio de Salazar, *maestro de capilla* in Mexico City from 1688 to 1715. Some of her *villancicos* were written in local dialects representing the variety of European, indigenous and African peoples living in New Spain at the time. Most often, Spanish or Portuguese traditions were simply reworked in an American setting, with new themes or lyrics in a native language. In the case of a *negro* or *negrilla*, for example, a *villancico* written in black dialect was set to music with systematic neo-African syncopation. There were, however, forms of music and dance that did not correspond to European models, like the *tocotín*, an indigenous dance, and the *portorrico de los negros* and *cumbees* of African origin. It is also clear that new trends and rhythms began to travel back to Europe from the colonies even in the early days and became very popular. Scholars argue, for example, over the origins of the Spanish *zarabanda*. Although considered a European dance form, some musicologists make a case for it as an American phenomenon that made its way to Europe very early in the sixteenth century.

Just as Afro-American and indigenous music were different from each other, music in the popular European tradition offered still further differences. Its basic rhythms during the colonial period were 6/8 and 3/4 and, in contrast to the pentatonic scale of indigenous peoples, Europeans used a seven-tone scale. They brought new instruments, of which the most significant, given their immediate popularity and the relative absence of this kind of instrument in indigenous America, were the stringed variety, the guitar, the violin and the harp. Of these, the most important were the *vihuela* and the guitar, which subsequently acquired many names and forms (*requinto, tiple, bandola, cuatro, guitarrilla, guitarrón, charrango, violão* and *cavaquinho*) and became the common instrument of the continent. Other instruments, like the piano, accordion and *bandoneón* came later, brought from Europe as new musical styles crossed the ocean.

The colonists developed a musical practice that would eventually be counted among the most basic traditions of Latin America. As fashions changed in Europe and new musical styles emerged, these too made their way across the Atlantic and underwent a similar process of adaptation. In Peru there are *criollo* versions of the waltz and an Inca foxtrot. In Brazil, the waltz has developed a form that seems to have little to do with its Viennese ancestor. In Paraguay, the waltz, the polka and the galop were often rendered in local style, with lyrics in Guaraní. Some of the most celebrated forms in the Hispanic tradition are those that have become associated with a national culture and a national identity. Although versions of it are danced in several countries of South America, the *cueca* is thought of as the national dance of Chile. The Spanish *zapateado* has many variants across the continent, but in the form of the *jarabe* is associated with Mexican national identity. The gaucho music of the southern cone and the Mexican *ranchero* style are representative of rural life and traditions in the countries where they have developed. And one of the most remarkable variants of an Hispanic tradition is the Mexican *corrido*. In a manner that recalls the popular *romances* of Spain of the late medieval period and the Renaissance, the *corrido* is a narrative song often used to tell historical or contemporary events. The Mexican Revolution was a source of many such songs, of which one of the most celebrated is *Adelita*, but there are also *corridos* on the nationalization of the petroleum industry and, more recently, on the drug lords and their trade, a development which serves to illustrate the continued vitality of the *corrido* in Spanish America. When sung to the accompaniment of a *mariachi* band, we seem to witness a quintessentially Mexican experience.

Art music and cultural nationalism after independence

By the end of the eighteenth century, church music and the structures that supported it had begun to fall into crisis and decay. For art music to flourish in the newly independent countries, it would need an infrastructure comparable to that which fostered the establishment and development of sacred music in colonial times. It would need theatres and concert halls, a receptive public and academies and conservatories to train performers, composers and musicologists. Just as sacred music thrived under the patronage of the Church, secular music would depend on other social institutions and the patronage of the State. It would also need a new purpose and recognition as a legitimate vehicle for the formation and expression of a culture. While European styles, each incorporating elements of local culture and history, including popular music, had already been canonized, secular art music in a Latin American style had yet to be fully established. Not only had local popular traditions still to become recognized as the legitimate expressions of a people, but they had yet to be adopted by composers capable of giving them high cultural form. Against this background, the history of art music in Latin America is partly a movement towards legitimacy: the struggle of a region to overcome the perception of marginality and to produce music that valorized the local.

The musical nationalism which this enterprise required did not surface until the late nineteenth century, when it was influenced by a rising consciousness of nationhood and European trends towards the incorporation of popular and folk forms and melodies into high art compositions. From the time of independence until well into the nineteenth century, the musical scene was dominated by music of European origin or written in the European style. Italian opera and light musical theatre in the form of the Spanish *zarzuela* prevailed on the stage even in places with a sophisticated musical culture, such as Mexico City,

Havana and Buenos Aires. In these cities, performances were staged by both touring and resident companies, and the repertoire included the latest Italian and French productions as well as works in the Italian style by local composers, such as the Mexican Aniceto Ortega (1823–75), who wrote *Guatimotzin* (1871), an Italianate opera on a romanticized Aztec theme. A taste for the opera had already formed in the Brazilian capital, Salvador, in the early eighteenth century and remained even after the capital was transferred to Rio de Janeiro in 1763. But it was in the latter city that opera flowered more profusely, undoubtedly stimulated by the presence of a royal court during much of the nineteenth century. During many of the years in that century there were regular opera seasons, which included the most recent European works and performances by some of the most celebrated European singers. In 1809, José Maurício Nunes Garcia had already had staged *Le due gemelle*, the first opera known to have been composed by a Brazilian, but Brazilian opera in the Italian style is more famously associated with the work of Antônio Carlos Gomes (1836–96). His first success, *A Noite do Castelo*, was staged in Brazil in 1861, but by 1867 he had already won success in Italy, where he had gone in 1864 and was to remain for most of his life. His composition style was almost entirely accommodated to European tastes, but it included American themes, most notably in *Il Guarany*, his greatest success, first performed in Milan at the Scala in 1870.

In addition to opera, the songs and piano music preferred by the bourgeoisie, performed in the setting of the salon, equally reflected European tastes. Symphonic and chamber music were less significant. In Argentina, for example, it was not until the end of the nineteenth century that greater prosperity allowed for an increase in the number of professional musicians and made it possible to mount musical performances, other than opera, on a large scale. These conditions also created a more propitious climate for the composition and performance of works by national composers. Of these, the most prominent was Alberto Williams (1862–1952), a prolific composer (112 opus numbers in total) whose compositions reflected the land, its people and the gaucho traditions of the *payadores*. His first collection of *Aires de la Pampa* (1893) included the first of the many *cielitos*, *gatos*, *vidalitas*, *milongas* and other popular songs and dances he would eventually compose, and they appeared just as *Martín Fierro* (1872) by José Hernández (1834–86) was becoming established in the national consciousness as an expression of the essential Argentinian. However, recognition of popular music as a form through which to construct and express a national identity was also taking root elsewhere. In Mexico, along with salon music, composers such as Juventino Rosas (1868–94) were writing arrangements of popular local dances in addition to the polkas, waltzes, mazurkas and schottisches that were the order of the day. In Brazil, some of the first stirrings of musical nationalism may be found in the piano piece *A Sertaneja* (1869), by Brasilio Itiberé da Cunha (1846–1913), which draws on several popular melodic traditions and dance forms, and in the work of Alexandre Levy (1864–92), in compositions such as *Tango Brasileiro* (1890), for piano, and *Suite Brésilienne* (1890), for orchestra.

Notwithstanding these beginnings, the full effects of nationalism were not felt until the early years of the twentieth century, when it was soon the most significant trend in art music in Latin America and remained so until about 1950, long after the fashion for musical nationalism had declined in Europe. Nationalism was not only a response to a process of identity formation which the cultures of all Latin American republics experienced in their way, but a response to changes in musical tastes and styles emanating from avant-garde Europe. It was not, therefore, an entirely introspective movement, but one in which New World cultures again showed their capacity for innovation based on the hybridization of local and foreign forms. The result was a productive period in composition and the formation of musical styles which brought recognition and legitimacy to the musical life of the continent by bringing its instruments and the immense variety of popular forms in indigenous, mestizo, *criollo* and Afro-American music more fully into the Western tradition. The most notable successes, at least in terms of their international impact, were in Mexico, Cuba and Brazil.

In Mexico, the early work of Juan M. Ponce (1882–1948) continued the Romantic nationalism of nineteenth-century salon music, but a period of residence in Paris (1925–33) changed his writing. In the tone poem *Ferial* (1940), for example, he sought to authenticate his representation of a marketplace by orchestrating for local instruments. For all his interest in popular and folk music, however, Ponce was more comfortable with the complex harmonies of a neoclassic style. A number of his compositions for guitar, written in this vein, were popularized by Andrés Segovia and belong to the standard repertoire for the instrument.

In contrast to Ponce, Carlos Chávez (1899–1978) was also affected by new European trends in music but wrote in a style considered profoundly non-European. His impact in Mexico did much to promote musical nationalism, while the international diffusion of his work significantly enhanced the standing of Latin American music as a whole. His music was thematically and technically innovative. He drew on mestizo folk traditions and popular urban music, and his understanding of indigenous music is a product of sustained study of its forms and history. Chávez's music in a Mexican style emerged in the context of the so-called Aztec Renaissance of the 1920s, immediately after the Revolution, when the formation of a national culture, including recuperation of the pre-Hispanic past, was undertaken as a state enterprise. His new music was also made possible by the unorthodox harmonies and orchestrations fostered by the European avant-garde. The authenticity of his reconstruction of pre-Cortesian music is questionable on several counts, but it certainly revolutionized contemporary music in the Americas. One of his earliest works in the new style is *El fuego nuevo* [The New Fire] (1921), a ballet based on Aztec ritual ceremonies held to propitiate the renovation of the sun at the end of its 52-year cycle.

In Cuba, the recognition and cultivation of Afro-Cuban culture had an impact on all the arts. In music, it was a source of rhythms and instrumentation, especially percussion, and was combined with the *guajiro* traditions of Hispanic Cuba. Its two most recognized exponents were Amadeo Roldán (1900–39) and Alejandro García Caturla (1906–40), who raised Cuban music to new levels through their mastery of prevailing European styles and their sensitivity to Cuban popular musical expression. In several countries, however, the formation of a national art music was impeded by late development of a suitable level of professional competence. In Peru, for example, there was no counterpart after independence to the creativity of the colonial period. European-style opera and salon music predominated and it was not until the beginning of the twentieth century, with composers such as Teodoro Valcárcel (1902–42), that local Hispanic and indigenous traditions received more serious attention.

Indigenous elements were far less significant in the formation of a national musical style in the countries of the Southern Cone of Latin America. In Chile, there is a rich indigenous heritage, but European traditions dominated. In the River Plate republics of Argentina and Uruguay, the tradition of the gaucho, as noted in the case of Argentina, had already begun to characterize national musical styles by the late nineteenth century. The leading figure in the nationalist movement of the 1930s in Argentina was Juan José Castro (1895–1968) whose *Sinfonía argentina* [Argentine Symphony] (1934) drew on several dance genres, including tango, then at the peak of its popularity. Alberto Ginastera (1916–83) was also noteworthy during the 1940s. His ballet *Estancia* [Country-House] (1941) represents scenes of rural life and includes sung and recited excerpts from *Martín Fierro*, while his *Obertura para el 'Fausto' criollo* [Overture for 'Fausto'] (1943) is an evocation of the *gauchesco* comic poem by Estanislao del Campo (1834–80). Both compositions show how national identity in Argentina had by this time already become associated with cultural codifications of the past in literary texts.

Nationalism in Brazilian music already had its precursors in the nineteenth century, but it was Alberto Nepomuceno (1864–1920) who advanced the movement to a point where a national musical expression seemed more possible. He composed in a variety of different idioms, but in pieces such as *Série Brasileira* (1897), he also demonstrated how music might serve as a form of expression of Brazilian life. Whatever Nepomuceno's success, however, it was overshadowed by the life and work of Heitor Villa-Lobos (1887–1959), Brazil's most important composer to date of music in the classical style and one of Latin America's most significant composers of the twentieth century. As a young man, Villa-Lobos became familiar with the varied musical traditions of Brazil through travels in the different regions of the country. At the same time, he also absorbed the influence of European composers, including the old masters, especially Bach, but also the more recent, such as Wagner, Puccini and the French composers. He wrote prodigiously, producing about two thousand compositions, and in many of them drew upon his familiarity with the European tradition and popular Brazilian music. He wrote operas, symphonies, ballets, suites for orchestra, concertos and pieces for solo instrument. Among his best known are his *Chôros*, named for a Brazilian country dance, a series of fourteen works written between 1920 and 1929, and the *Bachianas Brasilieras* (1930–44), a set of compositions for varied instrumental and vocal combinations, which use the contrapuntal techniques of Bach in conjunction with Brazilian musical traditions, and have long since found their place in the international concert and recording repertoire. The international stature acquired by Villa-Lobos during his own lifetime was matched by the recognition he received in his own country and the impact he had on its musical life in music education and administration.

Regardless of its allegiance to popular and folk music, the nationalist movement also owed much to the avant-garde, as we have already noted. Moreover, the new musical forms from Europe were pursued independently all the while that nationalism flourished. They grew in importance as the century progressed and produced several notable figures and movements, sometimes in direct opposition to nationalism, which came to be criticized for its facile appeal to the exotic. The Mexican Julián Carrillo (1875–1965) acquired international recognition for his contribution to sound experiments in the early decades of the century. In Chile, under the leadership of the composer and teacher Domingo Santa Cruz (1899–1987), institutional structures in support of music were strengthened considerably, in ways that channelled interests towards the European heritage and twentieth-century innovation. The formation of the *Instituto de Extensión Musical* at the University of Chile in 1940 further enhanced musical professionalism in Chile and was one of several institutions and groups formed at this time in different places in Latin America, such as the *Grupo Renovación* and *Agrupación Nueva Música* in Argentina and the *Grupo de Renovación Musical* in Cuba, whose purpose was to modernize musical practice in their countries. At the same time, nationalism in music was criticized more outspokenly for the alleged backwardness it fostered. By the 1950s and 1960s nationalism no longer dominated as it once had, but coexisted with international trends. Since then, an environment of musical eclecticism has emerged, consistent with the growth of the main urban centres of Latin America into large cosmopolitan cities. Like all cultural institutions, art music has also endured the political changes and economic upheavals and reverses of the last forty years. In some countries this has resulted in certain unique directions, as in Cuba, where progressive music prospered after the revolution of 1959 and the political alignment with the former Eastern Bloc opened Cuban music to the influence of the avant-garde of Eastern Europe. By contrast, the Andean countries have had greater difficulty in developing the institutions which would permit the kind of eclecticism characteristic of other centres, such as Mexico and Argentina, where a highly sophisticated musical scene allows composers to respond to their cultural or subjective interests in a range of styles which embraces every-thing from traditional nationalism to abstract experimentalism.

Contemporary sounds

When Alejo Carpentier wrote that Latin American music exploded into existence rather than evolved in coherent and measured patterns, he also argued that its greatest beauty and strength lay in its non-classical forms. For it is in the realm of semi-popular and popular music that the region's most salient feature, the hybrid interplay of European, American and African cultures, is most powerfully expressed. We need only review the musical history of one region, the Caribbean, and one island, Cuba, to see how explosive Latin American music has been as a popular phenomenon.

The nineteenth-century *contradanza habanera*, or simply *habanera*, evolved from the Spanish *contradanza*, which was danced in formations directed by a caller. Cuban music, however, was greatly influenced by refugees and migrants from Haiti after the Haitian Revolution of 1804, who brought the traditions of French and Franco-Caribbean music and dance with them. Following the French *contredanse*, the Cuban *habanera* developed into a dance for couples, acquired an Afro-Cuban syncopated rhythm and became very popular in nineteenth-century Europe. The *habanera* was followed by the *danzón*, even more strongly Afro-Caribbean in its rhythmic form. Along with the *bolero*, another European-derived genre from Cuba, *danzón* was soon popular throughout Latin America. The bolero, a romantic song of painful love and traitorous women, had become quintessentially Mexican by the mid-1930s. One of the best-known composers and performers of bolero of that time was Agustín Lara (1900–70), whose *Noche de ronda* is a classic of the genre. The bolero's greatest years were between 1930 and 1960, but its appeal is timeless, partly because of its masterful manipulation of nostalgia. Several generations of Latin American performers have adopted it or its 1950s derivative, *bolero filin* (from the English 'feelings') at some point in their careers and continue to do so. The hit film *Danzón* (1991), by the Mexican director María Navaro, featured bolero in all its glory and testified to its staying power.

In South America, *tango* has had a similar history. It, too, is a hybrid of neo-African and European elements. It evolved in the poor suburbs of Montevideo and Buenos Aires and by the beginning of the twentieth century was already associated with the cafés and brothels frequented by poor immigrants. The social habilitation of tango and its adoption by the middle class is a product of its acceptance in France, where Argentinian emigrés took it in about 1905, and where it spawned a European tangomania that endured until the outbreak of war in 1914. In Argentina, its popularity continued to grow and peaked in the late twenties and early thirties, enhanced by the sales of sheet music, recordings, radio and film. Like bolero in Mexico, tango is a song of nostalgia, treachery and disillusion, traditionally sung to guitar but also to a small orchestra of strings, piano and one or more *bandoneones*, a diatonic accordion now firmly associated with tango. Like bolero, it also had its stars, of whom the greatest was Carlos Gardel, whose death in a plane crash in Medellín, Colombia, in 1935, while still at the height of his fame only added to his legendary stature. The popularity of tango declined, even in Argentina, after the late forties and during the second half of the century. Yet, it has shown itself capable of further mutations. The new tango of Astor Piazzolla, combining elements of jazz and blues with traditional sounds and orchestrations revived it in the eighties and nineties at the same time as a younger generation of musicians in Argentina has fused it with contemporary pop forms.

Returning to the Caribbean, Cuba is also the home of rumba, a secular Afro-Caribbean musical genre, as opposed to religious Afro-Cuban music, associated with the widespread practice of *santería* and *palo monte*, two of the many syncretic neo-African religions in the Caribbean and Latin America. Rumba emerged towards the end of the nineteenth century as an urban dance genre. Traditionally, it consisted of one or two dancers accompanied by three *conga* drums, two pairs of tapped sticks, a lead singer and chorus. Its most popular form today is the *guaguancó*. Rumba is a complex form, involving a *clave*, or continuous pattern of beat overlaid by another. The lead singer sings a *canto*, introducing the theme of the rumba, and the other vocalists sing the *montuno*, or refrain, creating a call-and-response structure.

Rumba shares the *clave*, *montuno* and call-and-response structure with *son*, perhaps the best-known variety of Cuban music. *Son* emerged in the mountains of eastern Cuba, *campesino* music that, perhaps more than any other genre of music on the island, responded to its European and African history. The guitar and the *tres* (a three-string guitar) were the principal instruments, along with bongo drums, the *marimbula* (like the African 'thumb-piano') and *güiros* (a percussion instrument made from dried gourds). *Son* migrated to Havana, where it was first recorded in 1924 by the *Sexteto Habanero*. In the 1930s, the trumpet was added to the *conjunto de son*, which combined with the influence of rumba to create the sound of urban *son*. *El trío Matamoro*, one of Cuba's most famous *conjuntos*, responsible for many of the innovations that led to the ascendance of *son*, was formed in 1925 by Miguel Matamoro (1894–1971). By the forties and fifties, Cuban music had travelled to New York City, where musicians and bandleaders like Arsenio Rodríguez, Dámaso Pérez Prado, Machito

(Frank Grillo), Mario Bauzá, Benny Moré, Israel López (Cachao) and the Puerto Ricans Tito Puente and Tito Rodríguez created *mambo*, the big-band Latin sound, through the fusion of swing jazz with *son* and its relative, the *guaracha*. As it evolved in New York City, in contact with Puerto Rican *plena* and musicians like Rafael Cortijo and Ismael Rivera, as well as North American blues, jazz and rock, this music provided the basis for the *salsa* explosion of the 1960s.

The musical history of Latin America is one of travel and adaptation. Dominican *merengue*, already popular outside the island in the 1950s and made more so in the 1980s by Juan Luis Guerra and his group *4.40*, is performed around the world. Like the Cuban *danzón*, its origins can be traced to contact with the French *contredanse*. In the nineteenth century, local versions had already emerged in Puerto Rico, Venezuela and Colombia. As performed today, *merengue* is probably one of the most popular dances of the Caribbean, far outstripping salsa, for example, as a contemporary pop form. Yet, while Cuban and other Caribbean dances provide the most startling examples of Latin American music as a regionally and internationally popular phenomenon, one can also point to many others which have followed a similar trajectory: Mexican *rancheras* and *mariachi* music, Panamanian and Colombian *cumbias*, Brazilian samba and Andean melodies recognized the world over.

This success is not without its problems, however. There is the question of stereotypes that capitalize on the 'Latin sound', as well as the problem of appropriation and ownership. One might take a closer look at the discovery, by United States blues musician Ry Cooder, of Cuban music included on the 1997 Grammy-winning recording *Buena Vista Social Club*. Although supposedly lost to the world after the 1959 Cuban Revolution, the melodies and rhythms of this recording, and many of the featured musicians, have been familiar to Latin American audiences for several decades. Certainly, the very nature of popular music as a commodity of global markets makes it open to multiple influences. For this reason, musicologists often prefer to separate the popular from the traditional or folkloric, valorizing the latter as representative of a nation or culture and discounting the former as potentially corrupted by outside influences. These debates form an integral part of the development of popular music in Latin America. When Bossa Nova first emerged in Brazil in the late 1950s, critics charged that its stars, artists such as João Gilberto and Antonio Carlos Jobim, were corrupting traditional Brazilian samba with North American musical influences, especially jazz. The history of MPB, or *música popular brasileira*, a period of intense innovation in Brazilian popular music, which Charles A. Perrone dates from 1965 to 1985, highlights these tensions. The great Chico Buarque, for example, was often hailed as a representative of traditional Brazilian music against the founders of the Tropicália movement of the late 1960s, Gilberto Gil and Caetano Veloso, who argued that Brazilian popular music needed to be open to all influences, both traditional and pop, including rock music and its various forms of electronic instrumentation.

It has become increasingly difficult to sustain this valorization of the traditional over the genres of mass popular music. How do we classify the jazzed and rocked up versions of traditional Colombian *cumbias* by Colombian pop star Carlos Vives on his 1993 album *Clásicos de la provincia* [Classics from the Provinces], which was an international hit and brought traditional tunes to new audiences? Similarly, purists would argue that salsa is a Caribbean and Latin American phenomenon, forgetting its genesis in New York recording studios. The story of salsa is perhaps most illustrative of how popular music complicates the question of origins. Celia Cruz, one of the few women to make it to stardom as a salsa performer, has said that salsa is nothing more than Cuban *son*. On the one hand, this is correct, for salsa is *son* and *son* is Cuban. But, on the other, salsa is specific to a city, New York, and a decade, the sixties, just as ties with Cuba were about to be cut off by the United States embargo and as Cuban music and the big-band mambo sound were giving way to rock'n'roll.

While salsa's genetic pool is decidedly murky, its debt to the Caribbean, especially Afro-Caribbean music, is so profound that musicologists are never reluctant to claim it as authentically Latin American. Such is not the case with other genres, often listened to by millions but rarely mentioned in academic texts or cultural writings. *Nueva Ola*, for example, is a Puerto Ricanized version of sixties rock. Lucecita Benítez, Frankie Valentín, Myrna Pagán, Charlie Robles, Chucho Avellanet and others recorded in Puerto Rico and were popular throughout Latin America, singing what many considered to be pallid Spanish-language (and sometimes English-language) imitations of Anglo music, particularly offensive as a symbol of United States political and economic influence. However, one has only to listen to a recording by the *Zafiros*, a Cuban version of the Platters popular in the sixties and seventies, to see how much North American styles had been Latin Americanized. In Mexico, groups like *Los locos del ritmo*, *Los Teen Tops* and *Los Hooligans* were equally successful, as were artists such as Roberto Carlos of the *Jovem Guarda* or *iê-iê-iê* movement in Brazil.

Rock itself has followed a particularly interesting trajectory in Latin America. In Chile and Argentina, it came to signify resistance to dictatorship and social control. In Argentina, middle-class youth were the first to make rock their own and often suffered social and political oppression as a consequence. Branded 'subversives', 'drug-addicts' and 'delinquents', rock musicians and their fans were confronted with systematic censorship, harassment and imprisonment from approximately 1965, when Argentine rock first came into existence, until 1983, when the military junta collapsed after the Falklands/Malvinas War. Some important bands of the early 1970s were *Alma y Vida, Aquelarre, Color Humano, Pappo's Blues, Pescado Rabioso, Sui Generis* and *Vox Dei*. According to rock historians Osvaldo Marzullo and Pancho Muñoz, the cry of *se va a acabar, se va a acabar, la dictadura militar* (it's going to be over, it's going to be over, the military dictatorship) was chanted in unison by crowds attending rock concerts.

When the Malvinas/Falklands War broke out in 1982, the military government outlawed English-language music on the radio. Needing to find something to play, radio stations turned, ironically enough, to *rock nacional* as a more appropriately patriotic genre. Musicians like Fito Páez, who exploded onto the Argentine scene in the eighties, were instrumental in shaping the contemporary pop scene throughout the region. Today, Argentine, Spanish and Mexican rock dominate the Spanish-language market in Latin America and in Europe and rock music has also become a major cultural presence in Brazil. Chilean techno-pop, *Café Tacuba* and *Maná* from Mexico, *rockason* from Cuba – this music is highly commodified yet culturally marginalized, derivative but original, foreign but Latin American. More recently, rap music and its variations, like reggae-rap, sung in English and Spanish, have suffered the same kind of disdain and censorship that rock so often met in its earlier years. The association of rap with urban United States culture and with African-American culture in particular, has been loudly rejected by cultural nationalists loath to acknowledge it as a new local form of music.

Among the most popular artists in any genre are the balladeers, the performers of the *balada romántica*, like the Guatemalan Ricardo Arjona and José José from Mexico. One vintage Mexican singing star, Juan Gabriel, performs light pop, often syrupy and sentimental tunes, with more emphasis on vocals than instrumentation. Like other balladeers, he borrows from a vast range of traditional and local forms while performing a genre that has become so heterogeneous that national origins are almost immaterial. He borrows, for example, from bolero, *rancheras* and other Mexican and Caribbean genres, as well as tango and Anglo soft rock. It is no coincidence that Juan Gabriel was born and raised just across the Texas border in Juarez, Mexico. Like other Latino pop musicians, including those based in the United Stated, such as Gloria Estefán, the deceased Selina and Los Lobos, he has a vast audience which recognizes the different cultural modes put into play and knows bolero, as well as United States country music and rock, *rancheras* and the blues, soft rock and salsa.

Finally, one cannot speak of contemporary Latin American popular music without mentioning *Nueva Canción*, which combines folk traditions from many different regions (Chile, Argentina, Puerto Rico, Cuba, Nicaragua) with commercial forms and creates politically and culturally committed music. Some of its greatest performers have been the Chileans Violeta and Isabel Parra, and Victor Jara, the Cubans Pablo Milanés and Silvio Rodríguez of *Nueva Trova*, Mercedes Sosa of Argentina, the brother and sister duo from Nicaragua, *Guardabarranco*, Roy Brown from Puerto Rico, the groups Inti-Illimani and Illapu from Chile and *Flor de caña* in the United States. Because the music draws on local traditions and a heterogeneous mixture of contemporary elements, the sound of *Nueva Canción* is varied. It is also inextricably linked to the political history of Latin America since 1960. As a variety of music that sought to promote political change through the preservation and recuperation of regional and national identities, its composers and performers were often in the front line of political protest and resistance to authoritarianism and state violence. Victor Jara was killed during the dictatorship of Augusto Pinochet. Mercedes Sosa was barred from her native country for many years and the Chilean group Inti-Illimani lived in exile in Europe until the nineties. In Cuba, on the other hand, *Nueva Canción*, or *Nueva Trova*, was officially sanctioned and supported. Fidel Castro's revolutionary government chose to promote mass media cultural genres as part of a plan for large-scale political and ideological reform. In the tradition of the troubadours who sang about heroes and adventurers, *nueva trova* compositions told of revolutionary struggles and Third World liberation as well as more intimate themes. Silvio Rodríguez and Pablo Milanés are the two principal figures, although their appeal today is perhaps more nostalgic than revolutionary, even if they are national heroes and continue to draw huge crowds of all ages throughout Latin America.

The traditions of the troubadour and those of politically committed songwriters have a long history in Latin America and are established genres of its contemporary music. The story of Brazil's MPB, and the emergence of performers and artists such as Edu Lobo, Elis Regina, Chico Buarque, Caetano Veloso, Milton Nascimento, Gilberto Gil and Maria Bethânia, cannot be told without referring to the terrible years of the Brazilian military dictatorship which lasted from 1964 to 1985. The continuing popularity and creative energy of Latin American protest music is further testimony to the accuracy of Alejo Carpentier's affirmation about the vitality of Latin American music and its extraordinary capacity for transformation, its ability to respond to new social and political circumstances, and to incorporate new traditions and forms. Accidents and adaptation. Unexpected changes and surprises. Measured scales and distant tunes. From Carlos Chávez to Ricky Martin, from Andean folk-songs to Cuban rapper Athanai Castro, these characteristics have marked the music of the continent throughout its history. They have resulted in its distinctive sounds, the unique voices of many communities, hybrids of many sources, which have not only been heard around the world and have affected music worldwide, but which continue to adapt, to change and surprise us.

Further reading

Aparicio, Frances R., *Listening to Salsa: Gender, Latin Popular Music, and Puerto Rican Culture*, Hanover NH, 1998

Aretz, Isabel (ed.), *América Latina en su música*, México City and Paris, 1977

Austerliz, Paul, *Merengue: Dominican Music and Dominican Identity*, Philadelphia PA, 1997

Béhague, Gerard, *Music in Latin America: An Introduction*, Englewood Cliffs NJ, 1979

(ed.), *Music and Black Ethnicity: The Caribbean and South America*, Miami FL, 1994

Carpentier, Alejo, 'América Latina en la confluencia de coordenadas históricas y su repercusión en la música', in Isabel Aretz (ed.), *América Latina en su música*, México City and Paris, 1977, pp. 20–34

La música en Cuba, 4th edn, Mexico City, 1993

Figueroa, Frank M., *Almanaque de la música latinoamericana*, 2nd edn, St Petersburg, 1996

Flores, Juan, *From Bomba to Hip-Hop: Puerto Rican Culture and Latino Identity*, New York, 2000

Leymarie, Isabelle, *La música latinoamericana: ritmos y danzas de un continente*, Barcelona, 1997

Manuel, Peter, *Caribbean Currents: Caribbean Music From Rumba to Reggae*, London, 1995

Marzullo, Osvaldo and Pancho Muñoz, *Historia del rock nacional. Todo es historia* 19, no. 239 (1987): 6–29

McGowan, Chris and Ricardo Pessanha, *The Brazilian Sound. Samba, Bossa Nova and the Popular Music of Brazil*, Philadelphia PA, 1998

Olsen, Dale E. and Daniel E. Sheehy (eds.), *The Garland Handbook of Latin American Music*, New York and London, 2000

Perrone, Charles A. and Christopher Dunn, *Masters of Contemporary Brazilian Song. MPB 1965–1985*, Austin TX, 1989

(eds.), *Brazilian Popular Music and Globalization*, London, 2001

Santiago, Javier. *Nueva Ola portoricensis*, San Juan, 1994

Savigliano, Marta E., *Tango and the Political Economy of Passion*, Boulder, San Francisco and Oxford, 1995

Schechter, John M. (ed.), *Music in Latin American Culture*, New York, 1999

Stevenson, Robert, *La música colonial en Colombia*, trans. Andrés Pardo Tovar, Cali, 1964

Stigberg, David K., 'Foreign Currents During the 60s and 70s in Mexican Popular Music: Rock and Roll, the Romantic Ballad and the Cumbia', *Studies in Latin American Popular Culture* 4 (1985): 170–84

Taylor, Julie, *Paper Tangos*, Durham NC, 1998

Tumas-Serna, Jane, 'The *Nueva Canción* Movement and Its Mass-Mediated Performance Context', *Latin American Music Review* 13, no. 2 (1992): 139–215

Waxer, Lise (ed.), *Situating Salsa: Global Markets and Local Meaning in Latin Popular Music*, New York and London, 2000

11

The theatre space in Latin America

Practice and methodologies: space

This chapter offers an exploration of the development of the space for theatre in Latin America. It does not seek to give a detailed account of dramatists and plays, for there are now many sources for that information. Rather, it seeks, firstly, to understand the conditions for the production of theatre, and, secondly, to give a sense of the emergence of a dramatic art in Latin America. It aims also to facilitate an engagement with the thinking around the theatre, to open up for the reader some of the key ways in which this thinking has had an impact on the development of the art and to suggest a possible methodology for investigation.[1]

Speaking of the experience of making theatre in Chile over the period from the 1970s to the 1990s, the director Jaime Vadell says:

> For a while I went for simultaneity on stage: making the most of the possibility that exists in theatre that a number of things can go on at the same time, with no need to juxtapose them.
>
> A few of our productions were based on that idea, which found its best expression in *Una pena y un cariño* [One part sorrow, one part tenderness]. In that play, all at the same time, there was a folkloric spectacle (that was itself a show), a game of baby football, a shantytown meeting, a woman with her baby and a drama all of her own, and two wide boys trying to get in on the action. Six different spheres of action that ran parallel to one another. It was total chaos, and I don't know how we managed to pull it all together. Unfortunately, to do this, we needed a gigantic cast. There were 29 of us in that play.

Apart from poets you need impresarios who are either daring or mad. At that time there were none, but there was sufficient energy, which has been chipped away over time. If I could I would do it all over again. One idea was left on the drawing board and might be fun: a huge frieze around national or world reality. Perhaps the history of Chile, I don't know. But a frieze, that is to say, a spectacle that passes by as if it were on a conveyor belt, like an escalator, but flat. For example, a scene of O'Higgins triumphant in Chacabuco and, three scenes further on, embarking exiled for Peru. All without any commentary and without drama, but moving along like ducks in a fairground game.

I've done my sums: I would need 80 people, hundreds of costumes, props, etc., and a good few months in rehearsal. So that in the end a few critics turn up their noses at it, a friend tells you that they didn't get it, or, in the best of cases, a good friend tells you in solidarity that he almost died laughing. I'm grateful for the good will, but I swear that in all the plays I've ever done, I've never had the slightest desire to make anyone die laughing.[2]

In its generality this statement could have been uttered by many theatre directors: it is a statement of action, of intent, of ideas, of frustration, of reality. It highlights the constant juggling of a series of considerations before a play is actually produced and others after production – critical reception, public reaction. It also underlines in a vivid way the force of creativity. Here, the emphasis is on the spectacle, the intention of using the specific characteristics of stage performance. To the fore are the material aspects of the production, and the naming of the only resource left if there are none materially: energy. And, finally, there is the despair of countenancing an ambitious project for it to be all but ignored. Vadell's words name, in terms of the real experience of theatre, what I use as the basis of my analysis, that is, an awareness of the use of space, the ways in which theatre is above all the manipulation of a series of spaces, culminating in the occupation of the performance space.

A play such as *Una pena y un cariño* is part of the 'invisible' theatre of Latin America. Partly this is because the group works only in Chile. Also, the plays the group performs are often collectively created, so there is rarely a final 'text', and even if that were available it would not be easily readable for new stagings. There are many other reasons, but the point I want to make here is that this is the experience of the vast majority of Latin American theatre: it is invisible beyond performance. That is, it has not been translated for European and North American audiences, it has not entered an international canon. This has meant that there has been a lack of appreciation of Latin American theatre compared to the notable international acclaim for its prose and poetry.

How to write about theatre, in Raymond Williams's words, as a 'consideration of play and performance, literary text and theatrical representation, not as separate entities, but as the unity which they are intended to become?' In *Drama in Performance* Williams is concerned with the 'written work in performance: that is to say, the dramatic structure of a work, which we may realize when we read it as literature, as this actually appears when the play is performed'. In suggesting a means of analysing text and performance as eventual unity he talks of depending on 'the deliberate exercise of the imagination', where the controls for the accurate remembering or imagining of performance are 'the known general facts of performance and the existing texts'.[3] The idea of the study of theatre being the 'deliberate exercise of the imagination' is suggestive and creative. Because we have limited or no access to the written work in performance we are left with incomplete information for analysis, for when access is available only to the text we find ourselves dependent on only one element of the theatrical experience. In the Latin American context, analysis based on the text alone has tended to relegate plays to a category of inferior literature, with no universal validity and generally imitative of and inferior to European forms and trends. It has not allowed for a nuanced appreciation of how the embracing of practice and theory from abroad has been central to the development of theatre, nor does it create a framework for the study of the specific context. It also ignores the possibility of the absence of a final text. What I find particularly attractive in this context about Williams's notion of 'the deliberate exercise of the imagination' is that it allows for an engagement with the theatrical: for what is theatre if it is not the reading, translation and transformation of the 'text' into dramatic structures? It also serves to position the analyst beyond the immediate experience, engaged in something that is not literary analysis, but the attempt to enter and transmit the process of production and performance.

Recent criticism has engaged in exciting ways with this process and with the multiplicity of the experience of theatre – as text, as performance, as social reality – and there has been extensive debate around the historiography of Latin American theatre including the Latino/American experience in the United States.[4] Juan Villegas, one of the leading historians and theorists, argues for a new research model rooted in the study of the historical context of the performance act, believing that 'it is indispensable to consider the theatrical text as represented – acted – in a particular historical situation'.[5] This relates to a wider debate in which theatre is read as a form of cultural expression involved in the articulation of a series of different identities: national, ethnic, sexual. Prompted by having shared the experiences of many Latin American theatre practitioners, María Bonilla and Stoyan Vladich premise their book, *El teatro latinoamericano en busca de su identidad cultural* on the idea that 'theatre, as a structure of meaning, in its development and evolution, follows a road parallel to its culture, characterized by a search for identity'.[6] For them, this theatre, 'in a permanent search for its own aesthetic, is contradictory, violent and, consciously or not, makes evident in images the ideological sources of the artistic creation'. They do not see these as being produced 'by an aesthetic search by theatre groups, but by the confrontation of each group with historical reality, political, social and economic problems, lived at the moment of the production of the work'.[7] This approach is recognizable as a positioning of theatre as a critical meeting place for the aesthetic with 'reality', with what lies beyond the stage. Methodologically, Bonilla and Vladich trace the evolution of what they name as the five structural elements of theatre – author, director, actor, performance space and audience – in order to understand when and in what circumstances they form an aesthetic, ideological and poetic unity, 'formed by the search by a people for their own cultural identity, through images that interpret Latin American cultural reality theatrically'.[8] This unity is to be found in the nascent dialogues between groups and public in terms of interaction around the problems of Latin America. The questions they pose take us to the heart of one of the issues that has become a constant in Latin American theatre: the dynamic between the aesthetic and the political and their potentially contradictory demands.

In 1989 the Colombian director Santiago García (founder and director of the famous group, La Candelaria) wrote of the urgent need for a new Latin American *dramaturgia* (dramatic art): 'making theatre in our communities ("pueblos") is not a luxury, or some self-sacrificing spiritual effort, it is simply a necessity. But a necessity whose identifying feature of artistic urgency imposes a hazardous route of experimentation alongside the search for solutions in the midst of events that are generally quite incredible.'[9] He places artistic urgency alongside social necessity, and the 'hazardous route' refers as much to the practical difficulties of performance as to the search for aesthetically satisfactory results. He expresses eloquently the nature of this search, comparing it to other processes of artistic development, where there is evidence of the juxtaposition and super-imposition of styles, yet an overall artistic identity and unity, 'a result of a spirit of innovation that supersedes the assimilations, that, in turn, lose their imitative nature and are finally, for the artist (or the collective of artists), a stimulus for their desire for creativity and invention'. For García, contemporary Latin American theatre has demonstrated the capacity to assimilate forms from other cultures and transform them until they 'break the mould and find their own spontaneous and vital artistic flight'.[10]

What is fundamental here is the sense of the theatre experience as process, as assimilation, practice and innovation moving towards artistic unity. What Santiago García sees as emerging since the fifties, and connected with questions of identity, struggle and conflict, is a *dramaturgia latinoamericana*. He defines *dramaturgia*, the dramatic art, as the 'group of texts that form the theatre spectacle in its encounter with the audience', the written text being only one of these.[11] There is, he emphasizes, a complex and evolving dialogue with the dramatic art as developed and practised in other countries and cultures or in other times, and sees this as the source of a set of interrelations that make it possible to speak about Latin American theatre, established through the 'deep and dynamic' exchange between different experiences. By this he means that, as a result of festivals, prizes, publication, touring, there exist new points of contact and communication between the practitioners, texts and experiences that make up the dramatic art and, above all, the confidence that the art is not purely imitative of Europe, that it has established its own identity.

My approach to the study of theatre is based in the analysis of the different spaces – geographic, socioeconomic, historical/political, intellectual/creative – it occupies and manipulates. So, for example, in Chile under the Pinochet regime (as in other countries with repressive regimes), established groups had to endure sudden and unexplained police presence at rehearsals, the abduction of actors for hours at a time, fire bombs and death threats: they were being reminded of the limited and potentially dangerous space they were being allowed to occupy. Socially and economically, and in a wider context, the group in the shantytown that has to suspend rehearsals in order to have a collection to feed those who have walked there on an empty stomach emerges from and responds to a vastly different social reality from professional, commercial or subsidized companies. The same group will perform in venues that allow for no or very basic staging and this, along with the immediate demands of social circumstances, will inform the nature of the works they produce and the types of communication they seek to have with their audiences. Geographically, the inaccessibility of the central venues to all but a few speaks of the impact of geographical distance from the centre as well as of class, social and economic considerations that exclude lower sectors of the population. Here, in Domingo Piga's words, are the 'público mayoritario latente', the people who 'heroically go to the theatre' when there is a production of 'extraordinary interest'.[12] And, in the most unquantifiable of the spaces, the creative, the emergence of new movements, the writing and production of experimental works might be indicative of a vibrant artistic and intellectual space in which there is an established or growing space for the communication of ideas, for discussion, for innovation, as well as audiences willing to 'risk' this type of experience. Likewise an 'estética pobre' opens out for us the sense of a theatre that accommodates its ambitious aesthetic aims to its physical reality.

The play in performance, then, does not exist in isolation, it is interrelated with this broader set of spaces, each one of which has an impact on the process of production. And the moment of performance – with the visibility and 'complicity' in the experience of the author text (author), actor (director) and audience – becomes the meeting place of the key agents and their interaction with a series of external factors. And this is central to the difficulties of theatre production. When I started to study Latin American theatre I was struck by the number of times I read of periods of 'crisis', deemed to arise when one of the key elements – the playwright, the actor and the audience – failed. So, a dearth of national dramatists, poor box-office returns, or few notable actors or directors, or all three at once, would have critics lamenting the latest crisis. In the words of the Peruvian actor and director Luis Peirano, theatre is in constant crisis, caught 'between the urgent need to perform, no matter what, and the equally urgent need to change these performances. Our theatre lives as much from the weight of its inheritance as from the uncompromising insistence on utopia.'[13] This is the constant crisis of much of Latin American theatre: to be of the time in terms of reality and social and artistic aspirations, yet to exist in sociopolitical or cultural circumstances that have to be negotiated for each production.

This raises the question of the specificity of performance. The conditions for theatre mean that it seldom moves beyond invisibility, even in terms of national boundaries. The key point, I think, is that not every theatre product is visible, and that, more often than not, single events have a weight and significance that cannot be measured by anything other than their impact at a certain time with a certain audience. This, of course, makes theatre incredibly difficult to write about, and the question remains as to how to access the immediate experience as fully as possible. In many ways my approach, based on the analysis of the different spaces theatre occupies, corresponds to the models of Bonilla and Vladich; an insistence on historical and cultural context is in line with Villegas, and like Santiago García, I look to give a sense of the ways in which different *dramaturgias* communicate. But I must also rely on Raymond Williams's 'deliberate exercise of the imagination', for it demands the creative building upon a methodology in order to enter into the dramatic experience. In the rest of this essay I will look at three 'movements' in the twentieth century that have grown from thinking and practice in theatre: independent theatre, the university theatres and collective creation.

Independent and university theatres: the creation of the 'theatre environment'

Getting onto the street was easy, we concluded that out on the street there could be no economic conditions for getting together with the public, that there we had to be able to reconnect with the task, with the joy, with the possibility of joining together as a group and having a dialogue, with no 'states of siege' between us.

As far as the choice of material, all we had to do was to weigh up the idea of a 'new beginning'. Starting again . . . once more . . . beginning . . .

Juan Moreira was the beginning and the root of national theatre. In 1884/86 there appeared in the circus, the first real theatre in the River Plate. There was no theatre, in terms of the aesthetic vanguard and dramatic reflection of the audience before *Juan Moreira*, the archetypal drama of the dispossessed man pursued by the law.[14]

In 1983 the theatre group Teatro de la Libertad was formed in Buenos Aires, a product of the necessity, of the urgency to work in freedom after seven years of dictatorship. Their street theatre, *Juan Moreira*, had, its director tells us in the article cited above, more than eight hundred performances between 1984 and 1987. The performers sought to create a historical connection with a past theatre experience, one that would have the resonance of a new beginning, whose subject matter would refer to the moment, and that would be accessible to a mass audience, an audience not 'trained' in theatre going. They are acutely aware of the manipulation of symbols, both national and theatrical, and of space, in this case the reclaiming and occupation of public spaces for performance.

Significantly, the work of the Teatro de la Libertad refers to a sense that modern River Plate, or even Latin American, theatre 'began' with *Juan Moreira*, based on the novel by Eduardo Gutiérrez (1879). The show first came into being in 1884 when the Carlo brothers of the Circo Humberto had the idea of turning the novel into a pantomime, adapted by the novelist himself, and sought the collaboration of the Uruguayan Creole Circo Scotti-Podestá.[15] In the first instance the performance was in mime and circus acts recreated the life of the romantic hero, the gaucho Juan Moreira. In 1886 the Podestá brothers turned *Juan Moreira* into a pantomime with words and made their debut with it in the provinces. The audience, again, was 'popular' in origin, and did not have a theatre-going background, the most popular form of entertainment being the circus or the music hall. And again the spectacle was hugely successful, so much so that it moved to the theatres of Buenos Aires and Montevideo in 1889. This move transformed the play. As Adam Versényi says, '[t]he exigencies of performing on a proscenium stage meant that many of the innovative scenographic elements of the circus ring had to be discarded, and the new "cultured" bourgeois audience emphasized the distance from, rather than their common heritage with, the characters of the pantomime'.[16] The move meant a step away from the circus into more 'European' and certainly less popular forms of theatre.

This experience tells us quite a lot about the changing nature of theatre and performance. If we look at the question of space, we see elements that will be repeated over the century. The social space that this theatre occupies is, in the first instance, 'popular': this play does not come from the theatrical experimentation of a 'cultured' and educated group of artists, it comes from travelling players who build it from the elements of their circus act and maximize the use of their environment so that there are few barriers between actors and spectators, who are expected to participate as part of this tradition. The hero of the play is a character with whom there is an identification as a powerful symbol of a way of life that has resisted change and the imposition of the foreign. The language is local and is a vehicle for recognizable issues. Here are all the elements of the poetic unity Bonilla and Vladich seek out. But when the performance becomes a play and moves geographically to the theatres of the capital cities of Uruguay and Argentina, the social space changes, as does the nature of the theatre experience. Subsequently, the Podestá brothers performed a series of plays related to the gaucho question and in 1896 they definitively left their circus tent when they were given the rights to a work by the dramatist M. Leguizamón (1858–1935) on condition that it was performed in a theatre. Ironically, the piece, *Calandria*, is about a gaucho who gives up his old ways, is domesticated and settles down. As Bonilla and Vladich point out: '*Calandria* signals a fact: the gaucho has been assimilated into the established order. This accentuates the social implications if we think of the change in structure of the constitution of the public that went to the circus to see *Juan Moreira* and that which would go to the Victoria Theatre to witness the domestication of a gaucho, who, although nostalgic, is accepting of his new situation.'[17] Whether this was the first Latin American play or not becomes irrelevant as we see the ways in which the theatre process is built and theatre languages are established.

Most significantly, *Juan Moreira* signals the beginning of a period in which there is a closing, a completion, of the theatre triangle. Histories of Latin American theatre will take us back to pre-Colombian ritual, to the importance of performance in indoctrination and evangelization, creating links from conquest until the present moment, and I would agree that in terms of wider questions of theatricality and performance this continuity in ritual and ceremony exists. But it is only recently that there has been a consistent creative valorization of these non-European traditions, and they have been, above all, recaptured and developed in the 'popular' and 'new' theatres as alternative forms. Theatre – as a performance of a text on stage for a specific audience – is European in origin, 'just one mode of theatricality, limited to a cultural tradition'.[18] But it is this and the lack of recognition of the impact of the process of transculturation that has meant that theatre has occupied, in Grinor Rojo's words, the space of the 'género postergado', the belated genre: not recognized in its cultural and creative specificity.[19] The late eighteenth century saw the first European-style theatres being built in Mexico, Cuba, Argentina, Venezuela, Colombia, Guatemala, Bolivia and Chile. This is the theatre that was home for visiting and resident foreign companies, and for European theatre that toured with operettas, *zarzuelas, sainetes*. The establishing of national theatres meant that there was a progressive defining of the audience, the dominant model being that of bourgeois theatre, based on 'self-referential verbal discourse, restricted to the controlled space of the stage and its commercial seating arrangements, under the control of an impresario'.[20] The image emerges of an art that develops through its relationship to a Europeanized audience, exclusive of social and cultural spaces beyond that reality.

Yet, the nineteenth century set certain foundations for theatre, most certainly in the forms and the types of debates in which it was engaged. The battles for independence had seen questions of identity, of the tensions between the foreign, the creole and the indigenous, uppermost in many dramatists' work. The key forms of the late nineteenth century were Romanticism and *costumbrism*, akin to, but not a barren copy of, European forms. Romanticism and *costumbrism* provide more than anything a vision of a range of characters in the emergent nation states, they present structures of power relationships, give clues as to how the margins relate to the centre, show, through the mixing of politics, love and tragedy, the placing of the individual in a wider national structure. Theatre became one of the spaces deemed appropriate for the education of the public in new ideas, in new moralities, new ways of being.[21] And there is the beginning of a dramatic sensibility separate from the European: Luis Ambrosio Morante (1755–1837) set up a school for actors, João Caetano dos Santos established Brazil's first national group and in 1816 published his reflections on the art of acting *Lições Dramáticas* [Dramatic Lessons].

It was early in the twentieth century that the interaction with Europe began to have different repercussions. In many ways, *costumbrism* had represented its time, and the very nature of the form had allowed for its use all over the continent. Yet, Carlos Solórzano talks of it as 'carrying the seeds of its own destruction in that it began to distance Latin American theatre from a more universal vision of political and social problems'.[22] The 1920s is a period of artistic renewal when, according to Grinor Rojo, 'the new intellectuals were more interpreters than chroniclers of facts, more active thinkers than evasive archaeologists of the past' and out of this came new theatre expressions, responding to 'the historical contract between the individual and our people and the urgent demands of a world in which the purely local is in a process of disappearing'.[23] This awareness of socio-historic change and the perception of crisis in a theatre that did not seem to be capturing the moment provoked reflection on the nature of Latin American theatre, and it is during this period that movements emerge that articulate new ways of thinking and practice.

In Mexico, the group the Siete Autores Dramáticos, founded in 1923 around a season of plays at the Municipal Theatre, began to give a voice to a set of 'new values' that they perceived as necessary in the theatre.[24] They aimed to address these through the creation of a theatre movement that would provide the space through which to: act against the old forms of theatre and to renew practices; modernize production and the repertoire; go beyond the commercialization of mainstream theatre, which they saw as abusing the ignorance of the public or the emptiness of society; create a theatre art based on the key elements of acting, dramaturgy and direction; educate the audience through a repertoire that would give them access to the classics and modern international and national theatre. This is the first stage in the conscious creation of a 'theatre environment' that would also inform the creation of the university theatres. There is an acute awareness of theatre as occupying a series of different artistic spaces, and of the need to be consistent and coherent in the efforts to control and conquer these spaces. But, nevertheless, this is a stage in the development of the theatre when the practitioners are aware that the traditional triangle is not complete, and it is this that they perceived as a prolonged crisis. The thinking and conceptualization of theatre created a notion of an ideal, but the reality – both in terms of the lack of an audience ready to engage with such progressive practices and in terms of the practitioners able to produce them was still far behind – meant that the conditions did not allow for further experimentation.

The great achievement of the first experiments in independent (unsubsidized and non-commercial) theatre was to create a solid foundation for development, a language of criticism, evaluation and intention that would be echoed in a series of other theatre movements. The protagonists set up focal points for communication and exchange, often through theatre journals, nationally they organized theatre prizes and they aimed to take theatre geographically from the centre to the margins. And independent theatre companies sought to be in contact with their audiences, to identify preoccupations and problems and to deal with these in ways that would speak to and provoke the audience. They privileged theatre practice and the aesthetic over commercial success, initiating the move from the company to the greater collectivism and involvement of the group, and sought to express universal values in the creation of a tradition of the dramatic work as literary text. Independent theatre has given Latin America some of its most respected and internationally acclaimed directors (signalling the growing centrality of the director throughout the creative process): people like Leónidas Barletta (Teatro del Pueblo), Atahualpa del Cioppo (El Galpón, Uruguay), Carlos Giménez (Rajatablas, Venezuela), Xavier Villaurrutia and Celestino Gorostiza (Teatro Ulises, Mexico), Osvaldo Dragún (Fray Mocho) and the collective the Teatro Popular Ictus in Chile. One of the great successes, perhaps, was the Federación Uruguaya de Teatros Independientes (FUTI, 1947) created as a 'rallying point'[25] for often precarious independent companies. It provided a focal point for activity for those with a shared aesthetic and ideological base, and by 1960, the FUTI had its own *carpa* (circus marquee) that could hold more than six hundred and was available to member companies as a performance space that they could use as an active way of reaching wider audiences. The impact of these groups has been one of the driving forces for innovation, and has been the source of much of contemporary dramatic writing in Latin America. Thematically, Carlos Solórzano sees the early authors reacting against the isolating effect of the specificity of *costumbrism* and reclaiming the right to express themselves in any style and in any form including the avant-garde and the embracing of 'universalism'. (For example, Roberto Arlt (Argentina, 1900–42), Xavier Villaurrutia (Mexico, 1930–50), Carlos Felipe (Cuba, 1914–75), Nelson Rodrigues (Brazil, 1912–80).)

By the late thirties, there is a further impetus for the consolidation of the art in a number of countries. In Chile, this perceived need for a truly national art resulted in the founding of the university theatres. In a vibrant cultural atmosphere especially fostered in the universities and, from 1938, in the reforming atmosphere of the government of Pedro Aguirre Cerda, the space for expansion was created and one of the strongest of the continent's traditions of university theatre was founded. The Teatro de Ensayo de la Universidad de Chile and the Teatro Experimental de la Universidad Católica were founded in 1941 and 1943 respectively. Their aims were, to a striking degree, similar to those of the Siete Autores Dramáticos, the first of the independent theatres. Above all, they sought to foster 'un ambiente teatral', an environment in which theatre would function at a high artistic and professional level. This meant that they sought to educate and form 'men of the theatre' in all aspects of theatre production – design, stage-management, directing, acting – as well as using prizes, productions and festivals to encourage new dramatic works. They sought also to 'educate' the audience in a tradition of classical and modern theatre, and they used their institutional basis to set up professional theatre schools in which these aims could be achieved. The Chilean experience is one of the most important in university theatre, but there are other notable cases. The Peruvian university theatre followed this model and the Teatro Universitario de San Marcos was established in 1941, again in an atmosphere of state support: under José Luis Bustamante y Rivero, theatre had been put under the protection of the state and a Department of Theatre was formed, leading to the creation of the Escuela Nacional de Arte Escénica (ENAE: National School of Theatre Arts) and Companía Nacional de Comedias (National Drama Company).[26]

The creation of the university theatres alongside the development of the *teatro independiente* and some national theatre speaks of the attention given in different pockets of activity to the modernization of the art. The texts that emerge in the fifties and sixties move around a number of preoccupations expressed formally in a move from the *costumbrist* dependence on environment and 'literary archaeology' into the fascination with the psychological and the interplay between history and the individual, the defining of specific identities, the assimilation of Latin American languages on stage in the exploration of aspects of national realities in local ways. So, language is important: it is local, texts deal with problems of political crisis, with important social issues, key among these being marginality. Theatre in these spaces often expressed dissent, a lack of ease with reality, or sought to denude seemingly acceptable realities. The groups forged a space for theatre that was 'contestatario', questioning, demanding of response, committed to the idea of being a voice in public, if not always convinced of the power for the impetus to change. What we begin to find in key geographic areas in Latin America – Chile, Mexico, Cuba, Argentina – are the first works of many of the dramatists that dominate the second half of the twentieth century. To name a few: in Mexico, Emilio Carballido (b. 1925), Luisa Josefina Hernández (b. 1928); in Argentina, Carlos Gorostiza (b. 1920), Osvaldo Dragún (1929–99), Griselda Gambaro (b. 1928), Eduardo Pavlovsky (b. 1933); in Chile, Egon Wolff (b. 1926), Isidora Aguirre (b. 1919), María Asunción Requena (1915–86), Luis Alberto Heiremans (1928–64), Jorge Díaz (b. 1930); in Peru Sebastián Salazar Bondy (1924–65), Sarina Helfgott

(b. 1928); in Uruguay, Carlos Maggi (b. 1922), Carlos Legido (b. 1924); in Venezuela César Rengifo (1915–80), Isaac Chocrón (b. 1933), José Ignacio Cabrujas (b. 1937). Lists can say very little; the dramatists cited here are very different, but what does distinguish them – and they are only a small number from an extremely impressive group – is the creation of the well-made play. For here is the dramatic text as literary text intended for performance. This is the theatre triangle at its most cohesive, with the professional actor, dramatist/director and the complicit audience now well trained in theatre languages international and national. And this was the source of the next crisis.

Collective creation: the force of context

> Here, undoubtedly, is the point of growth of any drama of our century: to go where reality is being formed, at work, in the streets, in assemblies, and to engage at those points with the human needs to which the actor relates.[27]

If the new movements of the thirties sought to create a 'theatre environment', then the theatre that began to appear in the late fifties and early sixties sought to broaden the scope and reach of theatre, democratize it, move it beyond the traditional spaces and incorporate it into the lives of those who were not – and could not be – the audience in the central venues. In this respect, we cannot ignore the impact of the marginal on the centre in terms of artistic challenge and innovation. In Peter Brook's words, '[I]t is always the popular theatre that saves the day.'[28] (Remember *Juan Moreira*.) As Gerardo Luzuriaga pointed out in 1978, the question of popular/populist theatre 'is one of the most widely discussed in the theater of contemporary Latin America'.[29] He provides a synthesis of popular, political and educational theatres in Latin America, showing their persistence and diversity in terms of, for example, the conquest and the use of indigenous ritual and ceremony in evangelization, the emergent working class and workers' associations and the theatre of social protest in the early twentieth century, the presentation of the events and characters of the Mexican Revolution in tent shows and music halls, children's theatre, student and independent groups who 'used the dramatic arts as a weapon in their fight for reform', the integration of consciousness-raising theatre, the development of collective creation or documentary theatre. The range is massive but again the theatre is largely invisible, for it is in marginality and the fringe that it has been developed and, more recently, theorized.

In an essay that attempts to assess the nature of popular theatre, Domingo Piga highlights the problems of identifying the 'popular'. He traces the emergence of the notion of popular theatre to the Enlightenment ideals of eighteenth-century France and quotes Rousseau's notion of theatre as a festival for the whole population, where the audience would be converted into actors, creators in the spectacle, resting the theatre back from the elites that had commanded its space since the Renaissance. For Piga these ideas are at the root of the Latin American approach. He underlines the role of the relationship between the social and artistic spaces:

> There is a reciprocal dynamic: the theatre is born, as a theme-cum-problem, and as cast, from the people, it is a product of a certain society and it returns to the people, to that society. This is how it should be understood, as a live dialogue, face to face, between the creator and the public. We should not want to use the word spectator when we speak of popular theatre, because the public in this case is a participant, it is not merely limited to being a receiver, a spectator of what is seen and heard on the stage. In an authentic popular theatre if dialogue does not exist, the phenomenon of popular theatre does not exist.

This is crucial to the understanding of the way alternative theatres developed in the sixties, when the most important innovation is the form know as collective creation, which was, says Piga, the 'necessary response, the indispensable response to the lack of authors who could create the works that the age, its people and its problems demanded'.[30]

In 1981 in Caracas, at a meeting called the Second Encounter of Latin American and Spanish Theatre, practitioners of collective creation discussed its history. It was, they said, a 'new or alternative aesthetic, a solution to a crisis . . . a crisis of the structure of traditional commercial theatre and/or culture'. They identified three levels of this structure: production, internal relationships within the producing organization and the relationship with the public. In terms of production they outline the ways in which they challenged the privileging of the literary text as the 'fundamental code of performance'.[31] For them this had meant that internal systems of organization in a company (the dominant model for production through the nineteenth and twentieth centuries) determined the role of the director as a mediator between text and actors, resulting in the isolation of text, actor and author from each other. With regard to the audience, they had sought to rectify the 'minimal creative participation of the spectator', which, again, they attribute to an antiquated European and cosmopolitan model, suited to the proscenium arch theatre, the home of the theatre of the elites, and to the illusion of a universal theatre for a universal public. This they name as a form of colonialism, reductive and exclusive of local systems of culture and reality. The roots of collective creation lie in the radical response to this 'crisis' and in the conscious and theoretically based reconfiguration of the relationships between the audience and the actor, and the space beyond the theatre venue. The interaction between these spaces is 'the source of renovation of dramatic writing', able to create original texts that function as proposals for performance, within a system of theatre production that favours involvement: the group as opposed to the company. The systematizing and theorizing of their practice becomes a way of embarking upon a type of Latin American possessing of theatre, using 'modern sciences of expression and communication in order to build on languages that had been elaborated elsewhere'.[32] We return to Santiago García's vision of Latin American dramatic art as the 'group of texts that form the theatre spectacle in its encounter with the audience'.

Collective creation is not, of course, isolated in contemporary theatre, and it would be reductive to think of it as such. We need only think of North American groups like The Living Theatre, The San Francisco Mime Troupe, Bread and Puppet Theatre, or the Chicano theatre groups, Teatro Campesino and El Teatro Esperanza. And Latin American practitioners know well the debt they owe to, for example, Brecht, *commedia dell'arte* and the theatre of the Spanish seventeenth century: Enrique Buenaventura, whose 'new theatre' is one of the central axes of collective creation, used Lope de Vega's 'Arte nuevo de hacer comedias' (The New Art of Making Plays) as his 'historical antecedent'.[33] Practitioners such as Augusto Boal (Brazil), Enrique Buenaventura (Colombia), Santiago García, the members of the Teatro Popular Ictus (Chile), Escambray (Cuba), El Galpón (Uruguay) had long experience of 'traditional' theatre: they were real 'men of the theatre' in the mould of the independent and university theatres. In short, they had served their 'apprenticeship'. Let us look briefly at three key experiences.

In 1958 Enrique Buenaventura took over the directorship of the recently formed Escuela Departamental de Teatro (Regional School of

Theatre), from which he created the Teatro Experimental de Cali (TEC), one of the most significant contemporary groups in Latin America. During the first years he used authored works, and the play through which the group really began to challenge convention was *Los soldados* [Soldiers] (1966), based on a novel by Carlos Reyes about the brutal repression of strikers on banana plantations in 1928. This experience is the genesis of their later production, *La denuncia* [The Denunciation], which, through a courtroom trial, studies the sociopolitical structures that lay at the root of such repression. *Los soldados / La denuncia* are classic examples of collective creation, the text being questioned and transformed in performance by the audiences the group sought out (workers, peasants, students), and by the practice of the forum discussion after each show. In this instance, the forums showed that there was greater interest in the causes of the eventual massacre of strikers than the role of the soldiers.[34] The method that would become central to collective production is seen in embryo here: the investigation of the theme, the search for the argument, the 'thesis', structure and dramatic image, followed by staging, text and music, and the forum.[35] It is a method that was further theorized through discussion with the other great Colombian director, founder of the group La Candelaria (1966), Santiago García, and formed the theoretical and practical basis for the work of the influential Colombian 'new theatre'.

The Cuban group Escambray, formed in 1968 as an alternative to the important group Teatro Estudio, seem to embody 'the theatrical flowering that followed the Cuban revolution'.[36] In an effort to reach beyond the centre, they moved to the region of Escambray, where they used the reality and experience of local people as the source of their theatre. They developed a 'discover-action-debate formula'[37] which they first pioneered with their *La Vitrina* [The Showcase] by Albro Paz in 1971. The active intervention of the audience led them to develop a system know as 'parenthesis' through which they sought to incorporate the interventions of the audience who would then become 'creators' with the ability to transform the play. The practice of involving the audience creatively is also central to the work of Augusto Boal, the most famous of this group beyond Latin America.[38] The fundamental forms of Boal's theatre have been Image Theatre, Invisible Theatre and Forum Theatre. Image Theatre uses a still image of the participant's life, which is then 'sculpted' by other participants in order to discover what 'direction or intention is innate in them'.[39] Invisible Theatre, as the name suggests, is theatre that happens without the audience knowing. It is mounted in places where the event might have happened, for example a restaurant, a lift, a train, the street, and the aim is to provoke reaction in those watching so that they become involved, become part of the theatre, become what Boal calls 'spect-actors'. In Forum Theatre a show is performed as if it is a conventional play, the 'spect-actors' are asked if they are in agreement with the solutions offered on stage and when they answer no the play is performed a second time, becoming this time a type of fight or game, with the 'spect-actors' invited to stop the action where they believe it could be changed. If they cannot effectively change that action, the play will be resumed as in the first performance until another person takes over. In all of this a 'joker' directs the game, corrects errors and keeps the game going. Boal seeks to create a theatre of constant change, a theatre that rejects catharsis as a maintenance of the status quo. His theatre has had massive resonance beyond Latin America and he works largely beyond Brazil. What is important here, however, is that these are techniques shared across experiences of popular and collective theatre.[40]

The impact of collective creation in Latin America has probably been more important than any other creative innovation of the twentieth century. Of course, it has led to poor plays, bad scripts, propaganda, agit-prop, the age-old paternalism of the urban elite preaching revolution to the 'uneducated' peasant and worker. But there is also a great insistence on the development of a process that marries – in the best style of Brecht, Piscator, Dario Fo – the 'message' with the art, 'entretener transformando' transformation through entertainment.[41] Collective creation has been widely misrepresented as a form that does away with the script completely and that has done great damage to the dramatic author. But, collective creations are 'scripted', complex and theatrically intelligent, and groups do work with authored texts. The key point is that, even when working with a 'literary' text, this is only one of the codes of the *puesta en escena*, the performance. This allows for the incorporation of different traditions of spectacle, dance, ritual and music, involving and celebrating cultural hybridity. Yet, inevitably perhaps, the questions prompted by collective creation have provoked a new sense of 'crisis'. And this is around the question of the predominance of *puesta en escena* over the dramatic text and the role of the literary.

New crisis: The text and performance

In 1992 the Argentine dramatist Griselda Gambaro wrote of a perceived crisis in dramatic writing, 'compared to the notable flourishing of narrative we are at the present moment seeing a crisis in dramatic writing that, nevertheless, sits alongside one of the most brilliant periods of theatre in our century in terms of the creative display of its directors'.[42] She replaces the notion of crisis with the more appropriate question of visibility. The authored text renders its creator invisible as director and actors take it over, and the practices that have evolved around collective creation and the spectacle have seen a privileging of the role of the director over that of the author. Griselda Gambaro positions this new crisis in terms of dramatists' attempts to be a reflection of their respective countries, where the turbulence of their histories has put almost insurmountable obstacles in the way of artistic realization. The art, then, reflects the crises of these societies. Crisis is the price of a dramatic art whose thematic pool of sources is the real.

'I do not write texts, I write *mise-en-scène*', says Jaime Vadell in the paper quoted at the beginning of this essay, succinctly naming this crisis. And it is true that the spaces for theatre have opened up so much that it is no longer meaningful to speak only of 'theatre', and the terms 'performance' or 'theatricality' are much more expressive of the diversity of experience.[43] What contemporary theatre demonstrates are the complexities of the ways in which the space for performance, for the theatre experience, is once again being questioned and reconfigured. To end this chapter, I want to look at what this reveals about theatre practices by looking at one recent experience.

In the summer of 1999 the hottest show in London was *Villa Villa* by the Argentine group De la Guarda. The show, staged internationally, had been described variously as 'primitive' (in New York), a 'festival', 'sensory assault' (London), 'poetic acrobatics' (France), a type of theatrical rave.[44] For the performance, the audience is herded in promenade style, surrounded by deafening sound, and the action starts above: suggestive shapes and shadows, things plopping, falling, rolling on the suspended paper stage, then a burst of light and dark, of firework-like effects that also suggest the cosmic, the milky way. And finally, the actors, the mountaineers and acrobats, the anticipation and the expectation of being enthralled, not from theatre stalls, but in a type of playpen, a space shared with the actors, filled with natural and simple elements, 'things crafted by hand. Nothing sophisticated. Things you play with; paper, water, toys, balloons, the air, our bodies . . . a kiss', as described in the programme.

In their working methods De La Guarda ostensibly destroy the theatre triangle. They work with an audience as they elaborate the show, judging the possibilities of the space that they both occupy and how they interact in it. They say that they aim to go beyond a scripted language in order to provoke feelings and sensations. The absence of words, but the overwhelming presence of music, shouting, voicings, means, they say in their programme, an immediate and pure experience. 'We try to go faster than the minds of the audience.' The different relationships created – actor/actor, actor/audience – are not based on language, on the word; rather, they are based on the creation of intense communal energy, from which a transitory community might emerge. So it would seem that we have a space undemarcated by text, author, audience. Yet, in reality, there is a 'text', for the piece is minutely scripted and communication and timing between performers is of crucial importance; there are performers and there is an audience. But the space for intellectual articulation is disrupted, the conceptual space allowed by 'traditional' Western theatre is, ostensibly, destroyed.

De La Guarda's *Villa Villa* is a series of fragmented elements which are variously decipherable if we look at them from an awareness of possible theatre spaces. In the physical use of space, the acrobatics and clowning, and in the expectation of the participation of the audience, we can see the circus and the pantomime. In the actual 'scripting' we have a collective creation with the recognizable, if slightly modified, dimension of the incorporation of the audience in the development of the piece. Like many modern theatre pieces it seeks to bypass the uncertainty of the verbal, often creating surreal and absurd juxtapositions; the physical 'assault' on the audience is reminiscent of the theatre of cruelty of such as Antonin Artaud and Fernando Arrabal; the attempt to break down the fourth wall (anticipated in the seventeenth century by the Mexican Sor Juana Inés de la Cruz) has been a constant in theatre since Pirandello and Brecht, and has been central to the practice of popular and socially committed theatre in Latin America, especially in collective creation. Going beyond the performance space, there is a loss of the national context. The group's identity as Argentine loses importance: they transcend geographic and linguistic barriers (the piece was performed simultaneously in New York and London), they are international and, through the World Wide Web, potentially global, and prominent advertising makes them part of a commercial market. Yet, the historical and political context against which this is played out is, of course, that of the continuing repercussions of the 'dirty war' waged by the Argentine dictatorship against its own citizens from 1976–83, the subsequent transition to democracy and the rearticulation and repossession of lost languages and spaces.

In pieces such as this and many others,[45] theatre is made transparent, revealed as a space of intersecting systems of meaning and evocation, the privilege of location as primary source of meaning moving from one element to another, or losing significance totally. So, ironically perhaps, modern theatre is laying bare mechanisms that have always been part of the theatre experience, but have rarely been so consciously revealed on stage. Latin American theatre, caught still in the eternal crisis of realization and production has established, more than at any time in its history, multiple spaces for expression, performance, theatricality.

Notes

1. Some of the ideas explored in this essay were presented in the History of Spanish and Latin American Theatre Lecture, 'On Interpreting Space, Process and History in Latin American Theatre', Queen Mary College, University of London, March 2001.
2. Jaime Vadell, 'Creo que el teatro es espectáculo', *Revista Apuntes* 96 (1988): 76. Throughout this essay translations from the Spanish are mine and are intended to convey the meaning as well as the types of languages that have emerged in the study of Latin American theatre.
3. Raymond Williams, *Drama in Performance* with a new Introduction and Bibliography by Graham Holderness (Milton Keynes and Philadelphia PA, 1991), p. 18.
4. See particularly the journals dedicated to the study of Latin American Theatre, for example: *Latin American Theatre Review*; *Gestos. Teoría y práctica del teatro hispánico*; *Diógenes. Anuario Crítico del Teatro Latinoamericano*; *Apuntes*; *La Escena Latinoamericana*; the publications of the Centro Latinoamericano de Creación e Investigación Teatral (CELCIT). For excellent bibliographic information see: Herbert H. Hoffman, *Latin American Play Index*, vols. I and II (Metuchen NJ and London, 1983); Fernando de Toro and Peter Roster, *Bibliografía del teatro hispanomericano*, vols. I and II (Frankfurt am Main, 1985).
5. Juan Villegas, *Para un modelo de historia del teatro* (Irvine CA, 1997), p. 37.
6. María Bonilla and Stoyan Vladich, *El teatro latinoamericano: en busca de su identidad cultural* (San José, 1988), p. 9.
7. Ibid., pp. 11, 10.
8. Ibid., p. 73.
9. Santiago García, 'La urgencia de una nueva dramaturgia', *Tablas* 3 (1989): 5.
10. Ibid., 6.
11. Ibid., 7.

12. T. Domingo Piga, 'El teatro popular: Consideraciones históricas e ideológicas', in Gerardo Luzuriaga (ed.), *Popular Theater for Social Change in Latin America* (Los Angeles CA, 1978), p. 15.

13. Luis Peirano, 'La creación teatral en América Latina desde la perspectiva de la puesta en escena', *Revista Apuntes*, 96 (1988): 99.

14. Enrique Ducal, 'Apuntes finiseculares para la historia del teatro de grupos en la Argentina', *Diógenes. Anuario Crítico del Teatro Latinoamericano* 7 (1991): 7–38.

15. See Adam Versényi, *Theatre in Latin America. Religion, Politics, and Culture from Cortés to the 1980s* (Cambridge, 1993), pp. 72–8. See also Bonilla and Vladich, *El teatro latinoamericano*, pp. 62–6.

16. Verséyni, *Theatre in Latin America*, p. 177.

17. Bonilla and Vladich, *El teatro latinoamericano*, p. 66.

18. Juan Villegas, 'Closing Remarks', in Diana Taylor and Juan Villegas (eds.), *Negotiating Performance. Gender, Sexuality and Theatricality in Latino/a America* (Durham NC and London, 1994), p. 317.

19. Grinor Rojo, *Orígenes del teatro hispanoamericano contemporáneo* (Santiago de Chile, 1972), p. 21.

20. María de la Luz Hurtado, *Teatro chileno y modernidad: identidad y crisis social*, Ediciones de Gestos. Colección Historia del Teatro, 2 (Irvine CA, 1997), p. 49.

21. See, for example: in Chile, Daniel Barros Grez (1834–1904) and Alberto Blest Gana (1830–1920); in México, Marcelino Dávalos (1871–1923) and Federico Gamboa (1864–1939); in Cuba, José Jacinto Milanés (1814–63) and Gertrudis Gómez de Avellaneda (1814–73); in Brazil, Luis Carlos Martin Pena (1815–45), Manoel de Macedo (1820–82), José de Alencar (1828–77) and França Júnior (1838–90); in Uruguay, Florencio Sánchez (1875–1910).

22. Carlos Solórzano, 'Towards Cultural Independence and Diversity. An Introduction to Theatre in the Americas', in Don Rubin (ed.), *The World Encyclopedia of Contemporary Theatre*, vol. II: *Americas* (London and New York, 1998), p. 14.

23. Grinor Rojo, *Orígenes del teatro hispanoamericano contemporáneo*, p. 27.

24. The group was composed of Franciso Monterde, José Joaquín Gamboa, Carlos Noriera Hope, Víctor Manuel Díez Barroso, Ricardo Parada León and the brothers Carlos and Lázaro Lozano García. Grinor Rojo, p. 35.

25. 'Uruguay', in *The World Encyclopedia of Contemporary Theatre*, vol. II, p. 485.

26. *The World Encyclopedia of Contemporary Theatre*, vol. II, p. 364.

27. Raymond Williams, *Drama in Performance*, p. 171.

28. Peter Brook, *The Empty Space* (London, 1990), p. 73.

29. Gerardo Luzuriaga, Preface, *Popular Theater for Social Change in Latin America*, p. xv. There is now a substantial literature on the question of contemporary popular theatres, often grouped problematically under the title of 'teatro nuevo' or new theatre. It is impossible to enter into this discussion here, neither is it desirable for it would be necessarily reductive to do so, for the theatre is too diverse. For good overviews, see Diana Taylor, Adam Versényi and Beatriz Risk, *El nuevo teatro latinoamericano: una lectura histórica* (Minneapolis MN, 1987).

30. Piga, both quotations, p. 19.

31. Orlando Rodríguez, 'El teatro latinoamericano – 1958–1982 (Cuatro Facetas)', *Cuadernos de Investigación Teatral*, 27 (Caracas, 1988), p. 17.

32. Ibid. p. 18.

33. See Versényi, *Theatre in Latin America*, p. 163.

34. Versényi, *Theatre in Latin America*, p. 164, and Bonilla and Vladich, *El teatro latinoamericano*, p. 213.

35. Bonilla and Vladich, *El teatro latinoamericano*, p. 139.

36. *The World Encyclopedia of Contemporary Theatre*, vol. II, p. 223.

37. Ibid., p. 225.

38. See 'Augusto Boal', in María M. Delgado and Paul Heritage (eds.), *In Contact with the Gods? Directors Talk Theatre* (Manchester and New York, 1996), pp. 18 and 31. Boal has pioneered forms of revolutionary theatre for radical change right up to his 1990s 'Legislative Theatre', 'theatre as doing politics', after his election as a city councillor in 1992.

39. Augusto Boal, *Games for Actors and Non-Actors* (London and New York, 1992), p. xix. See also, Augusto Boal, *Theatre of the Oppressed* (New York, 1979).

40. For an interesting critique of Boal, see David S. George, 'Theatre of the Oppressed and Teatro de Arena: In and Out of Context', *Latin American Theatre Review* 28, no. 2 (1995): 39–54.

41. Domingo Piga, 'El teatro popular', p. 11.

42. Griselda Gambaro, 'Algunas consideraciones sobre la crisis de la dramaturgia', *Revista Apuntes*, 104 (1992): p. 87.

43. For an inclusive and provocative discussion of the validity of these terms see Taylor and Villegas (eds.), *Negotiating Performance*. They underline that there is no Spanish equivalent for the term performance, and Juan Villegas argues strongly for adopting the term, 'teatralidad'.

44. Web page, http://www.delaguarda.com.

45. In an unpublished essay, 'Claves estético-culturales del teatro latinoamericano' (1994), María de la Luz Hurtado mentions, for example, *Macunaíma* (Brazil), *Lila la mariposa* (Cuba), *Los músicos ambulantes* (Peru), *La Negra Ester* (Chile).

Further reading

Key journals with articles in English

Gestos. Teoría y práctica del Teatro Latinoamericano (Articles in English, Spanish and Portuguese)
Latin American Theatre Review (Articles in English, Spanish and Portuguese)

Books on Latin American theatre history

Boyle, Catherine, *Chilean Theater, 1973–1985. Marginality, Power and Selfhood*, New Jersey, 1992

Delgado, María M. and Paul Heritage (eds.), *In Contact with the Gods? Directors Talk Theatre*, Manchester and New York, 1996 [Chapter on Boal]

Graham-Jones, Jean, *Exorcising History. Argentine Theatre under Dictatorship*, London and New Jersey, 2000

Luzuriaga, Gerardo (ed.), *Popular Theater for Social Change in Latin America*, Los Angeles CA, 1978

Rubin, Don (ed.), *The World Encyclopedia of Contemporary Theatre*, vol. II. *The Americas*, London and New York, 1998

Taylor, Diana, *Theatre of Crisis. Drama and Politics in Latin America*, Kentucky, 1990

Taylor, Diana and Juan Villegas (eds.), *Negotiating Performance. Gender, Sexuality and Theatricality in Latino/a América*, Durham NC and London, 1994

Versényi, Adam, *Theatre in Latin America. Religion, Politics and Culture from Cortés to the 1980s*, Cambridge, 1993

Williams, Raymond, *Drama in Performance* (with a new introduction and bibliography by Graham Holderness), Milton Keynes and Philadelphia PA, 1991

12

Cinema in Latin America

> Dazzled by so many marvellous inventions, the people of Macondo
> did not know where their amazement began . . . They became
> indignant over the living images that the prosperous merchant Bruno
> Crespi projected in the theatre . . . for a character who had died and
> was buried in one film and for whose misfortunes tears of affliction
> had been shed would appear alive and transformed into an Arab in the
> next one.[1]

In this passage from the novel *Cien años de soledad* (*One Hundred Years of Solitude*), Gabriel García Márquez depicts the impact of 'modernity' on the previously isolated town of Macondo. New technologies of light, speed and sound – 'so many marvellous inventions' – are brought in on what is described as an 'innocent' yellow train, though this innocence is revealed to have more sinister implications as the imperial powers, in the form of the banana company, soon arrive and take charge of the region. A local merchant offers the first movie projection in town, with films and equipment bought in from outside: the very technology of cinema, its cost and sophistication, is seen to reflect and exacerbate the unequal development between 'peripheral' places like Macondo and the metropolitan centres. The new audiences would gradually learn the conventions of documentary and narrative cinema, but the immediate impact of the medium was thrilling, 'dazzling', 'amazing'. The people of Macondo have an immediate empathy with filmic melodrama – and melodrama would be one of the main structuring forces of Latin American cinema – but find the developing 'star' system, with celebrated actors in different roles, somewhat less believable. Cinema, which Macondo's mayor calls 'a machine of illusions', is here seen as a most powerful form of entertainment, instruction but also obfuscation. Films mainly come from abroad, although local merchants like Crespi, would realize that they could sometimes increase their prosperity not just as importers and distributors, but also as producers of films. Such adventurers, who would seek to develop national and regional projects, to tell individual and collective stories in a market that would soon become dominated by Hollywood, people the history of more than one hundred years of cinema in Latin America.

The silent era

Within very few months of the first projections of the Lumière brothers in Paris in December 1895, Lumière's cameramen had found their way by boat and rail to the major capital cities of Latin America. By August 1896, C. F. Bon Bernard and Gabriel Veyre were already showing the president of Mexico, Porfirio Díaz, the new moving images and were filming the president and his family and entourage. From there the rail networks could take agents to outlying cities and provinces: screenings were reported all over Mexico by early 1898. One of the most successful films projected was Méliès's *Arrivée d'un train* and local cameramen throughout the region would soon be taking pictures of their own trains arriving at different mainline stations, one of a number of defining, foundational, images that melded progress, movement, technology and invention.

A traveller to Brazil wrote in 1917: 'Sandwiched in between business, art, press, politics, are the omnipresent and irrepressible moving picture theatres, which here in Rio de Janeiro, as in every South American city and town from the top of the Andes to Patagonian Punto Arenas, give evidence by their number and popularity of the picture age in which we live.'[2] Cinemas gradually replaced the more itinerant forms of exhibition, where a cameraman would set up his own tent as viewing area, or else project at vaudeville shows, in the *carpas* or tent theatres that flourished in working-class districts. What was the viewing on offer? This consisted almost exclusively of foreign films, from the early newsreels and *actualités*, to the narrative cinema of French and Italian melodrama that dominated world markets up to the 1910s. From the mid-1910s, once the disputes of the Patents War had been resolved in the American film industry, and taking advantage of the near paralysis of European production in the First World War, Hollywood successfully invaded and took over world markets. US films could achieve such dominance because they generally covered costs in the home market, which contained about half of the world's movie theatres, and could thus be sold cheaply abroad.

The stars and the exotic locations of Hollywood films soon appeared in photo-journals and fan magazines all over Latin America. If we agree with Mexican critic Carlos Monsiváis that Latin American audiences went to the cinema not just to dream, but also to learn how to behave and think in modern ways, in a secular world, then the early, and still dominant, teacher was Hollywood.[3]

The space for the growth of Latin American cinema in this period would be found in newsreels and documentaries, covering areas of local public and private life that international cinema would not be much concerned with: regional themes, sporting competitions, military parades. They reflected the self-images of different societies, especially the world of the aristocracy: its fashions and power and its ease in the developing cities and in impressive rural landscapes. The cinema played a key role in imagining and depicting the 'modern' nation, as the many documentaries throughout the region celebrating the Centenary of Independence from Spain in 1910 would attest. Only in very exceptional circumstances would foreign newsmen or cameramen become interested in filming in Latin America.

One notable exception was during the Mexican Revolution, 1911–17, when US journalists and film crews vied to enlist in the armed struggle and follow the armies of the revolutionary generals. Pancho Villa became the first major star of the screen by signing an exclusive contract with Mutual Film Corporation for $25,000. This sum guaranteed that Villa would try to give the cameramen optimum filming conditions by fighting and scheduling executions in daylight wherever possible, and by agreeing to rerun battles if satisfactory images had not been obtained in the heat and dust of the battle. The US interest in the Revolution, however, should not be seen to overshadow the pioneering work done by Mexican cameramen during this time. Some of the best local cineastes, Salvador Toscano, the Alva brothers and Enrique Rosas, to name the most prominent, captured images of the revolutionary struggle. In other countries, newsworthy events also attracted the film maker. In Brazil, for example, there were a number of reconstructions of notable stories, sensational crimes (*Os estranguladores* [The Stranglers], directed by Antonio Leal in 1908) or more quirky tales such as *O comprador de ratas* ([The Rat Buyer], produced by Antonio Leal, 1908) where a government attempt to overcome disease by offering to buy dead rats leads to the local population in Rio breeding rats to sell to the government.[4] In 1918 Enrique Rosas made *El automóbil gris* [The Grey Car], reconstructing the daring robberies of a gang that had operated in Mexico City in 1915. Rosas had earlier filmed the executions of several of the gang members. The documentary style that had dominated in Mexico in the revolutionary period was combined with the conventions of early Hollywood gangster movies – including a number of impressive car chases – to great effect.

The telling of 'national' tales, or the adaptation of literary classics would form the basis of the first, albeit rudimentary, attempts at narrative cinema. In Argentina, Mario Gallo made a number of short features around key events of Argentine Independence (*La Revolución de Mayo* [The May Revolution], 1909; *El fusilamiento de Dorrego* [The Shooting of Dorrego], 1910), while Humberto Cairo, in *Nobleza gaucha* [Gaucho Nobility] (1915) would take up the symbol of the gaucho, the Argentine plainsman. As other chapters in this volume explain, the gaucho had developed throughout the nineteenth century as a literary symbol and as a protagonist of popular theatre, and was, by the 1910s, being transformed from an outsider into the main representative of the 'soul' of the Argentine nation, a figure that predated the mass immigration of the late nineteenth and early twentieth centuries.

The gaucho figure also illustrates how local cinema was developing by incorporating different culture traditions, in this case literature and theatre melodrama. Another story, the very stuff of melodrama, would tell of the difficult negotiations between traditional values and modernity. In the lyrics of tango, a dance that also became a song form in the 1910s, a (usually male) protagonist is often stranded in the world of modernity, singing nostalgically of the folks back home: his mother, his friends and his local neighbourhood, the barrio, which is the site of homespun wisdom. By contrast, an ingénu(e) is propelled into this modern world, often falling into the snares of corruption and prostitution. Even before the advent of sound, film makers such as José 'El Negro' Ferreyra would set a number of films in the *arrabales* or outskirts of Buenos Aires, one of the main sites of tango, and could on occasion persuade live orchestras to accompany the film. One film, *La muchacha del arrabal* [The Girl from the *Arrabal*] (1922), led to the recording of a notable tango of the same name, revealing once more the interpenetration of different areas of the culture industry as sound recordings and the growth of radio were helping to consolidate and reflect popular tastes.

The film heritage of Latin America in the silent era has been almost completely lost through neglect, indifference or lack of resources, which have been compounded by disasters of fire and flooding hitting key archives in, for example, Mexico City and Buenos Aires. Film historians have a few dozen prints to view and thus rely primarily on newspaper and journal accounts. These reveal the production of both documentary and fictional films in almost every country of Latin America, films that were able to capture a small percentage of the domestic market, in the interstices of the distribution and exhibition of Hollywood and European cinemas. They included the adaptation of literary classics, the more lachrymose the better, a strong influence of theatrical melodrama, a partial incorporation of Hollywood styles; and the presence of actors and actresses who had gained popularity in the vaudeville shows and circuses that dominated popular culture in the 1910s and 1920s. Some directors, almost always self-funded or supported by a local patron – the state intervened most infrequently at this time, and mainly in the role of film censor rather than film promoter – could build up a body of work. The most successful of these was the Brazilian Humberto Mauro, who was supported by the cultural maecenas, Adhemar Gonzaga, and made films like *Braza dormida* [Burned out Embers] (1928) and the stylish *Lábios sem bejos* [Lips Without Kisses] (1930), that explored the tensions between rural life (Mauro was from the outlying region of Cataguases) and the sophistication of modern urban centres such as Rio de Janeiro. There was little avant-garde exploration of the medium itself – vanguard culture in the twenties was expressed more clearly in literature and painting – though one notable exception was the abstract *Límite* [The Boundary] (1929) by the precocious eighteen-year-old Brazilian Mario Peixoto.

At the beginning of the sound era, therefore, Latin American cinema had a presence in cinemas in the region, albeit precarious. No one quite knew what the talkies would bring: would they lead to the invasion of the English language, or would foreign films be drowned out by the songs and linguistic gags of the contemporary Latin American vernacular?

Sound cinema: 1930–50

One immediate result of the coming of the talkies was the halting of film production in a number of Latin American countries that simply could not afford investment in the new technologies and technical expertise: it would take Venezuela, Colombia and Cuba, amongst others, a number of years to start making films with sound. By contrast, the main three film-producing nations, Argentina, Mexico and Brazil, tried to seize the advantages offered by this new situation. Hollywood did not develop a coherent global policy for several years: initially dubbing was not available because there was no way to mix sound. Almost in desperation, North American companies began to make Spanish-language versions of Hollywood films. In 1930, Paramount set up a huge studio near Paris, that, by working a 24-hour schedule, at one point turned out versions in a delirious twelve languages. This strategy was not successful. Local audiences wanted to see the Hollywood stars, not local stand-ins, while accent and dialect varied wildly: no Mexican audience, for example, would tolerate an Argentine accent or, worse still, a Madrid accent. As dubbing and subtitling techniques improved, Hollywood, emerging vigorously from the Depression, reconsolidated and increased its share of global markets. Yet there was still space for local producers to work with local material: song, dance, melodrama and comedy. These were the successful ingredients of early sound cinema in the region.

In Argentina the music was tango. The Paramount 'Hispanic' studios in France had already produced a number of features starring Latin America's first musical superstar, the Argentine tango singer, Carlos Gardel. These were mere vehicles for his singing, as local audiences well understood, for they often demanded that projections be suspended and the spool be rewound so that they could repeat the enjoyment of their favourite tangos such as 'Mi Buenos Aires querido' [My Beloved Buenos Aires]. Gardel, despite his reluctance, and inability, to learn English, was being groomed for English-language film markets at the time of his untimely death in an air crash in 1935. It was left to his friends in Buenos Aires, the singers, bandleaders and musicians, to star in Argentine tango films, directed with aplomb by Ferreyra and Manuel Romero, amongst others. In 1936, Romero teamed up with the cabaret singer, Libertad Lamarque, who wrote and starred in *Ayúdame a vivir* [Help Me Live] (1936), a tale of an innocent abroad in a world of duplicitous men and false glamour. The film used song as punctuation at moments of dramatic tension: the *melos* is very literally central to the drama. Critic Carlos Monsiváis has argued convincingly that melodrama in early Latin American cinema can be distinguished from Hollywood tear-jerkers like *Mildred Pierce* or *Written on the Wind* by their capacity for excess. In *Besos brujos* (1937; *Bewitching Kisses*), 'Libertad Lamarque grabs the swine that has carried her off and kisses him aggressively, repeatedly, while she exclaims: "give me back my kisses". Is it possible to go any further than this?'[5]

In Brazil, where Rio became the almost exclusive centre for film production in the thirties and forties, private producers exploited what would become a rich vein of popular culture, the *chanchada*, or musical comedy, which drew on vaudeville sketches as well as music and dance forms connected with carnival. The significantly named *Coussas nossas* [Our Things] (1931) displayed, in the face of Hollywood, 'our' Brazilian radio stars, orchestras, comedians and dancers. The indefatigable producer Adhemar Gonzaga brought to the screen the Miranda sisters, Portuguese immigrants who had become successful singers and hoofers. In *Alô Alô Brasil* (1935) and *Alô Alô Carnaval* (1936) Carmen Miranda emerged as a major star and made several more films and many records in Brazil before erupting onto the US stage and screen from 1939, where, her hair bedecked with fruit, she became a samba singing and dancing symbol of the 'Latin' in many Hollywood wartime productions, an exuberant example of the 'Good Neighbour' policy between the US and Latin America.

In Mexico, song was essential to the mood of the earliest sound melodramas. In Arcady Boytler's stylish *La mujer del puerto* (1931; *The Woman of the Port*), the protagonist, played by Andrea Palmer is betrayed by her fiancé, who causes the death of her father. Bereft, she drifts into prostitution and unwittingly sleeps with her long-lost brother in the dockside brothels of Vera Cruz. This plot – without the incest and with a more muted 'tragic' ending – was repeated in many Mexican *caberetera* or 'prostitute' films of the 1940s in particular. The songs were memorable, in particular the Marlene Dietrich-style husky lament by Palma 'I sell pleasure to men who come from the sea and leave at dawn. Why must I love?' Husky crooning in smoke-filled bars about the vicissitudes of love became the trademark of Mexico's favourite nightclub singer of the 1930s and 1940s, Agustín Lara, who composed boleros for the cinema and immortalized many of cinema's favourite melodramas and stars in song.

It would be another song form, the *canción ranchera*, which would give Mexican cinema its most popular film genre. In 1936, director Fernando de Fuentes – who had previously offered a complex and tragic portrayal of the Mexican Revolution in films such as *Vámonos con Pancho Villa* (1935; *Let's Go with Pancho Villa*) – brought out a bucolic pastoral fantasy, *Allá en el Rancho Grande* (1936; *Out on the Big Ranch*). Its vision of an imagined rural harmony and, in particular, its songs became enormously popular in Mexico and throughout Latin America and led to a proliferation of *ranchera* films. The main star to emerge in this genre was Jorge Negrete, the imperious *charro* who, in his sequined cowboy suits, sang

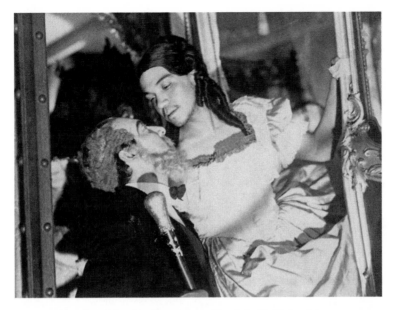

Figure 8 Manuel Medel and Mariano Moreno 'Cantinflas' in *El signo de la muerte*, 1939.

of love's conquests and failures. In this world of haughty disdain and impending danger, with every song a miniature melodrama, we are far from 'home, home on the range' of the singing cowboys of Hollywood movies. Another, less formidable, macho singing star was Pedro Infante, who became the figure of the resilience and honesty of the urban dispossessed in late 1940s films such as *Nosotros los pobres* [We the Poor] (1948). These figures could not only sing memorable songs; they also offered, in contrast to the Hollywood stars, a different style and physiognomy for 'being a man'.

Other, more picaresque, versions of male behaviour could be found in the comedians, especially the Mexican Cantinflas, who, from the late 1930s until his death in 1993, was a star throughout the subcontinent. His most successful roles were in the 1940s, in particular his depiction of the *pelado*, or scruffy streetwise neighbourhood wide-boy, who lived on his wits and managed to subvert, through verbal dexterity, the hierarchical structures of society. Cantinflas offered an extraordinary combination of physical elasticity and impossible contortions, arching eyebrows, leers and a use of language in which words, delivered at breakneck speed, went desperately in search of meanings, knocking over sense and polite society in an exhilarating rush. He would later use this humour at the service of the powers that he had once berated, but in his early days

Figure 9 Dolores del Río in *Flor silvestre*, 1943.

he was a subversive talent, whose jokes and gestures were repeated throughout Latin America. Other comics also gained a great popular following. The Argentine Niní Marshall frequently reprised several stock characters including Catita, the foul-mouthed disruptive daughter of Italian immigrants and Cándida, the *gallega* (Spanish) maid. In Brazil, the stars of *chanchada* and other film genres were Oscarito and Grande Otelo, who played quite subtly with hill-billy and racial stereotypes. Comedy remained a redoubt for national and popular sentiment in the face of Hollywood, a source of pride that there was a 'we', a community, who understood the gags, the double meanings and often improvised wordplay.

Latin America could also put forward its own, albeit reduced and somewhat under-publicized, 'star system': the singers, the comics and certain icons of beauty. The most conscious use of stars as emblems of a nation could be found in the work of the Mexican Emilio 'El Indio' Fernández – Mexico's John Ford – together with his cinematographer Gabriel Figueroa and scriptwriter Mauricio Magdaleno. El Indio persuaded the Mexican Hollywood star of the 1920s and 1930s, Dolores del Río, to return to Mexico in the early 1940s, where he teamed her with Pedro Armendáriz in a series of melodramas set at the time of the

Mexican Revolution. Figueroa, the most prolific cinematographer in the history of Latin American cinema, created a Mexico of lowering clouds, emblematic plants and the play of light and shadow, an elemental, atavistic world, where the main characters could play out dramas of loss and redemption, such as *Flor silvestre* [Wild Flower] (1943) and *María Candelaria* (1943). Here the Edenic couple, del Río and Armendáriz, communicate through a dialogue of elegant glances, with the hieratic, stoic beauty of del Río contrasted to the passion and tenderness of Armendáriz. Mexico's other major star of the 1940s, María Félix, offered a more tempestuous and aggressive image of the Mexican woman. In her third film *Doña Bárbara* (1943), based on the famous regionalist novel by the Venezuelan Rómulo Gallegos, Félix was given a part that she would repeat with variations over the next decade: *la doña*, the haughty self-reliant woman, *la devoradora*, the femme fatale. The narrative structures of her films, however, seek to reimpose the law of family and the state on the rebellious woman. This is seen most explicitly in El Indio Férnández's *Enamorada* [In Love] (1946), where, in a Mexican taming of the shrew, the rebellious Beatriz (Félix) first rejects, then falls for the young revolutionary general Reyes (Armendáriz) and follows him out to war. In a more pedagogical role, in *Río Escondido* (1947; *Hidden River*), Félix is sent by Mexican president Miguel Alemán – who plays himself in a cameo-role in the film, just as he would play a small cameo-role in Félix's off-screen life – to educate the illiterate Indian population in northern Mexico.

The cinematic representation of women was left primarily in the hands, and in the gaze, of men throughout this period, although recent scholarship has unearthed both the prints and also the life stories of directors such as the Mexicans Adela 'Perlita' Sequeyro and Matilde Landeta, who offered a different view on the stubbornly male domains of the *ranchera* film and the epic melodramas of the Mexican Revolution. In Landeta's 1949 film, *La Negra Angustias* ['Black' Angustias], a simple goatherd, brutalized by men, becomes a *coronela* in the revolutionary army and, in a rare touch of liberating revenge, orders the castration of her childhood rapist, before the iron laws of sentimental melodrama take over and she falls for a white, middle-class teacher. Angustias can, however, partially escape these laws by reasserting her own independence, riding out to do battle in the Revolution when this man abandons her. In Brazil, the actor, producer and director Carmen Santos produced a notable body of work, including directing the historical epic *Inconfidência*

Mineira [Conspiracy in Minas] (1947), while the multitalented Gilda de Abreu was a singer, actress and scriptwriter who directed the successful feature *O ebrio* [The Drunk] in 1947.

As both the quantity and quality of film production increased, especially in Mexico and Argentina, these films found ready markets in other countries in Latin America. The first attempts at sound cinema in countries such as Colombia and Peru followed the models of the *ranchera* and also the 'neighbourhood' films, with a preponderance of musical sketches. Cuban cinema was based on adaptations of popular radio soaps and also on the sounds of Caribbean music, especially in the performances of Rita Montaner, a multitalented actress, who starred in a number of rudimentary melodramas made by Ramón Peón. Other Cuban performers, most particularly the rumba dancer Ninón Sevilla, moved to Mexico and starred in several post-war dance-hall/prostitute movies, the most celebrated of which was *Aventurera* [Adventuress] (1949), a film – or rather an excessive performance by Sevilla – that would attract audiences worldwide, including the somewhat breathless attention of a young Francois Truffaut in *Cahiers du Cinéma* (1954). Cuba and Venezuela could offer exotic locations for Mexican film makers and local producers were often minor partners in co-productions. If there was any continuity in film production outside the 'big three' industries, this was to be found in documentary and particular newsreel.

Hollywood remained, however, the dominant force in the market and, as an arm of US commercial expansion, could deal quite ruthlessly with perceived threats to its market share, undermining attempts by individual countries to protect their fledgling industries through quotas or import tariffs. Cinema became an important element of US foreign policy during the Second World War when large grants – through Nelson Rockefeller's Office of the Coordinator of Inter-American Affairs – were given to its neighbour and ally Mexico to invest in studios and equipment. Perceived 'enemies' such as Argentina, however, that did not join the allied war effort until very late, were denied access to raw film stock, to such an extent that the Argentine film industry almost ground to a halt for several years. After the war, however, it was necessary to curb the success of Mexican cinema at home and in Latin America and to re-establish commercial domination in the region. Funds for production and new equipment dried up, whilst the distribution and exhibition sectors were flooded by US imports.[6] With more aggressive Hollywood marketing, Mexico found that it could maintain a market share only

Figure 10   Lima Barreto's *O cangaceiro*, 1953.

by producing quick, formulaic films known as *churros* after the doughy sweetmeat. It was time for a change.

The near impossibility of trying to compete with Hollywood in the studio production of quality films can be seen in the short-lived experiment of the Vera Cruz film company founded in Brazil in 1949. This company invested massively in the industry, building costly studios, importing new equipment and bringing over skilled European technicians. The project was posited on gaining access to international markets, which proved impossible, and it was too expensive to be maintained by the domestic market alone since Vera Cruz films cost about ten times that of average Brazilian movies. Up until 1954, Vera Cruz made eighteen films, the best known being Lima Barreto's *O cangaceiro* (1953; *The Bandit*), which was to have a great impact on the directors of the subsequent generation. In the end, however, the project was too overblown for domestic conditions. If it was very difficult to compete with Hollywood on its own terms, what were the alternatives for local cineastes?

Towards a 'new cinema'

The 1950s witnessed a slow but definite shift in the appreciation of cinema among intellectuals and middle-class sectors more generally, often fostered by the establishment of Cine Clubs and discussion groups. At the same time radical alternatives to the Hollywood studio system such as neorealism and the French 'new wave' were gaining attention and visibility. These developments chimed with the economic limitations and cultural and social aspirations of film makers in Latin America. We are talking here initially of minority groups: the majority of the film-going public of Latin America was watching, and would continue to watch, the popular formula films: masked wrestlers in Mexico (the hugely popular *Santo* films), B-movie thrillers, sex comedies (Isabel Sarli in Argentina), music and melodrama. A gap began to widen between popular taste and what intellectuals thought should be popular taste, but this was not clearly perceived in the enthusiasm for new ways of filming, that would soon become ever more practical with the introduction of lighter weight cameras. The streets could replace the studio, 'unmediated' social realities could be captured, non professionals playing 'the people' could replace the stars, individual voices, the 'politique des auteurs' could rebel against the bland anonymity of studio productions. Cine Clubs spread throughout Latin America and aspirant film directors, not satisfied by merely watching a screening of *Bicycle Thieves*, went to study at the centre of the neorealist movement, the Centro Sperimentale in Rome. Gabriel García Márquez was one of the earliest graduates, alongside the Cubans Julio García Espinosa, Tomás Gutiérrez Alea and the Argentine Fernando Birri. An even greater number would study at IDHEC (the Institut des Hautes Etudes Cinématographiques) in Paris, at the heart of the practices of the *nouvelle vague*.

With hindsight, the contours of a new movement can be perceived throughout the continent, but film makers were still working very much in isolation from each other. Mention should be made of several precursors to the 'new cinema' movements. In Brazil, Nelson Pereira dos Santos brought the production system of neorealism to Rio in *Rio 40 Graus* (1955; *Rio 40 degrees*) and *Rio Zona Norte* (1940; *Rio, Northern Zone*), focusing on the slum dwellers and the popular musicians of Rio. One young critic, Glauber Rocha celebrated this work and coined a phrase that would become the watchword of Cinema Novo in Brazil in the 1960s: he called it film making 'with an idea in the head and a camera in hand'. In Argentina, there were two directors who proposed very different models. Leopoldo Torre Nilsson was the *auteur* of aristocratic decadence. Informed by French new wave, Bergman and British directors such as Karel Reisz and Lindsay Anderson, and in close collaboration with his wife, the writer Beatriz Guido, he explored the decline of aristocratic and genteel society in Argentina in such films as *La casa del angel* (1957; *The House of the Angel*) and *La caída* (1959; *The Fall*). In the north of Argentina by contrast, Fernando Birri set up a university film school in Santa Fé and produced several neorealist works, including the documentary *Tiré die* (1958; *Throw Us a Dime*) and the fictional feature, *Los inundados* (1963; *Flooded Out*). In a corner of Mexico City, the maverick exile Spanish film maker Luis Buñuel made a series of features inside and outside the industry, which subverted all the dominant orthodoxies.

New cinemas

Informed by the stylistic revolutions in film making outlined above, the 'new' cinemas in Latin America grew up in the briefly optimistic conditions of the late 1950s and early 1960s in Latin America. Two models fuelled this optimism: the Cuban Revolution of 1959 and the myths and realities of non-revolutionary 'developmentalism' in countries such as Argentina or Brazil. Such optimism would be called into question by military coups in Brazil in 1964 and Argentina in 1966, but for a time it seemed that, especially with the model of Cuba as an exemplary, nationalist, anti-imperialist movement, and with the building of the modern city of Brasilia as a showcase of Brazilian modernity in the late fifties, new alternatives could be proposed and accomplished. In a climate of intensity and shared cultural and political horizons, in every country crucial problems were under debate: Could Cuba develop a state-led socialist cinema? Could a modus vivendi evolve between film makers and the state in 'dependent' capitalist societies? What were the conditions for production in conditions of scarcity? Which film languages and styles were most appropriate for different societies? What was the relationship between film makers (largely middle-class intellectuals) and the people they purported to represent?

The film makers were often the theorists of a movement that they claimed would, in contrast to Hollywood, be lucid, critical and realist, popular, anti-imperialist and revolutionary. Glauber Rocha in Brazil wrote of 'An Aesthetics of Hunger', Julio García Espinosa argued for an 'Imperfect Cinema' in Cuba, whilst the Argentines Solanas and Getino came up with the most widely quoted and disseminated formulation, that of a 'Third Cinema', that rejected both the 'first' cinema of

Hollywood and the 'second' cinema of national *auteurs* divorced from popular struggle. It is important to analyse these theoretical proposals in their historical context, rather than universalize them as the only 'true' path of Latin American cinema. Just as the term 'magical realism' in literature has become detached from its context and is now used, often as a term of abuse, to explain away the literature of a continent, so there has been a tendency, especially in much metropolitan criticism, to cover Latin American film production with the blanket term of Third Cinema. Third Cinema in Argentina and in Latin America refers to a few films in a short historical time frame: the sixties and early seventies.

New movements grew up in individual countries and film practitioners increasingly met in festivals and congresses throughout the region. From these meetings, but also from the general climate of liberation struggles throughout the Third World, there was talk of a Pan-American movement. Pan-Americanism has proved, however, to be a beguiling but elusive goal since the early independence movements of the nineteenth century: the development of cinema in Latin America is best understood by examining national situations, even though in the sixties there were a number of shared ideals and practices. Cuba proclaimed itself at the vanguard, setting up a national film institute, ICAIC, a well-respected film journal *Cine Cubano* and looking to develop documentary and fictional film in a climate of increasing shortages, with an early blockade of goods from the United States that denied access, amongst other things, to the latest Hollywood movies. Newsreel and documentary proved to be the most innovative area of development, especially in the work of Santiago Alvarez. Alvarez turned scarcity into a signifier, remodelling second-hand sources such as news photos and television clips and developing a poetic and politically effective film collage in such documentaries as *Now* (1965) and *Hasta la victoria siempre* (1967; *Until Victory, Always*). The most accomplished fictional film makers of the sixties were Tomás Gutiérrez Alea, in particular in *Memorias del subdesarrollo* (1968; *Memories of Underdevelopment*) and Humberto Solás, whose sprawling three part *Lucía* (1968) charted different historical moments of revolutionary development through the actions of its female protagonists. The bitter dispute over the role and function of artists and intellectuals within the Revolution, however, which mirrored economic and social debates in the decade, led to widespread exile and also to a hardening of government policies in the early seventies, to which the film industry was not immune.

Figure 11 Hemingway's house in *Memorias del subdesarrollo*, 1968.

The Cinema Novo movement in Brazil was perhaps the most complex and innovative in the region, and it was forced to adapt to very different political circumstances. Before the military coup of 1964, the young, largely Rio based, film makers of the sixties, Nelson Pereira dos Santos, Glauber Rocha, Ruy Guerra, Carlos Diegues and Joaquim Pedro de Andrade set their films in the main in the desolate north-east of Brazil, the deserted backlands, the *sertão*, with its poverty and history of mythical social bandits, the *cangaceiros*, and messianic leaders. The films ranged from Glauber's mythic *Deus e o diabo na terra do sol* (1963; *Black God, White Devil*) to Guerra's harshly realist *Os fuzis* (1963; *The Guns*) but all shared the belief that change was possible and that film makers could be in the vanguard of the movement for change. The military coup put an end to such populist dreams but for a time left-wing culture continued to flourish, albeit within state-defined limits, and film makers looked to find a place in the shadow of the 'philanthropic ogre', Octavio Paz's telling phrase for the nature of state power. It was a question of how to work within the limits of philanthropy and censorship and state terror, especially following a further coup in 1968. Glauber's *Terra em transe* (1967; *Land in Anguish*) offered an allegory of the limitations of the committed intellectual. Other film makers resorted to different forms of indirection and allusion. Joaquim Pedro de Andrade's *Macunaíma* (1969), was a popular comedy that used the metaphor of cannibalism to explore the 'devouring' nature of savage capitalism and neo-imperialism. Cinema Novo directors, despite the severity of dictatorship, managed to negotiate throughout the seventies what they perceived as an ethical relationship with state power and subsidies.

The strength and stability of state power in Mexico had always managed to defuse radicalism through co-option or coercion and the film industry was the most solid, if not cumbersome, in Latin America, with jealously guarded unionized interests. Changes were thus less striking, though a fledgling, more experimental, film making began to make progress in the sixties. In Argentina, a sophisticated group of young film makers used the city of Buenos Aires as the backdrop, or even a protagonist in films that explored middle-class anomie or alienation. The political and cultural environment radicalized under an obscurantist military regime that came to power in 1966. The most representative film of this populist radicalism, that looked to the return of the exiled president Juan Domingo Perón to save a situation that was becoming increasingly violent, was Fernando Solanas and Octavio Getino's *La hora de los hornos* (1966–8; *The Hour of the Furnaces*). This colossal four-hour work, in three parts, explored neo-colonialism and violence as the legacy of Argentina's economic and cultural dependency on Europe and posited radical Peronism as the answer to society's ills. Formally complex and ideologically Manichean, the film, and its accompanying tract, 'Towards a Third Cinema' became a clandestine rallying point against the dictator Onganía, and a model of activist film making.

In Chile, the 'democratic road' to socialism led to a victory of the *marxisant* Popular Unity coalition under Salvador Allende in 1970. The cultural and political effervescence of the years leading up to these elections saw the coming of age of Chilean cinema, with five features being made – four of them with the same camera – between 1968 and 1969. The two major directors to emerge were Raúl Ruiz, with his inventive, maverick, *Tres tristes tigres* (1968; *Three Sad Tigers*) and Miguel Littín, with the fictional/documentary reconstruction of the case of an illiterate murderer, *El chacal de Nahueltoro* (1968; *The Jackal of Nahueltoro*), who is seen as the victim of grinding rural poverty. These film makers would support Allende and try to construct a socialist film culture in the very few years that Popular Unity was allowed to govern, until the Pinochet coup of September 1973. A film maker who had studied in Chile in the early sixties, the Bolivian Jorge Sanjinés, began a lifelong preoccupation with how to make films that would adequately highlight the popular cultural and political struggles of Bolivia's workers, peasants and, in particular, indigenous peoples. His film cooperative Ukamau's most successful film was *Yawar Mallku* (1968; *Blood of the Condor*), which dramatized the sterilization of indigenous women by the US Peace Corps. But despite this success the group was not satisfied with their work. It was not enough to film in indigenous languages, with indigenous subjects. How could one find a filmic language that would illustrate the different, collective, non-individualistic, world-view of Quechua-Aymara peoples? Experiments that rejected close-ups and made, instead, extensive use of sequence shots (long takes with a still camera, with people moving in and out of the frame at middle distance) would seek to answer these questions at the level of form, while the group sought to maintain its work following a hardline military coup in 1971.

Throughout the region, therefore, the sixties and early seventies witnessed the development of radical film practices. Its moment of optimism, however, was to prove very brief. The 'hour of the furnaces', that was to light up and guide liberation struggles throughout the continent, was soon extinguished.

State repression, state-led development

From the early seventies, military dictatorships spread throughout the southern half of the continent. Banzer's coup in Bolivia in 1971 was followed by a military takeover in Uruguay, one of Latin America's most stable democracies, in 1973. The Pinochet coup in Chile took place several months later, while in Argentina, after the return of Perón in 1973 and his death less than a year later, the country spiralled into a near civil war, a violence that was extended and consolidated by the military that took power in March 1976. Film workers in these countries suffered the same fate as those in the wider community: imprisonment, murder, torture, exile or extreme censorship. In Cuba, the seventies witnessed a clamping down of artistic freedoms, while in Brazil, film makers walked the tightrope between state repression and state largesse. In Mexico, Colombia, Peru and Venezuela, the state encouraged the growth of the film sector. A few examples of these broad tendencies must suffice.

In Chile, following the Pinochet coup, domestic film production, which had not been extensive in the Popular Unity period of 1970–3, came to a complete halt and many directors and actors were forced into exile, some, like Littín, narrowly escaping with their lives.[7] In exile, paths diverged, though Chilean directors produced a remarkable body of work in exile, overcoming displacement and isolation in the host nations. Ruíz found his way to Paris, where he became, in very few years, one of the most innovative and highly regarded directors in Europe. Littín, by contrast, escaped to Mexico, where he received state support to make the Third World epic *Actas de Marusia* (1975; *Letters From Marusia*).

Ruíz's wife, Valeria Sarmiento, also developed a successful career as an editor and a director, one of several Chilean women cineastes to emerge in these years. As a broad generalization, women directors began to achieve prominence from the late 1970s, putting forward issues of gender that had largely been ignored in the first wave of new cinema in the 1960s, where politics had been the overwhelmingly pressing concern. In the severely censored world of Argentine cinema in the late seventies and early eighties, María Luisa Bemberg began her notable directorial career with two features that spoke of women's freedoms and containment, *Momentos* (1981; *Moments*) and *Señora de nadie* (1982; *Nobody's Wife*).

Her Argentine compatriot, Fernando Solanas, in contrast to Ruíz, had a much more isolated and limited experience in exile. His film on Argentine exiles in Paris, *Tangos, el exilio de Gardel* (*Tangos, the Exile of Gardel*) was started in 1981, but took until 1985 to complete, with co-production money from Argentina, which had returned to democracy in late 1983. In the film, Solanas plays a cameo as a director who literally explodes in frustration at all the setbacks he encounters. Jorge Sanjinés spent almost a decade outside Bolivia in the 1970s, but managed to stay working in the Andean region, where he succeeded in making *El enemigo principal* (1973; *The Principal Enemy*) in Peru and *Fuera de aquí* (1976; *Get Out of Here*) in Ecuador. The latter is an openly didactic film on imperialist penetration in Ecuador that, according to researchers at the University of Quito, was seen by an extraordinary three million people out of an eight million total population. In the main, however, it was foreign producers and distributors that benefited from these authoritarian conditions: the US Motion Picture Export Association recorded greatly increased profits in late seventies Argentina. No one, however, could profit from blatant censorship that banned certain foreign films and mutilated others through cuts.

In Brazil, by contrast, film makers found a way of working with the *dictablanda* – or 'soft' dictatorship – of the military government. While Cinema Novo could no longer claim to be an integrated movement for social change, its individual directors dominated film making throughout the seventies and eighties. They received support from Embrafilme, the state distribution agency that, in 1975, began to work in production and exhibition as well. Screen quotas for Brazilian films increased and the market share for Brazilian cinema went up from 15 to 30 per cent between 1970 and 1980. The runaway success of the period was Bruno Barreto's adaptation of Jorge Amado's raunchy novel, *Dona Flor e seus dois maridos* (1976; *Dona Flor and Her Two Husbands*), which, with over ten million viewers in Brazil and widespread international distribution, became the most successful film in Brazilian history. Other more sedate literary works were adapted to the screen, while the history of slavery proved the inspiration for Carlos Diegues's *Xica da Silva* (1977), and Tizuka Yamasaki explored Japanese migration to Brazil in *Gaijin: caminhos da liberdade* (1980; *Gaijin: Roads to Freedom*). Nelson Pereira dos Santos revised the early sixties Cinema Novo view that the 'people' were alienated masses that had to be educated out of false consciousness, in two films, *O amuleto de Ogum* (1974; *The Amulet of Ogum*) and *Na estrada da vida* (1980; *Road to Life*), that showed the vibrancy and strength of popular religion and popular music.

In Mexico, President Luis Echeverría, 1970–6, sought to woo intellectuals in the aftermath of the 1968 massacre of students demonstrating in Tlatelolco, Mexico City. This brought benefits to the film sector in terms of state subsidies for production, increased participation in distribution, and the establishment of a film school. The state funded some five features in 1971 and thirty-five by 1976. There was an attempt to foster a radical 'quality' cinema, in contrast to the comedies and adventure films that were the staple diet of private producers. Socially engaged topics included Ripsten's analysis of the persecution of Jews by the Inquisition in *El santo oficio* (1973; *The Holy Office*), Felipe Cazals's analysis of religious bigotry and fanaticism in *Canoa* (1975) and two films depicting early-twentieth-century history, Paul Leduc's depiction of the Mexican Revolution, *Reed, México Insurgente* (1970; *Reed, Insurgent Mexico*) and Marcela Fernández Violante's analysis of the anti-revolutionary Cristeros rebellion of the late twenties, *De todos modos Juan te llamas* (1975; *Whatever You Do, It's No Good*). Jaime Humberto Hermosillo's work, in contrast to those films that engaged with broad political subjects, followed a more intimate, but no less radical path, by exploring gender issues, in particular gay and lesbian concerns, that had been totally elided from the nationalist discourse of family and state. These promising developments were, however, interrupted in the next presidential term of office, 1976–82 when López Portillo entrusted the running of the film sector to his sister, Margarita, who proceeded to dismantle the Echeverría system.

Cuba's initial radicalism in film was tempered by hardline state policies towards culture in the seventies. ICAIC worked with historical representations, posing Cuban history as an unproblematic development from slave rebellions to revolution, while the present – with some notable exceptions such as Sara Goméz's *De cierta manera* (1974; *One Way or Another*), which dealt sensitively with gender issues and the marginality of the black population – was largely ignored. Experimentation in narrative was in the main abandoned, in favour of a more transparent style of 'revolutionary' adventure story and an increasingly Manichean political content. Other countries that had lacked any continuity in film culture, such as Peru, Colombia and Venezuela, began to offer state subsidies and the film makers emerged to take advantage of these conditions. Some of these directors, such as Román Chalbaud in Venezuela, and Francisco Lombardi in Peru, established very successful careers, whilst most others found it difficult to maintain a continuity in film making, for, whatever the advantages of state funding, cinema remained a high cost, precarious, activity. Few films could cover their costs in the home market, even fewer had access to wider markets, outside the somewhat limited world of international film festivals.

Redemocratization and neo-liberalism: towards 2000

Some general observations can be made about film culture in the period that covers the early eighties to the end of the millennium. There was a successful 'redemocratization' process throughout almost the whole region, a process that led to increased freedoms for film makers, but also to the sober awareness that the radical dreams of the sixties and early seventies had to be tempered by realism, and the marketplace. When the bones of Ernesto Che Guevara were disinterred in July 1997 and finally laid to rest, his image had moved from that of inspiration to revolution to that of honourable idealist. Bolivia, where he had been murdered, had elected in 1997 a broad civilian coalition led by the former dictator of the 1970s, General Hugo Banzer. The time was for mature deliberations and compromises, some unpalatable, as when successive democratic governments in Argentina would be forced to stop prosecuting the military for human rights abuses because of the fear of a military backlash.

If the term 'new cinema' could not be associated with revolutionary energy, it could more usefully refer to an increasing process of intro-spection, a move from the political to the personal. If the term 'new' had any currency in the eighties and nineties, it would have to be found in the ways in which film makers, in financially difficult and politically monochrome decades, managed to keep an individual and/or collective vision alive. The Colombian Sergio Cabrera found a metaphor for these circumstances in his 1993 success *La estrategia del caracol* (1993; *The Snail's Strategy*), which tells of a group of tenants in a large old house in Bogotá, who are threatened with eviction by a yuppie landowner. Cabrera offers a witty inflection on one of the oldest stories of Latin American cinema – the people of the 'neighbourhood' faced with a rapacious modernity – that avoids the sentimentality of melodrama and also the triumphalism of revolutionary optimism. Eventually the neighbourhood community is re-established in a 'new' space that is built from what has been salvaged and appropriated from the past, thanks to the creativity of different generations. Cabrera's vision for Latin American cinema is inclusive and gradualist, rather than proclaiming any radical break. The very act of film funding – it took Cabrera many years to complete the project – is in itself the strategy of a snail.

Cabrera's tenement world is also a metaphor for the nation, threatened by globalization and transnational capital. There has been an increasing tendency to see national cinema in Latin American as being swallowed up by globalization. Indeed, the Argentine critic Néstor García Canclini asked in 1993 whether there would be a Latin American cinema in the year 2000: 'What remains of national identities in a time of globalisation and interculturalism, of multinational co-production . . . of free trade agreements and regional integration?'[8] It remained the case, however, that there *was* a Latin American cinema in 2000 and that the nation remained the principal site for both the production and the reception of movies. There was an increase in co-productions with international production or distribution companies, though this was not new, but rather an exacerbation of the perennial problem of an under-financed industry seeking outside funding to hedge against almost inevitable losses in the home market. There were few directors who could move easily in and out of the national context or guarantee the interest of foreign investors. One such case, the exception rather than the rule, was the Mexican Alfonso Cuarón, whose art-house success *Solo con tu pareja* (1991), distributed in English as *Love in the Time of Hysteria*, led to a successful career in Hollywood in the late nineties. Cuarón returned to Mexico to make the 'coming of age' sex comedy *Y tu Mamá también* (*And Your Mother Too*) in 2001 before being put under contract to make the third *Harry Potter* movie. He had already displayed a great talent for adapting children's literature by bringing to the screen *The Little Princess* in 1996. Such examples – others might be the films of the Brazilian Walter Salles in the nineties, the continued pre-eminence of Raoul Ruíz in French cinema or the runaway international success of Iñárritu's Mexican feature, *Amores perros* (2001; *Love's a Bitch*) – tend to disguise rather than illustrate the very real obstacles that most film makers have always encountered in the region. An awareness of developments within the nation therefore remains the best way of keeping the period in focus.

Figure 12 Gael García Bernal in *Amores perros*, 2000.

One further shared concern across the region was the spiralling
decline in admissions throughout the 1980s, the closing of movie theatres
and what seemed like an inevitable and irretrievable loss of cinema
audiences to the 'private' consumption of television and video. This
decline was, however, stemmed in the nineties by the growth of multiplexes throughout the region, often situated in US-style shopping malls
in the more affluent parts of major cities. These malls – islands of safety,
atomized units, space capsules, where the dangers and complexities of
the street were kept at a distance – looked likely to change the urban
topography and the ways in which people occupied and used space
throughout the region. More local, privileged areas, as in the style of
Los Angeles, gradually displaced the historic centres of cities. In cinema,
neighbourhood cinemas were closed down and replaced by multiplexes
in these dispersed locations. More screens did not mean a greater variety
of movies, but rather that fewer, mainly Hollywood, films were simultaneously released in more locations. Increased ticket prices also determined who could go to the cinema with any regularity and who would be
limited, increasingly, to a diet of small-screen *telenovelas*, produced by the
big media corporations such as Televisa in Mexico and Globo in Brazil.
There had always been conflict in Latin America between producers and

exhibitors, and the multiplexes became another complex area of negotiation, where local films had to fight for screen time, usually without the protection of state-imposed screen quotas. Yet this situation, in the year 2000, was, at least, fluid, far from the prophecies of doom of the late eighties that saw Latin American cinema in irreversible decline.

The 'big three' film industries of Mexico, Argentina and Brazil had different strategies for the development of cinema in the late eighties and nineties. Mexico, under the presidency of Salinas de Gortari, 1988–94, witnessed radical changes in the relationship between cinema and the state. The impending NAFTA (North American Free Trade Association) agreement stipulated the need to open state enterprises to market forces and, as a result, state bodies working in film production, distribution and exhibition were privatized and closed-shop unions were forced to open up to competition from independent film companies. At the same time, the Mexican Film Institute, IMCINE, embarked on a policy of cofinancing certain projects, a strategy that proved successful for a limited period. More established directors consolidated their work and there emerged a new generation of talented directors including, for the first time in the history of Latin American cinema, a powerful group of women directors, Busi Cortés, María Novaro, Dana Rotberg, Guita Schyfter and Marisa Sistach. Novaro's *Danzón* (1991) became the most successful film of this group, perhaps by adhering to the tried and tested formula of 1940s Mexican cinema, that of combining melodrama with music and dance. But we are far from the sin and redemption of the fallen women of the earlier *cabaretera* films: *danzón*, a Caribbean dance rhythm, offers here a ludic element, the pleasure and elegance of popular dance. The star of this film, and of many others in the period, María Rojo, was elected to Congress in 1997, where she sought to promote positive legislation for the film industry.

The darker elements of melodrama would be found in the films of Arturo Ripstein who, together with his wife, the scriptwriter and, on occasion, co-director Paz Alicia Garcíadiego, produced in the nineties a sustained body of work unmatched in Latin America. His films are located in worlds that are closed, intense and incestuous. The preferred site of combat is the family, with domineering mothers who demand the most impossible sacrifices, or the couple – as in *Profundo carmesí* (1996; *Deep Crimson*) – alienated from society, caught up in their own, often horrific, rituals. The black humour of much of Ripstein's work chimes with the interests of other directors in the decade: this was a time when

Mexican cinema rediscovered a sense of humour after the more serious, overtly politicized films of the sixties and seventies. Perhaps the most successful formula was the comedic exploration of the sexual mores of young, attractive, middle-class protagonists, as in Cuarón's *Solo con tu pareja*, a farce about an energetic Lothario working in advertising, who is led to believe, through a medical report faked by one of his many rejected conquests, that he has AIDS. This was followed later in the decade by Antonio Serrano's box-office hit *Sexo, pudor y lágrimas* (1998; *Sex, Shame and Tears*), a slick bedroom comedy about the disintegrating relationships of modern couples.

Political satire became increasingly prominent as the power of the PRI began to weaken throughout the nineties, leading to the dismantling of one-party rule and the election of the right-of-centre PAN candidate, Vicente Fox, in 2000. The most successful Mexican release of 1996 was *Las delicias del poder* [The Delights of Power] directed by Iván Lipkies), starring Mexico's popular comic actress and film maker, María Elena Velasco, 'India María'. This farcical comedy, based around an electoral campaign that was taking place against the back-cloth of attempted political assassination, had a sharp contemporary relevance for Mexico that had seen the murder of two high-ranking PRI politicians in 1994. A more savage satirical indictment of the PRI was offered by Luis Estrada's, *La ley de Herodes* (2000; *Herod's Law*), which linked the party to corruption and murder. Herod's Law, to offer a somewhat antiseptic translation of a popular Mexican saying, means: whatever way, you're screwed. Mexico voted its way out of this conundrum, by rejecting the PRI at the 2000 elections, although whether the country and the film industry had finally repealed Herod's Law remained an open question.

In Argentina, the return to democracy in December 1983 saw a resurgence of cinema. Initially many films dealt with recent traumas: the Falkland /Malvinas war and, most insistently, the effects of the military dictatorship within Argentina and on the diasporic exile community. The Oscar award-winning *La historia oficial* (1985; *The Official Version*) offered an emblematic search for the truth of the military atrocities as a schoolteacher gradually discovers that her adopted daughter is really the child of one of the 'disappeared', whose grandmother is still searching for her. The film deployed many of the conventions of melodrama, a form derided by many political film makers of the sixties and seventies, in a most successful way. Another film not to shy away from the deployment of sentiment was María Luisa Bemberg's *Camila* (1984), the story of two lovers persecuted by an authoritarian government in the middle of the nineteenth century that served as an allegory for more recent traumas. Two films by Fernando Solanas, *Tangos: el exilio de Gardel* (1985; *Tangos, the Exile of Gardel*) and *Sur* (1988; *South*) dealt with the experience of exile and also with the internal exile of those who lived through the dictatorship. Unlike his earlier, openly didactic, hectoring, in *La hora de los hornos*, Solanas sought new forms that, by blending song, dance, the plastic arts, choreography and theatricality, sought to give pleasure to audiences as well as political instruction. As in the films of the thirties, tango represented the survival and transformations of national popular culture. Dozens of new and established directors made features in the new freedoms offered by democracy and sought to maintain visibility during the economic downturn in the late eighties and the severe neo-liberal economic conditions imposed by the Peronist President Menem in the 1990s. The urgency to depict the traumas of the recent past gradually gave way to a variety of different thematic concerns, from the freewheeling post-modernist work of Alejandro Agresti to the literary, lyrical fantasies of Eliseo Subiela, although some of the most impressive films of the nineties, including Bemberg's *De eso no se habla* (1993; *We Don't Talk About It*) and Lita Stantic's *Un muro de silencio* (1993; *A Wall of Silence*), returned insistently to areas of memory and forgetting. An earlier film by Bemberg, *Yo la peor de todas* (1990; *I The Worst of All*) had dealt with issues of censorship and intellectual persecution in the depiction of the seventeenth-century Mexican poet and nun Sor Juana Inés de la Cruz. A younger generation of directors emerged in the late nineties, working in neo-documentary style as well as in the more conventional forms of comedy and social satire, but their enthusiasm and momentum faced the stark realities of economic collapse, as from 2001 the Argentine economy plunged into its deepest ever crisis.

   In Chile, the election of a civilian government in 1990 after seventeen years of military rule had some benefits for film makers, most notably the easing of censorship. But the realities of a fractured intellectual community, the need to compromise with omnipresent military power and the chronic underfunding and under-representation of Chilean films in the domestic market were obstacles not easy to overcome. The few significant features made in the nineties were the result of co-production finance. They focused in the main on coming to terms with a recent past of dictatorship, exile and human rights abuses. Titles such as Gonzalo Justiniano's *Amnesia* (1993; *Amnesia*) and Patricio Guzmán's

Figure 13 Sor Juana (Assumpta Serna) renounces her intellectual work and writes 'I The Worst of All' in her own blood. From *Yo la peor de todas*, 1990.

La memoria obstinada (1997; *Obstinate Memory*) point to dominant issues of memory, forgetting and reconciliation, issues that were at the heart of the first Chilean feature premiered after the return to democracy, Ricardo Larraín's *La frontera* (1991; *The Frontier*). These concerns were similarly echoed in two major international features based on work by Chilean writers: *Death and the Maiden*, Roman Polanski's 1994 adaptation of Ariel Dorfman's play about torture and accountability and *Il postino* (1994), that dealt with the exile of the Chilean poet Pablo Neruda in the late 1940s and the lyrical and political power of his verse.

The Brazilian military's increasing *abertura* or 'opening' to democracy from the late 1970s and the return to democracy in the mid-eighties was accompanied by continued state support for the film industry. Critics of the period argue that despite some memorable films in the eighties, by veterans such as Nelson Pereira dos Santos (*Memórias do cárcere* 1984; *Memories of Prison*) or newcomers like Ana Carolina and Suzana Amaral, the 'state-dependent' model was entering into crisis, with jostling for patronage becoming more important than the quality of movie making.[9] But however misguided state funding had been, it had at least sustained film making for over twenty years. When President Fernando Collor de Mello dismantled Embrafilme in 1990, there was an immediate collapse in production: in 1992 only two Brazilian features were released. Collor was soon impeached on corruption charges and successive democratic governments – the interim term of Itamar Franco and the presidencies of Fernando Enrique Cardoso between 1995 and 2002 – witnessed a most successful attempt to revive the film industry, albeit through different financial incentives. Direct state funding was made available, but in the main money came from the private sector that made use of the fiscal incentives of significant tax breaks offered for film investment. Some two hundred feature films were produced between 1994 and 2000, although they had to fight for screen time in a country – and a region – still dominated by the power of Hollywood distribution. A few had widespread international success, in particular Bruno Barreto's *O que é isso companheiro* (1997; *Four Days in September*), a film that revisited radicalism of the late 1960s by depicting the kidnapping of the American Ambassador to Brazil, and Carlos Diegues's musical *Orfeu* (1999), the antidote to what Diegues referred to as the 'tourist cult' of Marcel Camus's 1959 movie, *Black Orpheus*. If Diegues's depiction of popular culture in the *favelas* or shantytowns at carnival time offered one element of continuity with the geographical and thematic interests of earlier Cinema Novo, Walter Salles's journey into the *sertão* in *Central do Brasil* (1998; *Central Station*), offered clear links to another area much favoured by Glauber Rocha among others in the early sixties: the *sertão* as a place of violence and poverty, but of ultimate redemption. In Salles's vision, the *sertão* becomes a place of reconciliation and harmony, far from the inhumanity and the dangers of modern city life. *Central Station*'s success at home and abroad seemed to represent the 'renaissance' of Brazilian film in the second half of the nineties, though the lurking economic and political crisis found a form in a number of features and documentaries, in particular Sérgio Bianchi's aptly titled *Crónicamente inviável* (2000; *Chronically Unfeasible*), where all aspects of the nation and, on a meta-textual level, all aspects of high production, 'quality' film making, are viewed as chronically unviable.

'Chronically unviable' would be the fear stalking many film makers in the region. Countries such as Peru, Colombia and Venezuela, that had seen a growth in film production in the 1980s, mainly as a result of state support, were subject to a colder, neo-liberal climate in the 1990s. Instead of talking about developing film industries, we can see the continuing work of tenacious individuals such as Francisco Lombardi in Peru, Jorge Sanjinés in Bolivia, Victor Gaviria and Sergio Cabrera in Colombia and Roman Chalbaud and Fina Torres in Venezuela, all making films against the odds. In the early nineties, with the dismantling of the Soviet Union and the Eastern Bloc, Cuba looked like the most chronically unviable place of all. Indeed, near bankruptcy and the threat of widespread civil unrest as a result of shortages, led to a severe hardening of political attitudes in the early nineties, a time that Castro called a 'Special Period in Time of Peace'. Cinema was not immune to ideological scrutiny. There was a temporary ban on Daniel Díaz Torres's *Alicia en el Pueblo de Maravillas* [Alice in Wonder Town] (1991): a town full of non-exemplary workers sent for re-education in an environment where reality and hallucination blur was not deemed to be an appropriate metaphor for the country, although many felt that the metaphor was particularly apt. As conditions eased, the veteran film maker Tomás Gutiérrez Alea made two films under the shadow of an incurable lung cancer: *Fresa y chocolate* (1994; *Strawberry and Chocolate*) that, for the first time in Cuban revolutionary cinema, explored the issue of homosexuality, and *Guantanamera* (1995), a meditation on death and a homage to the landscape and people of Cuba. There is a reference in *Guantanamera* to an Afro-Cuban legend about a god who forgot to invent death, but who would eventually rectify this error by sending a cleansing rain to end immortality. Perhaps in his last months of life, when the film was released, Alea was warning Castro about the dangers of going on forever, but by the turn of the century, the leader had yet to take this advice and, as international capital jostled to be on the ground for the next stage of Cuban 'development', money became available for cinema in terms of co-productions.

At the beginning of the new millennium, therefore, cinema was surviving and in some cases even thriving in the region through a mixture of stubbornness and creativity. One notable example was the Argentine film industry following the financial crash in 2001: despite these seemingly insurmountable odds, quality films continued to be produced. The Argentine director Carlos Sorín, dramatized this need to make movies in his 1985 feature, *La película del rey* (*A King and His Movie*). In it, a young film maker tries, increasingly desperately, to tell the story of Orélie Antoine de Tounens, a Frenchman who, in 1861, founded the kingdom of Araucania and Patagonia. The Frenchman's deranged utopian quest to achieve his goal is mirrored by that of the film maker, struggling with no money, a dwindling cast and an inhospitable terrain. Although he eventually has to abandon his film, the young director immediately becomes enthusiastic at the thought of another project. His irrepressible optimism and good humour, his inventiveness and creativity – he has to film, for example, a huge Indian uprising with only three ponies and a motley crew of unpaid extras – speaks to a century of film making in Latin America.

Notes

1. Gabriel García Márquez, *One Hundred Years of Solitude* (Harmondsworth, 1972), p. 209.
2. Clayton Sedgwick Cooper, *The Brazilians and Their Country* (New York, 1917).
3. Carlos Monsiváis, Carlos Bonfil, *A través del espejo: el cine mexicano y su público* (Mexico City, 1994).
4. For a discussion of this film and for an illuminating account of the silent era of Latin American cinema, which informs this chapter, see Ana M. López, '"A Train of Shadows": Early Cinema and Modernity in Latin America', in V. Schelling (ed.), *Through the Kaleidoscope: The Experience of Modernity in Latin America* (London, 2000), pp. 148–76.
5. Carlos Monsiváis, *Aires de familia: cultura y sociedad en América Latina* (Barcelona, 2000), pp. 66–7. My translation.
6. Seth Fine, 'From Collaboration to Containment: Hollywood and the International Political Economy of Mexican Cinema after the Second World War', in J. Hershfield and D. Maciel (eds.), *Mexico's Cinema: A Century of Film and Filmmaking* (Wilmington DE, 1999), pp. 123–63.
7. See Gabriel García Márquez, *Clandestine in Chile* (London, 1989), for an account of Littín's exile and subsequent return to Chile.
8. Néstor García Canclini, 'Will there Be Latin American Cinema in the 2000? Visual Culture in a Postnational Era', in Ann Marie Stock (ed.), *Framing Latin American Cinema: Contemporary Critical Perspectives* (Minneapolis MN, 1997), pp. 246–58.
9. See Randal Johnson, 'In the Belly of the Ogre', in John King, Ana López and Manuel Alvarado (eds.), *Mediating Two Worlds: Cinematic Encounters in the Americas* (London, 1993), pp. 211–12.

Further reading

Barnard, Tim and Peter Rist (eds.), *South American Cinema: A Critical Filmography 1915–1994*, New York, 1996

Berg, Charles Ramírez, *Cinema of Solitude: A Critical Study of Mexican Film 1967–1983*, Austin TX, 1992

Hershfield, Joanne, *Mexican Cinema/Mexican Woman, 1940–1950*, Tucson AZ, 1996

Hershfield, Joanne and David Maciel, *Mexico's Cinema: A Century of Film and Filmmakers*, Wilmington DE, 1999

Johnson, Randal, *The Film Industry in Brazil: Culture and the State*, Pittsburgh PA, 1987

Johnson, Randal and Robert Stam (eds.), *Brazilian Cinema*, New York, 1995

King, John, *Magical Reels: A History of Cinema in Latin America*, London, 2000

King, John, Ana López and Manuel Alvarado (eds.), *Mediating Two Worlds: Cinematic Encounters in the Americas*, London, 1993

King, John, Sheila Whitaker and Rosa Bosch (eds.), *An Argentine Passion: María Luisa Bemberg and Her Films*, London, 2000

Paranaguá, Paulo Antonio (ed.), *Mexican Cinema*, London, 1996

Pick, Zuzana, *The New Latin American Cinema: A Continental Project*, Austin TX, 1993

Pilcher, Jeffrey, *Cantinflas and the Chaos of Mexican Modernity*, Wilmington DE, 2001

Rashkin, Elissa J., *Women Filmmakers in Mexico: The Country of Which We Dream*, Austin TX, 2001

Stock, Ann Marie (ed.), *Framing Latin American Cinema: Contemporary Critical Perspectives*, Minneapolis MN, 1997

Xavier, Ismail, *Allegories of Underdevelopment: Aesthetics and Politics in Modern Brazilian Cinema*, Minneapolis MN, 1997

13
———————

Hispanic USA: literature, music and language

Hispanic people in the United States are no longer on the fringes of society. According to the US Census Bureau, 38.8 million lived north of the Rio Grande in 2002. That is only a record of those who are legally present. Many more, perhaps millions, are also part of the United States, although they are not yet full-fledged citizens. Not even the words used to define them are unproblematic. Too many educators, administrators and general readers are unclear as to what exactly the term 'Latino' means. Does it encompass all people with a Hispanic background, regardless of where they are born or currently live? Is the category of race a defining factor? Or is it class, nationality and language? Is Latino literature written exclusively in Spanish and delivered in translation? These misunderstandings are a symptom of a collective need to delineate – to some, simplify – a community that is only recently being considered, in statistics, by politicians and the media, as a single, semi-homogenized group. Thanks to journalists like Roberto Suro and Juan González, the definition is becoming more concrete in the public sphere, but not rapidly enough to dispel the scores of questions that abound concerning the background and unity of the minority. The term Latino has come to be used to refer to people of Hispanic background born and/or living in the United States. In terms of their size and their history, they are a minority group made of various national subgroups. The three largest are Mexican-Americans, Cuban-Americans and Puerto Ricans on the mainland, followed by smaller groups such as Dominican-Americans and Colombian-Americans. In the general imagination, for decades this minority has been addressed in a myriad of ways, from the 'Spanish-speaking people' to *hispanos* to Latins.

In any case, the number of visible and invisible people, regardless of what one calls them, is astonishing. They are reshaping the very texture of US society. They force us to revisit the past and to look to the future with renewed anticipation. To some this might look like a surprising, unexpected and recent phenomenon. But history tells us that Latinos have worked, learned, laughed and dreamed on US soil for centuries. And we continue to do so, changing America and being changed by it; adapting to the ways of the land and making the country more receptive to ourselves. Who is the Latino who has moved next door? Or, in reverse: how ought we, Latinos, understand the Anglos that surround us? These questions are at the heart of this essay. My purpose in it is to offer a map to their varied culture – past, present and future. I shall divide the content into three parts: literature, music and language. In the first part I will imagine a compendium that might help explain the paradigm of Latino and American letters: how do authors bridge that hyphen? The second part will focus on one aspect of the extraordinarily rich universe of Latino music, the *narcocorrido*. And part three will discuss the pros and cons of Spanglish, the hybrid of Spanish and English. Caution: these topics open but a minuscule window to appreciate the large vistas that constitute Latino culture. My hope is that they will be seen as trees in a magisterially florid forest.

The literary quest

In 'The Function of Criticism at the Present Time', Matthew Arnold suggested that criticism has to do with life in all its manifestations. He believed that its prime objective is the pursuit of truth not only in the realm of literature but also in that of politics and social theory. He clearly did not have in mind anthologies as a form of criticism. It was intellectual analysis of the kind displayed in *Culture and Anarchy* and *Literature and Dogma* that he was referring to when he stated that, in order to succeed, criticism ought to be 'a disinterested endeavor to learn and propagate the best that is known and thought in the world'.[1] But less than a century and a half after Arnold's lasting and provocative essay first appeared, there is little doubt that these ubiquitous artefacts, these portable libraries, are very much a branch of literary criticism.

Or are they? A quick stop at the neighbourhood bookstore allows us to glimpse at how the publishing industry in the United States is looking to promote anthologies. There are anthologies about almost every-thing imaginable, from Marilyn Monroe and Elvis Presley to eroticism in seventeenth-century France, from Chinese dissidents in Tiananmen Square to love-letters of famous politicians and young voices in the Palestine community. Very few of these volumes have a shelf-life of even a couple of years. Less a whole than a sum of parts, they do not come with a critical apparatus, nor are they comprehensive in scope and exhaustive in their selection criteria. They are somewhere between a book and a magazine, capitalizing on the curiosity of an audience with little time to read, that is more interested in the hors d'oeuvre than in the main course. The politics behind them are clear: marginalized sectors of the popu-lation (minorities, women, Third World nations, etc.) are far better repre-sented on the anthology bookshelf than in the section on general fiction.

It is useful to start with anthologies to see what Latino literature is and where it has come from. Latinos, one of the groups under-represented by New York publishing houses, are among those that have actually benefited from the frenzy to anthologize. Far more anthologies of Latino literature have been published by large and small publishing houses and by university presses in the last two decades than at any other period in the country's history. Their ancestors set the tone, from *El espejo / The Mirror: Selected Mexican-American Literature*, edited by Herminio Rios-C. and Octavio I. Romano-V. in 1969, to *Aztlán: An Anthology of Mexican-American Literature*, edited by theatre director Luis Valdez along with Stan Steiner in 1972. These anthologies, almost without exception, are destined for a trade market audience and place little emphasis on context. The reason is not difficult to grasp. Latino letters have only recently gone mainstream, and a symptom of mainstream life is the urge to anthologize, that is, to digest and digress. In addition, anthologies as a form of criticism have embraced minorities only when those minorities are seen to have built an internal social structure that turns literature into a form of conscious self-portrait, the way the emblematic Harlem Renaissance did with African-Americans.

In fact, it was not until the eighties that, as a result of government measures and also media attention, a sense of ethnic community emerged across national factions. But the quest for a centripetal force within the community has invariably been met with its centrifugal counterpart: ought Cuban-Americans, for instance, a majority of whom arrived in the United States after the Fidel Castro revolution of 1958–9, really be seen as part of the same minority as chicanos, whose life in the South-west precedes the arrival of the Mayflower? What do they share beyond a single language and a handful of historical highlights? For it to be truthful to its heterogeneous, multifaceted content, therefore, an all-encompassing critical anthology of Latino literature ought to address the parallel national histories and even the tension at the core of the minority. It must explore the parallel histories each of these subgroups has experienced prior to the media addressing them as a sum of parts. For centuries, literature was a more local affair, so there was no contact between a Latino author living in Albuquerque and another Latino author from a different national background living in New York. Even during the Civil Rights era, the relationship between chicanos and blacks in California was far more substantial than that between chicanos and Cuban-Americans. The sense of sameness, again, is a rather recent phenomenon. It is not surprising, then, that most anthologies up until 1985 chose to approach their content from a regional perspective.

In the early nineties, together with Harold Augenbraum, I put together a volume that selected material from a continental perspective: *Growing Up Latino: Memoirs and Stories*.[2] It was part of a trend that included the prolific anthological work of the poet Ray González, whose *magnum opus* in this genre was *Currents from the Dancing River*.[3] The true promoters of this trend, Nicolás Kanellos and Gary D. Keller, were active at least a decade earlier and today's generation builds upon their groundwork. Each edited a literary magazine that showcased new fiction, essays, and poetry. In 1980 and 1982, together with Francisco Jiménez, Keller edited a two-volume anthology, *Hispanics in the United States*, released by his own press, Bilingual Review, the first volume in Tempe and the second in Ypsilanti, Arizona.[4] Kanellos, the director of Arte Público Press, a small federally funded house that has been instrumental in the dissemination of chicano literature in particular, and Latino letters in general, published *A Decade of Hispanic Literature: An Anniversary Anthology*, also in 1982.[5] Kanellos's labour of love continued as he went on to create the 'Recovering the US Hispanic Literary Heritage' series, devoted to reissuing Latino classics from the seventeenth century to the present. The titles in the series include the work of precursors such as Jesús Colón and María Cristina Mena.

The foundational efforts of 'The Invaluable Ks', Keller and Kanellos, made it possible for the many editors that produced anthologies in the nineties, to consolidate the field and make it more flexible. A rotating move from the periphery of the publishing industry to New York took place as houses such as Alfred A. Knopf, Houghton Mifflin, Delta and Penguin, brought out anthologies devoted to women, poetry and growing-up stories. In some quarters, the transition was seen as an appropriation by the New England intelligentsia of work done, in particular, by chicanos. In fact, as this trend was occurring in the North-east, anthologies kept on appearing in the South-west from publishers like Chronicle Books and Mercury House in San Francisco and university presses like Arizona and New Mexico. At any rate, it was an inevitable move, simply because the nation's publishing centre, and a trend-follower, is New York in the same way that Hollywood is the nation's entertainment capital. It is a hand-me-down place: it capitalizes and exploits intellectual trends.

At any rate, the anthological paths that Keller and Kanellos opened, and their successors took, were more impressionistic than critical. At the time this editorial work was done, the dream was to showcase the new and established, and also the 'trendy' and commercial. The next step in the delineation of the Latino literary tradition, as I perceive it, is closer in spirit to the Matthew Arnold: there is a need to produce a hefty, CinemaScope-style volume that does not turn its back on the trade market but that also, to paraphrase Arnold, has as its basic goal to learn and propagate the best and most significant in Latino literature and to explain the communicating vessels between authors, œuvres, movements and regions. In other words, to generate an anthology that is as objective and balanced as possible but that, in its quest to define the tradition, does not obliterate the differences between the various groups. It should start at the time of the conquest and colonization of Florida and the South-west in the sixteenth century. In this section, figures like Alvar Núñez Cabeza de Vaca, the Spanish explorer and author of *Chronicle of the Narváez Expedition*,[6] should appear alongside 'El Inca' Garcilaso de la Vega on Florida, and other chroniclers and missionaries of New Mexico, Texas, Colorado and the Pacific Rim, such as Juan de Castellanos, Gaspar Pérez de Villagrá, Father Eusebio Francisco Kino and Fray Junípero Serra. The anthology should navigate history patiently and responsibly, and conclude with the youngest and most promising authors of our time. The nineteenth century was an age of American expansion. In 1848, the Treaty of Guadalupe Hidalgo was signed. For $15 million, the United States acquired two-thirds of the Mexican territory, and with it the population that lived there – what are the South-western states today. The impact of this event was profound, and artists reflected on it in newspaper columns, poetry, theatre, and serialized novels. Equally important, the nineteenth century was a time of intense nationalistic sentiment that produced emblematic figures like the Cuban José Martí, part of whose life was spent in New York and Florida, centres of Cuban exile. For him and for other Caribbean intellectuals, the year 1898 was a watershed, for it was then that the Spanish-American War was fought, forcing Spain to give up the colonies Cuba and Puerto Rico. Martí, Eugenio María de Hostos, José María de Heredia and Ramón Emeterio Betances, among other literary figures, found themselves involved in the events in one way or another. These figures ought to be represented.

Of course, the twentieth century has been by far the richest in literary terms. From Julia de Burgos to William Carlos Williams (who was Puerto Rican on his mother's side), from the activist voices of the Chicano Movement of the sixties, to mainstream figures like Oscar Hijuelos, Cristina García, Julia Alvarez and Sandra Cisneros, the diversity of Latino voices (poets, novelists, playwrights, film-makers) is substantial. Essential to the overall ambition of an anthology like the one I envision is its structure: its table of contents and chronology should be a parade of multinational voices but the book should also provide an intelligent apparatus so that the various subgroups (Mexican-Americans, Cuban-Americans, Puerto Ricans in the mainland) decipher their own respective paths as well. The frequently ignored oral aspect of the tradition, involving *corridos*, *merengues*, rap songs, street poets and so on, must also be explored.

Latino Studies as such is a fairly young discipline. It is nurtured by the decades-long efforts in Chicano, Puerto Rican, Cuban and Ethnic Studies, many of which came as a direct result of the struggle for self-definition in the sixties, especially in the South-west. The works of Américo Paredes on folklore on the US–Mexican border and the brothers José David and Ramón Saldívar on Chicano narrative have been decisive,[7] as have been Genevieve Fabre on the European perspectives that define Latino letters and Suzanne Oboler, Juan Flores, William Luis, Marc Zimmerman, Marguerite Fernández-Olmos, Ellen McCraken on issues of identity, gender and nationality, to offer only a brief list of academics whose energy is fully committed to the field and whose books have opened up the debate.[8] University presses can no longer afford to have a catalogue that ignores Latino Studies. Even the elitist publishing houses in New York are conscious of the explosion of academic curiosity and commitment we are witnesses to.

Similarly, as a category, Latino literature is fairly young when compared to the literatures of other American immigrant groups. Most of these groups have been part of the so-called melting pot for a long time and so have Latinos, although, as I have suggested, they have not been perceived as a single minority until recent years. Immigration has not ceased, nor is it likely to do so in the immediate future, because of the economic and political conditions in Latin America. The tension between the various national subgroups, as well as issues of race, class and gender, play an important role in the shaping of a collective identity. The debate about identity in particular takes different tones depending on who is speaking and where. Authors such as the chicano Rudolfo Anaya and the Cuban Pablo Medina ought to be read alongside Puerto Rican Piri Thomas and Dominican Junot Díaz. The juxtaposition of their œuvres allows for intriguing insights into the complexity of Latino identity north of the Rio Grande.

A list of crucial questions emerges: What are the links of these authors to the so-called 'magic realist' style south of the border? How does the tradition compare to the literature of other ethnic minorities in the United States, such as the Irish, the Italians, and the Jews? What have been its crucial influences and defining historical factors? Latino literature offers different challenges to its Latin American counterpart: Latinos are at once an extremity of Hispanic civilization in the United States and also an ethnic minority – north and south in one. In the end, the anthology should help to define and herald simultaneously the Latino literary tradition. In 1906 W. E. B. DuBois prescriptively announced that the twentieth century would be marked by the colour line. This twenty-first century, I am convinced, will be about plurality and cross-ethnic, multinational integration. In that sense, Latinos are a microcosm: a sum of heterogeneous parts yet also a whole. To be knowledgeable of this crucial portion of the population, to understand its internal diversity, is fundamental if democracy in the United States is to be strengthened.

Narcocorridos

I have mentioned the oral tradition at the heart of Latino culture, and I included the term *corrido*. In discussing Latino music, I want to use that term as a springboard. But I want to do so indirectly, by calling attention to a *corridista* of unique talent: Rosalino 'Chalino' Sánchez. He is not someone you are likely to know about. Yet his legendary role as the revitalizer of the *corrido* – as the Mexican border folk-song is known – is unquestionable among the 25 million people that inhabit the border territories that unite or separate Mexico and the United States. In fact, his reputation reaches far beyond, from his native state of Sinaloa to nearby Coahuila and Durango, and, emphatically, to the Mexican barrios of Los Angeles, where Chalino spent his most artistically fruitful years. Songs of his like 'El crimen de Culiacán' [The Crime of Culiacán] are listened to religiously on the radio in bars, birthday parties, malls and garages. His cassettes and CDs are astonishingly popular. By all accounts a mediocre singer with little stage charisma, he is nevertheless to Mexicans a folk hero of epic proportions. Soon after his mysterious death in Culiacán in 1992, more than 150 *corridos* about his plight were recorded. In the opinion of ethnomusicologists, this makes him the most written about *corrido* subject ever. The fact that the Anglo music establishment refuses to acknowledge Chalino's durability is, for me, proof of a deep distrust. He is a bestseller in a tradition whose luminaries often make it to the Billboard Latin chart, one that not only easily outsells tropical rhythms – salsa, *merengue*, *cumbia*, *bachata* – but also accounts for approximately a third of the overall Latin record sales in the United States. But the explanation of Chalino's anonymity among non-believers is more complex: together with scores of other solo *corridistas* and troupes, like Jenny Rivera and Los Hermanos Jiménez, like Los Pajaritos del Sur and Grupo Exterminador, he eulogized in his lyrics a symbol regularly vilified in the English-language media: the narcotrafficker.

Latino music is hot in the United States. Record stores across the nation have separate sections devoted to Celia Cruz and Tito Puente, Enrique Iglesias, Jennifer López, Marc Anthony and Shakira, *Los Super Seven*, La Trova Cubana and La Nueva Canción, as well as the deceased Selena. Even prominent figures such as David Byrne, Paul Simon and the Back Street Boys have released Spanish-language songs, so as not to be left behind. The audience for this music cuts across class, gender and ethnic lines: rich and poor, white and black, young and old, the rhythms are everywhere. And they have been everywhere for decades, for Latino music did not suddenly spring out of the blue. Already in the forties, Caribbean music was hip in the north-eastern states. This coincided with the arrival in Hollywood of Mexican divas such as Dolores del Río. Rancheros were not appealing, but cha-cha-cha, mambo, and rumba surely were. In their innocence, these styles, needless to say, are a far cry from the *narcocorrido*. It is not that Latino music has become politicized in the last decades: that was a change that took place in the sixties, as a result of the Civil Rights Movement and of the Cuban Revolution. No, *narcocorridos* offer a different type of politics: the celebration of drug cartels as saviors of the oppressed.

The protagonists of Chalino's songs and those by his peers are immigrants to the United States. They address head-on urgent political and social issues: poverty, drug traffic, injustice, discrimination and the disillusionments of a life built around the ever-evasive dollar bill. (The term *corrido* comes from *correr* 'to run'.) In one ballad a couple of girls disguise themselves as nuns and drive a van full of cocaine, which they claim is powdered milk for an orphanage in Phoenix. In another, two brothers, Carlos and Raúl, are the owners of a circus that uses unfair strategies to push other circuses out of business. The circus, of course, is an allegory of Mexico of the late eighties and early nineties: Carlos is an obvious reference to Carlos Salinas de Gortari, former president of Mexico, and Raúl, his drug-convict brother. These and other similar lyrics become part of one of the oldest rural musical traditions of the New World. They deliver a rough-and-tumble plot succinctly and without circumvolutions, offering a recognizable beginning that leads to a denouement, and follow a rhymed metre that is simple and straightforward. In that sense they are structurally similar to the British broadside, the cowboy songs of the South-west and gangsta rap. Instrumentally, though, they use accordion and guitar, although acoustics and percussion might also be added.

The *corrido* spread its influence in the nineteenth century but reached its apex in the Mexican Revolution that started in 1910, when political figures like Pancho Villa and Emiliano Zapata, as well as prototypes like the female soldier La Soldadera were the stuff of *corridos*. I have heard *corridos* about the bandit Tiburcio Vázquez and activist César Chávez, about the tejana singer Selena and the revolutionary Subcomandante Marcos, even about the scholar and folklorist Américo Paredes. These figures are extolled in a way that allows people to give expression to their emotion. There are also *corridos* that address historical events. In fact, the vitality of the form lies in the fact that no sooner does an important incident take place, than a song is already available to reflect on it. This immediacy is crucial: it grants it the quality of a news report. For instance, there is a *corrido* about the troublesome racial affair of police brutality in Los Angeles against Rodney King in 1992. More recently, I have listened to a *corrido* that recounts the tragedy of 11 September 2001, in New York City. There are also several movies based on *corridos*, including the highbrow *The Ballad of Gregorio Cortés*, directed by Robert Young. The *narcocorrido* is a slightly different item, however: once a sub-genre of the tradition, it has emerged since the seventies as the principal instrument to chronicle the odyssey of Mexicans across the Rio Grande in a drug-infested universe.

Let me return to Chalino and to another popular hero, the so-called 'Angel of the Poor': Jesús Malverde. These two figures strike me as real paradigms of complex popular sentiment. Malverde, for instance, is a type of magnet for collective faith, which allows people to live through violence and loss. Did he ever exist? How can one explain the fact that thousands of people stop regularly at his shrine in Culiacán to ask for a miracle, from recovery from an illness to protection against the federal police and the narcotraffickers? Scholars of various persuasions claim that he is a fusion of Catholic iconography and the biographical traces of a Sinaloan outlaw Heraclio Bernal, another representative of the oppressed, who was executed in 1909 by a mean-spirited governor and left to hang for weeks on a tree. But Eligio González, a composer and self-made entrepreneur devoted to the construction and administration of La Capilla, a chapel dedicated to honor Malverde, believes that the bandit's name was Jesús Juárez Maso, and that he became known as Malverde, 'because of the green (*verde*) pants in which he used to hide himself from the *rurales*, the rural police'.[9] In any case, Malverde, he explains, was a social bandit who, according to the legend, was severely wounded one day. His condition was desperate; he was almost dying. Suddenly, he decided to sacrifice himself by requesting that a friend turn him in so as to collect a reward posted on his name. Malverde then asked the friend to distribute the money among the dispossessed. He especially cared for those involved in the drug trade, thus his nickname 'El Narcosantón', an unofficial narco-saint.

González is known in Sinaloa for handing out wheelchairs and coffins, and for officiating at funerals. In La Capilla he has placed various *narco-corridos* about Malverde on sale. Also available are human-size busts of him. Given that no material evidence of the bandit has ever been available, González commissioned a local sculptor to make the figurines. He says: 'Since at that time Pedro Infante and Jorge Negrete were popular [Mexican movie stars], I said to him, "Look, [Malverde] was a good-looking boy, white, and so that people will identify with him, make him somewhere in between Pedro Infante and Jorge Negrete".'[10] González also describes Malverde's miracles. For instance, the Sinaloan government decided to construct a state office building on the land where people met to pay tribute to 'El Narcosantón'. A huge protest ensued, that lasted two years. In that time stones jumped like popcorn on the ground, machinery frequently broke down, and other mishaps occurred. In the end, the building was finished, but the faith among the people was by then unquenchable. An extract of the famous 'Corrido a Jesús Malverde' follows:

> Voy a cantar un corrido de una historia verdadera,
> De un bandido generoso que robaba dondequiera.
> Jesús Malverde era un hombre que a los pobres ayudaba,
> Por eso lo defendían cuando la ley lo buscaba.

> I am going to sing a *corrido* of a true story,
> Of a generous bandit who robbed wherever he went.
> Jesús Malverde was a man who helped the poor,
> Because of that, they protected him when the law was after him.

Truth, generosity and bravado . . . Most of the *narcocorridos* are similar in tone: they celebrate the semi-fictitious adventures of a righteous person, usually a male, who dared to fight against the establishment. It is as if the best of Mexico, its source of endurance, was built against the odds. The lyrics by composers like Paulino Vargas, Julián Garza and Jesse Armenta, are fatalistic in nature: they recount fateful, bloody encounters, in which individuals avenge themselves in order to leave their dignity intact. *Dignidad*, indeed, is what the *narcocorridos* are about: the supremacy of honor.

In what has been described as 'a journey into the music of drugs, guns, and guerrillas', the music of the US–Mexico border emerges from a half-finished modernity, a place where the drug business has radically transformed people's daily routine, yet it has left untouched the sense of morality. The people Elijah Wald, the author of *Narcocorrido*, comes across are never appalled by the consumption of narcotics. Why should they? As a bystander tells him, that is someone else's problem. Their immigrant's sole concern is with survival: *la sobrevivencia*. In *The Labyrinth of Solitude*, Octavio Paz once described Mexicans as unafraid of death. The *narcocorrido* seems proof of this observation. Malverde, for instance, is anything but a submissive figure. He is eager to subvert official rule, although he knows his subversion will ultimately be ineffectual. He does not fit the pattern of a Stallone/Rocky archetype, who is able to overcome, with charisma and stamina, every obstacle placed before him.

In the end, the mythical Rocky of the Sylvester Stallone movies is taken to be the underdog that becomes an undisputed bell-wether. No such emblem exists in the Spanish-language drug culture: in this ballad, as in 'The Wetback's Tomb', 'The Circus' and countless others, the concept of the underdog is alien to such a degree that the Spanish language does not even have an approximate translation for the term. Malverde is a source of endurance. In the end, though, the establishment – the gringos, the corrupt politicos – prevail. Still, confrontation is embraced by *corridistas*: for them, it is better to have a dignified death than a life lived on one's knees. Sooner or later, society finds a way to pay tribute to the martyr. In the case of Malverde, his timelessness is to be found not only in La Capilla and the handsome busts on sale but also in the Denny's-like cafeterias called Coco's Malverde and Chic's Malverde, as well as in businesses like Malverde Clutch & Brakes. And this timelessness has a corporate dimension in the shape of the marketing arrangement that Eligio González has established with Pepsi-Cola. Local distributors give the saint's caretaker discounts so he can sell soda at concerts and dances (of *narcocorridistas*), allowing him to keep the profits for 'El Narcosantón'. Once during a large encampment of campesinos outside the state building that lasted two months, González is said to have sold four thousand cases of Pepsi.

Of the myriad troubadours of the *corridos*, probably the most emblematic is Chalino. His impact among youths is so strong that there is a trend towards Chalino-sound-alikes that, demographically and in ambition, eclipse even the Elvis Presley mania. In ten minutes a record-store owner might display cassettes and CDs by twenty-five different so-called 'chalinitos'. There is no doubt that it is the myth, the way people project their own dreams onto Chalino's life, that holds the clue to his celebrity. For he was a warrior, and that is how every immigrant male, no matter the background, wants to see himself: as a fearless combatant. He was killed in a shootout at the age of thirty-one. This was not, of course, at all unexpected: almost to the end of his days he carried with him a pistol and he made sure everyone noticed it. His wore distinctive clothing: a cowboy hat, white or striped shirt, dark slacks, and boots, accompanied by ostentatious jewellery (rings, necklaces, watches) that is de rigueur among narcotraffickers. He spoke with a distinctive Sinaloan rancho accent: for instance, he said 'te fuites' for 'you left', rather than 'te fuiste'. '[Chalino] looked straight out of the mountains', a devotee assures us, 'one more of those shy, fierce men drinking in the cantinas and carrying drugs across the border in suitcases, ready to do the jail time with quiet fatalism, or to kill someone over a woman or a thoughtless remark'.[11]

From Sinaloa he moved north not only in search of work, but because he needed to run away from the law. Apparently, Chalino at the age of fifteen had gone to a party where he found the man who raped his sister Juana four years earlier and killed him on the spot. He followed the harvests up through California to Oregon, finally settling in Inglewood, a Mexican-immigrant satellite town around Los Angeles. He was sent to prison in Tijuana for a series of petty crimes and it was there that he came across contraband smugglers with guitars. He began to write *corridos* with them. It was his first exposure to composition. Back in Los Angeles, he traded in marihuana and cocaine, but stopped the moment his musical career – which lasted only a total of four years – took off. He asked a *norteño* band to record his lyrics, but was unhappy with the result, so he tried his own luck in front of the microphone at the studio. Soon his cassettes were selling like hot potatoes. In *True Tales from Another Mexico* (2000), journalist Sam Quiñones reconstructs Chalino's roving path, reflecting on his success in packed clubs, cantinas and *quinceañera* (fifteenth birthday) parties. Soon everyone, from *coyotes* to wetbacks, was endlessly replaying his albums, in which he collected songs made to order on *narcotraficantes* of any stature. Eventually, after a performance in Coachella, twenty miles east of Palm Springs, a drunk unemployed 33-year-old jumped onstage and fired a 25-mm pistol into Chalino's side, injuring him. The incident was reported on the programme *ABC World News Tonight*, another case of Anglos showing interest not at the artistic quality of the performance, but at the violence. Chalino's reputation as a *valiente*, a brave macho, was bolstered by the incident. But his reputation as a dare-devil and a singer of revenge followed him, and sooner rather than later caught up with him. Probably filled with regret, he gave up his gun collection shortly after the wounding incident and he also sold the rights to his music for the lump sum of $115,000. These were the last acts of a singer whose subject matter often got him in trouble. In May, after a packed performance back in Culiacán, he and some relatives were stopped by armed men driving in Chevrolet Suburbans. An hour later, a couple of campesinos found his body, dumped by an irrigation canal near a highway. The mystery of his death remains unsolved. In a world of lawless landscapes such as the one Chalino inhabited, it is likely to remain unsolved. A stanza in homage to him reads:

Para cantar estos versos voy a quitarme el sombrero,
Para contar la tragedia de un amigo y compañero.
Chalino Sánchez ha muerto, que Dios lo tenga en el cielo.

To sing these verses I will take off my hat,
To recount the tragedy of a friend and companion.
Chalino Sánchez has died, may God have him in heaven.

News of his death spread far and wide through the radio, television and even e-mail. But in the migrant communities it was through *narcocorridos* that the tragedy was widely disseminated. It had been through these ballads that Chalino had become famous and it was in them that he was subsequently immortalized. This to me adds another crucial aspect: 'In the Mexican badlands', Quiñones argues, 'where the barrel of a gun makes the law, for generations dating back to the mid-1800s the *corrido* recounted the worst, best, and bloodiest exploits of men.'[12] Indeed, the *corridos* are the newspapers of an illiterate people. And they are something else: for migrants weary of corrupt politicians, this is a literary form that is alive orally for those unexposed to the written word. This is a form, needless to say, that is authentically democratic, one in which people express themselves in full.

Democracy is not a system the immigrants have been exposed to. They run away from dictatorial regimes, looking for a better future elsewhere. They often do not find it. Still, the *corrido* allows them a sense of freedom. What has maintained the tradition alive in the border region is the fact that workers with scarcely a cent to spare are eager to pay a composer what is for them a lot of money to tailor-make them a ballad about their own journey. Chalino's career flourished in large measure thanks to the endless commissions he satisfied from his avid customers. In the melodic tales he told about them, their anonymity was suddenly unlocked. This was nothing if not liberating. Through the *corrido* the labourer, pushed to oblivion by History (with a capital 'H'), was allowed the key to a room of his own: *un donnadie*, a nobody, unexpectedly got the chance to become *un alguien*, a somebody, at least for the few minutes that Chalino's stanzas lasted. And in taped form, replayed time and again, they could last forever. Producer Abel Orozco put Chalino's contribution in perspective: 'Before, they'd only do *corridos* about legendary figures. Now people want to hear about themselves while they're alive. Although they may be nobodies, they want to make themselves known. *Corridos* have become, over the last several years, a little less news and a little more publicity for common people. They're fifteen minutes of fame that they pay for themselves.'[13]

The gravitas of Spanglish

Chalino the Mexican immigrant: isn't he an American hero too? The answer, not surprisingly, depends on who is asked the question. Xenophobia is rampant in the United States, and conservative forces are likely to respond with a rotund *no*. Even other non-Mexican Latinos, such as the Cubans in Miami, might not feel any empathy towards him. But there is little doubt that Chalino is an emblematic figure, one that enables the scholar to zoom in on the cultural expressions of Latino life in the United States. For a chance to zoom out, I suggest taking a look at a larger-than-life topic: the language of Latinos, more specifically, through Spanglish. In the next several pages, I will attempt to explain what precisely this linguistic phenomenon is about. Where does it begin and end? Who are its speakers and promoters? By focusing on this phenomenon, the reader will hopefully get a clearer picture of the hyphenated existence that Latinos live every day in the United States: between English and Spanish, between Hispanic and Anglo-Saxon civilizations.

Once asked by a reporter for his opinion on *el espanglés*, one of the ways used to refer to Spanglish south of the border – some others are *casteyanqui, inglañol, argot sajón, español bastardo, papiamento gringo*, and *caló pachuco* – Octavio Paz, the Nobel Prize-winning Mexican author of *The Labyrinth of Solitude*, is said to have responded: 'ni es bueno ni es malo, sino abominable' (It isn't correct or incorrect, it's awful).[14] Indeed, the common assumption has it that Spanglish is a bastard jargon that is part *Span*ish and part En*glish* but has neither gravitas nor a clear identity. It is spoken (or, better, broken) by people of Hispanic descent in the United States, not only by the uneducated and intellectually unsophisticated, but also by the middle and upper classes. They are no longer fluent in the language of Cervantes but have also failed to master that of Shakespeare. So, to use an expression of Langston Hughes, these people wonder as they wander without a sense of direction.

The trouble with this view is that it is frighteningly near-sighted. It refuses to acknowledge that languages are never static but are in constant regeneration. They are enriched by the challenges their speakers face in history, the way they constantly accommodate their verbal skills to unforeseen possibilities. Around the tenth century, Spanish was a hodge-podge of vulgar Latin and regional dialects in the Iberian peninsula. By the time of Lope de Vega, Góngora and Quevedo, some five hundred years later, and after the bloody Reconquista by the Catholic crown, the syntax was more or less on the road to standardization and the transnational respectability of *el castellano* – its origins in the province of Castile – as an imperial tongue was unquestionable. But the so-called discovery of the New World opened a formidable door and the inclusion of terms used by Indian tribes who spoke Mayan, Huichol, Tarascan, Arucanian, Guaraní and Quechua needed to be considered. So lexicons made room for them, though not without the purists' despairing cries. To this day, the tension between the various modalities of Spanish, not only from one end of the Atlantic ocean to the other, but all across the Americas, highlights a most durable asset: its flexibility. Likewise, the arrival of the barbarous Saxons and Jutes in Britain around 450 AD, and their interaction with the Celts and the Normans, gave room to the language known as English, but the process was unhurried. By the time of Geoffrey Chaucer's *The Canterbury Tales*, it had undergone a normalized syntactical course, but some grammatical patterns were still untouched. *Cawdrey's Table Alphabeticall*, published in 1604, was the first attempt to offer a systematic approach to vocabulary. But when Dr Samuel Johnson embarked on his dictionary in the eighteenth century, there was still, in his own view, much to be cleansed: Gallicisms had a 'pervasive' influence and authors, from Milton to Dryden, often spelled the same word in different ways. The English used today in Australia is not the same one employed in Nigeria, New Zealand and India. The differences are not only geographical: Nigerian English, as any other, is in constant revolution.

After Chinese, English today is the largest language of the globe in terms of number of speakers: a total of 350 million; it is followed by Spanish with 250. In the Americas the two languages cohabit promiscuously, and increasingly the result of that cohabitation is Spanglish. It is unavoidable everywhere in the Hispanic world, particularly in the United States. It spreads effortlessly thanks to the help it receives from two major 24-hour TV networks in Spanish, the World Wide Web, rap and rock music, newspapers like *El Diario / La Prensa* in New York, *El Miami Herald* in Miami, and *La Opinión* in Los Angeles and the more than five hundred radio stations *en español*, far more than the total number of stations in

El Salvador, Nicaragua, Costa Rica, Guatemala and Honduras together. 'My son is espoliadísimo', a popular soap-opera actress remarks on air to a television talk-show host. Or, 'Conviértase en inversor con Continental National Bank', claims an ad in Dade County, Florida, 'porque hoy más que nunca, tiempo is money'. And a street sign in La Villita, a Chicago neighbourhood, reads: 'Apartments are selling like pan caliente and apartments de verdad'.

The verbal resources of society are infinite in their mutability. 'Standard' and 'informal' codes are always in tension. Spanglish is still an informal code, but evidence shows that its acceptability is growing rapidly. People used to think that it amounted to little more than the coinage of a handful of fresh terms. But linguists and other specialists show it is in the process of defining its own syntax. At the word-stock level, Spanglishisms – once called *anglicismos* – are omnipresent all over the globe, from the *gofres* (waffles) of Madrid to the *guachiman* (guard) of Caracas and the soccer *réferi* (referee) in Guadalajara. This is not to say, of course, that the phenomenon has not grown in relevance. Many of them might be traced back many decades and even a century. For instance, Constantino Suárez, in his *Vocabulario cubano*, released in Havana in 1920, included dozens of terms used in the Caribbean, among the African population in particular, that we would easily acknowledge as varieties of Spanglish: *faite* (fight), for instance, and *tifiar* (to steal). These terms were incorporated into Cuban idiom as they arrived with the fleets of British pirates and merchants stationed in the island's ports for long periods of time. Many of these terms have gone out of use, replaced by neologisms. More than seventy years later, the popular *Clave: Diccionario del Uso del Español Actual*, coordinated by Concepción Maldonado González, published in Madrid in 1996 and available across the Americas, has a much higher percentage of these kinds of terms – I've estimated 15 percent of the total. They include *anti-baby* (contraceptive pill), *videometraje* (video movie) and *tolerado* (accepted). But in the United States the use of Spanglish goes far beyond the coinage of neologisms.

Latinos in the United States are also the fifth largest concentration of Hispanics worldwide, surpassing demographically the overall population of countries like Venezuela and Uruguay, and equalling the size of Spain. To some this transformation might look like a surprising, unexpected phenomenon, but this is not the case: Latinos have been an integral part of American society for centuries, ever since the Spanish explorers first set foot in Florida and what is today the South-west. Some are immigrants while others have never moved; instead, the United States came to them, first in 1848, then in the aftermath of the Spanish-American War. The largest waves of immigration are concentrated in the twentieth century, when huge masses moved from south to north in the continent. The roots, therefore, can be found in the geography of republics that range from Colombia to the Dominican Republic. Since these republics have been more or less racially mixed from the start, the native citizens of Hispanic descent and also the immigrants that have settled in the United States, from the middle of the nineteenth century to the present, are a racial hybrid: mestizos, whites, Africans and Asians. Almost all of them are unified by a common language, Spanish, although Brazil, the Guayanas and portions of the Caribbean Basin also, speak Portuguese patois, French or English. Class also allows for a study in contrast: immigrants to *El Norte*, whether from Havana, Managua or Bogotá, have come from the lower, middle and upper strata in Latin America. This hodgepodge has given room to questions of identity explored earlier in this chapter.

Perhaps it is not at all extraordinary that the deceptive sense of newness gives way to an atmosphere of anxiety and even xenophobia in Hispanic and Anglo enclaves, in particular towards the dissemination of Spanglish. Its impact announces an overall *hispanización* of the entire society whereas in the Americas it generates fear that the region's tongue, seen by many as the last bastion of cultural pride, is being taken over by American imperialism. Left-wing militants in Latin America, infatuated as they still are with an ideology that harks back to José Enrique Rodó's *Ariel* (1900), believe something must be done to counter-attack its influx and influence – 'Muera Hollywood! Muera el espanglés!' On the other side of the border, their right-wing opponents fear that their own nation is in the course of a sharp decline that entails a switching of tongues. But a language cannot be legislated; it is the freest, most democratic, form of expression of the human spirit. And so, every attack against it serves as a stimulus, for nothing is more inviting than what is forbidden. Today musicians and literati use Spanglish without apology in novels, poems, non-fiction. . . . The emphasis depends on the author's acculturation: at times it does not go beyond a handful of intertwined Spanish *voces*. On other occasions, though, it becomes a full-blown dialect, as in the work of scores of authors north and south of the Rio Grande, such as Tato Laviera, Guillermo Gómez-Peña (responsible, along with Enique

Chagoya and Felicia Rice, for the *Codex Espangliensis*),[15] Juan Felipe Herrera, Rolando Hinojosa and Giannina Braschi. This is the opening paragraph of 'Pollito Chicken', a story by Ana Lydia Vega from Puerto Rico included in *Vírgenes y mártires*. It shows to what extent the languages, Spanish and English, are intertwined:

> Lo que la decidió fue el breathtaking poster de Fomento que vio en la travel agency del lobby de su building. El breathtaking poster mentado representaba una pareja de beautiful people holding hands en el funicular del Hotel Conquistador. Los beautiful people se veían tan deliriously happy y el mar tan strikingly blue y la puesta del sol – no olvidemos la puesta de sol a la Winston-tastes-good – la puesta de sol tan shocking pink en la distancia que Suzie Bermiúdez, a pesar de que no pasaba por el Barrio a pie ni bajo amenaza de ejecución por la Mafia, a pesar de que prefería mil veces perder un fabulous job y morir de hambre por no coger el Welfare o los food stamps como todos esos lazy, dirty, no-good bums que eran sus compatriotas, Suzie Bermiúdez, repito, sacó todos sus ahorros de secretaria de housing project de negros – que no eran mejores que los New York Puerto Rican pero por lo menos eran New York Puerto Rican – y abordó el 747 en raudo y uninterrupted flight hasta San Juan.[16]

I once heard Ana Celia Zentella, a specialist in its syntax and the author of *Growing Up Bilingual*, describe the individual Spanglish-speaker as 'two monolinguals stuck at the neck'.[17] It is a haunting, beautiful image that makes me think of Stevenson's *Dr. Jekyll and Mr. Hyde* – one body, two selves. But is it accurate? Many Spanglish-speakers are indeed bilingual. 'Hablamos los dos', an interviewee told Zentella in broken Spanish, we speak both languages, Spanish and English. And yet, many are not fully active in either of them, orally or in written form. The syntax and grammar of one spill all over into the other and vice versa and the degree of instantaneous self-translation is unequivocal. There was a time when this miscegenation was seen socially as unacceptable. Richard Rodriguez, in his autobiography *Hunger of Memory*, described the 'shame' of Spanish-speaking children in California in the fifties. He saw it as a private language but also a language of isolation: 'Like those whose lives are bound by the barrio, I was reminded that Spanish marked my separateness from *los otros, los gringos* in power.'[18] English, he was told, was the nation's official code of communication, and should be used at all times. Fortunately such a sense of shame is long gone. And in Mexico and South America too the *zeitgeist* has changed with the fall of the Berlin Wall and the dismantling of Communism. Marxism is no longer an ideology with much zest. Neo-liberalism has been welcomed, and with it a middle-class laissez-faire mentality. The result is that today Spanglish-speakers are no longer ashamed of their speech. It is not an either/or issue any longer.

To seize upon the potential of Spanglish, it is crucial to understand the metabolism of both Spanish and English. Antonio de Nebrija, the first to compile a grammar of the language that one day would give birth to Francisco de Quevedo, Pablo Neruda and Jorge Luis Borges, famously said of Spanish that it was always a tool of empire. An imperial tool, indeed, with a clear-cut goal – to spread the mission of the Iberian knights and missionaries in 'uncivilized' lands – and it was forced onto the population. In the colonial period, though, to civilize meant to re-educate, to evangelize, and slowly to incorporate the region and its inhabitants into the sphere of influence of the Catholic crown. The language was used to proselytize. But as ethnolinguist Angel Roseblatt has argued in his lucid *El español de España y el español de América* (1962), not even on this side of the Atlantic was it simply transplanted; instead, it adapted to the new reality by incorporating terms that came from pre-Columbian tongues, such as *aguacate* and *tenzontle*. Indeed, for over five hundred years Spanish has twisted and turned in a most spontaneous fashion from the Argentine pampa to the rough roads of Tijuana. Today it is as elastic and polyphonic as ever, allowing for a wide gamut of possibilities that go beyond mere localisms. A person in Madrid might easily communicate with his counterpart in Caracas, but numerous nuances – from meaning to accent to emphasis – distinguish them. These nuances are also apparent in the many versions of Spanish spoken north of the Rio Grande, Mexican, Cuban, Puerto Rican and so forth, and within these categories are different regionalisms, such as the immigrant Spanish from Nuevo León, Oaxaca or Jalisco, for example. Add to this the *español novomexicano* that is different from its many counterparts, such as the *tejano*, *kanseco* and *californio* Spanish. The result, clearly, is a babelesque jumble.

In 1994 I published an essay entitled 'Translation and Identity', in which I explored the verbal dimension of the conquest of Mexico.[19] It is, I am convinced, a little-known aspect of the encounter between Europe and the pre-Columbian world that ought to be analysed in further detail. For the conquest not only gave room to a political, military and social colonization of millions that belonged to a gamut of Indian tribes that spoke languages such as Mayan, Huichol and Tarascan in Mexico to Arucanian, Guaraní and Quechua in South America. It was, equally importantly, an act of linguistic subjugation. The Spanish language spoken in the continent that ranges from Ciudad Juárez to Tierra del Fuego is an acquired artefact, a code of communication that serves as a weapon to control and re-educate. The fact that Sor Juana Inés de la Cruz and Jorge Luis Borges wrote their poems and stories in Cervantes's tongue does not mean, obviously, that they wrote *in* translation. Their Spanish was as much theirs as it was the property of Benito Jerónimo Feijóo, Miguel de Unamuno and Federico García Lorca. But the language as such had not come into being in the Americas the way it had in the Iberian peninsula. In the Americas it was a foreign imposition, a sign of the imperial expansion of the Catholic kingdoms of the monarchs Isabella and Ferdinand.

It is no sheer coincidence that 1492, the *annus mirabilis* in Iberian history, was not only the moment when the Jews were expelled from the peninsula and when Columbus sailed across the Atlantic in search of an alternative route to the Indies. This was also the year in which Antonio de Nebrija (*c.* 1441–1513), a respected scholar at the University of Salamanca, published the first *Gramática* of the Spanish language. At the same time he released his *Diccionario latino–español* and, shortly after, in 1495, he came out with its counterpart, the *Vocabulario español–latino*. The climate was ripe in Spain not only for the consolidation of Castile and Aragón to become a single Catholic empire but it was also a most crucial time for the centralization of political and social power. The *Reconquista* – Reconquest – that had lasted since the crusades of the eleventh century, was finally complete. And its completion brought with it a sense that Castilian Spanish was called upon to become the unifying tongue of the whole kingdom. There followed a period of intense intellectual and artistic fertility, the 'Golden Age' of Spanish arts and literature, when mystical poets, playwrights and novelists, such as Fray Luis de León, Santa Teresa de Jesús, Lope de Vega, Francisco de Quevedo, Calderón de la Barca, Luis de Góngora and, especially, Miguel de Cervantes, gave the world a taste of the baroque sophistication of Spanish courtly and country life. By devoting himself to the standardization and cataloguing of spelling and to the study of the syntax and grammar of Castilian Spanish, Nebrija legitimated a language whose speakers were only recently self-conscious of its scope. The vulgar Latin of the Roman Empire, which is different from the classical Latin of authors like Ovid and Seneca, gave room to a tongue – part of the family of Romance languages that includes Italian and Romanian, influenced by Celtic and

German, and by the Slavic varieties respectively – with a distinct flavour. This fact is crucial in the understanding of Spanglish too, for Spanish as such became a language of power, a language with an army, the moment Spain concentrated its strength and announced itself to other countries as a well-defined nation. To become one, a nation needs a set of symbols, a shared history and centralized power structure, and a single, commonly understood, language. Spanish became that language. Through it, Spain spread its world-view in northern Africa, Turkey, the Philippines and all over the Caribbean and the Americas. Nebrija was part of this move to consolidate and homogenize. The first official full-length dictionary of the Spanish language appears in another significant year, 1611, almost exactly in between the release of the two parts of *Don Quijote de la Mancha*, which appeared in 1605 and 1615 respectively. It is a dictionary prepared under the shadow of the Holy Office of the Inquisition, as most intellectual matters were then, by a lexicographer named Sebastián de Covarrubias Orozco (1539–1613), who, like Nebrija and also Fray Luis de León, Calderón and later Miguel de Unamuno, was attached to the University of Salamanca.

Like that of any language, the birth of Spanglish is not too difficult to locate. Between 1492 and the middle of the nineteenth century, the encounter of the two *Weltanschauungs*, Anglo-Saxon and Hispanic, produced a bare minimum of verbal miscegenation. The chronicles of conquest and conversion penned by Cabeza de Vaca and 'El Inca' Garcilaso all had their target readership mainly in the Iberian peninsula. They are composed in a Castilian Spanish coloured by a few regionalisms. The picture changed dramatically in the Mexican South-west between 1810 and 1848. Early on, Napoleon sold Louisiana to the United States. Soon after, the arrival of Anglo-Americans into Arizona, Texas, New Mexico and California began to transform the region. Missions were secularized, the Santa Fe Trail was opened by William Bicknell in 1822 and trade became attractive in spite of exorbitant taxes by Mexican officials. It was in those years that Texas became Americanized, with a population that quadrupled between 1820 and 1830, mostly as a result of new Anglo arrivals. The dialogue between Spanish and English increased as an obvious consequence. With the Treaty of Guadalupe Hidalgo the population that lived in those territories in Arizona, California, New Mexico and so on, switched citizenship from one day to the next. Article VIII of the document in English is clear about the physical status of these people. 'Mexicans now established in territories previously belonging to

Mexico', it stated, 'and which remain for the future within the limit of the United States, as defined by the present treaty':

> shall be free to continue where they now reside, or to remove at any time to the Mexican Republic, retaining the property which they possess in the said territories, or disposing thereof, and removing the proceeds wherever they please; without their being subjected, on this account, to any contribution, tax or charge whatsoever.

> Those who shall prefer to remain in the said territories, may either retain the title and rights of Mexican citizens, or acquire those of citizens of the United States. But they shall be under the obligation to make their election within one year from the date of the exchange of ratifications of this treaty: and those who shall remain in the said territories, after the expiration of that year, without having declared their intention to retain the character of Mexicans, shall be considered to have elected to become citizens of the United States.

> In the said territories, property of every kind, now belonging to Mexicans, not established there, shall be inviolably respected. The present owners, the heirs of these, and all Mexicans who may hereafter acquire said property by contract, shall enjoy with respect to it, guaranties equally ample as if the same belonged to citizens of the United States.[20]

Curiously, no mention is made anywhere in the document of the inhabitant's 'madre lengua' or mother tongue, although it was said in newspaper reports that, since language is an unalienable civil right, 'it shall be respected thoroughly'. History, however, is written not by the conquered but by the victors; soon English became the dominant tongue of business and diplomacy in the newly acquired south-western lands. But the usage of Spanish in schools and the household did not altogether vanish. Newspapers such as *El Clamor Público* in Albuquerque and *El Nuevo Mundo* in San Francisco serve as testimony to the relevance of the tongue. *El hijo de la tempestad* by Eusebio Chacón, the oral history of Eulalia Pérez and the call-and-response *El trovo del viejo Vilmas y Gracia*, the anonymous *Los Comanches*, are examples of its vitality.

The syncretism intensified with the Spanish-American War, in which Spain lost control of its colonies in the Caribbean, Cuba and Puerto Rico, as well as in the Philippines, and the United States replaced the Spanish empire as a global power. Spanish was out, at least politically; English was in. But again, the usage of Feijóo's tongue did not altogether cease. By then, Key West and New York had become magnets of immigration and Puerto Rican and Cuban communities had solid roots in them. But it was clear that, as the so-called American Century was about to begin, the communication code had changed. From 1901 until the end of the millennium, scholars like Ricardo Alfaro, Francisco Santamaría, Washington Llorens, Elena Mellado de Hunter and Juan José Alzugaray Aguirre published dictionaries of Anglicisms with increasing frequency all across the Hispanic world – in particular in Mexico, Cuba, Argentina and Spain.[21] This, surely, is a symptom of the verbal cross-fertilization experienced from north to south. Words like lasso, bookaroo, rodeo, amigo, mañana and tortilla made it into English; likewise, gringo, mister and money began to be used in Spanish. The Nicaraguan poet Rubén Darío, the anointed leader of the *modernista* poetic movement that swept the Americas between 1885 and 1915, denounced the oppressiveness of the English language in one of his poems:

> ¿Seremos entregados a los bárbaros fieros?
> ¿Tantos millones de hombres hablaremos inglés?
> ¿Ya no hay nobles hidalgos ni bravos caballeros?
> ¿Callaremos ahora para llorar después?
>
> Will we surrender to the fierce barbarians?
> Will so many millions speak English?
> Are there no longer noble hidalgos and brave knights?
> Will we be silent now so as to cry later?[22]

The extent to which Spanish in the New World originally penetrated Iberian Spanish is illustrated by an anecdote about Nebrija. In 1492 he included in his *Diccionario latino-español* the Latin term *barca* for a small rowboat. Then the *Vocabulario español–latino*, its companion volume, was released in 1595, the Indian term *canoa*, from the Nahuatl, was listed, followed by the Latin definition. Evidently, in those three years, the impact of pre-Columbian languages on Iberian Spanish made itself felt. The Salamanca grammarian was only a conduit through whom the verbal flux from across the Atlantic began to manifest itself.

Today numerous Nahuatl words like *molcajete, aguacate* and *huipil* (from *mulcazitl, ahuacatl* and *huipilli,* respectively) are accepted by the Real Academia Española as *Americanismos*. The repression by the Spanish conquistadores of the Indian population did not leave room for the formation of a slang, defined by J. E. Lighter, editor-in-chief of the Random House *Dictionary of American Slang*, as 'an informal, nonstandard, nontechnical vocabulary composed chiefly of novel-sounding synonyms for standard words and phrases'.[23] Five hundred years after the

'Conquest', Spanglish is indeed just that – a vital social code, one whose sheer bravura is revolutionizing both Spanish and, to a lesser extent, English. There is not one Spanglish, however, but many. Issues of nationality, age and class are factors in this variety. The multiplicity is clear in the United States, where the language spoken by Cuban-Americans is different from the so-called Dominicanish- and Nuyorrican-spanglish. Localisms abound, not only geographical (*Istlos*, for instance, is Spanglish for East Los Angeles, just as *Sagüesera* is South West Street in Miami) but also ethnic (*chale* is a chicano expression of disagreement, and *chompa* is Nuyorican for jumper). At Amherst College, a few colleagues and I did an experiment not long ago: in a single room, we invited to meet for the first time four Spanglish speakers from different backgrounds: Miami, Chicago, Brownsville and Los Angeles. The only guidelines we set for them were that they should not to be too formal but should communicate in a comfortable way. The result was astounding: as soon as the participants familiarized themselves with each other the conversation flowed easily, although the speakers often felt compelled to define, in impromptu fashion, a certain term or expression so as not to alienate the rest. Within fifteen minutes, a sense of linguistic community was perfectly tangible.

And this is only at the national level. 'Ganga Spanglish' (*ganga*, from 'gang'), as the jargon spoken by urban youngsters is known, introduces other differences. Take, for example, rapper lyrics, such as these by *KMX Assault*:

> Mi abuelita says la vida es dura
> Levántate Boricua! Wakin' up es la cura
> Orgulloso, proud of my heritage
> Echar Pa'lante with my people is my imperative

> This Boricua will; endeavor to be clever
> got to succeed to make our kids' lives better
> We need this new breed to lead the way
> for all Puerto Ricans in the USA.

The next example is entitled 'Locotes', by the popular group Cypress Hill. It is part of their album *III Temple of Moom*:

> It's the locote coming out the bote
> I got a new jale jacking in the noche
> Give me your ferja
> In your pocket or they'll carry ya
> Off and burry ya in the eastside area

Trucha! And you don't stop 'til I'm done
Now the puercos got me on the run
You don't want to turn your back on me

Check it out ese you're looking
At the jefe
Of that clica with the big bad trece
I teach you a lesson, no question
Get your ass out now you're passing out
When you look at the cuete

Now the puercos got me on the run
from varrio to varrio
Looking for anybody, Oh Cesario
Hanging out with Mario
Looking for a place to hide

Don't turn your back on a vato like me
Cuz I'm one broke motherfucka in need
Desperate! What's going on in the mente
Taking from the rich not from my gente
Look at that gabacho slipping
Borracho from the cerveza
He's sipping
No me vale, madre
Gabacho pray to your padre
This is for the time you would
Give me the jale.

Terms like *ese* (dud), *clica* (circle of friends), *gabacho* (white person), and *jale* (job) are unique to inner-city Chicano Spanglish. These and other *voces* hold a resemblance to *tocho cheli* and the slang from Mexican streets. They are recurrent in *raperos en español* such as *Latin Alianza, Chicano 2 Da Bone, Latin Lingo* and *Dr Loco's Rockin' Jalapeño Band*. They are in sharp contrast with the more sophisticated verbal modulation used by high-brow poets like Giannina Braschi. From her novel *Yo-yo Boing!*:

   – Abrela tú.
   – ¿Por qué yo? Tú tienes las keys. Yo te las entregué a tí. Además, I left mine adentro.
   – ¿Por que las dejaste adentro?
   – Por que I knew you had yours.
   – Por qué dependes de mí?
   – Just open it, and make it fast. Y lo peor de todo es cuando te levantas por la mañana y te vas de la casa y dejas la puerta abierta. Y

todo el dinero ahí, desperdigado encima de una gaveta en la cocina, al lado de la entrada. Y ni te das cuentas que me pones en peligro. Yo duermo hasta las diez. Y entonces me levanto y me visto rápidamente y cuando voy a abrir la puerta me doy cuenta que está abierta. Es un descuido de tu parte. Dejar la puerta abierta. Alguien puede entrar y robarme y violarme. Y tú tan Pancho, Sancho, ni te importa.

– ¡Claro que me importa. Eso sí fue un descuido.

– Sí, ¿y lo otro no lo es? Scratch the knob and I'll kill you.[24]

Numerous Spanish terms come from sports: *los doubles* (tennis), *el corner* and *el ofsait* (soccer), *el tuchdaun* (American football), *el nokaut* (boxing). And then, of course, there is Cyber-Spanglish, the cybernetic code used frequently by Internet users. The United States is expected to have 150 million surfers in 2005. Countries like Mexico, Argentina and Colombia have far fewer users, but their link to the World Wide Web is also solid. Terms like *chatear* (to chat), *forwardear* (to forward) and *el maus* (computer mouse) are indispensable north and south of the Rio Grande as well as in Spain and in the Caribbean. This clearly is another facet of the verbal phenomenon, used across national and even class lines.

In 1997 Günther Haensch, author of *Diccionarios del español en el umbral del siglo XXI*,[25] made a list of the dozens of lexicons in the Americas that have attempted to reflect the many different examples of social and ethnic Spanish slang spoken at the continental level, such as *germanía*, *lunfardo*, *ciboney* and *guay*, as well as sexual idioms, euphemisms and insults. (What is courteous might be said in any tongue, Maimonedes said, but what it means needs a new language.) Many of those lexicons include Spanglish terms, although they don't necessarily identify them as such. The task of collecting these 'Spanglishisms', an effort that ought to be both transnational and also inter-ethnic, has remained undone, in part because public awareness has kept Spanglish as a fluid form of communication always about to disappear. For years it has been perceived as a transitional stage for Spanish speakers in the process of acquiring English. But it is clear now that Spanglish is more than a transitional stage; in fact, it is an end in itself. Also aggravating is the fact that, through Hollywood and pop culture in general, the impact these days of English on every language – from Arabic to Bengali, from Piedmontese to Norwegian – is equally strong, yet nowhere but in the United States is a new form of communication taking shape with equal stamina.

The site, obviously, is no coincidence. From the outset the United States has received immigrants. Each immigrant group arrives with its own language. The overall pattern, though, is more or less the same: by the time the immigrants' grandchildren come along, English has all but taken over. But Latinos have broken this pattern. The reasons are manifold. In comparison with other groups, it is very difficult to pinpoint which is the first, second and third generation. This is because, as is the case with Native Americans, many chicanos did not actually come to the United States; instead, the United States came to them with the sale of the South-west in the middle of the nineteenth century. Other Hispanics have come at different periods: the Mexicans in the twenties and onward; Puerto Rican *jíbaros* and Cuban-American émigrés in the sixties; the Salvadoran and Nicaraguans in the late seventies and eighties . . . So, for decades, the influx has not stopped, injecting new life into the Spanish language. This endurance is magnificent: no other immigrant group in the United States has held on to its original tongue for so long.

In any case, Spanglish won't go away, 'no va pa'tras'; instead, as time goes by it will consolidate its status. It is not a haphazard jumble of words but, as Zentella and other specialists such as C. Alvarez and L. Torres point out, it is fixing its own morphosyntax.[26] The question, thus, is no longer what it is but where it is going. Might it grow to become a full-size language? Is it likely to become a threat and even replace Spanish altogether? (English, the lingua franca, is obviously not at stake.) These questions point to a puzzling future. Predicted to reach 50 million in the next decade, Latinos are an integral part of the United States, in spite of the xenophobic reaction they often get. It is said by the US Census Bureau that by the year 2025, if not sooner, one out of every four Americans will have Hispanic ancestry. This is an astonishing fact. By then Latin America will no longer end in the Rio Brave, nor will the United States begin in the Rio Grande. No, one will be *inside* the other: la América hispana y la América sajona merged into a single whole.

Notes

1. Quoted in L. Trilling (ed.), *The Portable Matthew Arnold* (New York, 1949), p. 261.
2. H. Augenbraum and I. Stavans (eds.), *Growing Up Latino: Memoirs and Stories* (Boston, 1993).
3. R. González (ed.), *Currents from the Dancing River: Contemporary Latino Fiction, Nonfiction and Poetry* (San Diego CA, 1994).
4. G. Keller and F. Jiménez (eds.), *Hispanics in the United States* (Tempe and Ypsilanti AZ, 1980).

5. N. Kanellos (ed.), *A Decade of Hispanic Literature: An Anniversary Anthology* (Houston, TX, 1982).

6. A. N. Cabeza de Vaca, *Chronicle of the Narváez Expedition* (New York, 2002).

7. See A. Paredes, *With His Pistol in His Hand: A Border Ballad and Its Hero* (Austin TX, 1958); R. Saldivar, *Chicano Narrative: The Dialectics of Difference* (Madison WN, 1990); J. D. Saldivar, *Border Matters: Remapping American Cultural Studies* (Berkeley CA, 1997).

8. See, for example, S. Oboler, *Ethnic Labels, Latino Lives: Identity and Politics of (Re)presentation in the United States* (Minneapolis MN, 1995), and J. Flores, *Divided Borders: Essays on Puerto Rican Identity* (Houston, 1993).

9. Quoted in E. Wald, *Narcocorrido: A Journey into the Music of Drugs, Guns and Guerrillas* (New York, 2001), p. 63.

10. Ibid., p. 67.

11. Ibid., p. 72.

12. Quoted in S. Quiñones, *True Tales from Another Mexico: The Lynch Mob, the Popsicle Kings, Chalino and the Bronx* (Albuquerque NM, 2001), p. 13.

13. Ibid., pp. 27–8.

14. Quoted in J. Ramos, *The Other Face of America: Chronicles of the Immigrants Shaping Our Future* (New York, 2002), p. 202.

15. G. Gómez-Peña with E. Chagoya and F. Rice, *Codex Espangliensis: From Columbus to the Border Patrol* (San Francisco CA, 2000).

16. A. L. Vega, with C. Lugo Filippi *Vírgenes y mártires* (Bio Pedras, Puerto Rico, 1981).

17. A. C. Zentella, *Growing up Bilingual: Puerto Rican Children in New York* (Malden MA, 1997).

18. R. Rodríguez, *Hunger of Memory: The Autobiography of Richard Rodríguez* (New York, 1983), p. 52.

19. I. Stavans, 'Language and Identity', in *The Essential Ilan Stavans* (New York and London, 2000), pp. 231–40.

20. Quoted in R. Griswold de Castillo, *The Treaty of Guadalupe Hidalgo: A Legacy of Conflict* (Norman OK, 1990), p. 78.

21. See, for example, R. Alfaro, *Diccionario de americanismos* (Madrid, 1964); F. Santamaría, *Diccionario general de americanismos*, 3 vols. (Mexico City, 1942).

22. R. Darío, 'Los cisnes', in E. Mejía Sánchez (ed.), *Poesía* (Caracas, 1977), p. 263.

23. J. E. Lighter (ed.), *Dictionary of American Slang*, vol. I, A–G (New York, 1994), p. xi.

24. G. Braschi, *Yo-yo Boing!* (Pittsburgh PA, 1998), p. 2.

25. G. Haensch, *Los diccionarios del español en el umbral del siglo XXI* (Salamanca, 1997).

26. See C. Alvarez, 'Code Switching in Narrative Performance: Social, Structural and Pragmatic Function in the Puerto Rican Speech Community in East Harlem', in C. Klee and L. Ramos García (eds.), *Sociolinguistics of the Spanish-Speaking World: Iberia, Latin America, and the United States* (Tempe AZ 1991); L. Torres, 'Code-Mixing as a Narrative Strategy in a Bilingual Community', in *World English* 11, 2/3 (1992): 183–93.

Further reading

Augenbraum, H., with Margarite Fernández Olmos (eds.), *The Latino Reader: An American Condition from 1542 to the Present*, Boston MA, 1997

Delgado R. and J. Stefancic (eds.), *The Latino/a Condition: A Critical Reader*, New York, 1998

Gonzales, J., *Harvest of Empire: A History of Latinos in America*, New York, 2000

Stavans, I., *The Hispanic Condition. The Power of a People*, New York, 2001
   Spanglish: The Making of a New American Language, New York, 2003

Index

Note: Italicized page numbers refer to notes, tables and illustrations.

Lightning Source UK Ltd.
Milton Keynes UK

177748UK00001B/80/P